1,001 Questions & Answers For the GMAT

Dr. Nancy L. Nolan

Paperback, electronic and CD-ROM versions published by:

Magnificent Milestones, Inc.
www.ivyleagueadmission.com

ISBN 978-1-933819-59-4

Disclaimers:

(1) This book was written as a guide; it does not claim to be the definitive word on GMAT™ preparation. The opinions expressed are the personal observations of the author based on her own experiences. They are not intended to prejudice any party. Accordingly, the author and publisher do not accept any liability or responsibility for any loss or damage that have been caused, or allegedly caused, through the use of information in this book.

(2) The GMAT is a registered trademark of the Graduate Management Admission Council (GMAC), which sponsors the test and decides how it will be constructed, administered and used. Neither Dr. Nolan nor Magnificent Milestones, Inc. is affiliated with the GMAC.

(3) Admission to business school depends on several factors in addition to a candidate's GMAT™ scores (including GPA, recommendations, interview and essays). The author and publisher cannot guarantee that any applicant will be admitted to any specific school or program if (s)he follows the information in this book.

Dedication

For students everywhere;
may the size of your dreams be exceeded only
by your tenacity to attain them.

Acknowledgements

I am deeply indebted to the students, professors, counselors and admissions officers who have shared their perceptions and frustrations about the GMAT™. This book, which was written on your behalf, would not be nearly as powerful without your generous and insightful input.

I also want to thank my colleagues at www.ivyleagueadmission.com for providing a constant source of support, along with the best editorial help in the business.

1,001 Questions & Answers

For the GMAT

Table of Contents

Chapter 1: Introduction to the GMAT

To achieve a top score on the GMAT, students should follow a three-step plan:

- Learn the concepts that are on the test
- Learn the tips, traps and strategies of the test writers
- Learn to work faster and smarter by taking timed practice tests

We address Steps 1 and 2 in our companion publication, *Guerrilla Tactics for the GMAT: Secrets and Strategies the Test Writers Don't Want You to Know*. From our experience, no one should take the GMAT without mastering these techniques, which can make the difference between a great score and a mediocre one.

This publication addresses Step 3, which is to build your confidence, speed, and test-taking strategies by taking mock exams under actual testing conditions. From our experience, working with sample questions isn't enough; you need to attack the questions *exactly* as they are presented on the GMAT. By design, we have organized 1,001 GMAT questions in the identical format you will see on the exam:

Verbal Sections present 41 multiple choice questions in one 75-minute segment, including:

Critical Reading questions
Critical Reasoning questions
Sentence Correction questions

Quantitative Sections present 37 questions in one 75-minute section, including:

Mathematical word problems
Data Sufficiency questions
Data Interpretation questions

Let's be honest; the content of the GMAT isn't particularly difficult. With unlimited time, many students could attain a top score on the exam. The biggest challenge is working at a fast enough pace to:

1. answer as many "easy" questions as possible
2. formulate an intelligent guessing strategy

From our experience, there is no way to accomplish these goals without working through hundreds of practice questions under actual test conditions. Ultimately, it isn't just about timing. It's about knowing your own particular strengths in each section and developing a plan to maximize them.

And that's the aspect of test preparation that few "experts" acknowledge; one size does NOT fit all. *No two students have the same strengths and weaknesses, which means that no two preparation plans will be the same.* Ultimately, it's up to YOU to identify the areas in which you need work, and to focus your time accordingly. The 1,001 questions and answers in this publication are a great start.

Use the information in whatever way makes sense to YOU. If you want to assess the level of difficulty of the math questions, use a few of the Quantitative sections as a general review of the math topics on the GMAT. Check out the typical vocabulary words that show up in the reading passages and the grammatical concepts that are tested over and over again on the exam. Don't stop until you have them down cold. Then, before the day of the test, complete several sections under timed conditions. Make sure that you can work hard enough, smart enough and fast enough to earn your desired score.

As you scroll through the practice sections, you may notice that we have included a disproportionate number of quantitative questions. Why? Because the GMAT tests more than 15 different math concepts; they also increase the level of difficulty by presenting simple concepts as word problems, which require significant experience to master. In contrast, the verbal section tests significantly fewer concepts, which requires a smaller number of sample questions.

Finally, if you discover that you need additional help to prepare for the GMAT, we are proud to offer the following publications:

1. Guerrilla Tactics for the GMAT: Secrets and Strategies the Test Writers Don't Want You to Know presents the underlying math and grammar concepts that are tested, along with the tricky ways the test writers will try to confuse you.

2. For students who need additional practice for the quantitative section of the exam, *Math Word Problems for the GMAT: When Plugging Numbers into Formulas Just Isn't Enough* offers a complete review of the thirty types of word problems you are likely to see. Learn how to answer these questions quickly and accurately on the day of the test.

3. Finally, for students who are comfortable with the concepts on the GMAT and **really** want to challenge themselves before the big day, we are delighted to offer *The Toughest GMAT Practice Test We've Ever Seen*. Use this publication – and complete the mock exam - AFTER you have completed your preparation program. See how your performance compares to those of other highly competitive students. For an exam this important, why leave your preparation to chance?

Chapter 2: 1,001 Sample Questions for the GMAT

From our experience, the best way to build your confidence and speed before the GMAT is to take mock exams *under actual testing conditions*. Accordingly, that is how we have arranged the 1,0001 GMAT questions and answers:

The **12 Verbal Sections** each present 41 multiple choice questions in one 75-minute segment, including:

Critical Reading questions
Critical Reasoning questions
Sentence Correction questions

The **14 Quantitative Sections** each present 37 questions in one 75-minute section, including:

Mathematical Word Problems
Data Sufficiency questions
Data Interpretation questions

At the end of each section, we present a comprehensive answer key (including explanations) for those questions.

Use these practice questions to:

a.   analyze your strengths
b.   overcome your deficiencies
c.   master the tricks and traps of each section of the exam
d.   get the score you deserve

Directions: *The passage below is followed by questions based on its content. Answer the questions, based on what is* stated *or* implied *in the passage and any introductory material that may be provided.*

Passage 1

Long after the fighting and violence had ceased, the civil war that followed the disintegration of the U.S.S.R. left its people in a state of social, political and economic uncertainty. As a young man in Tbilisi, Georgia, Vladimir Ingo was intrigued by the challenges that would accompany the transition from a communist regime to a free market economy. Although there would undoubtedly be problems relating to unemployment, corruption and a lack of infrastructure, the influx of foreign and U.S. investments would also create exciting opportunities for those who were prepared to seize them. Georgia's development into a thriving free market economy, in which the public and private sectors would enjoy unprecedented growth and prosperity, offered a once-in-a-lifetime chance for young people to guide the area's financial and social re-development.

9

Of the former Soviet nations, Georgia faced unique challenges in its transition to a free economy. Although it attracted significant foreign investments, its residents were unprepared to manage these resources. This scenario created a strong demand for American-educated financial executives to lead and manage companies in the private sector that would provide solutions in the public's best interest.

14

Unfortunately, as Ingo predicted, the underlying challenges defied simple solutions. In 2001, the United States provided a loan guarantee to a leading bank in the Republic of Georgia to provide residential mortgage lending through the Overseas Private Investment Corporation (OPIC). On a theoretical basis, this meant that residents, for the first time, would be able to enjoy the financial and psychological benefits of home ownership. Additionally, tax reforms were implemented in 2003 to establish favorable conditions for local and foreign investors. Yet progress remained hindered by several practicalities, including widespread unemployment and a limited access to credit. Even now, about half of the 5 million residents of Georgia survive on less than $30 a month. In such an impoverished environment, in which people struggle to buy food, the idea of buying a home or qualifying for credit is beyond comprehension.

24

To succeed in a transitional economy, most individuals, small businesses and micro-entrepreneurs need funding, education and ongoing economic support. Under Ingo's direction, the United States Agency for International Development (USAID) completed a business plan for a non-profit organization (NGO) that would provide micro-finance, credit/services and loans to small businesses and Georgian entrepreneurs. The NGO will assess the overall infrastructure of the Georgian financial system, provide targeted technical assistance and customized financial training to micro-finance entities. Ultimately, it will expand access to capital for micro, small, and medium-sized enterprises in Georgia, which will foster innovation and increase the number of high-paying jobs in the underserved Akhalkalaki region. In the long run, these small businesses will play a key role in expanding the Georgian economy.

34

The USAID plan also addresses the implications of corruption, which has hindered Georgia's economic development and undermined the trust of many supporting international organizations. Despite the efforts of the World Bank and the International Finance Corporation (IFC), along with social advocate George Soros, most Georgians have simply lost faith in the government's ability to enforce its own laws and regulations. Years after the fall of communism, many refuse to pay taxes. Under Ingo's guidance and direction, the USAID NGO will support a new anti-corruption campaign that emphasizes education and implementation. To instill confidence in the younger generation, the campaign will implement a program at schools and universities and offer credits to students who volunteer at the NGO. With government support and leadership, including an ongoing awareness program, Georgia can finally eradicate the cancer of corruption and fulfill its social, political and economic potential.

45

1. The main idea of this passage is:

     a.   to discuss the effects of corruption in Georgia
     b.   to praise Vladimir Ingo's managerial skills
     c.   to discuss the challenges Georgia faces to transition to a free market economy
     d.   to discuss American opportunities to invest in Georgia
     e.   to restore the faith of Georgian citizens in their government

2. According to the author, which of the following factors does NOT influence home ownership in Georgia:

    a.   the availability of credit
    b.   level of foreign investment in the region
    c.   low wages
    d.   high unemployment
    e.   unstable property values

3. In Line 32, the word *underserved* most nearly means

    a.   uneducated
    b.   undeveloped
    c.   old
    d.   inner city
    e.   widespread

4. According to the author, what is the primary purpose of the NGO?

    a.   to eradicate corruption in Georgia
    b.   to provide subsidies to impoverished citizens
    c.   to inspire consumer confidence
    d.   to finance and support small business development
    e.   to create jobs

5. According to the passage, corruption has impacted the people of Georgia in several negative ways. Which of the following was NOT mentioned as a ramification of corruption?

    a.   Loss of confidence in law enforcement
    b.   Refusal to pay taxes
    c.   Public protests and demonstrations
    d.   Undermined the trust of international organizations
    e.   Slowed economic development

6. The author of the passage infers that Ingo

    a.   owns a small business in Georgia
    b.   was behind the OPIC initiative
    c.   is committed to re-building the Georgian economy
    d.   is a corrupt political official
    e.   has underestimated the problems in Georgia

7. The author's tone can best be described as

    a.   grave
    b.   neutral
    c.   disappointed
    d.   puzzled
    e.   optimistic

Passage 2

Despite the worldwide progress of the women's rights movement, women in all nations continue to face an uphill battle to achieve an equal measure of legislative representation. Although the percentage of women in political office differs from country to country, current research indicates that their likelihood of being elected depends on three factors: quotas, party ideology and districting.

5

Some state governments and political parties facilitate female legislative representation by using quotas, or affirmative action, to guarantee that a certain percentage of women are represented in the legislature. In India, for example, the ruling Congress party has mandated that 15 percent of its candidates in state elections be women. Likewise, political parties in Venezuela, Sweden, Norway and Germany maintain similar requirements. Quotas for women have a greater impact in the Proportional Representation (PR) system, in which seats in parliament are allotted in proportion to the votes each party receives, which creates an incentive for a political party to broaden its appeal to the public by including more women on its list of candidates. As a result of these mandated quotas, twice as high a proportion of women are elected to public office in PR systems than in Single Member District (SMD) electoral systems, in which the electorate typically favors the incumbent, who is usually male.

16

Existing poll data suggest that party ideology, particularly leftism, may also facilitate female legislative representation. In European countries with a strong Marxist-Socialist or Communist tradition, leftist parties take the lead in nominating and electing women. Although European leftist parties have always placed a greater emphasis on equality, after surviving numerous political, economic, and religious upheavals, other European countries have also become receptive to philosophies or ideologies that promote social justice. Ironically, although leftist parties took the lead in nominating women to political office, their historical performance indicates that they elect only slightly more women than parties on the right. This overall gain for women may be attributed to the party's fear of losing an electoral advantage.

25

Districting may also help women obtain greater legislative representation. Recent research suggests that women are uncomfortable with the adversarial political culture fostered by the single-member district systems, in which parties do not have to negotiate with each other to implement their legislative programs. In such a highly competitive environment, candidates often resort to using negative campaigns against each other. Historically, women have lacked the confidence and desire to participate in the gladiatorial contests that characterize these elections. Even if they triumph, women are likely to be adversely judged because such confrontational behavior contradicts the underlying social expectations that they be peacemakers, rather than gladiators. Instead, women tend to prefer the PR system, which fosters a consensus-seeking political culture in which parties must negotiate to pass legislation. Women tend to thrive in this type of interactive environment, in which they can use their communications skills and interpersonal strengths the same way they do in their family relationships.

37

Quotas, party ideology, and districting are only three of the complex factors that help to facilitate female representation in legislatures across the globe. Ironically, although women comprise fifty percent of every country's population, scholars have only recently begun to examine the different electoral arrangements on a worldwide basis, to determine the implications for women in their quest for political office. As the research continues, the results will inevitably provide women with a greater voice in government, where they can bring attention to critical issues that have been ignored by male-dominated legislatures. An influx of feminine dignity and intelligence will unquestionably benefit the governments in which women participate and the communities in which they live.

46

8. What is the main idea of the passage?

   a. Socialist countries are more committed to equality than democracies.
   b. Quotas, party ideology and districting have dramatically improved female representation in government.
   c. Although women are under-represented in most legislatures, they have much to offer the political process.
   d. Equality for women will never be achieved in legislative representation.
   e. Women are temperamentally unsuited for an adversarial political culture.

9. According to the author, what countries use affirmative action to guarantee a certain percentage of women in the legislature?

   a. Sweden, Germany, Bolivia, India, Pakistan
   b. Venezuela, Germany, Sweden, Norway, Bolivia
   c. Bolivia, Venezuela, Sweden, India, Norway
   d. Pakistan, India, Norway, Germany, Venezuela
   e. India, Norway, Sweden, Germany, Venezuela

10. What reason does the author give to explain the higher percentage of women in the PR electoral system (SMD electoral system?

    a.   countries that use the PR system are more committed to sexual equality.
    b.   the PR system favors parties that champion social justice.
    c.   the PR system favors incumbents, who are mostly women.
    d.   the PR system creates an incentive for a party to broaden it appeal by electing women.
    e.   The SMD system is ripe with corruption, which has turned most voters away.

11. According to the author, why do Socialist countries tend to have a higher percentage of women in the legislature?

    a.   the party's fear of losing an electoral advantage
    b.   women are less likely to accept bribes
    c.   women outnumber men in Socialist countries
    d.   women are wealthier and better educated in Socialist countries
    e.   the party believes that women representatives are more easily manipulated than men

12. In Line 30, what does *"gladiatorial"* mean?

    a.   effusive
    b.   intrepid
    c.   negotiable
    d.   adversarial
    e.   corrupt

13. According to the author, which of the following does NOT explain why women are uncomfortable with political campaigns?

    a.   Lack of confidence
    b.   Tend to be peacemakers
    c.   Thrive in interactive environments
    d.   Fear adverse judgments
    e.   Poor educational credentials

14. The author's tone suggests that his attitude toward women in the legislature is:

    a.   scornful
    b.   apathetic
    c.   enthusiastic
    d.   pessimistic
    e.   dismissive

15. The author cites all of the following as feminine strengths EXCEPT:

    a.   intelligence
    b.   strong analytical skills
    c.   good communication skills
    d.   peacemakers
    e.   dignity

Directions: The questions in this section are based on the reasoning contained in brief statements or passages. For some questions, more than one of the choices could conceivably answer the question. However, you are to choose the one that provides the most complete and accurate answer. You should not make assumptions that are implausible, superfluous, or incompatible with the passage.

16. Geology professor: In the past decade, miners have not discovered any new goldmines on the earth's surface. Auxiliary increases in gold production will be extremely limited, because most current mines have nearly depleted their resources. But global demand for gold has been increasing steadily, largely due to the production of rare European coins. Hence, a severe global shortage of gold, which will dramatically increase the price of gold futures, is nearly certain.

What is the purpose of the geologist's claim that auxiliary increases in gold production will be extremely limited?

    a.   It is the main conclusion of the geologist's argument.
    b.   It is a counter premise, which the geologist uses to amplify his initial statement.
    c.   It is an intermediate conclusion, which the geologist presents as evidence for his main conclusion.
    d.   It is a biased opinion that is not rooted in fact.
    e.   It is historical data used to introduce the actual evidence.

17. Attorney: To determine the validity of his client's personal injury claim, my opponent wants to review 300 other cases in which the complainant suffered a similar type of injury. He will personally contact all 300 victims to verify whether or not they were permanently paralyzed from using my client's product over the past ten years. But this type of after-the-fact inquiry is unfair and capricious because it does not consider the numerous other factors that influence the respondents' health, including age, lifestyle, and pre-existing conditions. Therefore, I submit that that the results of the attorney's review should not be accepted into evidence because they will unfairly prejudice the jury.

Which of the following, if true, would most help to justify the attorney's argument?

    a.   Many of the previous complainants settled their cases out of court because the evidence was slim.
    b.   The admission of hearsay evidence is precluded by state law.
    c.   Several previous juries were unduly swayed by the results of identical reviews.
    d.   The defendant in the case waived his right to a jury trial on similar charges in the past.
    e.   It is impossible to determine cause and effect ten years after an injury.

18. All babies cry. This entity is crying. Therefore, it must be a baby.

Which of the following uses a similar type of reasoning?

    a.   All nails have heads. This item has a head. Therefore, this item must be a nail.
    b.   All mothers eat cheese. This woman is eating. Therefore, this woman likes cheese.
    c.   All houses need heat. This house is cold. Therefore, this house lacks heat.
    d.   All dogs have legs. This creature is running. Therefore, this creature has legs,
    e.   All students must read. This student loves fiction. Therefore, this student is literate.

19. If this library has a good history collection, it will contain a copy of *John Adams* by T.T. Wyatt. The collection does contain a copy of *John Adams*, therefore, the library has a good history collection.

The logic of the above argument is most nearly paralleled by which of the following?

    a.   If there is a cat in the barn, there must be food for it to eat. There is a cat in the barn, so the barn must contain food.
    b.   Either nitrogen or argon is the lightest element of the periodic table. Nitrogen is not the lightest element of the periodic table, so argon must be the lightest element of the periodic table.
    c.   Whenever it snows, the cars get wet. The cars are not wet. Therefore, it has not snowed.
    d.   If diamonds are the most expensive minerals in the universe, then emeralds simply provide a contrasting color in most mines. Since emeralds provide a contrasting color in most mines, it follows that diamonds are the most expensive minerals in the universe.
    e.   If Steve is taller than Bev, and if Bev is taller than Emily, then Steve is also taller than Emily.

20. Gina cannot fly American Airlines because their flight to Phoenix is overbooked. She also cannot fly US Air, because they will not accept her frequent flyer miles. So, the only airline she can take to her class reunion is United, which is the only commuter airline that provides non-stop service between Tulsa and Phoenix.

The argument depends on which of the following assumptions?

  a. United is the only airline that offers non-stop service between Tulsa and Phoenix, other than American Airlines and US Air.
  b. United Airlines has a frequent flyer program.
  c. The US Air flight is not overbooked.
  d. The American flight is overbooked because it offered a special fare for those attended the class reunion.
  e. American Airlines would have accepted Gina's frequent flyer miles.

21. Evidence suggests that women in colonial America wore jewelry that was far more beautiful and ornate than earlier settlers. It seems, therefore, that colonial women were not as destitute as historians previously thought.

Which one of the following statements, if true, most seriously weakens the argument?

  a. Colonial women made their own jewelry for little or no cost.
  b. Historians based their judgment on hundreds of pieces of jewelry.
  c. Early settlers, although wealthy, did not place a high value on luxury items such as jewelry.
  d. Colonial women traded the jewelry for essential food and supplies.
  e. The jewelry in question included once-in-a-lifetime pieces such as wedding and engagement rings.

22. According to epidemiologists, the United States population is struck by a global pandemic, such as typhoid fever or swine flu, on an average of once every fifty years. The last such incident occurred in 2009, when the swine flu claimed the lives of several Americans who lived along the Texas-Mexico border. Hence, we can reasonably expect that the United States population will not be struck by another pandemic until 2059, when public health experts will be better prepared to predict and treat the patients who are affected by the illness. Hence, it would be foolish to allocate immediate funds to swine flu research in the near future, when we face more pressing needs, such as the rapid proliferation of HIV/AIDS.

The reasoning in the argument is most subject to criticism on what grounds?

  a. It implies that some diseases are more important than others.
  b. It does not consider the theoretical value of epidemiological research, only the preventive value.
  c. It does not consider the health status of people outside the United States.
  d. It fails to provide valid statistical data to support its claims.
  e. It uses evidence about the average frequency of a pandemic to make a specific prediction about when the next pandemic will occur.

23. All cars need gas. This car stopped running. Therefore, this car has no gas.

Which of the following uses a similar type of reasoning?

  a. All cats like meat. This cat refused to eat. Therefore, this cat prefers fish.
  b. All mothers are rich. This woman bought a new car. Therefore, this woman is rich. .
  c. All students need money. This student stopped spending. Therefore, this student has no money.
  d. All dogs have legs. This creature cannot walk. Therefore, this creature has no legs,
  e. All students need books. This student bought books. Therefore, this student can read.

24. Ten girls at an eating disorder clinic were evaluated for depression. The physician who examined them discovered that girls who were anorexic or bulimic were significantly more likely to be clinically depressed than random samples of the general population. These findings support the conclusion that girls with eating disorders are at serious risk for depression.

Which one of the following statements articulates the most critical weakness in the physician's method ?

> a. He confused correlation with causation.
> b. He generalized from a very small sample to a large population.
> c. His statistical methods were flawed.
> d. He did not publish his study in a peer-reviewed journal.
> e. He limited his subjects to girls.

25. According to psychologists, daytime soap operas have fallen into disfavor because they reflect outdated sexual roles and standards. Younger viewers, who are more sexually precocious than their parents and grandparents, cannot relate to contrived situations that depict women as helpless victims. Yet I submit there is a more likely reason for the decline in soap opera ratings. Contemporary teens can choose from several hundred television channels, while previous generations had only three channels. When presented with a plethora of entertainment choices on the small screen, the audience drifted to more interesting alternatives than daytime soap operas.

The argument does which of the following?

> a. Discredits the argument of the psychologists by manipulating the use of statistics.
> b. Presents an alternative explanation for the phenomenon the psychologists observed.
> c. Provides additional evidence to support the conclusion of the psychologists.
> d. Attempts to undermine the argument of the psychologists by using circular reasoning.
> e. Attempts to discredit the argument of the psychologist by using flawed reasoning.

Directions: The following sentences test correctness and effectiveness of expression. Part of each sentence (or the entire sentence) is underlined; beneath each sentence are five ways of phrasing the underlined material. Choice A repeats the original phrasing; the other four choices are different. If you think the original phrasing produces a better sentence than the alternatives, select choice A; if not, select one of the other choices. In making your selection, follow the requirements of standard written English, such as grammar, choice of words, sentence construction, and punctuation. Your selection should result in the most effective sentence – clear and precise, without awkwardness or ambiguity.

Example: Most teenagers struggle to be free both of parental domination but also from premature responsibilities.

> *a. both of parental domination but also from premature responsibilities.*
> *b. both of parental domination and also from premature responsibilities.*
> *c. both of parental domination and also of premature responsibilities.*
> *d. of parental domination and premature responsibilities.*
> *e. both of parental domination and their premature responsibilities as well.*

The correct answer is Choice D.

26. Convicted felons in Florida, regardless of their subsequent good deeds, never have and never will be allowed to vote in local, state and national elections.

> a. never have and never will be allowed
> b. neither have nor will be allowed
> c. have never and will never be allowed
> d. never have been allowed and never will be allowed
> e. never have had anyone allow them and never will have anyone allow them

27. When they competed in the Olympics, Barb and Jane acted <u>as though they were strangers, despite the fact that they had been</u> running partners for several years.

    a.   as though they were strangers, despite the fact that they had been
    b.   like complete and utter strangers, although they had been
    c.   kind of like strangers, despite being
    d.   as though they were strangers, although they had been
    e.   estranged, despite having been.

28. Rachel and Amy will join <u>Cara and I</u> at the mall on Tuesday.

    a.   Cara and I
    b.   Cara and me
    c.   I and Cara
    d.   me and Cara
    e.   both I and Cara

29. <u>Each of the ten pageant finalists hoped that they would win the crown, the scholarship and the brand news sports car.</u>

    a.   Each of the ten pageant finalists hoped that they would win the crown, the scholarship and the brand new sports car.
    b.   Each of the ten pageant finalists hoped that they would win the crown and scholarship, especially the brand new sports car.
    c.   Each of the ten pageant finalists hoped that they would win the crown, and with it, the scholarship and brand new sports car.
    d.   Each of the ten pageant finalists hoped that she would win the crown, the scholarship and the brand new sports car.
    e.   Each of the ten pageant finalists hoped that she would win the crown, which brought with it a scholarship and brand new sports car.

30. After careful consideration, Jake and Jennifer chose a wedding menu of tossed green salad, French onion soup, roast beef au jus, <u>along with a fabulous chocolate cake.</u>

    a.   along with a fabulous chocolate cake
    b.   including a fabulous chocolate cake
    c.   and a fabulous chocolate cake
    d.   in addition to a fabulous chocolate cake
    e.   with a fabulous chocolate cake

31. <u>Seeing the police car, the beer bottles were immediately tossed from the car by the worried teens.</u>

    a.   Seeing the police car, the beer bottles were immediately tossed from the car by the worried teens.
    b.   The beer bottles, after seeing the police car, were immediately tossed from the car by the worried teens.
    c.   The worried teens, after seeing the police car, tossed from the car the beer bottles, immediately.
    d.   Seeing the police car, the worried teens immediately tossed the beer bottles from the car.
    e.   The beer bottles were immediately tossed from the car by the worried teens, who saw a police car.

32. Hilary Clinton, <u>the Senator from New York, and most famous of all First Ladies, who we all agree is</u> one of the most famous and notorious women of the twenty-first century.

    a.   the Senator from New York, and most famous of all First Ladies, who we all agree is
    b.   who is the Senator from New York and famous First Lady, who we all agree is
    c.   the Senator from New York and the former First Lady, is also agreed to be
    d.   the Senator from New York and the most famous of all First Ladies, is also, we agree,
    e.   is the Senator from New York, and the most famous of all First Ladies, is

33. The Department of State worked diligently <u>to develop a consistent policy regarding emigration into the</u> United States.

    a.   to develop a consistent policy regarding emigration into the
    b.   to develop consistent policies regarding emigration into the
    c.   to make consistent the policies regarding emigration into the
    d.   to develop a consistent policy regarding immigration into the
    e.   to make consistent policies about immigration from the   .

34. After a prolonged delay, <u>in which the airport was paralyzed by eight inches of snow, the flight to Jamaica was cleared for take-off.</u>

    a.   in which the airport was paralyzed by eight inches of snow, the flight to Jamaica was cleared for take-off.
    b.   in which the airport was paralyzed by eight inches of snow, the flight from Jamaica took off.
    c.   in which eight inches of snow paralyzed the airport, the airline cleared the flight to Jamaica for take-off.
    d.   in which the airport was paralyzed by eight inches of snow, the airport allowed the flight to Jamaica to take-off.
    e.   in which eight inches of snow paralyzed the airport, the flight to Jamaica was cleared for take-off.

35. <u>In his written decision on the landmark case, Judge Reynolds eluded to previous case law on a similar topic, which supported his own personal views.</u>

    a.   In his written decision on the landmark case, Judge Reynolds eluded to previous case law on a similar topic, which supported his own personal views.
    b.   In his written decision on the landmark case, Judge Reynolds alluded to previous case law on a similar topic, which supported his own personal views.
    c.   Judge Reynolds eluded to previous case law in his written decision on the landmark case, which supported his own personal views.
    d.   In his written decision on the landmark case, Judge Reynolds was lucky to find previous case law that supported his own personal views, which he eluded to.
    e.   When writing his decision on the landmark case, Judge Reynolds alluded to previous case law, which supported his own personal views.

36. <u>Carrie considered suing the unscrupulous vendor, but she went no farther than veiled threats.</u>

    a.   Carrie considered suing the unscrupulous vendor, but she went no farther than veiled threats.
    b.   Carrie considered suing the unscrupulous vendor, but she went no farther than making veiled threats.
    c.   Although Carrie considered filing a lawsuit against the unscrupulous vendor, she went no farther than making veiled threats.
    d.   Carrie went no further than making veiled threats against the unscrupulous vendor, but she considered suing them.
    e.   Carrie considered suing the unscrupulous vendor, but she went no further than making veiled threats.

37. The reason why Americans don't worry about their weight <u>is because they have little time to exercise, compared with most other cultures</u> on earth.

    a.   is because they have little time to exercise, compared with most other cultures
    b.   is that they have little time to exercise, compared with most other cultures
    c.   is because they have little time to exercise, compared to most other cultures
    d.   is that they have little time to exercise, compared to most other cultures
    e.   is they lack time to exercise, compared with most other cultures

38. Because of an airline mix-up, several attendees missed the conference at which the agenda for future meetings were presented.

    a. Because of an airline mix-up, several attendees missed the conference at which the agenda for future meetings were presented.
    b. Due to an airline mix-up, several attendees missed the conference at which the agenda for future meetings was presented.
    c. Because of an airline mix-up, several attendees missed the conference for which the agenda for future meetings were presented.
    d. Due to an airline mix-up, several attendees missed the conference, which would present future meeting schedules.
    e. Because of an airline mix-up, several attendees missed the conference that explained the future agenda.

39. If Zachary would have lain in that bed for one more minute, he might have developed horrible bedsores, which would have exacerbated his existing health problems.

    a. If Zachary would have lain in that bed for one more minute, he might have developed horrible bedsores, which would have exacerbated his existing health problems.
    b. If Zachary had lay in that bed for one more minute, he might have developed horrible bedsores, which would have exacerbated his existing health problems.
    c. If Zachary would have lay in that bed for one more minute, he might have developed horrible bedsores, which would exacerbate his existing health problems.
    d. If Zachary had laid in that bed for one more minute, he might have developed horrible bedsores, which would exacerbate his existing health problems.
    e. If Zachary had lain in that bed for one more minute, he might have developed horrible bedsores, which would have exacerbated his existing health problems.

40. Her husband wanted to wash the car before his wife had come home from the mall.

    a. Her husband wanted to wash the car before his wife had come home from the mall.
    b. Her husband had wanted to wash the car before his wife would of come home from the mall.
    c. Her husband wanted to wash the car before his wife come home from the mall.
    d. Her husband wanted to wash the car before his wife came home from the mall.
    e. Her husband had wanted to wash the car before his wife would have come home from the mall.

41. The mayor of Dallas gave the secretarial job to the person whom achieved the highest score on the keyboard test.

    a. to the person whom
    b. to the person who
    c. to whom
    d. to whoever
    e. to whomever

Verbal 1: Answer Key for Verbal 1

Critical Reading

1. Answer choice C is correct. The passage describes the challenges that Georgia will face to make a successful transition to a free market economy.   Choices A, D and E are too narrow in scope to be the main idea. Choice B is incorrect, because the transition has not yet succeeded; hence, it is too soon to evaluate Ingo's leadership skills with 100% clarity.

2. The correct answer is E. All of the other factors are mentioned in the paragraph about home ownership.

3. The correct answer is B. Thus far, the area has not attracted business interest or investment.

4. Answer choice D is correct. Although all of the other factors are mentioned in the passage, they are not the *main* function of the NGO. Its underlying goal is to provide micro-financing for small businesses and entrepreneurs, which will create jobs and reduce unemployment. The subsidies are not intended for impoverished individuals.

5. The correct answer is C. All of the other answer choices were mentioned in the final paragraph of the passage.

6. The correct answer is C. The passage discusses Ingo's familiarity with Georgia's challenges and his commitment to conquering them.

7. The correct answer is E. The final sentence confirms the author's sense of optimism about the plan to re-build Georgia.

8. Choice C is correct. The other choices are too broad or narrow to be the main idea.

9. Choice E is correct. The answer countries are listed in Line 9 of the passage.

10. Choice D is correct. The answer is presented in Lines 11 –12 of the passage.

11. Choice A is correct. The answer is presented in Line 24 of the passage.

12. Choice D is correct. In this context, *gladiatorial* means adversarial.

13. Choice E is correct. The answer is presented in Lines 31 – 36 of the passage.

14. Choice C is correct. In the final paragraph, the author expressly states the benefits that women will bring to the legislature.

15. Choice B is correct. The passage includes all of the other answer choices.

Critical Reasoning

16. Choice C is correct. The claim is an intermediate conclusion that the geologist uses to support his main (larger) conclusion about severe gold shortages.

17. The attorney believes that the review will unfairly influence the jury. If similar juries had already been negatively impacted by an identical study, it would greatly bolster the attorney's argument. Choice C is correct.

18. The original argument is in the following form: "All X do Y. This does Y. Therefore, this must be an X." Choice A is correct.

19. The argument is in the form "If A, then B. B, therefore A". Choice D is also an argument that has the same form.

20. Choice A is correct. The argument presumes that United is the only commuter airline that offers non-stop service between Tulsa and Phoenix, other than American Airlines and US Air.

21. Choice A is correct. The jewelry, although beautiful, was not necessarily expensive.

22. Choice E is correct. The past frequency of pandemics cannot be used to predict the likelihood of a specific pandemic happening in the future.

23. The original argument is in the following form: "All X need Y. This A stopped doing Z. Therefore, this X has no Y." Choice C is correct.

24. The argument generalizes from a very small sample to the entire human population. If the women at the hospital are NOT typical of the general population, then the conclusion to the argument is weakened. Choice B captures this sentiment.

25. Choice B is correct. The argument presents an alternative explanation for the decline in soap opera

ratings.

Sentence Correction

26. This sentence is awkward because of the compound verb structure, which includes two different tenses. Additionally, the subject and verb are separated by a long modifying phrase. The correct answer is D, which fully states each phrase and includes the correct tense for each verb (never have *been* allowed and never will *be* allowed).

27. Choice D is correct. The other answer choices introduce new errors (or additional information that was not in the original sentence).

28. In choosing between *I and we*, students should use the same pronoun they would use if Cara was not mentioned in the sentence.   The correct pronoun is *me*, which is answer choice B.

29. Choice D is correct. The word *each* is singular, which requires the singular pronoun *she*.

30. The original sentence contains an error in parallelism. The menu items must all be presented consistently in the sentence. Hence, answer choice C is correct.

31. Choice D is correct. The sentence contains a misplaced modifier. It is also written in the passive voice. Only choice D corrects both mistakes without making an additional one.

32. This is not a sentence because it lacks a verb. Answers C, D and E correct the problem, but Choice D does it best.

33. Choice D is correct. The correct combinations of pronoun and verb are *immigrate into* and *emigrate from*.   Only Choice D uses the correct combination.

34. Choice C is correct, because is converts both passive verbs to active form, without changing the meaning of the sentence.

35. Choice B is correct. The original sentence uses the word *elude* instead of *allude*.   *Elude* means to avoid, while *allude* means to refer.

36. Choice E is correct. The original sentence uses *farther* instead of *further*. *Farther* refers to distance, while *further* refers to degree.

37. Choice D is correct. It is grammatically incorrect to use the expression "the reason why is because." Hence, only answer choices B, D and E are viable possibilities. Of these, B and E contain the error *compared with*, instead of *compared to*. Hence, choice D is correct.

38. Although this sentence contains many potential idiomatic traps, the error is actually in the subject-verb agreement. The word *agenda* is singular; the verb should therefore be *was presented*, not *were presented*. Choice B is correct.

39. The correct choice is A, which uses the correct verb form, *had lain*.   This sentence uses the verb *lay* in a hypothetical "if" clause, which requires the unusual form *had lain*.

40. The original sentence includes the wrong verb tense. Choice D is correct (*came home)*.

41. Choice D is correct. The correct wording of the sentence should be: The mayor of Dallas gave the secretarial job *to whoever* achieved the highest score on the keyboard test.

Directions: *The passage below is followed by questions based on its content. Answer the questions, based on what is stated or implied in the passage and any introductory material that may be provided.*

Passage 1

The most prominent error in conversation is not saying too little that amounts to much, but too much that amounts to little. Talkativeness is a characteristic more common of the ignorant than of the wise. Shenstone says, "The common fluency of speech in many men and women is due to a scarcity of matter and a scarcity of words; for whoever is master of a language and has a mind full of ideas, will be apt, in speaking, to hesitate upon the choice of both; but common speakers have only one set of ideas and one set of words to clothe them in— and these are always ready at the mouth. Just so people can come faster out of a church when it is almost empty, than when a crowd is at the door!" But although, according to the old proverb, "a still tongue denotes a wise head," the faculty of speech should not be neglected, merely because it may be misused.

9

Conversation is not a gift bestowed only upon those whom genius favors; on the contrary, many men eminent for their fluency of style in writing have been noted for habitual taciturnity in their intercourse with society. Hazlitt remarked, that "authors should be read, not heard!" Charles II of England, not only the wittiest of monarchs, but one of the liveliest of men, is said to have been so charmed in reading the humor of Butler's "Hudibras," that he disguised himself as a private gentleman and was introduced to the author, whom, to his astonishment, he found to be one of the dullest of companions. On the other hand, some of the humblest men with whom one falls into company, possessed of but little variety, and less extent of information, are highly entertaining talkers. The particular topic of remark does not form so essential a part of an interesting conversation, as the words and manner of those who engage in it. Robert Burns, sitting down on one occasion to write a poem, said: "Which way the subject theme may gang, let time or chance determine; perhaps it may turn out a song or probably a sermon."

21

In the same manner, the subject of a conversation need not be made a matter of study or special preparation. Men may talk of things momentous or trivial, and in either strain be attractive and agreeable. But quitting the consideration of the thought, to refer to the mode of its expression, it must be remarked and insisted that to "murder the king's English" is hardly less a crime than to design against one of the king's subjects. If committed from ignorance, the fault is at least deplorable; but if from carelessness, it is inexcusable. The greatest of sciences is that of language; the greatest of human arts is that of using words. No "cunning hand" of the artificer can contrive a work of mechanism that is to be compared, for a moment, with those wonderful masterpieces of ingenuity, which may be wrought by him who can skillfully mould a beautiful thought into a form that shall preserve, yet radiate its beauty.

31

A mosaic of words may be fairer than inlaid precious stones. The scholar who comes forth from his study a master of the English language is a workman who has at his command hardly less than a hundred thousand finely-tempered instruments, with which he may fashion the most cunning device. This is a trade which all should learn, for it is one that every individual is called to practice. The greatest support of virtue in a community is intelligence; intelligence is the outgrowth of knowledge; and the almoner of all knowledge is language. The possession, therefore, of the resources, and a command over the appliances of language, is of the utmost importance to every individual. Words are current coins of the realm, and they who do not have them in their treasury, suffer a more pitiable poverty than others who have not a penny of baser specie in their pocket; and the multitude of those who have an unfailing supply, but which is of the wrong stamp, are possessed only of counterfeit cash, that will not pass in circles of respectability.

42

1. What is the main point of the passage?

    a.   Language is a universal tool that unites us all
    b.   The most intelligent among us are linguists
    c.   Language is a precious gift that should be cultivated and used with care
    d.   Conversational flow should not be restricted by the participants
    e.   Writing requires time and effort to master

2. Which of the following most accurately expresses Shenstone's sentiments?

   a. Those who speak the best know the most
   b. Those with the least to say tend to speak the most
   c. Words allow the common man to speak with mastery
   d. Speaking in church is boorish and ill-advised
   e. Words are common, but language is an art

3. In Line 9, what does "*faculty*" mean?

   a. Teacher
   b. Hyperbole
   c. Example
   d. Staff
   e. Power

4. In Line 11, what does "*taciturnity*" mean?

   a. Flowery
   b. Reluctance
   c. Boastful
   d. Circumspect
   e. Humility

5. According to the author, which of the following best describes the reaction of Charles II of England to Butler?

   a. He found Butler charming and witty
   b. He found both the man and his work to be woefully overrated
   c. He enjoyed Butler's work but found him dull in person
   d. They became close companions upon their first meeting
   e. They shared a love of intelligent discourse

6. According to the author, what is inexcusable?

   a. Disrespecting the King of England
   b. Making careless grammatical mistakes
   c. Speaking too much
   d. A lack of education
   e. Using a cunning hand

7. According to the author, what is the relationship between language and words?

   a. Language is a virtue of intelligence, while words are an outgrowth of knowledge
   b. Words are a virtue of intelligence, while language is the almoner of knowledge
   c. Language is the greatest of sciences and using words is the greatest human art
   d. Language is the greatest art, which relies upon the science of words
   e. Language supports the virtue of a community through the mosaic of words

8. In Line 34, what does "*instruments*" mean?

   a. Words
   b. Letters
   c. Books
   d. Thoughts
   e. Tools

9. In Line 36, what does "*almoner*" mean"?

    a.   Virtue
    b.   Goodness
    c.   Source
    d.   Antipathy
    e.   Benevolence

10. According to the author, which of the following is the best example of "counterfeit cash"?

    a.   Illiteracy
    b.   Apathy
    c.   Slang
    d.   Education
    e.   Verbosity

Passage 2

In English legal practice, the written statement given to a barrister to form the basis of his case is called a brief; it was probably so-called because it was the first copy of the original writ. When a barrister assumes the responsibility for a case when it comes into the court, all of the preliminary work, such as the drawing up of the case, serving papers, and marshalling evidence, is performed by a solicitor, so that a brief contains a concise summary of the case that the counsel has to plead, with all material facts in chronological order, and frequently such observations thereon as the solicitor may think fit to make, the names of witnesses, with the "proofs," that is, the nature of the evidence which each witness is ready to give, if called upon. The brief may also contain suggestions for the use of counsel when cross-examining witnesses called by the other side.

10

Accompanying the brief may be copies of the pleadings and of all documents material to the case. The brief is always endorsed with the title of the court in which the action is to be tried, with the title of the action, and the names of the counsel and of the solicitor who delivers the brief. Counsel's fee is also marked. The delivery of a brief to counsel gives him authority to act for his client in all matters which the litigation involves. The result of the action is noted on the brief by counsel, or if the action is compromised, the terms of the compromise are endorsed on each brief and signed by the leading counsel on the opposite side. In Scotland a brief is called a memorial.

18

In the United States the word has, to a certain extent, a different meaning, a brief in its English sense not being required, for the American attorney exercises all the functions distributed in England between barristers and solicitors. A lawyer sometimes prepares for his own use what is called a "trial brief" for use at the trial. This corresponds in all essential particulars with the "brief" prepared by the solicitor in England for the use of counsel. But the more distinctive use of the term in America is in the case of the brief "in error or appeal," before an appellate court. This is a written or printed document, varying according to circumstances, but embodying the argument on the question affected. Most of the appellate courts require the filing of printed briefs for the use of the court and opposing counsel at a time designated for each side before hearing.

28

In the rules of the United States Supreme Court and circuit courts of appeals, the brief is required to contain a concise statement of the case, a specification of errors relied on, including the substance of evidence, the admission or rejection of which is to be reviewed, or any extract from a charge excepted to, and an argument exhibiting clearly the points of law or fact to be discussed. This form of brief, it may be added, is also adopted for use at the trial in certain states of the Union which require printed briefs to be delivered to the court.

35

The "brief-bag," in which counsel's papers are carried to and from court, now forms an integral part of a barrister's outfit, but in the early part of the 19th century the possession of a brief-bag was strictly confined to those who had received one from a king's counsel. King's counsel were then few in number, were considered officers of the court, and had a salary of £40 a year, with a supply of paper, pens and purple bags. These bags they distributed among rising juniors of their acquaintance, whose bundles of briefs were getting inconveniently large to be carried in their hands. These perquisites were abolished in 1830. English brief-bags are now either blue or red. Blue bags are those with which barristers provide themselves when first called, and it is a breach of etiquette to let this bag be visible in court. The only brief-bag allowed to be placed on the desks is the red bag, which by English legal etiquette is given by a leading counsel to a junior who has been useful to him in some important case.

46

11. What is the main point of the passage?

     a.   To compare and contrast a legal brief in England to one in the United States
     b.   To explain the original of "brief bags" in the British legal system
     c.   To differentiate among solicitors, barristers, and attorneys
     d.   To explain the legal definition of a brief
     e.   To compare and contrast the British and American legal systems

12. According to the passage, a brief in England is endorsed with all of the following EXCEPT:

     a.   Title of the court
     b.   Title of the action
     c.   Names of the counsel and solicitor
     d.   Name of the district or circuit judge presiding
     e.   Counsel fee

13. According to the passage, what is a brief "in error or appeal"?

     a.   A written document submitted by an attorney to the U.S. court of appeals
     b.   A written document submitted by a U.S. attorney to the opposing counsel
     c.   A written document submitted by a solicitor in England to the opposing counsel
     d.   A written document submitted by a barrister in England to the opposing counsel
     e.   A written response from the U.S. Supreme Court in response to an attorney's "trial brief"

14. In Line 41, what does "*perquisites*" mean?

     a.   Accoutrements
     b.   Privileges
     c.   Briefcases
     d.   Professional attire
     e.   Obligations

15. All of the following are true about "brief bags" EXCEPT:

     a.   They are used in England to carry counsel's papers to and from court
     b.   In the 19th century, they were only distributed to a select few by the King's counsel
     c.   They are either red or blue
     d.   It is a breach of etiquette for a blue bag to be visible in court
     e.   In England, they now form an integral part of a solicitor's outfit

Directions: *The questions in this section are based on the reasoning contained in brief statements or passages. For some questions, more than one of the choices could conceivably answer the question. However, you are to choose the one that provides the most complete and accurate answer. You should not make assumptions that are implausible, superfluous, or incompatible with the passage.*

16. All fats that are oxidized and dehydrogenated are used for frying, so there are frying fats that are polyunsaturated.

The conclusion of the argument follows logically if which one of the following is assumed?

     a.   All polyunsaturated fats are oxidized.
     b.   Some fats are oxidized but not dehydrogenated.
     c.   Some fats that are oxidized and dehydrogenated are polyunsaturated.
     d.   Some dehydrogenated fats are polyunsaturated, but not oxidized.
     e.   Ideally, all fats should be polyunsaturated.

17. Some students are athletes. All athletes are limber. Therefore, this student must be limber.

Which of the following uses a similar type of flawed reasoning?

    a. All houses have walls. Some houses are large walls. Therefore, large houses must have walls.
    b. Some flyers are travelers. All travelers are old. Therefore, this flyer must be old.
    c. Some months have thirty days. All months have four weeks,   Therefore, last month had thirty days.
    d. Some fruits are fattening. An orange is a fruit. Therefore, an orange must be fattening.
    e. All plants are green. Some weeds are orange. Therefore, this plant must be a weed.

18. Most beauty pageants are open to any contestant with musical talent and great physical beauty. Previously, the talent competition was worth 40% of the contestants' overall score. Since 2005, however, the talent competition has only been worth 10% of the contestants' overall score.

Which of the following conclusions is most strongly suggested by the paragraph above?

    a. Most singers and dancers are not beautiful enough to win a pageant.
    b. Most beauty pageant winners are not talented enough to play a musical instrument.
    c. The personal interview is now worth more than the talent portion of the competition.
    d. The talent requirement was an anachronism that demeaned women.
    e. Other factors besides musical talent are more important to the pageant judges.

19. Stephanie cannot write the article because she has already accepted another freelance assignment. Francesca, on the other hand, cannot write the article because she is not fluent in Italian. So, the article must be assigned to Bonnie, who is the only *Newsweek* editor in the Berlin office, other than Stephanie and Francesca.

The argument depends on which of the following assumptions?

    a. The editors in the Berlin office do not need to speak Italian.
    b. *Newsweek* editors are permitted to accept freelance assignments.
    c. The article must be written by a *Newsweek* editor in the Berlin office.
    d. Bonnie does not accept freelance assignments.
    e. Stephanie, Bonnie and Francesca are all freelance journalists.

20. Patients with heart disease are far more likely to eat red meat than healthy people. Therefore, patients with cancer are also far more likely to eat red meat than healthy people.

The flawed reasoning in the argument above most closely parallels the reasoning in which of the following?

    a. The rise in employment sparked an increase in the number of foreclosures in most communities. Therefore, the property tax revenues in these communities will inevitably decline.
    b. As sugar becomes more expensive, products that use it, such as chocolate and ice cream, will also increase in cost.
    c. Skinny people are far more likely to eat whole grains and fresh fruits and vegetables. Therefore, they are less likely to gain weight.
    d. The cost of roses will rise dramatically in the fall. Therefore, tulips and daisies will also cost significantly more in the fall.
    e. Pine trees are significantly more likely to rot in wet weather. Therefore, furniture manufacturers use less of it for lower-priced items.

21. In making cupcakes, Jill could easily substitute high fructose corn syrup for granulated sugar without adjusting her recipe. However, I think she should replace the granulated sugar with dark molasses, although it would increase the caloric content. The enhanced flavor that molasses would add to the cupcakes is well worth the extra calories.

Which one of the following is an assumption on which the argument depends?

a. Cupcakes can easily be made with different types of sugars.
b. Jill should base her selection of sugar on flavor and caloric content.
c. More bakers should use molasses when they bake cupcakes.
d. Molasses are higher in calories than high fructose corn syrup.
e. Granulated sugar and high fructose corn syrup are equal in calories.

22. Last season, the producers of *American Idol* conducted an interesting study. Six of the twelve finalists knew that their performances at dress rehearsal were being recorded and that portions of the tape might be aired on a subsequent episode of the series. However, the other six finalists did not know that their dress rehearsals were being recorded. When they reviewed the subsequent tapes, the producers discovered that the six contestants who knew they were being recorded performed significantly better than the six who did not.

This situation supports which one of the following propositions?

a. Subjects perform better if they are evaluated independently, rather than as part of a group.
b. The study is flawed, because singing is a creative endeavor that cannot be evaluated in an objective manner.
c. Subjects perform better when they do not know that they are being evaluated.
d. The study is flawed, because the performances at dress rehearsal are, by nature, works in progress.
e. Subjects perform better when they know they are being observed.

23. Most chefs who are efficient bakers are meticulous, but some non-meticulous chefs are very efficient bakers. In addition, every efficient baker is a good fry cook.

Which one of the following statements follows logically from the statements above?

a. Some good fry cooks are chefs.
b. Every meticulous chef is a fry cook.
c. Some good fry cooks are meticulous.
d. Every good fry cook is meticulous.
e. The efficient bakers who are also good fry cooks are also meticulous.

24. Jack: Firing nurses who cross the picket line is profoundly unfair. Such nurses are trying to take care of the patients who rely upon them.

Jill: The nurses *should* be fired because they are violating union policy. By doing so, they are betraying their peers on the nursing staff.

Which one of the following statements is more strongly supported by the exchange between Jack and Jill?

a. Jack and Jill disagree over the amount of power that a union should have in a hospital setting.
b. Jack believes that the patients should be the nurses' top priority, while Jill believes their loyalty should be to the union.
c. Jill is a union steward, while Jack is a part-time worker.
d. Jill's priority is money, while Jack's priority is service.
e. Jack and Jill disagree about the philosophical nature of the nursing profession.

25. Either Bill or Bob will win the election. Bill did not win, so Bob must have won the election.

The logic of the above argument is most nearly paralleled by which of the following?

     a. Either the library or the bookstore will have a good mystery collection. The library has a copy of *Blood Simple* by Robin Cook. Therefore, the library has a good mystery collection.
     b. If the cat is scratching, he is infected with fleas or ticks. There are no fleas in the pantry, so the cat must be infested with ticks.
     c. Either Stan or Sara is taller than Ben, and Ben is taller than Elliott. Therefore, Stan is taller than Elliott.
     d. If it snows or rains, the cars get wet. The cars are wet. Therefore, it might have snowed.
     e. Either oxygen or nitrogen is the lightest element of the periodic table. Oxygen is not the lightest element of the periodic table, so nitrogen must be the lightest element of the periodic table.

Directions: The following sentences test correctness and effectiveness of expression. Part of each sentence (or the entire sentence) is underlined; beneath each sentence are five ways of phrasing the underlined material. Choice A repeats the original phrasing; the other four choices are different. If you think the original phrasing produces a better sentence than the alternatives, select choice A; if not, select one of the other choices. In making your selection, follow the requirements of standard written English, such as grammar, choice of words, sentence construction, and punctuation. Your selection should result in the most effective sentence – clear and precise, without awkwardness or ambiguity.

Example: Most teenagers struggle to be free <u>both of parental domination but also from premature responsibilities.</u>

a. both of parental domination but also from premature responsibilities.
b. both of parental domination and also from premature responsibilities.
c. both of parental domination and also of premature responsibilities.
d. of parental domination and premature responsibilities.
e. both of parental domination and their premature responsibilities as well.

The correct answer is Choice D.

26. <u>Prison as well as restitution was the thief's dismal fate.</u>

     a. Prison as well as restitution was the thief's dismal fate.
     b. First prison, then restitution, will be the thief's dismal fate
     c. He will be punished by prison as well as restitution.
     d. Prison and restitution was the thief's dismal fate.
     e. As his fate, he endured dismal prison as well as restitution.

27. Neither Jeremy nor Nicholas <u>were at the party when Karen arrived</u>.

     a. were at the party when Karen arrived
     b. were at the party when Karen arrives
     c. was at the party when Karen arrived
     d. were at the party for Karen's arrival
     e. was at the party for Karen to arrive

28. Every flight attendant <u>except Jenny and she</u> was delayed by bad weather.

     a. except Jenny and she
     b. except Jenny and her
     c. accept Jenny and she
     d. besides she and Jenny
     e. accept for her and Jenny

29. One cannot win the lottery if you don't buy a ticket.

    a. One cannot win the lottery if you don't buy a ticket.
    b. You cannot win the lottery if one doesn't buy a ticket.
    c. He cannot win the lottery if you don't buy a ticket.
    d. You cannot win the lottery if you don't buy a ticket.
    e. One cannot win the lottery if a ticket is not bought.

30. The editor rejected the manuscript because it was pompous, offensive and lacking in style.

    a. it was pompous, offensive and lacking in style.
    b. It was pompous, it offended her and lacked style.
    c. of its pomposity, offensive and lack of style.
    d. of its pomposity, offensiveness and lacking of style.
    e. it was pompous, offensive and style-lacking.

31. According to Gary, a stove is needed for the senior center in good condition.

    a. a stove is needed for the senior center in good condition.
    b. a stove in good condition is needed for the senior center
    c. a stove is needed by the seniors, preferably in good condition.
    d. the senior center needs a stove in good condition.
    e. the stove that is needed for the senior center is in good condition.

32. A special interest group comprising members of the Republican Party, Right to Life advocates and miscellaneous religious groups hoping to influence the President's decision on reproductive freedom.

    a. A special interest group comprising members of the Republican Party, Right to Life advocates and miscellaneous religious groups hoping to influence the President's decision on reproductive freedom.
    b. A special interest group included members of the Republican Party, Right to Life advocates and miscellaneous religious groups whom hoped to influence the President's decision on reproductive freedom.
    c. A special interest group, including members of the Republican Party, Right to Life advocates and miscellaneous religious groups, hoped to influence the President's decision on reproductive freedom.
    d. A special interest group comprising members of the Republican Party, Right to Life advocates and miscellaneous religious groups were hoping to influence the President's decision on reproductive freedom.
    e. A special interest group hoped to influence the President's decision on reproductive freedom, included members of the Republican Party, Right to Life advocates and miscellaneous religious groups.

33. After every parent/teacher conference, David's parents chastised him about his greatest weakness: his refusal to conform with societal norms.

    a. After every parent/teacher conference, David's parents chastised him about his greatest weakness: his refusal to conform with societal norms.
    b. After every parent/teacher conference David's parents chastised him about his refusal to conform with societal norms, which was his greatest weakness.
    c. After every parent/teacher conference, David's parents chastised him about his refusal to conform to societal norms, which was his greatest weakness.
    d. David's greatest weakness was his refusal to conform with societal norms; after every parent/teacher conference, his parents chastised him about it.
    e. After every parent/teacher conference, David's parents chastised him about his refusal to conform to societal norms, which were his greatest weakness.

34. The fledgling mail order company, which was financed with borrowed money, was devastated when more then 30% of holiday buyers requested a refund.

    a. which was financed with borrowed money, was devastated when more then 30% of holiday buyers requested a refund.
    b. which was financed with borrowed money, was devastated when more then 30% of holiday shoppers demanded refunds.
    c. which the owners financed with borrowed money, was devastated when more then 30% of holiday buyers demanded a refund.
    d. which the owners financed with borrowed money, was devastated when more than 30% of holiday buyers requested a refund.
    e. which was financed with outstanding loans, was devastated when more than 30% of holiday shoppers were dissatisfied with their purchases.

35. Opponents to gun control realize that they cannot hope to effect the public as vehemently as they wish without alienating their representatives in Washington.

    a. they cannot hope to effect
    b. they cannot try to affect
    c. they cannot hope to effecting
    d. they cannot hope to affect
    e. they cannot hope to have an affect on

36. Once the stress of dieting and exercise are over, the players can return to their gluttonous ways.

    a. Once the stress of dieting and exercise are over, the players can return to their gluttonous ways.
    b. After the stress of dieting and exercise are over, the players can resume their gluttonous ways.
    c. After the stress of dieting and exercise are over, the players can return to their gluttonous ways.
    d. Once the stress of dieting and exercise is over, the players can return to their gluttonous ways.
    e. Once the stress of dieting and exercise is over, the players can return to gluttoning.

37. Buying only clothing made in the United States is admirable, so says my mother.

    a. Buying only clothing made in the United States is admirable, so says my mother.
    b. My mother says that we should buy clothing that is made in the United States.
    c. According to my mother, it is an admirable goal to buy clothing that is made in the United States only.
    d. My mother admires people who only buy clothing made in the United States.
    e. According to my mother, an admirable goal is to only buy clothing we make here in the United States.

38. The entrepreneur that built the mini-mall has requested a permit to add six hundred parking spaces.

    a. The entrepreneur that built the mini-mall has requested a permit to add six hundred parking spaces.
    b. The entrepreneur who built the mini-mall has requested a permit to add six hundred parking spaces.
    c. The entrepreneur that built the mini-mall has requested a permit to add a parking lot big enough to fit six hundred cars.
    d. A permit to add six hundred parking spaces was requested by the entrepreneur who built the mini-mall.
    e. After building the mini-mall, the entrepreneur requested a permit to add a six hundred car parking lot.

39. If Benjamin Franklin <u>were to walk the halls of a modern university, he would be delighted by</u> the novels uses of electricity, particularly computer and Internet applications.

    a.   were to walk the halls of a modern university, he would be delighted by
    b.   was to walk the halls of a modern university, he would be delighted by
    c.   were to walk the halls in a modern university, he would have to be delighted by
    d.   was to walk the halls of a modern university, he would delight to see the
    e.   were to walk the halls in a modern university, he would be delighted in

40. <u>The school officials attributed the low GMAT scores to the fact that not one of the more than five hundred students were graduates of the online review class.</u>

    a.   The school officials attributed the low GMAT scores to the fact that not one of the more than five hundred students were graduates of the online review class.
    b.   The school officials blamed the low GMAT scores to the fact that not one of the more than five hundred students were graduates of the online review class.
    c.   The school officials attributed the low GMAT scores to the online review class, which only one of the more than five hundred students were graduates of.
    d.   The school officials attributed the low GMAT scores to the fact that not one of the more than five hundred students would have graduated the online review class.
    e.   The school officials attributed the low GMAT scores to the fact that not one of the more than five hundred students was a graduate of the online review class.

41. <u>Also on the agenda is a presentation by Jane Bowers on salt reduction and a discussion about our upcoming Christmas party in Martha's Vineyard.</u>

    a.   Also on the agenda is a presentation by Jane Bowers on salt reduction and a discussion about our upcoming Christmas party in Martha's Vineyard.
    b.   The agenda is a presentation by Jane Bowers on salt reduction and a discussion about our upcoming Christmas party in Martha's Vineyard.
    c.   Also on the agenda are a presentation on salt reduction by Jane Bowers and a discussion about our upcoming Christmas party in Martha's Vineyard.
    d.   The agenda includes a presentation by Jane Bowers on salt reduction and our upcoming Christmas party in Martha's Vineyard.
    e.   Also on the agenda is a discussion with Jane Bowers on salt reduction and our upcoming Christmas party in Martha's Vineyard.

Answer Key for Verbal Section 2

Critical Reading

1. The passage explains the importance of language in society, including the need to master it in order to speak and write effectively. The best answer is choice C – the others are incorrect in focus and scope.

2. According to Shenstone, those with the least to say tend to speak the most. Choice B is correct.

3. In context, the word "faculty" means power. Choice E is correct.

4. Taciturnity means reluctant or disinclined to talk. Choice B is correct.

5. In paragraph two, Lines 13 -15, the author reveals that Charles enjoyed Butler's work but found him dull in person. Choice C is correct.

6. According to Line 26, carelessness in grammar is inexcusable. Choice B is correct.

7. The passage directly states (in Lines 26 – 27) that language is the greatest of sciences and using words is the greatest human arts. Choice C is correct.

8. In the passage, the word "instruments" refers to the words a person uses to make is point. Choice A is

correct.

9. In the passage, the word "almoner" means the source or distributor of knowledge. Choice C is correct.

10. According to the passage, "counterfeit coins" are words that are either incorrect or ill-suited to the situation. Choice C, slang, is the best answer.

11. Choice A is correct. The other answer choices are too broad or narrow in scope.

12. Choice D is correct. The other answer choices are all mentioned in Lines 11 – 14.

13. Choice A is correct. The answer is presented in Lines 23 – 25.

14. Choice B is correct. In context, perquisites means privileges.

15. Choice E is correct. All of the other answer choices are presented in Lines 36 – 45.

Critical Reasoning

16. Choice C is correct. The argument only makes sense if we assume that some fats that are oxidized and dehydrogenated are polyunsaturated.

17. The original argument is in the following form: "Some X are Y. All Y are Z. Therefore, this X must be Z." Choice B is correct.

18. Choice E is correct. The passage tells us that the talent portion of the pageant has been reduced from 40% to 10% of the contestants' overall scores. However, we do not know the other criteria upon which the contestants are being judged. Thus, the only logical answer choice is E.

19. Choice C is correct. The argument presumes that the article must be written by a *Newsweek* editor in the Berlin office.

20. Choice D is correct. The argument presumes that an event that occurs for one item will also occur for similar items.

21. Choice D is correct. The argument depends on the assumption that molasses contain more calories than high fructose corn syrup.

22. Choice E is correct. The singers who knew they were being observed performed better than those who did not.

23. This argument is as convoluted as you are likely to see on the GMAT. Choice C is correct. The original argument is in the form: "most A (chefs) who are B (efficient bakers) are C (meticulous), but some non-C As (non-meticulous chefs) are B (efficient bakers). In addition, every B (efficient baker) is a D (good fry cook)." Therefore, logically, we can state that some D (good fry cooks) are C (meticulous), which is Choice C.

24. Choice B is correct. Jack believes that the patients should be the nurses' top priority, while Jill believes their loyalty should be to the union.

25. Choice E is correct. The arguments both have the form "A or B. Not A., therefore B."

Sentence Correction

26. This example is notable for two reasons. First, it contains a prepositional phrase that makes the singular subject *prison* appear to be plural. Because of this trick, many students do not see that the sentence is correct as originally written (A). By simply adding commas or parentheses, the difference is significantly easier to discern:

Prison, as well as restitution, was the thief's dismal fate.
Prison (as well as restitution) was the thief's dismal fate.

27. Although this sentence includes two singular names, the subject is singular because they are joined by *neither* and *nor*. Hence, the correct answer is C, which uses the singular verb *was*.

28. Prepositional phrases require objects, rather than subjects. Hence, the correct pronoun is *her*, not *she*. Answer choice B is correct. Note that the writers also tried to confuse students by using the word *accept* in two of the answer choices.

29. In this case, the writers use pronouns inconsistently in the original sentence (*one, you*). The correct answer must use one or the other, but not both. The best choice is D.

30. The sentence is correct as written.   Choice A is correct.

31. There are two errors in this sentence. First, the verb is in the passive voice. Second, the modifier *in good condition* should be closer to the word it modifies, which is *stove*. The best correction is D.

32. This is not a sentence because it lacks a verb. Choice C is the best correction.

33. Choice C is correct. The original sentence contains an incorrect verb/preposition combination (it should read *conform to*, rather than *conform with*).

34. Choice D is correct. The correct phrase is *more than*, not *more then*. Choice D also replaces a passive verb (*was financed*) with the active form (*financed*).

35. *Effect* is a noun that means *a result*, while *affect* is a verb that means *to influence*. The correct answer is D.

36. The subject of the sentence (*stress*) is singular and requires a singular verb (*is*). The correct answer choice is D.

37. Choice D is correct.

38. Choice B is correct. The entrepreneur is a person; hence, the correct descriptor is *who*, not *that*.

39. The sentence is correct as originally written. Choice A is correct.

40. The original sentence has an error in subject / verb agreement. The subject (*one*) is singular and requires a singular verb (*was*). Choice E is correct.

41. The original sentence has an error in subject-verb agreement. The verb should be *are* to reflect that there are two items on the agenda. Choice C is correct.

Directions: *The passage below is followed by questions based on its content. Answer the questions, based on what is* <u>stated</u> *or* <u>implied</u> *in the passage and any introductory material that may be provided.*

Passage 1

In theory, governments provide a significant source of a people's collective political identity as well as the main arena in which individuals can organize for political action. Yet, in actuality, the type of government is a key indicator of how effective that political action will be. In the United States, individuals who are frustrated by the presidential system often suggest that Americans would be better served if the U.S. adopted a parliamentary system of government. Although both systems are democratic, the differences between them would create major changes in American politics if the U.S. completely switched over to a parliamentary system. Assuming, for example, that the U.S. adopted a unicameral parliamentary political system with a Proportional Representation (PR) electoral system, its citizens would immediately enjoy greater government efficiency, accountability, an increase in voter turnout and less waste of taxpayer money.

10

The fusion of powers in a parliamentary system creates a supreme legislative, executive, and judicial authority that can develop policies in a straightforward manner, without the checks and balances of a presidential system. In the U.S., where power is fragmented by the separation of powers, Congress is not obligated to pass legislation that the President proposes. Likewise, every bill passed by Congress must be reviewed by the President, who can either veto it or sign it into law. This process, which can be further complicated by the judicial branch, creates significant barriers that can slow down or halt the passage of law.

17

In contrast, the parliamentary system in Great Britain has fused its executive and legislative branches into the cabinet, the controlling and directing body of parliament, which operates by majority rule. To implement policy, the majority party expresses its power through the cabinet to bring about its desired legislation. In effect, if the cabinet enjoys party solidarity, it does not need to wonder if its policy will be stalled in the legislature or other branches of government. As long as the majority of cabinet members support the proposed legislation, parliament can implement policy quickly and effectively.

24

Candidates in a parliamentary system are also more likely to be held accountable for the promises they make when they run for office than candidates in a presidential system. After all, once the majority seizes power in the parliament, they enjoy the complete control of the cabinet. Voters, consequently, know exactly who to blame for their current situation: the party or parties in power. In contrast, voters in a presidential system are seldom sure who to blame because the fragmented system creates so many independent sources of power that an unhappy policy cannot be blamed on any one of them. As a result, voters who cannot accurately reward or blame their elected officials may vote less on policy-related criteria and more on a candidate's personality.

32

In many countries, the cabinet must report regularly to parliament about how it is managing the affairs of the state, which provides an extra level of accountability that is missing in a presidential system. In Great Britain, the Prime Minister must appear before parliament each week to answer blunt and direct interrogations from the opposition. The U.S. presidential system, however, does not have an equivalent forum in which the executive branch must account for its actions on a regular basis. Sadly, history suggests that when public officials cannot be held accountable, it becomes easier for them to spend public money or initiate policy contrary to their election promises.

40

Changing the U.S. electorate system from a Single Member District Plurality system (SMDP) to a Proportional Representation (PR) would most likely increase voter turnout, because it would eliminate the idea that any individual vote is wasted. In a PR system, people vote for parties, whose percentage of seats in the legislature is equivalent to the percentage of the electoral vote the party receives. To illustrate, picture the United State as one large state consisting of only one district and only 100 available seats in parliament. Each party running for a seat would create a list of their top 100 members, who would be their potential candidates. However, the number of actual candidates that the party would eventually send to parliament would depend on the percentage of votes that the party received. In this scenario, if a party received 20 percent of the votes in the election, it would secure 20 seats in parliament, which would go to the top 20 candidates on its list. Likewise, if a party received 50 percent of the votes, it would secure 50 seats in parliament, which would go to the top 50 candidates on its list.

52

In contrast, a SMDP system divides the state or country into several districts that have separate elections for their representatives. The resulting legislature includes the candidates who won a plurality of the vote in their respective districts. If the population of a district heavily favors a candidate from one particular party, the people from an opposing or minority party may feel that their vote is wasted, since their candidate can't possibly win the election. Far too often, people get discouraged by the SMDP system and eventually stop voting, which reduces the overall turnout. In a PR system, however, people are more willing to participate because they know that their vote will contribute to a percentage of seats obtained in the legislature, even if their party does not receive the majority of the votes.

61

By eliminating specific district representatives, the PR system would also reduce taxpayer spending on projects that only benefit one district. In the SMDP system, representatives may try to divert state money to pet projects that reward their own districts for their vote. Instead, the PR system features candidate lists that are organized state-wide, whereby candidates envision the nation as a single district whose efficient and effective representation is in their party's best interest. Consequently, the PR system creates a political environment that encourages a spirit of mutuality, rather than selfishness.

68

Although the current system of presidential government in the United States is effective, it could benefit from several of the components in the parliamentary and PR systems. In theory, the parliamentary system offers improved accountability and efficiency, and limits the waste of taxpayer money on pet projects. However, the current U.S. election process is a cherished and deeply entrenched part of American culture that dates back to the Constitution. Despite its inherent flaws, most U.S. citizens are satisfied with the presidential system and are not sufficiently motivated to change. In the absence of a political crisis, it is highly unlikely that Americans will champion the parliamentary system as a viable alternative.

76

1. What is the main point of the passage?

    a. The PR electorate system of government is superior to the presidential system.
    b. With minor concessions, the U.S. can improve its electorate process by adopting certain points of the PR electorate system,
    c. An SMDP electorate system is superior to the PR system.
    d. Although the parliamentary system of government offers several benefits to citizens, the U.S. is unlikely to adopt it in the near future.
    e. The U.S. electorate process offers its citizens a unique set of checks and balances that should not be compromised.

2. In Line 2, what does "*arena*" mean?

    a. chambers
    b. stage
    c. meeting place
    d. stadium
    e. forum

3. According to the passage, U.S. citizens would enjoy many benefits if they adopted a PR electoral system of government. Which of the following is NOT one of those benefits?

    a. Less waste of taxpayer money
    b. Greater accountability
    c. Greater representation for women and minorities
    d. Increased voter turnout
    e. Greater government efficiency

4. According to the author, to what can the slow pace of the legislative process in the U.S. be attributed?

    a. The solidarity of the Cabinet
    b. the fusion of powers created by a supreme legislative, executive and judicial authority
    c. the President's right to veto any bill passed by Congress
    d. the staggered election years for Senators and Congressman, which can affect the support for any given bill
    e. the tendency of Congressmen to vote along party lines, which creates an adversarial political environment

5. In Great Britain, how are policies passed?

    a.   by special approval of the Prime Minister
    b.   exclusively by the legislative branch
    c.   by majority rule in all three branches of government
    d.   by majority rule in the cabinet
    e.   by a public election

6. According to the author, why do voters in the U.S. vote according to a candidate's personality?

    a.   they support the special interests of that candidate
    b.   they are more intuitive than citizens in other countries
    c.   they are influenced by political advertisements, which emphasize the candidate's personality
    d.   they do not feel that they can hold the candidates accountable for policy success or failure
    e.   they trust their candidates more than citizens in other countries

7. According to the passage, why are British officials less likely to spend public money?

    a.   They are given limited spending authority compared to U.S. officials
    b.   The Prime Minister makes all budgetary decisions
    c.   They are more frugal by nature
    d.   They are given a specific budget each year which cannot be adjusted for any reason
    e.   They must account for their actions on a regular basis

8. Which of the following statements is NOT true about the PR system?

    a.   Each district has a separate election for its representatives
    b.   It eliminates the idea that a single vote is wasted
    c.   People vote for parties, rather than candidates
    d.   It usually increases voter turnout
    e.   The percentage of seats a party receives in the legislature is equivalent to the percentage of the electoral vote the party receives

9. In Line 63, what does "*pet*" mean?

    a.   bi-partisan
    b.   pork barrel spending
    c.   special interest
    d.   corrupt
    e.   covert

10. According to the author, under what circumstances would the U.S, change its current system of government?

    a.   The emergence of a viable third political party
    b.   An amendment to the Constitution
    c.   A political crisis
    d.   To eliminate the national debt
    e.   The successful impeachment of the President

Passage 2

The most dangerous fault that any food can have is that it shall be tainted, or spoiled, or smell bad. Spoiling, or tainting, means that the food has become infected by some germs of putrefaction, generally bacteria or molds. It is the poisons, called ptomaines, or the toxins produced by these germs which cause the serious disturbances in the stomach, and not either the amount or the kind of food itself. Even a regular "gorge" upon early apples or watermelon or cake or ice cream will not give you half so bad, nor so dangerous, colic as one little piece of tainted meat or fish or egg, or one cupful of dirty milk, or a single helping of cabbage or tomatoes that have begun to spoil, or of jam made out of spoiled berries or other fruit.

8

This spoiling can be prevented by strict cleanliness in handling foods, especially milk, meat, and fruit; by keeping foods screened from dust and flies; and by keeping them cool with ice in summer time, thus checking the growth of these "spoiling" germs. The refrigerator in the kitchen prevents colic or diarrhea, ice in hot weather is one of the necessaries of life. Smell every piece of food to be eaten, in the kitchen before it is cooked, if possible; but if not, at the table avoid everything that has an unpleasant odor, or tastes odd, and you will avoid two-thirds of the colic, diarrhea, and bilious attacks which are so often supposed to be due to eating too much.

15

11. According to the passage, which of the following is NOT considered a source of dangerous food spoilage?

    a.   Moldy egg
    b.   Unclean milk
    c.   Rotting cabbage
    d.   Unripe fruit
    e.   Jam made from rotting berries

12. In Line 2, what does "*putrefaction*" mean?

    a.   Vile
    b.   Colitis
    c.   Contamination
    d.   Reproduction
    e.   Disintegration

13. According to the passage, which of the following is NOT an effective way to prevent food spoilage?

    a.   Avoiding food with unpleasant smells
    b.   Avoiding raw meat
    c.   Refrigerating milk, meat, and fruit
    d.   Protecting food from flies and dust
    e.   Extreme cleanliness while handling perishable foods

Directions: The questions in this section are based on the reasoning contained in brief statements or passages. For some questions, more than one of the choices could conceivably answer the question. However, you are to choose the one that provides the most complete and accurate answer. You should not make assumptions that are implausible, superfluous, or incompatible with the passage.

14. Doctors at a medical seminar were asked to evaluate the event's schedule, location and topic selection to determine whether changes would increase attendance the following year. A majority of the evaluations recommended that the event be held on a weekend, instead of during the week. Based upon the results of the evaluations, the sponsors of the seminar decided to use a weekend schedule the following year.

Which of the following selections, if true, would support the sponsors' decision to change to a weekend schedule next year?

    a.   Approximately 50% of the doctors who received evaluation forms completed their forms and turned them in.
    b.   Other seminar sponsors have made changes in their programs based on comments they received in evaluation forms.
    c.   The same percentage of doctors who returned the evaluation forms wanted the weekend schedule.
    d.   A weekend seminar schedule would make commuting easier for the participants.
    e.   A significantly larger percentage of doctors who preferred the weekend schedule returned their evaluation forms than the doctors who preferred the weekday evening schedule.

15. The number of citations issued to drunk drivers has dramatically decreased in recent years. In 2005, 4,444 citations were issued to individuals for this infraction. In 2009, however, only 2,777 citations were issued. These statistics prove that local enforcement agencies have seriously neglected their monitoring of drunk driving practices since 2005.

Which one of the following does the author assume in reaching his conclusion?

    a. Monitoring and enforcement of drunk driving violations became more lax due to a change in the political climate in Washington, D.C.
    b. The decrease in the number of citations was not due to a reduction in the number of drunk drivers on the road.
    c. Authorities focused more on enforcing the ban on liquor sales to minors than on monitoring drunk driving on the roads.
    d. Local enforcement agencies suffered from a reduction in personnel during the period 2005 - 2009.
    e. For several years prior to 2005, in excess of 1,850 citations per year were issued in connection with drunk driving.

16. The stark frugality of Pennsylvania's Amish population suggests that people in the Northeast are more practical and conservative than people in other parts of the country.

The reasoning in the argument is vulnerable to criticism on what grounds?

    a. It does not consider Amish residents in other states.
    b. It generalizes from a small sample that is not unrepresentative of the whole.
    c. It ignores the influence of religion on people's lifestyle choices.
    d. It uses circular reasoning.
    e. It fails to define the term "Northeast."

17. The number of uninsured Americans has dramatically increased in recent years. In 2001, 20 million Americans had no medical insurance. In 2006, however, 50 million Americans had no insurance. These statistics prove that 30 million Americans lost their medical insurance between 2001 and 2006.

Which one of the following does the author assume in reaching his conclusion?

    a. The rising number of uninsured Americans will create an unprecedented economic crisis.
    b. Due to financial constraints, fewer employers offer medical insurance as an employee benefit.
    c. The increase in the number of uninsured Americans was not due to the increase in population.
    d. Between 2001 and 2005, hospitals reported a similar increase in the number of uninsured patients.
    e. For several years prior to 2001, most Americans received health coverage from their employers.

18. Evidence suggests that Harry spends far more money than necessary on health and beauty items such as shampoo and mouthwash. It seems, therefore, that Harry is frivolous with money and not committed to saving.

Which one of the following statements, if true, most seriously weakens the argument?

    a. Harry has dentures and a crew cut.
    b. Harry must maintain his appearance because he works in the entertainment industry.
    c. Harry buys all of his health and beauty products for half price at a wholesale warehouse.
    d. Shampoo and mouthwash are free at most hotels and gyms that Harry frequents.
    e. Harry favors two-in-one products that eliminate clutter in the bathroom.

19.   Everything that is bold and majestic fails to please her, so there are things that fail to please her that are purple.

The conclusion of the argument follows logically if which one of the following is assumed?

   a.   Some majestic things are purple, but not bold.
   b.   Some things that are bold and majestic are purple.
   c.   Some bold things are purple, but not majestic.
   d.   All purple things fail to please her.
   e.   Everything bold is purple.

20.   Today's pediatricians inoculate children against dozens of viruses and diseases. As a result, most children have developed immunity against infections that would have killed them a generation ago. Hence, if scientists discover a new disease, it will be unlikely to kill as many children as it would have in 1900.

Which of the following, if true, would most weaken this argument?

   a.   Few physicians outside the U.S. engage in medical research.
   b.   Research studies are heavily funded by pharmaceutical firms, which have a vested interest in promoting vaccines.
   c.   Not all diseases have vaccines or cures.
   d.   The cost of inoculations has become prohibitive for many families.
   e.   Although they enjoy a better diet, today's children are more vulnerable to environmental factors, such as pollution, climate change, and exposure to toxins.

21.   Over the past decade, the demand for calcium supplements has risen by 10% each year. At the same time, the demand for oyster shells, from which natural calcium is extracted, has slowly decreased by the same amount.

If the statements above are both true, which of the following statements must also be true?

   a.   The mineral content of oyster shells has increasingly been linked to cancer
   b.   Calcium is absorbed more efficiently by the body if it is taken with Vitamin D
   c.   The price of calcium supplements has decreased significantly in the past 10 years
   d.   Increasingly, manufacturer are making calcium supplements from synthetic sources, rather than from oyster shells
   e.   A nutritional expert recently recommended that all women increase their consumption of calcium

22. All mothers enjoy shopping for clothes. Jenny loves shopping for clothes. Therefore, Jenny must be a mother.

Which of the following statements uses a similar type of reasoning?

   a.   All entrepreneurs must write business plans to raise funding for their ventures. Corporation X made $1 million in profits during their first year of business. Therefore, the CEO of Corporation X must be an entrepreneur.
   b.   All circles are round. Figure X is round. Therefore, Figure X must be a circle.
   c.   All dogs have fleas. Rover takes anti-flea medication. Therefore, Rover must be a dog.
   d.   Every cat has claws. Animal X has claws. Therefore, Animal X could be a cat.
   e.   All science majors must take two literature classes. Rachel is taking a class in literature. Therefore, Rachel must be a science major.

23. Drinking Gatorade should increase a cyclist's athletic performance, since cyclists who win many races tend to drink more Gatorade at the finish line than cyclists who finish poorly.

The flawed pattern of reasoning in the argument above is most similar to that in which of the following?

   a. Shopping for shoes improves one's mental health, since it increases the release of neurotransmitters in the brain that are linked to positive emotions.
   b. Reading fiction will improve a student's writing skills, since students who read more than five pleasure books per year tend to have high grades in their creative writing classes.
   c. Attending school in the summertime will improve one's grades, because it reinforces key concepts on a year-round basis.
   d. Shopping on line is a solitary pursuit, although people who do it do not seem to miss the hustle and bustle of conventional malls.
   e. Marrying young is ill-advised, because people tend to mature later than they originally expected.

24. Geriatric physicians predict that as baby boomers approach retirement age, they will try to extend their longevity by engaging in rigorous exercise. That will inspire them lead to switch from sedentary hobbies like reading to more active pursuits such as ballroom dancing and rock climbing. Thus, these experts conclude, the likelihood of athletic related injuries will dramatically increase in the elderly population. Although this premise has merit, it fails to consider another factor: as people age, their metabolism slows down, which encourages them to engage in less strenuous and sedentary activities, which have a lower risk of athletic related injuries.

The argument does which of the following?

   a. Agrees with the conclusion of the geriatric physicians, but suggests that they are overly optimistic.
   b. Attempts to undermine the argument of the geriatric physicians by using circular reasoning.
   c. Attempts to undermine the argument of the geriatric physicians by drawing an alternative conclusion from their premises.
   d. Disagrees with the underlying premises of the geriatric physicians' argument.
   e. Discredits the argument of the geriatric physicians by manipulating the use of statistics.

25. Jamie joined the Miami Police Academy, despite the rule against enrollment by active military.

Which one of the following can be inferred from the argument?

   a. The Miami Police Academy discriminates against veterans.
   b. Soldiers are overqualified for the Miami Police Academy.
   c. Jamie was discharged from the military.
   d. Jamie is an active member of the military.
   e. Jamie is training to be a police officer.

Directions: The following sentences test correctness and effectiveness of expression. Part of each sentence (or the entire sentence) is underlined; beneath each sentence are five ways of phrasing the underlined material. Choice A repeats the original phrasing; the other four choices are different. If you think the original phrasing produces a better sentence than the alternatives, select choice A; if not, select one of the other choices. In making your selection, follow the requirements of standard written English, such as grammar, choice of words, sentence construction, and punctuation. Your selection should result in the most effective sentence – clear and precise, without awkwardness or ambiguity.

Example: Most teenagers struggle to be free both of parental domination but also from premature responsibilities.

a. both of parental domination but also from premature responsibilities.
b. both of parental domination and also from premature responsibilities.
c. both of parental domination and also of premature responsibilities.
d. of parental domination and premature responsibilities.
e. both of parental domination and their premature responsibilities as well.

The correct answer is Choice D.

26. Either Mary or him is lying.

   a. Either Mary or him is lying.
   b. Either Mary or he is lying.
   c. Either him or her are lying.
   d. Either he or Mary are lying.
   e. Either him or Mary is lying.

27. Joe and Harry ran down to the lake when they heard that a school of catfish were easy prey.

   a. Joe and Harry ran down to the lake when they heard that a school of catfish were easy prey.
   b. Joe and Harry ran to the lake when they heard that a school of catfish were easy prey.
   c. Joe and Harry ran down to the lake when they heard that a school of catfish was easy prey.
   d. Joe and Harry, upon hearing that a school of catfish was easy prey, run to the lake.
   e. Joe and Harry ran down to the lake because they hear a rumor about a catfish being easy prey.

28. Bethany offered the rich dessert to whoever she wanted.

   a. Bethany offered the rich dessert to whoever she wanted.
   b. Bethany offered the rich dessert to whomever she wanted.
   c. Bethany offered whoever the rich dessert, as she wanted.
   d. Bethany offered everyone the rich dessert, simply because she wanted.
   e. Bethany offered whomever she wanted the rich dessert.

29. Mr. Davis has no objection to him joining the class if he is willing to complete the assignments.

   a. to him joining the class
   b. if he will join the class
   c. for him to join the class
   d. if he were to join the class.
   e. to his joining the class.

30. After scoring poorly on the SAT, David decided to walk home and then lie down for an hour, and then call a few friends.

   a. and then lie down for an hour, and then call a few friends.
   b. lie down for an hour, and then calling a few friends.
   c. lay down for an hour, and then call a few friends.
   d. lying down for an hour, and then calling a few friends.
   e. lie down for an hour, and then call a few friends.

31. After hiding behind the sofa for ten minutes, much to our dismay, the birthday girl already knew about the surprise party.

   a. After hiding behind the sofa for ten minutes, much to our dismay, the birthday girl already knew about the surprise party.
   b. Much to our dismay, after hiding behind the sofa for ten minutes, the birthday girl already knew about the surprise party.
   c. Much to our dismay, after hiding behind the sofa for ten minutes, we discovered that the birthday girl already knew about the surprise party.
   d. After hiding behind the sofa we discovered that the birthday girl already knew about the surprise party for ten minutes, much to our dismay.
   e. The birthday girl already knew about our surprise party, after hiding behind the sofa for ten minutes, much to our dismay.

32. After careful investigation, the teacher concluded that John's aggressive behavior was provoked from a bully in the class.

   a. After careful investigation, the teacher concluded that John's aggressive behavior was provoked from a bully in the class.
   b. After carefully investigating John's behavior, the teacher concluded that John's was aggressive because he was provoked from a bully in the class.
   c. After carefully investigating John's aggressive behavior, the teacher concluded that it was provoked by a bully in the class.
   d. After careful investigation, the teacher concluded that John was acting aggressive because of provoking from a bully in the class.
   e. After careful investigation, the teacher concluded that John's aggressive behavior was provoked by a bully in the class.

33. Being that the hotel was over-booked, we stayed over until the next morning, when vacancies were available.

   a. Being that the hotel was over-booked, we stayed over
   b. In view of the fact that the hotel was over-booked, we stayed over
   c. Since the hotel was over-booked, we stayed over
   d. Because the hotel was over-booked, we stood over
   e. Being that the hotel was over-booked, we stood over

34. IRS auditors stormed the corporate offices of ABC Corporation, on account of an anonymous report of accounting irregularities.

   a. IRS auditors stormed the corporate offices of ABC Corporation, on account of an anonymous report of accounting irregularities.
   b. IRS auditors stormed the corporate offices of ABC Corporation because of an anonymous report on accounting irregularities
   c. IRS auditors stormed the corporate offices of ABC Corporation because of an anonymous report full of accounting irregularities.
   d. IRS auditors stormed the corporate offices of ABC Corporation in response to an anonymous report that accused the company of accounting irregularities.
   e. IRS auditors stormed the corporate offices of ABC Corporation in response to accounting irregularities.

35. After the award ceremony, the five scholarship recipients congratulated each other on their good fortune.

   a. the five scholarship recipients congratulated each other on their good fortune.
   b. the five scholarship recipients congratulated each other on account of their good fortune.
   c. the five scholarship winners congratulated each other on enjoying the same good fortune.
   d. the five scholarship winners congratulated one another on their good fortune.
   e. the five scholarship winners, who enjoyed the same good fortune, congratulated one another.

36. In the winter, the number of heart attacks from snow shoveling is astonishing.

   a. In the winter, the number of heart attacks from snow shoveling is astonishing.
   b. In the winter, an astonishing number of heart attacks occur because of snow.
   c. An astonishing number of people suffer heart attacks in the winter from shoveling snow.
   d. In the winter, snow shoveling causes astonishing heart attacks.
   e. Heart attacks occur because of snow shoveling in the winter at an astonishing rate.

37. <u>Cathy has not and she will not</u> take illegal drugs.

    a.   Cathy has not ever and she will not
    b.   Cathy has never yet and never will
    c.   Cathy never has or will
    d.   Cathy has not taken and she will not
    e.   Cathy never has and she never will

38. <u>Because Gina had laid in bed</u> for several months after her accident, she developed atrophy in her leg muscles.

    a.   Because Gina had laid in bed
    b.   Because Gina lies in bed
    c.   Because Gina is laying in bed
    d.   Because Gina has lay in bed
    e.   Because Gina had lain in bed

39. <u>Rachel enjoyed modern dance for its gracefulness, musicality and because it told a story.</u>

    a.   Rachel enjoyed modern dance for its gracefulness, musicality and because it told a story.
    b.   Rachel enjoyed modern dance for its grace, musicality and because it told a story.
    c.   Rachel enjoyed modern dance because of its gracefulness, musicality and because it told a story.
    d.   Rachel enjoyed modern dance because it was graceful, musical, and a story.
    e.   Rachel enjoyed modern dance for its gracefulness, musicality and storytelling.

40. <u>We took a bus to the history museum which carried more than two thousand passengers.</u>

    a.   We took a bus to the history museum which carried more than two thousand passengers.
    b.   We took a bus to the history museum that carried more than two thousand passengers.
    c.   We took a bus to the history museum which held more than two thousand passengers.
    d.   We took a bus that carried more than two thousand passengers to the history museum.
    e.   We were part of two thousand passengers who took a bus to the history museum.

41. <u>After living in Hawaii for most of his life, where temperatures are seldom below freezing.</u>

    a.   After living in Hawaii for most of his life, where temperatures are seldom below freezing.
    b.   After living in Hawaii for most of his life, the temperatures are seldom below freezing.
    c.   By living in Hawaii for most of his life, the temperatures are seldom below freezing.
    d.   For most of his life in Hawaii, where the temperatures are seldom below freezing.
    e.   He lived in Hawaii for most of his life, where the temperatures are seldom below freezing.

Answer Key for Verbal Section 3

Critical Reading

1. Choice D is correct. The other choices are either too broad or narrow in scope.

2. Choice E is correct. In this context, *arena* is a forum, or opportunity to exchange ideas.

3. Choice C is correct. All of the other answer choices are mentioned in the passage.

4. Choice C is correct. The answer is presented in Lines 14 – 16.

5. Choice D is correct. The answer is presented in Lines 18 – 23.

6. Choice D is correct. The answer is presented in Lines 28 - 31.

7. Choice E is correct. The answer is presented in Lines 33 – 36.

8. Choice A is correct. The other answer choices are presented in the sixth paragraph, Lines 41 – 51.

9. Choice C is correct. In this context, a *pet issue* is a special interest.

10. Choice C is correct. The answer is presented in the final sentence of the passage.

11. Choice D is correct. The answer is stated in Lines 4 – 7.

12. Choice E is correct. In context, *putrefaction* means disintegration.

13. Choice B is correct. The other answer choices are presented in Lines 9 - 14.

Critical Reasoning

14. The best way to strengthen this argument is to prove that the results of the survey accurately reflect the feeling of the entire group. Choice C is correct because it strengthens the connection between the sample and the general population.

15. The unstated assumption is that the reduction in the number of citations was *not* due to a reduction in the number of drunk drivers on the road - it was strictly because local law enforcement agencies did not give the issue the appropriate amount of attention. Choice B is correct.

16. Choice B is correct. The sample is small and biased.

17. The argument tells us that the number of uninsured Americans increased between 2001 and 2006. As evidence, the author cites the specific number of people who lacked medical insurance. The unstated assumption that the author makes is that the increase in the number of uninsured was *not* due to an increase in population - it was strictly because the original people they polled had lost their insurance between 2001 and 2006. Choice C is correct because it correctly states this assumption.

18. Choice C is correct. To weaken the argument, we need to find an answer choice that disputes the claim that Harry spends far more money than necessary on health and beauty items. Choice C does that.

19. Choice B is correct. The argument only makes sense if we assume that some bold and majestic things are purple.

20. In this case, the correct answer is elegant in its simplicity. The argument presumes that scientists will discover cures or vaccines for all new illnesses, which is not necessarily the case. Choice C is correct.

21. The question is asking us to infer why these two seemingly contradictory events have occurred. Choice D offers a plausible answer. If the demand for calcium increases at the same time that the demand for natural calcium decreases, then the source of the calcium must be non-natural, or synthetic.

22. The correct answer choice also use the argument All X do Y. This does Y. Therefore, this must be an X. Of the five possibilities, Choice B is the best answer. The other four answers all deviate slightly from the original argument.

23. The original argument has the form "doing A should cause B, since people who B also tend to A." Choice B is correct.

24. Choice C is correct. The argument accepts the premise of the geriatric specialists, but draws an alternative conclusion from it.

25. In this case, we are dealing with an inference question. The correct answer choice will be a piece of information that is essential to the argument; without it, the argument will no longer make sense. In this case, the correct choice is D. The argument infers that Jamie is an active member of the military.

Sentence Correction

26. The full version of the sentence is *Either Mary is lying or he is lying.* Both subjects require the verb *is.* Hence, the correct answer choice is B.

27. The word *school* is singular and requires the singular verb *was.* The only answer choice that makes this correction without creating additional errors is C.

28. In this sentence, the word *whoever* (which is a subject) is incorrectly used as an object of the preposition *to.* The word *whomever* should be used instead. Answer choice B is correct.

29. In this sentence, we have a pronoun *(him)* modifying a gerund *(joining).* The sentence is incorrect in its original form, because the pronoun should be in the possessive case *(his,* not *him)* to properly modify the noun. *Mr. Davis has no objection to his joining the class.* The correct answer choice is E.

30. In this question, David's three activities after the SAT must be presented in a consistent manner. The proper combination of verbs is *walk* home, *lie* down and *then call.* Answer choice E is correct. The writers added an additional level of difficulty by including the verb *lie,* which is often used incorrectly as *lay.* To answer this question correctly, students needed to catch the error in parallelism **and** avoid the incorrect verb trap.

31. This sentence has a misplaced modifier; it also omits the subject of the sentence. The correct answer is C, which solves both problems.

32. Choice E is correct. The correct phrase is *provoked by,* not *provoked from.*

33. The expression *being that* is always wrong. The correct answer is C, which substitutes the word *since.*

34. Choice D is correct. It eliminates the awkward (and incorrect) phrase *on account of;* it also clarifies the reason the IRS agents stormed the office.

35. Choice D is correct. The original sentence contains an incorrect word choice. *Each other* should be used when referring to two people, while *one another* should be used when referring to more than two people. Choices D and E make this correction, but Choice D does so succinctly.

36. Choice C is correct. It contains a strong, active verb; it places the adjective *astonishing* in front of the correct noun; finally, it retains the meaning of the original sentence.

37. In this sentence, the correct answer must include both forms of the verb *to take.* The only answer choice to do so is D, which is correct. The resulting sentence correctly presents both verb tenses: *Cathy has not taken and she will not take illegal drugs.*

38. The correct answer must match the verb tense in the second half of the sentence. Answer choice E is correct: *Because Gina had lain in bed for several months after her accident, she developed atrophy in her leg muscles.*

39. The original statement includes an error in parallelism. Choice E is correct. The statement should read: *Rachel enjoyed modern dance for its gracefulness, musicality and storytelling.*

40. The original sentence includes a misplaced modifier, which suggests that the museum carries the passengers, rather than the bus. The sentence should be re-written to place the modifier closer to the word that it modifies: *We took a bus that carried more than two thousand passengers to the history museum.* Choice D is correct.

41. The original statement is not a complete sentence. Choice E offers the best correction.

Directions: *The passage below is followed by questions based on its content. Answer the questions, based on what is* <u>stated</u> *or* <u>implied</u> *in the passage and any introductory material that may be provided.*

Passage 1

Civilization in its onward march has produced only three important non-alcoholic beverages--the extract of the tea plant, the extract of the cocoa bean, and the extract of the coffee bean. Of these three, coffee is universal in its appeal. In fact, for millions of people, coffee is no longer a luxury or an indulgence; it is a corollary of human energy and human efficiency. People love coffee because of its two-fold effect--the pleasurable sensation and the increased efficiency that it produces.

6

On a socioeconomic basis, coffee is a surprisingly democratic beverage. Not only is it the drink of fashionable society, but it is also a favorite beverage of the men and women who do the world's work, whether they toil with brain or brawn. It has been acclaimed "the most grateful lubricant known to the human machine," and "the most delightful taste in all nature." Yet, ironically, no "food drink" has ever encountered so much opposition as coffee. Given to the world by the church and dignified by the medical profession, nevertheless, it has also suffered from religious superstition and medical prejudice. During the thousand years of its development, coffee has experienced fierce political opposition, nonsensical fiscal restrictions, unjust taxes, irksome duties; but, surviving all of these, it has triumphantly moved on to a foremost place in the catalog of popular beverages.

15

But coffee is something more than a beverage. It is one of the world's greatest adjuvant foods whose unique flavor and aroma give it unique palatability and comforting effects. Men and women drink coffee because it adds to their sense of well-being. It not only smells good and tastes good to all mankind, heathen or civilized, but all respond to its wonderful stimulating properties. The chief factors in coffee goodness are the caffeine content and the caffeol. Caffeine supplies the principal stimulant, which increases the capacity for muscular and mental work without a harmful reaction. In contrast, the caffeol supplies the indescribable Oriental fragrance that entices us through the nostrils, forming one of the principal elements that make up the lure of coffee. There are several other constituents, including certain innocuous so-called caffetannic acids, which, in combination with the caffeol, give the beverage its rare gustatory appeal.

25

The year 1919 awarded coffee one of its brightest honors. An American general said that coffee shared with bread and bacon the distinction of being one of the three nutritive essentials that helped win the World War for the Allies. So this symbol of human brotherhood has played a not inconspicuous part in "making the world safe for democracy." Yet, like all good things in life, the drinking of coffee may be abused. Indeed, those having an idiosyncratic susceptibility to alkaloids should be temperate in the use of tea, coffee, or cocoa. In every high-tensioned country there is likely to be a small number of people who, because of certain individual characteristics, cannot drink coffee. To suit these people who are caffeine-sensitive, coffee makers have developed a curious collection of so-called coffee substitutes, which are "neither fish nor flesh, nor good red herring." Most of them have been shown by official government analyses to be sadly deficient in food value--their only alleged virtue. One contemporary attacker of the national beverage bewails the fact that no palatable hot drink has been found to take the place of coffee. The reason is not hard to find. There can be no substitute for coffee. Dr. Harvey W. Wiley has ably summed up the matter by saying, "A substitute should be able to perform the functions of its principal. A substitute to a war must be able to fight. Sadly, a coffee substitute will never be the nectar of the Gods that I lovingly call coffee."

40

1. What is the main point of the passage?

    a. To explain the botanical origin of coffee
    b. To explain why the church and the medical profession oppose excessive consumption of coffee
    c. To explain the practical role of caffeine and caffeol
    d. To explain the pitfall of caffeine-sensitivity
    e. To explain why coffee is the most popular beverage in the world

2. In Line 3, what does "*corollary*" mean?

    a. Inkling
    b. Essence
    c. Opponent
    d. Factor
    e. Source

3. According to the author, coffee has experienced all of the following EXCEPT:

   a. Political opposition
   b. Fiscal restrictions
   c. Unjust taxes
   d. Legal prejudice
   e. Religious superstition

4. In Line 16, what does "*adjuvant*" mean?

   a. Supportive
   b. Universal
   c. Affordable
   d. Aromatic
   e. International

5. According to the author, what is the role of caffeine in coffee?

   a. It gives coffee its gustatory appeal
   b. It makes coffee a medical nuisance
   c. It increases the drinker's mental and physical capacity
   d. It is one of the principal elements that make up the lure of coffee
   e. It can easily be replaced by a synthetic compound in coffee substitutes

6. According to Dr. Harvey W. Wiley, which of the following words or expressions best describes coffee substitutes?

   a. Clever and sophisticated
   b. Woefully inadequate
   c. A necessary evil
   d. Somewhat undesirable
   e. Medically superior

7. From this passage, we can infer that the author.......

   a. Works for a coffee manufacturer
   b. Acknowledges the political opposition to coffee
   c. Is sensitive to high doses of alkaloids such as caffeine
   d. Is enthusiastic about coffee
   e. Believes that caffeine-sensitivity is just a myth

8. In which of the following was this passage most likely published?

   a. A history book about the World Wars
   b. A cookbook
   c. An article in a food magazine
   d. A medical journal
   e. A psychology textbook

Passage 2

The evolution of American democracy into a government by public opinion, enlightened by the open discussion of political questions, was in no small measure aided by a free press. That too, like education, was a matter of slow growth. A printing press was brought to Massachusetts in 1639, but it was under the control of an official censor and limited to the publication of religious works. Forty years elapsed before the first newspaper appeared, bearing the curious title, "Public Occurrences Both Foreign and Domestic," and it had not been running very long before the government of Massachusetts suppressed it for discussing a political question.

8

Publishing, indeed, seemed to be a precarious business; but in 1704 there came a second venture in journalism, "The Boston News-Letter," which proved to be a more lasting enterprise because it refrained from criticizing the authorities. Still the public interest languished. When Benjamin Franklin's brother, James, began to issue his "New England Courant" about 1720, his friends sought to dissuade him, saying that one newspaper was enough for America. Nevertheless he continued it; and his confidence in the future was rewarded. In nearly every colony a gazette or chronicle appeared within the next thirty years or more. Benjamin Franklin was able to record in 1771 that America had twenty-five newspapers. Boston led with five. Philadelphia had three: two in English and one in German.

17

The idea of printing, unlicensed by the government and uncontrolled by the church, was, however, slow in taking form. The founders of the American colonies had never known what it was to have the free and open publication of books, pamphlets, broadsides, and newspapers. When the art of printing was first discovered, the control of publishing was vested in clerical authorities. After the establishment of the State Church in England during the reign of Elizabeth, censorship of the press became a part of royal prerogative. Printing was restricted to Oxford, Cambridge, and London; and no one could publish anything without previous approval of the official censor. When the Puritans were in power, the popular party, with a zeal that rivaled that of the crown, sought, in turn, to silence royalist and clerical writers by vigorous censorship. After the restoration of the monarchy, control of the press was again placed in royal hands, where it remained until 1695, when Parliament, by failing to renew the licensing act, did away entirely with the official censorship. By that time political parties were so powerful and so active and printing presses were so numerous that official review of all published matter became a sheer impossibility.

30

In America, likewise, some troublesome questions arose in connection with freedom of the press. The Puritans of Massachusetts were no less anxious than King Charles or the Archbishop of London to shut out from the prying eyes of the people all literature "not mete for them to read;" and so they established a system of official licensing for presses, which lasted until 1755. In the other colonies, where there was more diversity of opinion and publishers could set up in business with impunity, they were nevertheless constantly liable to be arrested for printing anything displeasing to the colonial governments. In 1721, the editor of the "Mercury" in Philadelphia was called before the proprietary council and ordered to apologize for a political article, and for a later offense of a similar character he was thrown into jail.

39

A still more famous case was that of Peter Zenger, a New York publisher, who was arrested in 1735 for criticizing the administration. Lawyers who ventured to defend the unlucky editor were deprived of their licenses to practice, and it became necessary to bring an attorney all the way from Philadelphia. By this time, the tension was high, and the approbation of the public was forthcoming when the lawyer for the defense exclaimed to the jury that the very cause of liberty itself, not that of the poor printer, was on trial. The verdict for Zenger, when it finally came, was the signal for an outburst of popular rejoicing. Already the people of King George's province knew how precious a thing is the freedom of the press.

47

Thanks to the schools, few and scattered as they were, and to the vigilance of parents, a very large portion of the colonists could read. Through the newspapers, pamphlets, and almanacs that streamed from the types, the people could follow the course of public events and grasp the significance of political arguments. An American opinion was in the process of making—an independent opinion nourished by the press and enriched by discussions around the fireside and at the taverns. When the day of resistance to British rule came, government by opinion was at hand. For every person who could hear the voice of Patrick Henry and Samuel Adams, there were a thousand who could see their appeals on the printed page. Men who had spelled out their letters while poring over Franklin's "Poor Richard's Almanac" lived to read Thomas Paine's thrilling call to arms.

57

9. What is the main point of the passage?

   a. To explain the popularity of political literature in colonial America
   b. To explain the evolution of censorship in England
   c. To illustrate the legal penalties for authors and publishers who failed to honor the censorship laws in colonial America
   d. To explain the importance of literacy in colonial America
   e. To discuss the importance and evolution of the free press in colonial America

10. In Line 9, what does *"precarious"* mean?

    a.   Illegal
    b.   Derivative
    c.   Capricious
    d.   Unsteady
    e.   Pedantic

11. The passage mentions all of the following newspapers EXCEPT:

    a.   New England Courant
    b.   The Philadelphia Times
    c.   Public Occurrences Both Foreign and Domestic
    d.   The Mercury
    e.   The Boston News-Letter

12. According to the passage, why did official censorship end?

    a.   Due to the increased availability of printed material, the government could no longer review all published material
    b.   The government benefited financially from the fees that were generated by licensing printing presses
    c.   The State Church relaxed its moral standards regarding published materials
    d.   Royalist and clerical writers staged a coup in 1695
    e.   The high literacy rate increased the demand for printed materials

13. In Line 35, what does *"impunity"* mean?

    a.   Government sanctions
    b.   Little or no supervision
    c.   Wanton abandon
    d.   Religious or spiritual fervor
    e.   Exemption from punishment

14. Which of the following is NOT true about the Peter Zenger case?

    a.   He was a New York publisher
    b.   His original attorneys were deprived of their law licenses
    c.   The final verdict was in favor of Zenger
    d.   He was arrested in 1735 for criticizing the church
    e.   The case was tried in King George's province

15. According to the author, what role did literacy have in the American Revolution?

    a.   It allowed people to document the events in writing for future generations
    b.   It allowed people to follow and understand the significance of political arguments
    c.   It allowed the church and government to influence people by publishing propaganda
    d.   It had little influence because people could not afford to buy printed matter
    e.   It allowed people to read the ballot when they voted in national elections

Directions: The questions in this section are based on the reasoning contained in brief statements or passages. For some questions, more than one of the choices could conceivably answer the question. However, you are to choose the one that provides the most complete and accurate answer. You should not make assumptions that are implausible, superfluous, or incompatible with the passage.

16. Steve cannot perform at the party because he was grounded by his parents. Tim, on the other hand, cannot perform at the party because he has laryngitis. So, the gig will be handled by Ryan, who is the only drummer in the marching band other than Steve and Tim.

The argument depends on which of the following assumptions?

   a. If Steve had not been grounded, he would have performed at the party.
   b. Steve does not have laryngitis.
   c. The other members of the marching band already declined the gig.
   d. Drumming is a difficult skill that few students have mastered.
   e. The gig can only be performed by a drummer in the marching band.

17. For many years, historians insisted that Native American women in the 1800s adhered to a rigid vegetarian diet, including roots, nuts, and berries. However, a recent study of their remains suggests that this might not be true. Hair samples from a Native American female revealed significant levels of Vitamins D and K, which the human body cannot product on its own; further, the only dietary source of these vitamins is red meat. Therefore, it is likely that Native American women from the 1800s consumed a meat-based diet, rather than vegetarian fare.

Which of the following, if true, would strengthen this conclusion the most?

   a. A recent nutritional study suggests that the human body can manufacture minute amounts of Vitamin D in frigid climates.
   b. The levels of Vitamin D and K in the hair samples from the Native American female were identical to those from women in Europe who eat a meat-based diet.
   c. When scientists re-ran the analyses on the same samples, they obtained identical results.
   d. When scientists examined hair samples from the bodies of several other Native American women, they obtained identical results.
   e. Twelve years after scientists examined the hair samples and published their results, no one has disputed them.

18. Maria rented the apartment, despite their restrictions against dogs.

Which one of the following can be inferred from the argument?

   a. The landlord owns a dog.
   b. Maria owns a dog.
   c. Maria dislikes dogs.
   d. Maria disliked the apartment.
   e. Maria did not read her lease.

19. An author who was writing a book about left-handedness solicited participants for a survey in *USA Today*. One-hundred readers who were left-handed agreed to be interviewed and assessed for certain personality traits. As the writer suspected, the interview results and personality assessments showed that Southpaws were more emotional and accident-prone than random samples of the general population. These findings support the conclusion that people are affected by their natural handedness.

Which one of the following selections, if true, points out the most critical weakness in the method used by the author to investigate left-handed characteristics?

   a. Left-handed children are typically more emotional than their right-handed siblings.
   b. The interviews and assessments were performed by an outside firm, not by the author.
   c. People who saw the newspaper ad were not more likely to be left-handed than the number of Southpaws in the general population.
   d. The author's bias against left-handed people reinforced his initial impression of their character traits.
   e. Readers who were not emotional and accident-prone were less likely to respond to the author's newspaper ad or participate in the study.

20. The best way to solve our company's present financial crisis is to lower prices, improve our commitment to customer service, and increase our budget for advertising. I challenge anyone who disagrees with me to prove that my plan will not work.

A flaw in the preceding argument is that it

   a.   requires a background in economics to understand
   b.   is unnecessarily argumentative
   c.   attempts to shift the burden of proof to those who object to the plan
   d.   fails to provide statistical evidence to show that the plan will actually succeed
   e.   relies upon a controversial economic theory

21. Of course Sara supports the war. She's a Marine.

Which one of the following uses reasoning that is most similar to the above argument?

   a.   Of course Jeff is a thief - he stole from me. I will never trust him again.
   b.   In the past, Liberals have prevented ratification of any nuclear arms limitation treaties with the Middle East, so they will undoubtedly prevent the ratification of the current treaty.
   c.   Following his conscience, Congressman Elliott voted against the pro-life bill, knowing that it would doom his chances for reelection.
   d.   Of course I pay my fair share of taxes. The IRS garnishes my wages.
   e.   Mr. Ryan is the police commissioner, so it stands to reason that he would support the NRA's position on gun control.

22. Twelve years after graduation, Harvard medical school alumni completed surveys about their individual participation in the school's honors program. The results for the survey were curious. Eighty percent of the respondents reported that they had participated in the honors program, when the actual number of students who had participated was only 35%.

Which one of the following provides the most helpful explanation for the apparent contradiction in these survey results?

   a.   Several respondents misread the survey.
   b.   A disproportionately high number of students who participated in the honors program responded to the survey.
   c.   Not all honors program participants responded to the survey.
   d.   Almost all Harvard medical students who participated in the honors program twelve years earlier responded to the survey.
   e.   The honors program was a prestigious activity that only the best students were invited to join.

23. The only psychologists invited to appear on *Oprah* are those that the producers believe will inspire viewers to buy Oprah's new book about the Law of Attraction. So, most Jungian psychologists will not be invited to appear on *Oprah*.

The conclusion above follows logically if which one of the following is assumed?

   a.   Oprah does not wish to invite speakers with alternative viewpoints on her show.
   b.   The Law of Attraction is not taught in most doctoral programs that train Jungian psychologists.
   c.   The primary purpose of Oprah's show is to sell books.
   d.   The producers do not believe that Jungian psychologists will inspire viewers to buy Oprah's book.
   e.   True experts on the Law of Attraction eschew traditional programs in psychology.

24. If exmars are the smallest subatomic particles in the universe, then xyclops are needed to hold exmars together. Since xyclops are needed to hold exmars together, it follows that exmars are the smallest subatomic particles in the universe.

The logic of the above argument is most nearly paralleled by which of the following?

   a. If this library has a good mystery collection, it will contain a copy of *Blood* by Robin Cook. The collection contains a copy of *Blood*, therefore, the library has a good mystery collection.
   b. If there is a monster in the attic, the attic must contain hot food for him to eat. There is a monster in the attic, so the attic must contain hot food.
   c. Either oxygen or argon is the lightest element of the periodic table. Oxygen is not the lightest element of the periodic table, so argon must be the lightest element of the periodic table.
   d. If Sara is taller than Ben, and if Ben is taller than Elliott, then Sara is also taller than Elliott.
   e. Whenever it snows, the cars get wet. The cars are not wet. Therefore, it has not snowed.

25. Students who participate in high school drama productions often become doctors. Therefore, participating in high school drama must somehow influence students to attend medical school.

Which selection contains the same type flaw as that contained in the passage above?

   a. Professional bowlers tend to have large biceps. Therefore, professional bowlers typically have large hands.
   b. Teenage girls who smoke often become unwed mothers. Therefore, there is something in cigarettes that enhances the fertility of teenage girls.
   c. During the hottest part of the day, cats do not play. Therefore, cats must play before dawn.
   d. Joggers tend to run slower when they wear rubber soled shoes than when they wear leather soled shoes. Therefore, joggers win more races when they wear leather soled shoes.
   e. Soap operas can impact the fashion choices of high school girls. Therefore, if a popular vixen on a soap wears short leather skirts, then high school girls will also start wearing short leather skirts.

Directions: *The following sentences test correctness and effectiveness of expression. Part of each sentence (or the entire sentence) is underlined; beneath each sentence are five ways of phrasing the underlined material. Choice A repeats the original phrasing; the other four choices are different. If you think the original phrasing produces a better sentence than the alternatives, select choice A; if not, select one of the other choices. In making your selection, follow the requirements of standard written English, such as grammar, choice of words, sentence construction, and punctuation. Your selection should result in the most effective sentence – clear and precise, without awkwardness or ambiguity.*

Example: *Most teenagers struggle to be free both of parental domination but also from premature responsibilities.*

   a. *both of parental domination but also from premature responsibilities.*
   b. *both of parental domination and also from premature responsibilities.*
   c. *both of parental domination and also of premature responsibilities.*
   d. *of parental domination and premature responsibilities.*
   e. *both of parental domination and their premature responsibilities as well.*

The correct answer is Choice D.

26. According to Mom, a large quantity of clothing and accessories are on sale at Macy's Department Store.

   a. According to Mom, a large quantity of clothing, shoes and accessories are on sale at Macy's Department Store.
   b. According to Mom, a large quantity of clothing, shoes and accessories is on sale at Macy's Department Store.
   c. Mom claims that a large quantity of clothing, shoes and accessories are on sale at Macy's Department Store.
   d. A large quantity of clothing, shoes and accessories are on sale at Macy's Department Store, according to Mom.
   e. According to Mom, Macy's Department Store is selling clothing, shoes and accessories on sale.

27. Even before the Friars rehearsed their dance performance, <u>they knew that they were not prepared</u> for such an important performance.

    a.   they knew that they were not prepared
    b.   he knew that they were not prepared
    c.   they knew that they had not been prepared
    d.   they knew that he was not prepared
    e.   they had known that they were not prepared

28. <u>That which we cannot do without is that which binds us.</u>

    a.   That which we cannot do without is that which binds us.
    b.   That we cannot do without binds us to it.
    c.   Which we cannot do without binds us to it.
    d.   What we cannot do without is that which binds us.
    e.   We are bound by what we cannot do without.

29. <u>Because of the treacherous road conditions, all residents were advised to stay home, except for policemen, firemen and military personnel like us.</u>

    a.   Because of the treacherous road conditions, all residents were advised to stay home, except for policemen, firemen and military personnel like us.
    b.   Due to treacherous road conditions, all residents were advised to stay home, accept for policemen, firemen and military personnel like us.
    c.   Because of treacherous road conditions, all residents were advised to stay home, except for us police, firemen and military.
    d.   Because of treacherous road conditions, all residents were advised to stay home, except for policemen, firemen and we military personnel.
    e.   Because of the treacherous road conditions, only policemen, firemen and military personnel like us were allowed on the road; all other residents were advised to stay home.

30. Despite the challenges of rising health care costs, <u>the quality of care in Australia is significantly higher than most Asian nations.</u>

    a.   the quality of care in Australia is significantly higher than most Asian nations
    b.   the quality of Australian health care is significantly higher than most Asian nations
    c.   the quality of care in Australia is significantly higher than Asia
    d.   the quality of health care in Australia is significantly higher than health care in most Asian nations
    e.   the quality of care in Australia is significantly higher than the quality of care in most Asian nations

31. <u>The movie did not realistically portray the struggles of the pioneers in the 1800's, which I saw at the metroplex last weekend.</u>

    a.   The movie did not realistically portray the struggles of the pioneers in the 1800's, which I saw at the metroplex last weekend.
    b.   The movie did not realistically portray the 1800's struggles of the pioneers; I know, because it saw it last weekend at the metroplex.
    c.   Last weekend's movie did not realistically portray the struggles of the pioneers in the 1800's at the metroplex.
    d.   The movie, which I saw last weekend at the metroplex, did not realistically portray the struggles of the pioneers in the 1800's.
    e.   I saw a movie last weekend that did not realistically portray the struggles of the 1800's pioneers at the metroplex.

32. The visiting professor, whose recent publications on women's suffrage in Guatemala, were recently published by *Redbook.*

    a.   The visiting professor, whose recent publications on women's suffrage in Guatemala, were recently published by *Redbook.*

    b.   The recent publications of the visiting professor, which were about women's suffrage in Guatemala, were recently published in *Redbook.*

    c.   *Redbook* recently published the visiting professor's publications about women's suffrage in Guatemala.

    d.   *Redbook* recently published articles about the visiting professor's suffrage in Guatemala.

    e.   *Redbook* recently published articles about women's suffrage in Guatemala, which were written by the visiting professor.

33. Dylan refuses to invest in stocks because his father was defrauded by a con man during the 1987 stock market crash.

    a.   Dylan refuses to invest in stocks because his father was defrauded by a con man during the 1987 stock market crash.

    b.   Dylan refuses to invest in stocks because of the 1987 stock market crash.

    c.   Because a con man defrauded his father, Dylan refuses to invest in stocks during the 1987 stock market crash.

    d.   To avoid being defrauded by a con man like his dad, Dylan refused to invest in stocks after the 1987 stock market crash.

    e.   A con man defrauded Dylan's father during the 1987 stock market crash; as a result, Dylan refuses to invest in stocks.

34. In spite of Brittany's objections, the hairdresser applied a dark henna to her hair, which made her look tired and drawn.

    a.   In spite of Brittany's objections,

    b.   Not listening to Brittany's objections,

    c.   Ignoring Brittany's objections,

    d.   Although Brittany clearly vocalized her vehement objections,

    e.   Closing her mind to Brittany's objections

35. Whose to decide whether or not a child should receive medical care for a life threatening Illness: the parents, the physician, or the insurance company?

    a.   Whose to decide whether or not a child should receive medical care for

    b.   Whose to decide whether or not a child receives medical care for

    c.   Whose to decide if a child should receive medical care for

    d.   Who is to decide whether or not a child should receive medical care for

    e.   Whom will decide whether or not a child should receive medical care for

36. Oncologists often claim that it is them, not surgeons or cardiac specialists, that save more patient's lives.

    a.   it is them, not surgeons or cardiac specialists, that save more patient's lives.

    b.   it is they, rather than surgeons or cardiac specialists, that save more patient's lives.

    c.   they, rather than surgeons or cardiac specialists, save more patients' lives.

    d.   they save more patients' lives than surgeons or cardiac specialists.

    e.   they save most patients' lives, compared to surgeons or cardiac specialists.

37. Rebecca had to borrow a copy of *West Side Story* from the local library, <u>thinking that she didn't know where her own copy was at.</u>

    a.   thinking that she didn't know where her own copy was at.
    b.   because she didn't know where her own copy was at.
    c.   on account of she didn't know were her own copy was at.
    d.   because she didn't know where to find her own copy at.
    e.   because she didn't know where her own copy was.

38. Jane could easily have gotten accepted into a better law school if she <u>would have studied</u> more as a college student.

    a.   would have studied
    b.   studied
    c.   had studied
    d.   had been studying
    e.   would of studied

39. Lori's angry outburst the night before her wedding <u>resulted in her guests premature retreat</u> from the rehearsal dinner.

    a.   resulted in her guests premature retreat
    b.   caused her guests premature retreat
    c.   was the cause of her guests premature retreat
    d.   caused her guests to retreat premature
    e.   caused her guests' premature retreat

40. <u>To address the needs of tsunami victims, a fund was established by the World Bank in ten countries to buy disaster relief supplies</u>.

    a.   To address the needs of tsunami victims, a fund was established by the World Bank in ten countries to buy disaster relief supplies.
    b.   To address the needs of tsunami victims in ten countries, a fund was established by the World Bank to buy disaster relief supplies.
    c.   To address the needs of tsunami victims, the World Bank established a fund to buy disaster relief supplies in ten countries.
    d.   To address the needs of tsunami victims, a fund was established by the World Bank to buy disaster relief supplies in ten countries.
    e.   To buy disaster relief supplies for tsunami victims, a fund was established by the World Bank in ten countries.

41. Because they could not afford to stay in a hotel room <u>for the duration of their trip, Frank and Jane opted to stay in a hostile at the base of the Alps</u>.

    a.   for the duration of their trip, Frank and Jane opted to stay in a hostile at the base of the Alps.
    b.   for the duration of their trip, Frank and Jane stayed in a hostile at the base of the Alps.
    c.   Frank and Jane opted to stay in a hostile at the base of the Alps for the duration of their trip.
    d.   at the base of the Alps, Frank and Jane opted to stay in a hostile for the duration of their trip.
    e.   for the duration of their trip, Frank and Jane opted to stay in a hostel at the base of the Alps.

Answer Key for Verbal Section 4

Critical Reading

1. Choice E is correct. The main point of the passage is to explain the worldwide appeal of coffee.

2. Choice E. In context, corollary means source.

3. Choice D is correct. All of the other answer choices are mentioned in Lines 12 – 14.

4. Choice A is correct. In context, adjuvant means helpful or supportive.

5. Choice C is correct. The answer is stated in Lines 20 – 21.

6. Choice B is correct. Dr. Wiley feels that coffee substitutes are woefully inadequate.

7. Choice D is correct. The author is overwhelmingly enthusiastic about coffee's appeal.

8. Choice C is correct. The passage contains basic information and is light in tone; it was written for a general audience.

9. Choice E is correct. The other options are either to broad or narrow in scope.

10. Choice D is correct. In context, precarious means uncertain or unsteady.

11. Choice B is correct. All of the other answer choices are mentioned in the passage.

12. Choice A is correct. The answer is presented in Lines 26 – 29.

13. Choice E is correct. In context, impunity means exempt from punishment.

14. Choice D is correct. He was arrested for criticizing the administration, not the church. The other answer choices are all mention in Lines 40 – 46.

15. Choice B is correct. The answer is presented in Lines 49 – 50.

Critical Reasoning

16. The argument presumes that the gig can only be performed by a drummer in the marching band. Choice E is correct.

17. For this argument, the best way to strengthen the conclusion is to obtain identical results for several additional Native American women. Choice D is correct.

18. In this case, the correct answer choice will be a piece of information that is essential to the argument; without it, the argument will no longer make sense. In this case, the correct choice is B. The argument infers that Maria owns a dog.

19. Choice E is correct. The argument generalizes from a very small sample to the entire human population. If the participants who responded are NOT typical of the general population, then the conclusion is weakened. Choice E captures this sentiment.

20. Choice C is correct. This argument is incomplete because it offers no proof. Without evidence to support the position, the author shifts the burden of proof to those who are brave enough to challenge him.

21. This argument is fallacious and unfair because it assumes that all Marines support the war. Some Marines, however, may have moral, ethical, or philosophical reasons for opposing the war. The argument suggests that a person's profession determines his/her opinion. Choice E is the correct answer, because it does the same thing.

22. Choice B is correct because it best explains the apparent contradiction.

23. Choice D is correct. The argument presumes that Oprah's producers do not believe that Jungian psychologists will inspire viewers to buy Oprah's book on the Law of Attraction.

24. The argument is incorrect and in the form "If A, then B. B, therefore A". Choice A is correct, because it has the same form. Choice B has the form: "If A, then B. A, therefore B". This argument is valid and different from the original one. Choice C has the form: "A or B. Not A. Therefore, B". Choice D has the form: "If A > B and B > C, then A > C." Finally, choice E has the form: "If A, then B. Not B. Therefore, not A."

25. Choice B is correct, as it uses the same false correlation. Other choices lead to unwed parenthood besides smoking cigarettes. Likewise, doctors are inspired to attend medical school for reasons other than their high school drama class.

Sentence Correction

26. The word *quantity* is singular and requires the singular verb *was*. The only answer choice that makes this correction without creating additional errors is B.

27. The verb tense should be the past perfect tense, which indicates that an action or event was completed before another action or event began. Choice E is correct.

28. Choice E is correct. The original sentence is an overwritten (and somewhat pompous) version of a very simple concept.

29. Choice A is correct. The original sentence contains no errors.

30. Choice E is correct. In the original sentence, the two concepts are not presented in a parallel manner. In Choice E, it is clear that the sentence is comparing the *quality of care* in the two locations.

31. Choice D is correct. The original sentence contains a misplaced modifier.

32. This is not a complete sentence because it lacks a verb. The best revision is Choice C, which uses an active verb.

33. This question is tricky because it is subtle. The correct answer is Choice E, which corrects the passive verb by separating the two phrases by a semi colon. The other choices that correct the verb either omit information or add new errors.

34. The correct answer is choice C, which eliminates the incorrect opening (*in spite of*), without changing the meaning of the sentence or adding details that were not originally there.

35. The original sentence contains an incorrect pronoun. Choice D is correct.

36. Choice D is correct. Choice E is tempting, but it introduces the word *compare*, which implies something more than the original sentence.

37. Choice E is correct. The word *at* is unnecessary, because *where* already indicates location.

38. In this sentence, the correct verb is *had studied*, which is answer choice C.

39. In this sentence, the word *guests* fails to denote the possessive form. The only two answer choices that make this correction are D and E. Choice D, unfortunately, creates a new error by using the word *premature* incorrectly. The correct answer choice is E.

40. The original sentence contains a passive verb that should be re-written in the active voice. Choice C is correct.

41. The original sentence includes the incorrect spelling of the word *hostel,* which changes the entire meaning of the sentence. Choice E is the best revision

Directions: *The passage below is followed by questions based on its content. Answer the questions, based on what is stated or implied in the passage and any introductory material that may be provided.*

Passage 1

On a theoretical basis, fruits and vegetables are considered to be kindling foods, which supply certain mineral elements that are not present in sufficient proportions in the coal foods, such as meats, starches, and fats. Furthermore, the product of fruit and vegetable digestion and burning in the body helps to neutralize the waste products from meats, starches, and fats. Thirdly, fruits and vegetables have a overwhelmingly beneficial effect upon the blood, the kidneys, and the skin. In fact, their reputation for "purifying the blood" and "clearing the complexion" is really well deserved. The keenness of our liking for fruit at all times, and our special longing for greens and sour foods in the spring, after their scarcity in our diet all winter, is a true sign of their wholesomeness.

9

Not the least of their advantages is that fruits and vegetables contain a large proportion of water; and this, though diminishing their fuel value, supplies the body with a naturally filtered and often distilled supply of this necessary element of life. One of the best ways to avoid that burning summer thirst, which leads you to flood your unfortunate stomach with melted icebergs, in the form of ice water, ice cold lemonade, or soda water, is to take an abundance of fresh fruits and green vegetables.

15

Many vegetables contain small amounts of starch, but few of them enough to count upon as fuel, except potatoes, which must rightfully be classified with the coal foods. Most fruits contain a certain amount of sugar-- how much can usually be estimated from their taste, and how little can be gathered from the statement that even the sweetest of fruits, like ripe pears or ripe peaches, contain only about eight per cent sugar. They are all chiefly useful as flavors for the less interesting staple foods, particularly the starches. In fact, our instinctive use of them to help down bread and butter, or rice, or puddings of various sorts, is a natural and proper one. Like vegetables, fruits also contain various salts which are useful in neutralizing certain acid substances formed in the body.

24

Soldiers in war, or sailors upon long voyages, who are fed a diet consisting chiefly of salted or preserved meat, with bread or hard biscuit and sugar, but without either fruits or fresh vegetables, are likely to develop a disease called scurvy. Little more than a century ago, hundreds of deaths occurred every year in the British and French navies from this disease, and the crews of many a long exploring voyage--like Captain Cook's—or of searchers for the North Pole, have been completely disabled or even destroyed entirely by scurvy. It was discovered that by adding to the diet fruit, or fresh vegetables like cabbage or potatoes, scurvy could be entirely prevented, or cured.

32

But how much real fuel value do fruits and vegetables have? In order to get the nourishment contained in a pound loaf of bread, or a pound of roast beef, you would have to eat: twelve large apples or pears, four and one-half quarts of strawberries; a dozen bananas, seven pounds of onions; two dozen large cucumbers; ten pounds of cabbage; or one-half bushel of celery. Notwithstanding their slight fuel value, there are few more valuable and wholesome elements in the diet than an abundant supply of fresh fruits and green vegetables. If at all possible, all people should have a garden, if only the tiniest patch, and grow them for their own use, both because of their wholesomeness and freshness when so grown, and because of the valuable exercise in the open air, and the enjoyment and interest afforded by their care.

41

1. What is the main point of the passage?

    a.   To explain the fuel value of fruits and vegetables
    b.   To discuss the nutritional value and health benefits of fruits and vegetables
    c.   To compare the nutritional value of kindling foods to coal foods
    d.   To explain the cause and prevention of scurvy
    e.   To explain the nutritional deficiencies of fruits and vegetables

2. In Line 3, what does "*neutralize*" mean?

    a.   Incite
    b.   Deodorize
    c.   Defuse
    d.   Accelerate
    e.   Putrefy

3. According to the author, all of the following are coal foods EXCEPT:

   a. Potatoes
   b. Meats
   c. Starches
   d. Kale
   e. Fats

4. According to the author, which of the following is NOT a health benefit of fruits and vegetables?

   a. They improve human vision
   b. They improve the complexion
   c. They purify the blood
   d. They supply water to the body
   e. They supply mineral elements

5. According to the author, what is the chief use of fruits?

   a. They sweeten food without adding a significant amount of sugar
   b. They provide an inexpensive source of protein, compared to meats, starches, and fats
   c. They neutralize acids in the body
   d. They enhance the complexion because they are low in fat
   e. They flavor less interesting foods, such as starches

6. According to the author, all of the following will help to prevent scurvy EXCEPT:

   a. Potatoes
   b. Cabbage
   c. Tallow
   d. Pears
   e. Celery

7. From the passage, we can infer that the author.....

   a. Believes that fruits and vegetables provide too little food value to justify their cost
   b. Believes that kindling foods are inferior to coal foods
   c. Is enthusiastic about the importance of fruits and vegetables in the human diet
   d. Believes that pesticide use destroys the benefits of fruits and vegetables
   e. Believes that a vegan diet is far superior to one that includes meats, starches, and fats

Passage 2

The origin of the corset is lost in remote antiquity. The figures of the early Egyptian women show clearly an artificial shape of the waist produced by some style of corset. A similar style of dress must also have prevailed among the ancient Jewish maidens; for Isaiah, in calling upon the women to put away their personal adornments, says: "Instead of a girdle there shall be a rent, and instead of a stomacher (corset) a girdle of sackcloth." Homer also tells us of the cestus of Venus, which was borrowed by the haughty Juno with a view to increasing her personal attractions, that Jupiter might be a more tractable and orderly husband. Coming down to the later times, we find the corset was used in France and England as early as the 12th century.

8

The most extensive and extreme use of the corset occurred in the 16th century, during the reign of Catherine de Medici of France and Queen Elizabeth of England. With Catherine de Medici a thirteen-inch waist measurement was considered the standard of fashion, while a thick waist was an abomination. No lady could consider her figure of proper shape unless she could span her waist with her two hands. To produce this result a strong rigid corset was worn night and day until the waist was laced down to the required size. Then over this corset was placed a steel apparatus called a corset-cover, which reached from the hip to the throat, and produced a rigid figure over which the dress would fit with perfect smoothness.

16

During the 18th century corsets were largely made from a species of leather known as "Bend," which was not unlike that used for shoe soles, and measured nearly a quarter of an inch in thickness. About the time of the French Revolution, a reaction set in against tight lacing, and for a time there was a return to the early classical Greek costume. This style of dress prevailed, with various modifications, until about 1810 when corsets and tight lacing again returned with threefold fury. Buchan, a prominent writer of this period, says that it was by no means uncommon to see "a mother lay her daughter down upon the carpet, and, placing her foot upon her back, break half a dozen laces in tightening her stays."

24

It is reserved to our own time to demonstrate that corsets and tight lacing do not necessarily go hand in hand. Distortion and feebleness are not beauty. A proper proportion should exist between the size of the waist and the breadth of the shoulders and hips, and if the waist is diminished below this proportion, it suggests disproportion and invalidism rather than grace and beauty.

29

The perfect corset is one which possesses just that degree of rigidity which will prevent it from wrinkling, but will at the same time allow freedom in the bending and twisting of the body. Corsets boned with whalebone, horn or steel are necessarily stiff, rigid and uncomfortable. After a few days wear, the bones or steels become bent and set in position, or, as more frequently happens, they break and cause injury or discomfort to the wearer.

34

About seven years ago, an article was discovered for the stiffening of corsets, which has revolutionized the corset industry of the world. This article is manufactured from the natural fibers of the Mexican Ixtle plant, and is known as Coraline. It consists of straight, stiff fibers like bristles bound together into a cord by being wound with two strands of thread passing in opposite directions. This produces an elastic fiber intermediate in stiffness between twine and whalebone. It cannot break, but it possesses all the stiffness and flexibility necessary to hold the corset in shape and prevent its wrinkling.

41

We congratulate the ladies of today upon the advantages they enjoy over their sisters of two centuries ago, in the forms and the graceful and easy curves of the corsets now made as compared with those of former times.

44

8. What is the main point of the passage?

    a.   To argue against the use of corsets for medical reasons
    b.   To justify the use of Coraline in the manufacture of corsets
    c.   To explain the historical preference for an artificially small waistline
    d.   To mock the ancient standard of beauty in European culture
    e.   To discuss the historical evolution of the corset in women's fashion

9. In Line 5, what is a "*cestus*"?

    a.   Dress
    b.   Wig
    c.   Girdle
    d.   Stocking
    e.   Wardrobe

10. The author mentions the use of corsets in all countries EXCEPT:

    a.   Egypt
    b.   Greece
    c.   France
    d.   Italy
    e.   England

11. In Line 11, what does "*abomination*" mean?

    a.   Disgrace
    b.   Obesity
    c.   Distress
    d.   Menacing
    e.   Uncouth

12. From Lines 9 - 15 in the passage, what we can conclude about Catherine de Medici?

    a. She was a fashion icon in Italy
    b. She used a corset-cover to attain a thirteen-inch waist
    c. She abolished the use of corsets due to their extreme discomfort
    d. She imported special leather called Bend to make her corsets
    e. She was a strong enthusiast of classic Greek costume

13. According to the author, all of the following are true EXCEPT:

    a. Corsets boned with whalebone are stiff, but comfortable
    b. Distortion and feebleness are not beauty
    c. The perfect corset prevents wrinkling, but allows the body to twist and bend
    d. Corsets and tight lacing do not necessarily go hand in hand
    e. An artificially small waist suggests disproportion and invalidism

14. Which of the following is NOT true about Coraline?

    a. Coraline is manufactured from the natural fibers of the Ixtle plant
    b. Coraline cannot break
    c. Coraline is an elastic fiber that is stiffer than whalebone
    d. Coraline revolutionized the corset industry
    e. Coraline possesses the required stiffness and flexibility to hold a corset in shape.

15. What is the tone of the passage?

    a. Ambivalent
    b. Aghast
    c. Lackadaisical
    d. Factual
    e. Incredulous

Directions: The questions in this section are based on the reasoning contained in brief statements or passages. For some questions, more than one of the choices could conceivably answer the question. However, you are to choose the one that provides the most complete and accurate answer. You should not make assumptions that are implausible, superfluous, or incompatible with the passage.

16. Thanks to the internet, consumers have unprecedented access to quality information about diet, nutrition, and exercise. As a result, most have an excellent idea of the lifestyle choices they should make to maintain a desirable weight. Hence, as the internet continues to expand, consumers will be significantly less likely to be overweight.

Which of the following, if true, would most weaken this argument?

    a. Not all consumers have internet access.
    b. Despite the availability of good information, consumers rarely use it to make good lifestyle choices.
    c. Most obese people have physical constraints against exercise.
    d. Funding for nutritional researchers is increasingly scarce.
    e. Most nutritional web sites are funded by weight loss firms, which have a vested interest in promoting their company's products.

17. Either restrictions must be placed on gun ownership or the gangs in this country will use them to destroy society. Since this consequence is unthinkable, we must restrict gun ownership.

What is the flaw in this conclusion?

    a.   Gangs do not want to destroy society.
    b.   The author does not offer an option between the two alternatives.
    c.   Guns are not a real threat to our way of life.
    d.   Most gang members do not own guns.
    e.   The author uses circular reasoning,

18. In 2006, a large state university raised its tuition and fees by 5% for most undergraduate students. The following year, school administrators imposed an additional 5% tuition hike for the same undergraduate students. Despite these consecutive tuition hikes, the total amount of money collected by the university in tuition and fees remained constant until 2007, when it decreased dramatically.

Each of the following, if true, could help to resolve the apparent discrepancy described above EXCEPT:

    a.   Beginning in 2007, the tuition and fees for scholarship students were deposited into a different account, which artificially deflated the number that was reported in the study.
    b.   The increase in tuition and fees caused a drop in enrollment in 2007.
    c.   The tuition increases were waived for all students who pre-enrolled for classes.
    d.   The total enrollment at the university increased dramatically in 2007.
    e.   In 2007, the university eliminated several undergraduate programs, which had formerly attracted hundreds of students.

19. Physician: a prestigious medical journal recently ran an article about the reaction of the members of the American Medical Association (AMA) to national health care reform. The author quoted three prominent physicians, all of whom expressed their fervent support for socialized medicine. These quotations gave the impression that all members of the AMA support a radical change in our current medical system. However, the author of the article failed to mention that the three physicians he interviewed were all from Canada, where socialized medicine is the norm.

Which of the following principles best explains the physician's argument?

    a.   Most U.S. physicians do not favor a radical change in the current medical system.
    b.   The author of the article was not a member of the AMA; as such, his assessment of their position was flawed.
    c.   The article was misleading, because it was written by a lobbyist for the pharmaceutical industry, who supports radical health care reform.
    d.   The article was misleading, because it presented the biased views of three physicians as being representative of those of an entire group.
    e.   The article was misleading, because the Canadian doctors had not been advised that they would be quoted in the interview.

20. Martians can learn much from workers on other planets. On Saturn, for example, many employers provide racket ball equipment and courts for their employees to use. Few employers on Mars have similar facilities. Studies show that workers on Saturn are more productive than those on Mars. Thus, it must be concluded that the productivity of Martians will lag behind their counterparts on Saturn until mandatory racket ball programs are introduced.

The conclusion of the argument is valid if which one of the following is assumed?

    a.   Racket ball will improve the Martians' health.
    b.   The productivity of all workers can be increased by racket ball.
    c.   Racket ball is an essential factor in the Saturn worker's superior productivity.
    d.   Saturn workers are happier than Martian workers.
    e.   Corporations on Mars don't have the funds to build elaborate racket ball courts.

21. All models enjoy fashion. Coral loves fashion. Therefore, Coral must be a model.

Which of the following statements uses a similar type of reasoning?

   a. All squares are rectangles. Figure B is a square. Therefore, Figure B must be a rectangle.
   b. All actresses are thin. Claire is an actress. Therefore, Claire must be thin.
   c. Every cat has claws. Animal X has claws. Therefore, Animal X could be a cat.
   d. All entrepreneurs pay taxes. Bill pays taxes. Therefore, Bill must be an entrepreneur.
   e. All students write papers. Some students read books. Therefore, all students must be literate.

22. During the late 1980s, when mutual fund companies were rapidly expanding their share of the financial services industry, the Kidder-Peabody brokerage house surveyed one hundred stock owners and asked them if they would be more willing to buy individual securities or a mutual fund. Seventy percent of the respondents said that they preferred to buy individual stocks. On the basis of this survey, Kidder-Peabody decided to continue brokering only individual stocks. Yet during the 1990s, Kidder-Peabody lost even more market share to mutual fund companies.

Which one of the following, if it were determined to be true, would best explain this discrepancy?

   a. Only 10 percent of the investors who received the survey bothered to reply.
   b. Cabot Brokerage, which conducted a similar survey with similar results, continued to broker only individual stocks and also lost more of their market share to mutual fund companies.
   c. The surveyed clients who preferred individual stocks also preferred asset-backed securities.
   d. Kidder-Peabody determined that it would be more profitable to broker individual stocks.
   e. Eighty percent of the clients who responded to the survey wanted to buy individual stocks, rather than mutual funds.

23. Kittens need additional immunizations as they age. Therefore, puppies must also need additional immunizations as they age.

The flawed reasoning in the argument above most closely parallels the reasoning in which of the following?

   a. Cable costs and utility bills are due at the end of the month. Therefore, we should pay the water bill at the same time as well.
   b. Typists base their rate on the length and complexity of a document. Therefore, court reporters should also base their rates on the length and complexity of a document.
   c. Supermarkets require sixty parking places per one-thousand square feet of store space. Therefore, older supermarkets should increase their parking areas to comply with the new rule.
   d. Movie Gallery charges 99 cents for every new release, except for documentaries, which are 50 cents each. Therefore, Netflix should lower its prices to be more competitive with Movie Gallery.
   e. Hot dogs contain far less fat if they are boiled rather than fried. Therefore, hamburgers should not be fried unless absolutely necessary.

24. During the 1970's, both priests and nuns wore conservative dress to church services. However, Father Dave did not.

In presenting her position, the author does which one of the following?

   a. Makes a contradiction.
   b. Attacks the motives of her opponents.
   c. Uses the positions of noted social commentators to support her position
   d. Claims that her position is correct because others cannot disprove it.
   e. Argues in a circular manner.

25. ARIEL: If top-tier recruiters want to hire extraordinary students, they will interview the ones at our university. Since we have not been contacted by top-tier recruiters, we may conclude that none have visited our campus.

AMBER: Or, perhaps, they did not think the students at our university are extraordinary.

How is Amber's response related to Ariel's argument?

    a. She misses Ariel's point.
    b. She attacks Ariel personally rather than her reasoning.
    c. She support's her Ariel's conclusion, but not her logic.
    d. She points out that Ariel made an unwarranted assumption.
    e. She uses circular reasoning.

26. Senators Gary Hart and Bob Kerry advocate the legalization of medicinal marijuana. These leaders would not propose a social policy that is likely to be harmful. So there is little risk in experimenting with a three-year legalization of medicinal marijuana.

In presenting her position, the author does which one of the following?

    a. Assumes a position of moral superiority.
    b. Attacks the motives of her opponents.
    c. Argues in a circular manner.
    d. Uses the positions of elected officials to support her position.
    e. Claims that her position is correct because others cannot disprove it.

Directions: *The following sentences test correctness and effectiveness of expression. Part of each sentence (or the entire sentence) is underlined; beneath each sentence are five ways of phrasing the underlined material. Choice A repeats the original phrasing; the other four choices are different. If you think the original phrasing produces a better sentence than the alternatives, select choice A; if not, select one of the other choices. In making your selection, follow the requirements of standard written English, such as grammar, choice of words, sentence construction, and punctuation. Your selection should result in the most effective sentence – clear and precise, without awkwardness or ambiguity.*

Example: *Most teenagers struggle to be free both of parental domination but also from premature responsibilities.*

a.   both of parental domination but also from premature responsibilities.
b.   both of parental domination and also from premature responsibilities.
c.   both of parental domination and also of premature responsibilities.
d.   of parental domination and premature responsibilities.
e.   both of parental domination and their premature responsibilities as well.

The correct answer is Choice D.

27. Either Sara or you are guilty.

    a. Either Sara or you are guilty.
    b. Either Sara or you is guilty.
    c. Either Sara is guilty or you are guilty.
    d. Either you or Sara are guilty.
    e. Either Sara is guilty or you is guilty.

28. There remain many arguments in favor of women becoming stay-at-home mothers.

    a. There remain many arguments in favor of women becoming stay-at-home mothers.
    b. There remains many arguments in favor of women becoming stay-at-home mothers.
    c. There remain many arguments to favor women becoming stay-at-home mothers.
    d. There remains many arguments that favor women becoming stay-at-home mothers.
    e. There remain many arguments in favor of women to become stay-at-home mothers.

29. If a husband wants to send his wife a dozen roses, <u>they can order them from a local florist</u>.

    a.   they can order them from a local florist
    b.   they can order it from a local florist
    c.   he can order them from a local florist
    d.   they can order them at a local florist
    e.   one can order them from a local florist

30. The teacher claimed <u>that everyone will be punished for their misdeeds</u>.

    a.   that everyone will be punished for their misdeeds.
    b.   if everyone will be punished for their misdeeds.
    c.   about everyone being punished for their misdeeds.
    d.   that everyone will be punished for his misdeeds.
    e.   that everyone should be punished for his misdeeds.

31. The night after their breakup, Janis tried to get Steve jealous <u>in a revealing outfit by walking through a restaurant full of people.</u>

    a.   in a revealing outfit by walking through a restaurant full of people
    b.   by walking in a revealing outfit full of people in a crowded restaurant
    c.   by walking through a restaurant in a revealing outfit full of people
    d.   by wearing a revealing outfit walking through a restaurant full of people
    e.   by walking through a restaurant full of people while she was wearing a revealing outfit

32. <u>If a snowbird lives in Florida during the winter months, when temperatures are cold up north and in Chicago during the summer months, when Florida is as hot as an oven.</u>

    a.   If a snowbird lives in Florida during the winter months, when temperatures are cold up north, and in Chicago during the summer months, when Florida is as hot as an oven.
    b.   If one lives in Florida during the winter months, the temperatures are cold up north, and in Chicago during the summer months, when Florida is as hot as an oven.
    c.   A snowbird lives in Florida during the winter months, when temperatures are cold up north, and in Chicago during the summer months, when Florida is as hot as an oven.
    d.   If a snowbird lives in Florida during the winter months, when temperatures are cold up north, and in Chicago during the summer months, when Florida is as hot as an oven.
    e.   If a snowbird lives in Florida during the winter months, when temperatures are cold up north, then in Chicago during the summer months, when Florida is as hot as an oven.

33. Ryan refuses to buy footwear at Macys because <u>he was sold a pair of shoes that fell apart within two weeks.</u>

    a.   he was sold a pair of shoes that fell apart within two weeks.
    b.   he was sold by the clerk a pair of shoes that fell apart within two weeks.
    c.   he was sold a pair of shoes that two weeks later fell apart.
    d.   they sold him a pair of shoes that fell apart within two weeks.
    e.   a pair of shoes that were sold to him fell apart within two weeks.

34. <u>Although he tried to hide it, Dave was completely disinterested in Joe's story about his summer vacation.</u>

    a.   Although he tried to hide it, Dave was completely disinterested in Joe's story about his summer vacation.
    b.   Although he tried to hide it, Dave was disinterested in hearing Joe's story about his vacation.
    c.   Dave was completely disinterested in Joe's story about his summer vacation, but he tried to hide it.
    d.   Dave tried to hide his complete disinterest in Joe's story about his summer vacation.
    e.   Although he tried to hide it, Dave was completely uninterested in Joe's story about his summer vacation.

35. Before he left for the mall, <u>Dave asked Carla if she wanted to accompany him.</u>

    a.   Dave asked Carla if she wanted to accompany him.
    b.   Dave asked Carla if she wanted to go.
    c.   Dave asked Carla whether she wanted to accompany him.
    d.   Dave asked Carla if she wanted to come with him.
    e.   Dave asked Carla whether she wanted to come with.

36. <u>Although Bob and Ted worked together on the science project, Bob's conclusions were completely different than Ted's.</u>

    a.   Although Bob and Ted worked together on the science project, Bob's conclusions were completely different than Ted's.
    b.   Despite working together on the science project, Bob's conclusions were completely different than Ted's.
    c.   Although Bob and Ted worked together on the science project, Bob's conclusions were completely different from Ted's.
    d.   Although they worked together on the science project, Bob and Ted reached conclusions that were completely different than each other's.
    e.   Bob and Ted, who worked together on the science project, reached conclusions that were completely different than each other.

37. Shortly after their guests arrived, Dina and Tom realized that they <u>had prepared nowhere near the amount of food they needed</u> to feed the entire group.

    a.   had prepared nowhere near the amount of food they needed
    b.   had prepared nowhere near the amount of food they would need
    c.   had prepared not enough food they would need
    d.   had not prepared the amount of food they would need
    e.   had not prepared enough food

38.   <u>The children play quieter after lunch when I feed them a heavier snack.</u>

    a.   The children play quieter after lunch when I feed them a heavier snack.
    b.   The children play quietly after lunch when they have ate a heavier snack.
    c.   The children play quietly after lunch when I feed them a heavier snack.
    d.   The children play most quiet after lunch when I feed them a heavier snack.
    e.   I feed the children a heavier snack to get them to play quiet after lunch.

39. <u>Going to school and keeping up with homework are important to academic success.</u>

    a.   Going to school and keeping up with homework are important to academic success.
    b.   Going to school and keeping up with homework is important to academic success.
    c.   For academic success, what is important is going to school and keeping up with homework.
    d.   Go to school and keep up with homework are academic success.
    e.   Going to school and doing your homework will lead to academic success.

40. <u>What happens is going to surprise all of you.</u>

    a.   What happens is going to surprise all of you.
    b.   What happens is going to surprise you.
    c.   What will happen is going to surprise all of you.
    d.   What happens is going to be a surprise.
    e.   What happens is a surprise for all of you.

41. <u>My father, mother and sister insists that Christopher Columbus died in 1532, despite all evidence to the contrary.</u>

    a.   My father, mother and sister insists that Christopher Columbus died in 1532, despite all evidence to the contrary.
    b.   Christopher Columbus died, insist my father, mother and sister, in 1532, despite all evidence to the contrary.
    c.   Despite contrary evidence, my father, mother and sister insists that Christopher Columbus died in 1532,
    d.   My parents and sister insists that Christopher Columbus died in 1532, despite all contrary evidence.
    e.   My father, mother and sister insist that Christopher Columbus died in 1532, despite all evidence to the contrary.

Answer Key for Verbal Section 5

Critical Reading

1. Choice B is correct. The objective of the passage is to discuss the nutritional value and health benefits of fruits and vegetables.

2. Choice C is correct. In context, neutralize mean to defuse or render harmless.

3. Choice D is correct. All of the other choices are listed in the passage as coal foods.

4. Choice A is correct. All of the other answer choices are mentioned in the passage.

5. Choice E is correct. The answer is presented on Line 20.

6. Choice C is correct. All of the other answer choices are mentioned it the passage.

7. Choice C is correct. The author is enthusiastic about the importance of fruits and vegetables in the human diet.

8. Choice E is correct. The main point of the passage is to discuss the historical evolution of the corset in women's fashion.

9. Choice C is correct. In context, cestus means girdle.

10. Choice D is correct. All of the other countries are mentioned in the passage.

11. Choice A is correct. In context, abomination means disgrace.

12. Choice B is correct. The answer is stated directly in Lines 9 – 15.

13. Choice A is correct. All of the other answer choices are mentioned in the passage.

14. Choice C is correct. All of the other answer choices are mentioned in Lines 35 – 40.

15. Choice D is correct. The author presents his case in a clear and factual manner.

Critical Reasoning

16. The argument presumes that the availability of the information will translate into actual lifestyle changes, which is not necessarily the case. Choice B is correct.

17. The argument offers two options: either restrict gun ownership or lose society. Yet there certainly may be other alternatives, including one that society can tolerate. Choice B is correct.

18. In this question, the test writers have increased the level of difficulty by using the word "except," which

requires you to select the answer that does NOT resolve the discrepancy. Choice D is correct – it is the only choice that does not offer a plausible explanation for the results.

19. The author's concern was that the author based his conclusion of the views of three Canadian physicians who were biased on the topic of health care reform. Accordingly, they did not represent the views of the entire AMA. Choice D is correct. Bear in mind, answer choices A, B, C and E might very well be *true*, but they do not answer the question that is being asked. Many students are distracted by these answers, which relate to the argument in a reasonable way, yet are actually nothing more than extraneous information.

20. The unstated premise of the argument is that racket ball is an integral part of productivity and that workers on Saturn are more productive than those on Mars because they play more racket ball. The correct answer is C.

21. The argument in the question stem can be symbolized as follows: All models (all X) enjoy fashion (do Y). Coral loves fashion (this one does Y). Therefore, Coral must be a model (therefore, this one must be an X). Of the five possibilities, Choice D is the best answer. The other four answers all deviate slightly from the original argument.

22. The argument generalizes from the survey to the general population, so the reliability of the projection depends on how representative the sample is. Choice E is best, because it points out that the one hundred people who participated in the survey did not represent the entire investment community.

23. The argument presumes that a requirement in one situation should be the same for a similar situation. Choice B is correct. The other answer choices all have a slightly different form.

24. The author's argument is a contradiction. Choice A is correct.

25. Choice D is the correct answer because it acknowledges Ariel's unwarranted assumption – that the students at their university are extraordinary enough to attract the attention of top-tier recruiters. Amber's response acknowledges that this may not be the case.

26. The author's only evidence is that respected people agree with her position. Choice D is correct, as she is appealing to the authority of others.

Sentence Correction

27. When two subjects that would normally command different verbs are joined by *or/nor,* the subject that is *closer to the verb* determines the person. In this case, the subject *you* is closer to the verb than *Sara*. Hence, the verb must agree with the subject *you*. But what about Sara? Here's where it's important to remember the directions at the beginning of this section of the GMAT. The writers have asked you to select the BEST way to correct this awkward sentence, which is to place the correct verb next to each singular subject: *Either Sara is guilty or you are guilty*. The correct answer is C.

28. Choice A is correct. The sentence is correct as originally written.

29. In this sentence, the pronoun *they* (which is plural) refers to the word *husband* (which is singular). To correct this sentence, the subject and pronoun must match in number. Hence, the correct answer choice is C, which uses the singular pronoun *he*.

30. The word *everyone* is always singular, so it requires a singular pronoun in this sentence. Answer choices D and E are the only ones that use *his* instead of *theirs*. Choice E, however, changes the meaning of the sentence by changing the word *will* to *should*. Therefore, the correct answer choice is D.

31. Choice E is correct. This sentence has a misplaced modifier that confuses its meaning. Unfortunately, the answer choices that move the modifier closer to its subject are even more confusing than the original sentence. The best answer is therefore choice E, which lengthens the sentence, but clarifies its meaning.

32. This is not a sentence because it lacks a subject in its main clause. Choice C is the best correction.

33. In this question, the phrase *he was sold* includes a passive verb, which should be expresses as an

active verb.   Choice D is correct.

34. Choice E is correct. *Disinterested* means objective or unbiased, while *uninterested* means not caring about something or someone.

35. Choice C is correct. The original sentence makes a common error by using the word *if* instead of *whether*. (*Whether* introduces a choice, while *if* introduces a condition.)

36. Choice C is correct. The original sentence contains the erroneous expression *different than*, which should be *different from*.

37. Choice E is correct. The phrase *nowhere near* is cumbersome; instead, be definitive by stating *not enough*.

38. The correct way to modify the verb is by using the adverb *quietly*. Answer choice C is correct.

39. Choice A is correct. The sentence is correct as written. Choice E, although dramatically correct, changes the meaning of the sentence.

40. The correct revision is Choice C, *what will happen*.

41. The subject and verb in the original sentence do not agree. Choice E is the best revision.

Directions: *The passage below is followed by questions based on its content. Answer the questions, based on what is* <u>stated</u> *or* <u>implied</u> *in the passage and any introductory material that may be provided.*

Passage 1

The eleventh century, during which feudal power rose to its height, was also the period when a reaction set in among the townspeople against the nobility. The spirit of Rome revived with that of the bourgeois and infused a feeling of opposition to the system which followed the conquest of the Teutons. "But," says M. Henri Martin, "what reappeared was not the Roman municipality of the Empire, stained by servitude, although surrounded with glittering pomp and gorgeous arts, but it was something coarse and almost semi-barbarous in form, though strong and generous at its core, and which, as far as the difference of the times would allow, rather reminds us of the small republics which existed previous to the Roman Empire."

8

Two strong impulses, originating from two totally dissimilar centers of action, irresistibly propelled this great social revolution, with its various and endless aspects, affecting all of central Europe, and being more or less felt in the west, the north, and the south. On one side, the Greek and Latin partiality for ancient corporations, modified by a democratic element, and an innate feeling of opposition characteristic of barbaric tribes; and on the other, the free spirit and equality of the old Celtic tribes rising suddenly against the military hierarchy, which was the offspring of conquest. Europe was roused by the double current of ideas which simultaneously urged her on to a new state of civilization, and more particularly, to a new organization of city life.

16

Italy was naturally destined to be the country where the new trials of social regeneration were to be made, but she presented the greatest variety of customs, laws, and governments, including the Emperor, Pope, bishops, and feudal princes. In Tuscany and Liguria, the march towards liberty was continued almost without effort; whilst in Lombardy, on the contrary, the feudal resistance was most powerful. Everywhere, however, cities became more or less completely enfranchised, though some more rapidly than others. In Sicily, feudalism swayed over the countries, but in the greater part of the peninsula, the democratic spirit of the cities influenced the enfranchisement of the rural population. The feudal caste was in fact dissolved; the barons were transformed into patricians of the noble towns which gave their republican magistrates the old title of consuls.

25

The Teutonic Emperor in vain sought to seize and turn to his own interest the sovereignty of the people, who had shaken off the yokes of his vassals: the signal of war was immediately given by the newly enfranchised masses and the imperial eagle was obliged to fly before the banners of the besieged cities. Happy indeed might the cities of Italy have been had they not forgotten, in their prosperity, that union alone could give them the possibility of maintaining that liberty which they so freely risked in continual quarrels amongst one another.

31

1. What is the main point of the passage?

   a. Despite the opposition, Italians refused to relinquish their freedom
   b. The Italian social revolution was guided by two strong, but mutually opposing, forces
   c. Without unity, the Italian cities were unable to maintain their liberty
   d. The eleventh century was a period of great wealth and refinement in Italy
   e. The democratic spirit in Italian cities eventually conquered the feudalistic tendencies in rural areas

2. According to the author, what followed the conquest of the Teutons?

   a. Opposition to the system
   b. The fall of the bourgeois
   c. The rise of the nobility
   d. Cultural refinement
   e. A widespread commitment to education and literacy

3. According to M. Henri Martin, the entity that appeared in Italy after the fall of the Roman Empire was characterized by all of the following EXCEPT:

    a. Coarseness
    b. Generosity
    c. Semi-barbaric
    d. Stained by servitude
    e. Strength

4. According to the author, which two impulses propelled the European social revolution?

    a. Celtic conquests versus Greek and Latin democracy
    b. Celtic barbarism versus Greek and Latin corporations
    c. Celtic military versus Greek and Latin barbarism
    d. Celtic conquest of Greek and Latin democracy
    e. Celtic spirit of freedom and equality versus Greek and Latin opposition

5. In Line 17, what does "*regeneration*" mean?

    a. Dedication
    b. Revision
    c. Renewal
    d. Exploration
    e. Blending

6. According to the author, Italian society in the eleventh century included all of the following EXCEPT:

    a. Feudal princes
    b. Sicilian priests
    c. Bishops
    d. Emperor
    e. Pope

7. According to the author, in what place was feudal resistance most powerful?

    a. Tuscany
    b. Rome
    c. Liguria
    d. Lombardy
    e. Sicily

8. In Line 21, what does "*enfranchised*" mean?

    a. Free
    b. Wealthy
    c. Educated
    d. Political
    e. Patrician

9. In Line 27, to what does the word "*yokes*" refer?

    a. Garments
    b. Ideology
    c. Weapons
    d. Values
    e. Oppression

10. What is the author's tone in the passage?

    a. Superior
    b. Ironic
    c. Neutral
    d. Aghast
    e. Conciliatory

Passage 2

At first glance, they were the perfect family. Dad was an executive at the Enron Corporation, while Mom worked at the same firm. Then, the company, and their lives, crashed down around them because of an illegal scheme that left millions of stockholders empty-handed. In a deal that requires prison time and a forfeiture of over $24 million to the government in ill-gotten gains, Andy and Lea Fastow eventually plead guilty to charges of fraud and tax evasion. As expected, the Fastows have earned little sympathy from the thousands of Enron employees who lost their careers, life savings and retirement dreams in this sordid debacle. Barring a miracle, few will ever earn back what Ken Lay's merry gang of thieves has stolen from them.

8

Enron's problems began with revelations that its chief financial officer was running partnerships that allowed the company to keep half a billion dollars in debt off its books. The precipitous fall in Enron's stock price was the result of fraud, as executives cashed out their stock positions while falsely reassuring shareholders that business was booming. The international accounting firm Arthur Anderson also engaged in deceptive behavior by helping Enron hide hundreds of millions of dollars of losses and by destroying documents that would have been helpful to the subsequent criminal investigation.

15

Many people are now questioning how in the world this could have happened. A better question is why the government didn't implement better regulations to *prevent* it. Considering the behind-the-scenes practices at both firms, the debacle was inevitable. After beginning as a traditional energy producer/seller in 1985, Enron gained permission from the Federal Energy Regulatory Commission to trade energy futures and derivatives. Unfortunately, Enron opted to cheat, rather than play by the rules. Instead of letting the free market decide energy future prices, Enron set up nearly 3000 offshore companies, many of which they treated as partnerships.

22

These offshore companies provided Enron with the perfect ruse to manipulate energy prices and, at the same time, hide its own debts. When states like California came to Enron to lock in energy contracts, Enron would show them contracts it had signed with its offshore "partners" that locked them in at increasingly astronomical prices. Viewing what appeared to be legitimate contracts with others, Enron's customers had no choice but to submit to Enron's extortive energy prices.

28

For many years, Enron circumvented the magic of the marketplace and set its own price for energy, wildly inflating the stock price. Greedy Enron executives saw no end to the possibilities for its offshore entities. By transferring its obligations to some of the these shell companies, they were able to show Wall Street profits, when in fact the company was being looted into insolvency by its top managers. When the uncontrollable meltdown of Enron's scheme began in December 2001, the world learned that Enron's apparent success had been little more than a complex illusion.

35

To restore the public's faith in corporate America, the federal government needs to quickly undo every "loophole" that Enron exploited in its convoluted scheme. Offshore partnerships should be banned. Government investigators should be granted free access to a firm's books and audit them on a regular basis. Firmer laws must be implemented to govern an accounting firm's relationship with its clients. No single company should ever be in a position to set the price for energy, nor should they be allowed to show non-existent profits to Wall Street.

42

As devastating as the Enron scheme has been to thousands of displaced employees and millions of bilked stockholders, it has taught the entire world a cynical lesson about the power of greed and the need for governmental regulation in the minutia of everyday corporate life. Thanks to Enron, many potential investors will never be willing to invest a dime in a publicly held company. Worse than their tarnished reputations and their prolonged jail sentences, this is the sad legacy that the Fastows have left us.

48

11. What is the objective of the passage?

    a.   To explain the criminal actions of the Fastows
    b.   To explain the intricacies of insider trading
    c.   To explain how and why the Enron scandal occurred
    d.   To explain how the government can prevent similar scandals
    e.   All of the above

12. In paragraph one, what is the author's tone?

    a.   wry
    b.   forlorn
    c.   insightful
    d.   resigned
    e.   neutral

13. In line 10, what does *"precipitous"* mean?

    a.   uncertain
    b.   unexpected
    c.   irregular
    d.   dangerous
    e.   steep

14. According to the passage, what was Arthur Anderson's role in the Enron scandal?

    a.   Cashed out their stock positions early
    b.   Set up shell corporations offshore
    c.   Manipulated the price of energy in California
    d.   Destroyed documents about the case
    e.   Submitted forged documents to government investigators

15. In line 25, to whom does the author refer as *"partners"*?

    a.   The company's shareholders
    b.   The CEO and Board of Directors
    c.   The Arthur Anderson accounting firm
    d.   Enron's energy customers
    e.   The shell companies offshore

16. Which of the following was NOT part of the Enron scandal?

    a.   Government agents accepted bribes from Enron executives
    b.   Most employees lost their jobs and retirement savings
    c.   Accounting firm helped company hide losses
    d.   Executives falsely inflated the corporate profits
    e.   Company illegally manipulated the price of energy

17. In the passage, the author makes several suggestions to prevent a similar scandal in the future. They include all of the following EXCEPT:

    a.   Firmer laws to regulate accounting firms
    b.   Offshore partnerships should be banned
    c.   The government should have the right to inspect the books of companies on a regular basis
    d.   The government should set the price for energy contracts
    e.   Stronger penalties for white collar crime

18. In line 45, what does *"minutia"* mean?

    a. prospectus
    b. finances
    c. litigation
    d. paper trail
    e. details

19. According to the author, what is the worst part of the Fastows' legacy?

    a. Employees lost their jobs and retirement savings
    b. Public afraid to invest in stock market
    c. California overpaid for energy contracts
    d. They must serve mandatory prison terms
    e. Public humiliation and embarrassment

20. Which of the following statements best expresses the author's opinion about corporate accounting?

    a. Most accounting firms are honest and do not require extra scrutiny.
    b. The government must establish and enforce stronger laws to govern the actions of accountants to rebuild the public trust in corporations.
    c. The government should establish stronger laws to govern the accounting policies of energy companies.
    d. The government should devote more resources to investigating illegal offshore entities.
    e. Scandals like Enron, although devastating, are rare. No sweeping changes in accounting practices are necessary.

Directions: *The questions in this section are based on the reasoning contained in brief statements or passages. For some questions, more than one of the choices could conceivably answer the question. However, you are to choose the one that provides the most complete and accurate answer. You should not make assumptions that are implausible, superfluous, or incompatible with the passage.*

21. In baseball, hitting a grand slam is a skill that only players with great batting averages can achieve. Wade Boggs was a great player, so even though he did not have a great batting average, he would have excelled at hitting grand slam home runs.

Which one of the following contains a flaw that most closely parallels the flaw contained in the passage?

    a. Eighty percent of the freshmen at Yale eventually receive a bachelor's degree. Kyle is a freshman at Yale, so he will probably complete his studies and receive a bachelor's degree.
    b. If the police don't act immediately to quell the disturbance, it will escalate into a riot. However, since the police are understaffed, there will be a riot.
    c. The meek shall inherit the earth. Sara received an inheritance from her father, so she must be meek.
    d. During the Great Depression, the rich and the poor both had to sacrifice. However, Rick's family was wealthy, so they continued to purchase luxury goods.
    e. All parrots are birds and all birds excrete nitric oxide. Therefore, all birds that excrete nitric oxide are parrots.

22. Professor: a prestigious educational journal recently ran an article about the need for foreign language training at the university level. The author quoted four prominent experts, all of whom supported mandatory requirements for both English and Spanish classes. These quotations gave the impression that all faculty members support the need for training in both languages. However, the author of the article failed to mention that the four experts he interviewed were all from Venezuela, where both English and Spanish are spoken.

Which of the following principles best explains the professor's argument?

a. Most faculty members in the U.S. do not favor mandatory classes in Spanish.
b. The author of the article does not speak Spanish; accordingly, his assessment of their position was flawed.
c. The article was misleading, because it was written by a language professor.
d. The article was misleading, because the experts the author consulted only spoke one language.
e. The article was misleading, because it presented the biased views of four experts as being representative of those of an entire group.

23. All kittens and puppies at Space Coast Rescue must be spayed or neutered before they are placed for adoption. Jane's cat is spayed, so it must be from Space Coast Rescue.

What is the flaw in this conclusion?

a. It presents contradictory evidence.
b. It uses circular reasoning.
c. It presumes that Jane lives on the Space Coast.
d. It ignores the possibility that Jane's cat was from another source.
e. The conclusion is not flawed.

24. Jill loves seafood. She was raised on the coastline.

Which one of the following uses reasoning that is most similar to the above argument?

a. Karen loves swimming. She is an athlete.
b. Babies drink plenty of milk. They need extra protein.
c. Fruit grows in tropical climates. Florida is in the tropics.
d. Harry eats plenty of steak. He lives on a farm in Kansas.
e. Jay is allergic to seafood. He cannot eat shrimp.

25. In a recent survey, one thousand college seniors were asked to choose between two options. In the first scenario, the students would be guaranteed a job in their field after graduation at a starting salary of $50,000 per year. In the second scenario, the one thousand graduates would be forced to compete for eight hundred positions, which offered a starting salary of $75,000 per year. Although the students had a "sure thing" with the first option, they overwhelmingly indicated that they preferred the second option.

Which one of the following, if true, would best explain these results?

a. The students who owed significant student load debt were more likely to choose the first option.
b. The students were willing to sacrifice a high salary for a secure position.
c. The students were willing to sacrifice security for the chance to earn a higher salary.
d. The guaranteed positions were mostly in the public sector.
e. In the current economy, many students preferred to attend graduate school than enter the job market.

26. Students at a local university were asked whether or not they would consider buying their textbooks in electronic form, rather than in hardback or paperback form, if the prices were competitive. A majority of the respondents claimed that they preferred to buy hardback or paperback textbooks, rather than their electronic counterparts. Based upon the results of the survey, publishing companies declined to make their textbooks available in electronic form.

Which of the following, if true, provides the most support for the publishers' decision?

    a. Hardcover textbooks have a higher resale value than electronic textbooks.
    b. Electronic textbooks are ecologically friendly.
    c. Hardcover textbooks are more expensive than their electronic counterparts.
    d. Students who purchase electronic textbooks are not allowed to print the documents.
    e. At schools that offer students a choice between hardcover and electronic textbooks, nearly 90% of the students purchase the hardcover textbooks.

27. Zachary bought a condo on Walden Pond. Therefore, Zachary must have paid $100,000.

Which of the following correctly states the omitted assumption in the argument?

    a. Zachary paid $100 per square foot for his condo.
    b. Zachary's neighbor paid $100,000 for a condo on Walden Pond.
    c. All condos at Walden Pond are the same size.
    d. All condos at Walden Pond cost $100,000.
    e. Zachary recently inherited $100,000.

28. Before the Civil War, civil plaintiffs could present their cases to a judicial panel if they paid a fee to the court and their complaints met the criteria of existing case law. At first, the number of civil cases was small. Eventually, the judicial panel invented new types of laws that generated additional cases and greater revenues for the court.

Which of the following conclusions is most strongly suggested by the paragraph above?

    a. The judicial panel decided most cases in a capricious manner.
    b. Without adequate representation, the defendant rarely prevailed.
    c. Before the Civil War, the judicial panel had greater power than other branches of government.
    d. In making decisions, the judicial panel was motivated partially by economic considerations.
    e. Early legal decisions, when taken collectively, formed a coherent body of law.

29. Twelve thousand patients with seafood allergies were evaluated for a variety of viral infections. The physicians who examined them discovered that 90% of the patients with seafood allergies also tested positive for the Epstein Barr virus. These findings support the conclusion that seafood allergies cause the Epstein Barr virus.

Which one of the following selections, if true, points out the most critical weakness in the method used by the physician?

    a. He confused correlation with causation.
    b. He generalized from a very small sample to a large population.
    c. He used circular reasoning.
    d. He did not publish his study in a peer-reviewed journal.
    e. He intentionally chose a biased population for his study.

Directions: The following sentences test correctness and effectiveness of expression. Part of each sentence (or the entire sentence) is underlined; beneath each sentence are five ways of phrasing the underlined material. Choice A repeats the original phrasing; the other four choices are different. If you think the original phrasing produces a better sentence than the alternatives, select choice A; if not, select one of the other choices. In making your selection, follow the requirements of standard written English, such as grammar, choice of words, sentence construction, and punctuation. Your selection should result in the most effective sentence – clear and precise, without awkwardness or ambiguity.

Example: Most teenagers struggle to be free <u>both of parental domination but also from premature responsibilities.</u>

a.   both of parental domination but also from premature responsibilities.
b.   both of parental domination and also from premature responsibilities.
c.   both of parental domination and also of premature responsibilities.
d.   of parental domination and premature responsibilities.
e.   both of parental domination and their premature responsibilities as well.

The correct answer is Choice D.

30. <u>Dan lives in the house across from Jane, which is adjacent to the green log cabin owned by Desmond Harris</u>.

    a.   Dan lives in the house across from Jane, which is adjacent to the green log cabin owned by Desmond Harris.
    b.   Dan lives in the house across from Jane's house, which is adjacent to the green log cabin owned by Desmond Harris.
    c.   Dan lives in the house across from Jane's, which is adjacent to the green log cabin owned by Desmond Harris.
    d.   Dan lives in the house across from Jane, which is next to the green log cabin that is owned by Desmond Harris.
    e.   Dan lives across from Jane, in a house, and adjacent to the green log cabin owned by Desmond Harris.

31. Women who avoid social gatherings <u>never have nor ever will be</u> gregarious.

    a.   never have nor ever will be.
    b.   never have been, and never will be,
    c.   never have and never will be
    d.   have never and will never be
    e.   never have been gregarious and never will be

32. <u>Dr. Bancroft has designated Nurse Smith as one of the employees who are going to receive special training in handle hazardous waste</u>.

    a.   Dr. Bancroft has designated Nurse Smith as one of the employees who are going to receive special training in handle hazardous waste.
    b.   Dr. Bancroft has designated Nurse Smith as someone who will receive special training in hazardous waste.
    c.   Dr. Bancroft has designated Nurse Smith as one of the employees who will receive special training in handling hazardous waste.
    d.   Dr. Bancroft designated Nurse Smith to receive special training in handling hazardous waste, as one of the few employees.
    e.   Dr. Bancroft designated Nurse Smith as one of the employees to receive special training in hazardous waste.

33. <u>By the time the doctor returned her call, Mrs. Stevens had all ready gone into labor</u>.

    a.   By the time the doctor returned her call, Mrs. Stevens had all ready gone into labor.
    b.   By the time the doctor returned her call, Mrs. Stevens had already gone into labor.
    c.   When the doctor returned her call, Mrs. Stevens had all ready gone into labor.
    d.   By the time the doctor had returned her call, Mrs. Stevens had all ready gone into labor.
    e.   Mrs. Stevens had all ready gone into labor when the doctor returned her call.

34. Being that the attorneys were not prepared, they requested a three-week continuance from the Judge.

    a. Being that the attorneys were not prepared, they requested a three-week continuance from the Judge.
    b. Being that the attorneys were not prepared, they asked the Judge for a continuance of three weeks.
    c. Being that the attorneys were not prepared for three weeks, they requested a continuance from the Judge
    d. Because the attorneys were not prepared, they requested a three-week continuance from the Judge.
    e. Because they were behind, the attorneys requested a three-week continuance from the Judge.

35. Jessie could of gone to the prom with Bryan, but she didn't know he was interested.

    a. Jessie could of gone to the prom with Bryan, but she didn't know he was interested.
    b. Jessie could have gone to the prom with Bryan, if she would have known he was interested.
    c. Jessie could have gone to the prom with Bryan, if she could have known he was interested.
    d. Jessie would of gone to the prom with Bryan, but she didn't know he was interested.
    e. Jessie could have gone to the prom with Bryan, but she didn't know he was interested.

36. To prevent insect bites, Connie wears long sleeves, a floppy hat, along with a gallon of insecticide with DEET.

    a. long sleeves, a floppy hat, along with a gallon of insecticide with DEET.
    b. long sleeves, and a floppy hat and a gallon of insecticide with DEET.
    c. long sleeves and a floppy hat with a gallon of insecticide with DEET.
    d. long sleeves, a floppy hat, and a gallon of insecticide with DEET.
    e. long sleeves and a floppy hat, with a gallon of insecticide with DEET.

37. Along with language, economics and political persuasion, sociologists insist that culture, including eclectic views on spirituality, are integral to personality development.

    a. Along with language, economics and political persuasion, sociologists insist that culture, including eclectic views on spirituality, are integral to personality development.
    b. Along with language, economics, political persuasion, and culture, sociologists insist that spirituality is integral to personality development.
    c. Sociologists insist that language, economics, political persuasion, and culture, including eclectic views on spirituality, is integral to personality development.
    d. Along with language, economics and political persuasion, sociologists insist that culture, including eclectic views on spirituality, is integral to personality development.
    e. Sociologists insist that personality development depends upon eclectic views on language, economics, political persuasion, culture, and spirituality.

38. Cheetahs, pandas and leopards are all popular at the zoo, but leopards have the larger audience appeal.

    a. Cheetahs, pandas and leopards are all popular at the zoo, but leopards have the larger audience appeal.
    b. Of the three animals – cheetahs, pandas and leopards – pandas have the larger audience appeal.
    c. Pandas have more appeal than cheetahs and leopards with the audience.
    d. Although cheetahs, pandas and leopards are all popular, pandas have the larger audience appeal.
    e. Cheetahs, pandas and leopards are all popular at the zoo, but pandas have the largest audience appeal.

39. Once a teenager starts to smoke, it will most likely he will continue to do so.

    a. Once a teenager starts to smoke, it will most likely he will continue to do so.
    b. Once a teenager starts to smoke, he will most likely continue to do so.
    c. Once a teenager starts smoking, it is likely one will continue to do so.
    d. Once a teenager starts to smoke, it is most likely they will continue to do so.
    e. Once a teenager smokes, it likely to continue.

40. The models will double their workouts in their efforts at slimming down before the show.

    a. The models will double their workouts in their efforts at slimming down before the show.
    b. Before the show, the models will double their workouts in their efforts at slimming down.
    c. The models will double their workouts in their efforts to slim down before the show.
    d. The models, in their efforts at slimming down, will double their workouts before the show.
    e. Before the show, to double their efforts to slim down, the models will double their workouts.

41. The new owners of Channel One, including media mogul Rupert Murdoch, held an international news conference to lie out their strategy for reporting domestic terrorist attacks.

    a. to lie out their strategy for reporting domestic terrorist attacks.
    b. to lay out their strategy for reporting domestic terrorist attacks.
    c. to lie out the strategy by which they will report domestic terrorist attacks.
    d. to lay out their domestic strategy.
    e. to lie out their strategy to report domestic terrorist attacks.

Answer Key for Verbal Section 6

Critical Reading

1. Choice C is correct. The main point of the passage is stated in the final line. If the Italian cities had unified rather than quarreled, they might have maintained their liberty.

2. Choice A is correct. The answer is on Line 3.

3. Choice D is correct. The answers are mentioned in Lines 4 – 6.

4. Choice E is correct. The answer is presented in Lines 11 – 14.

5. Choice C is correct. In this context, regeneration means renewal.

6. Choice B is correct. All of the other answer choices are mentioned in Lines 18 – 19.

7. Choice D is correct. The answer is presented in Line 20.

8. Choice A is correct. In this context, enfranchised means free.

9. Choice E is correct. In this context, the word yokes means oppression.

10. Choice C is correct. The author presents the information in a neutral tone.

11. Choice E is correct. The passage covers all of these points.

12. Choice D is correct. In the first paragraph, the author is resigned to the fact that the Fastows' victims will not recover their losses or forgive the Enron executives who defrauded them.

13. Choice E is correct. In this concept *precipitous* means steep,

14. Choice E is correct. Arthur Andersen submitted forged document to investigators to try to hide Enron's actual financial status.

15. Choice E is correct. In this context the *partners* were the phony offshore entities that Enron established.

16. Choice A is correct. All of the other answer choices were mentioned in the passage.

17. Choice E is correct. All of the other answer choices were mentioned in the passage.

18. Choice E is correct. In this context, *minutia* means details.

19. Choice B is correct. According to the author, the worst consequence of the scandal is that it made the American public afraid to invest in the stock market.

20. Choice B is correct. The author favors stronger laws to regulate accounting practices to prevent future scandals.

Critical Reasoning

21. The argument clearly contradicts itself, so the correct answer choice will contradict itself in a similar manner. Choice D is the correct answer. It begins by stating that both the rich and the poor had to sacrifice during the Great Depression, but it ends by stating that a wealthy family (Rick's) did not curtail spending.

22. The author's concern was that the author based his conclusion of the views of four experts who were biased on the topic of language studies. Accordingly, they did not represent the views of other faculty members. Choice E is correct.

23. The argument ignores the possibility that Jane's cat was from another source. Choice D is correct.

24. This argument presumes that a person's place of residence determines his/her dietary preferences. Choice D uses the same reasoning.

25. Choice C is correct. The students were willing to sacrifice security for the chance to earn a higher salary.

26. The best way to strengthen this argument is to prove that the results of the survey accurately reflect the feeling of the general student population. Choice E is correct because it strengthens this connection.

27. In this argument, the assumption is that all condos at Walden Pond cost $100,000, which is Choice D.

28. Choice D is correct. By increasing the number of legal cases, the judicial panel increased its power AND generated significant revenue. A natural conclusion is that the desire for economic gain fueled the expansion. Choices A, B, C and E are not supported by the text.

29. Choice A is correct. The physician presumed that one factor caused the other, without providing any evidence to support that conclusion.

Sentence Correction

30. The correct revision is Choice B, *across from Jane's house*.

31. Choice E is correct. The sentence includes two phrases with different verb tenses; hence, each must be stated in full: Women who avoid social gatherings *never have been gregarious and never will be* gregarious.

32. The original sentences contains the incorrect form of the verb *handling*. Choice C is the best correction.

33. The correct revision is Choice B (*had already*, not *had all ready*).

34. The phrase *being that* is always wrong. Choice D makes the best revision (*because*).

35. The original sentence includes an incorrect verb form. Choice E offers the best revision (*could have gone*, not *could of gone*).

36. Choice D is correct. The original sentence has an error in parallelism. The correct list of items should

read: To prevent insect bites, Connie wears long sleeves, a floppy hat, and a gallon of insecticide with DEET.

37. The word culture is singular, which requires the singular verb *is*. Choice D is correct, because it makes this correction without changing the meaning of the sentence.

38. Choice E is correct. When three or more items are being compared, the correct term is *largest*, not *larger*.

39. Choice B presents the best revision (*he will most likely*).

40. The original sentence uses an infinitive instead of a gerund. The sentence should read: *The models will double their workouts in their efforts to slim down before the show.* Choice C is correct.

41. The correct choice is B which uses *lay* versus *lie*.

Verbal Section 7:   75 minutes   41 questions

Directions: The passage below is followed by questions based on its content. Answer the questions, based on what is <u>stated</u> or <u>implied</u> in the passage and any introductory material that may be provided.

Passage 1

In and of itself, competition can be a healthy ingredient in the workplace, which produces better quality products or services at the lowest possible price. It can also stimulate the search for new technologies or better ways to satisfy customers. Pushed to extremes, however, competition can often reach an intensity that results in unethical practices and detrimental consequences.

5

Such intense competition, along with the desire to maximize profits and personal wealth, lead the formerly successful Enron Corporation down an unethical and illegal path. In the early days, Enron experienced significant growth and gained substantial credibility as a natural gas company. Later on, however, most of its successful operations were replaced by the illusion of successful initiatives. Over time, executives were no longer able to generate large profits, and, in fact, gambled away a substantial part of the company's financial resources. As a result, Enron's top executives began to actively borrow funds from Wall Street investors to make up the difference. The company's financial deficits, however, were effectively hidden from the investment bankers, as well as the remainder of the financial community.

14

As a result of many unwise and unethical domestic and foreign investments, extravagant corporate expenditures by the enterprise's top executives and a series of scandals involving irregular mark-to-market accounting procedures, Enron filed the largest bankruptcy in the American history on December 2, 2001.

18

Most people don't realize that Enron, like many other American corporations, possessed its very own Code of Ethics, in which the company tried to position itself as an international employer, a creator of innovative energy solutions, as well as a global corporate citizen. It assured all of its employees that these great responsibilities were not taken lightly by the corporation's executive management, which was committed to conducting itself in a respectful manner. The Code of Ethics continued to explain that Enron felt very strongly about its core values; it demanded that its employees treat each other as they would like to be treated themselves. Further, the Code of Ethics emphasized the importance of honoring all promises to clients and corporate prospects. Finally, it listed open communication and excellence at the top of its list of core values. Most impressively, all employees, including executive managers, were held to the same standards in respect to the company's vision and values. As required by most firms, Enron also mandated a signed compliance form that verified that each employee would adhere to the stipulated corporate standards.

30

Upon the approval of the company's Board of Directors, Enron's Chairman, Kenneth Lay presented the Code of Ethics in July 2000. Ironically, on May 25th, 2006, Mr. Lay was convicted of one count of conspiracy, three counts of securities fraud, three counts of bank fraud and two wire fraud counts. In addition, Mr. Lay was found guilty of signing misleading audit representation letters and making false statements and presentations to securities analysts and rating agencies.

36

Subsequently, Jeffrey K. Skilling, Enron's former Chief Executive Officer since February 2001, was also found guilty of nineteen (out of twenty-eight) felony charges filed against him during the financial collapse of the corporation. Just to name a few, the courts found Skilling guilty of one count of conspiracy, one count of insider trading, five counts of making false statements and presentations to securities analysts and twelve counts of securities fraud.

42

Lastly, Enron's former Chief Financial Officer, Andrew S. Fastow, played a key role in hiding the corporation's massive losses through the mark-to-market and creative accounting practices. On October 31, 2002, Fastow was found guilty of seventy-eight counts of conspiracy, money laundering and fraud. In exchange for his testimony against other Enron top executives, Andrew Fastow agreed to serve a ten-year prison term. Kenneth Lay and Jeffrey Skilling faced up to 185 years in prison for their fraudulent activities and conspiracy at Enron. Lay, however, died of a heart attack before his sentence could be imposed.

49

There are many lessons to remember from the story of Enron's rise, prominence, and financial collapse. Although some people feel it is an account of justified achievement, growth, innovation, and creativity, most agree it is an unfortunate (but true) testimony of human greed, ambition, competitive deceit, and arrogance. Enron's story shows that the company's Code of Ethics didn't really mean anything because it was not applied equally to everyone in the corporation. There must be a genuine and strong commitment from top management to reinforce and support the principles and values that are set forth in a corporate Code of Ethics. Further, funds should be made available in each corporate budget to conduct ethics training (and possibly hire ethics officers) to communicate, implement, and integrate the ethical behavior into the firm's culture.

58

1. According to the author, all of the following are positive effects of competition EXCEPT:

    a.   more educated workforce
    b.   better ways to satisfy customers
    c.   better quality products
    d.   lowest possible price
    e.   improves the search for new technologies

2. In Line 12, what does "*deficit*" mean?

    a.   expenditure
    b.   subterfuge
    c.   impairment
    d.   deficiency
    e.   disadvantage

3. According to the author of the passage, which of the following is NOT a reason for Enron's bankruptcy?

    a.   Irregular accounting procedures
    b.   Unethical foreign investments
    c.   Extravagant executive expenses
    d.   Tax evasion
    e.   Bank fraud

4. In Line 34, what does "*audit*" mean?

    a.   government
    b.   examination
    c.   repercussion
    d.   regulatory
    e.   seizure

5. According to the author, which of the following best conveys the value of a corporation's Code of Ethics?

    a.   It assures Wall Street investors of a firm's mission and goals
    b.   It attracts the right type of employee at all levels of the organization
    c.   It is only valuable if top managers support and reinforce its principles
    d.   It is an essential public relations tool
    e.   It has no intrinsic value

6. What is the tone of the passage?

    a.   apathetic
    b.   vainglorious
    c.   dejected
    d.   incredulous
    e.   objective

7. Which of the following is the best title for the passage?

    a.   The Criminal Consequences of Enron
    b.   How Top Enron Managers Betrayed Their Corporate Code of Ethics
    c.   How Enron Fell from Grace
    d.   Fraud at Enron: The New Corporate Culture
    e.   Enron: The Aftermath

Passage 2

About five miles from Warwick are the ruins of Kenilworth Castle, the magnificent home of the Earl of Leicester. Geoffrey de Clinton, in the reign of Henry I, built a strong castle and founded a monastery here. It was afterwards the castle of Simon de Montfort, and his son was besieged in it for several months, ultimately surrendering, when the king bestowed it upon his youngest son, Edward, Earl of Lancaster and Leicester. Edward II, when taken prisoner in Wales, was brought to Kenilworth, and signed his abdication in the castle, being afterwards murdered in Berkeley Castle. Then it came to John of Gaunt, and in the Wars of the Roses was alternately held by the partisans of each side. Finally, Queen Elizabeth bestowed it upon her ambitious favorite, Dudley, Earl of Leicester, who made splendid additions to the buildings.

9

It was here that Leicester gave magnificent entertainment to Queen Elizabeth, including a series of pageants that lasted seventeen days and cost $5000 a day--a very large sum for those times. The queen was attended by thirty-one barons and a host of retainers, and four hundred servants, who were all lodged in the fortress. The attendants were clothed in velvet, and the party drank sixteen hogsheads of wine and forty hogsheads of beer every day, while to feed them ten oxen were killed every morning. There was a succession of plays and amusements provided, including the Coventry play of "Hock Tuesday" and the "Country Bridal," with bull-and bear-baiting, of which the queen was very fond. The display and hospitality of the Earl of Leicester were intended to pave the way to marriage, but the wily queen was not to be thus entrapped.

18

The castle is now part of the Earl of Clarendon's estate, and he has taken great pains to preserve the famous ruins. The great hall, ninety feet long, still retains several of its Gothic windows, and some of the towers rise seventy feet high. These ivy-mantled ruins stand upon an elevated rocky site commanding a fine prospect, and their chief present use is as a picnic-ground for tourists. Not far away are the ruins of the priory, which was founded at the same time as the castle. A dismantled gate-house with some rather extensive foundations are all that remain. In a little church near by the matins and the curfew are still tolled, one of the bells used having belonged to the priory.

26

Few English ruins have more romance attached to them than those of Kenilworth, for the graphic pen of the best story-teller of Britain has interwoven them into one of his best romances, and has thus given an idea of the splendors as well as the dark deeds of the Elizabethan era that will exist as long as the language endures.

30

8. What is the main point of the passage?

   a. To discuss the romantic significance of the English ruins
   b. To discuss the ownership and use of Kenilworth Castle from ancient times until modern day
   c. To discuss Queen Elizabeth's romance with the Earl of Leicester at Kenilworth Castle
   d. To explain the Earl of Clarendon's efforts to restore Kenilworth Castle to its original beauty
   e. To document the architectural genius of Geoffrey de Clinton

9. The passage mentions all of the following about Edward II EXCEPT:

   a. Taken prisoner in Wales
   b. Signed his abdication at Kenilworth Castle
   c. Murdered in Berkeley Castle
   d. Son of the Earl of Lancaster and Leicester
   e. Besieged in Kenilworth Castle

10. In Line 7, what does "*partisans*" mean?

   a. Rulers
   b. Servants
   c. Opponents
   d. Followers
   e. Clergy

11. Which of the following is NOT true about Queen Elizabeth's pageants?

    a.   The pageants were designed to convince the Queen to marry the Earl of Clarendon
    b.   The pageants cost $5000 per day
    c.   The Queen's attendants were clothed in velvet
    d.   Ten oxen were killed every morning to feed the guests
    e.   The Queen's barons, retainers, and servants were lodged in the fortress

12. According to the passage, what is currently the primary use of Kenilworth Castle?

    a.   A church
    b.   An historic bell tower
    c.   A picnic ground for tourists
    d.   The current home of the Earl of Clarendon
    e.   A private residence of the British royal family

13. In Line 22, what does "*priory*" mean?

    a.   Tower
    b.   Ruins
    c.   Estate
    d.   Castle
    e.   Monastery

14. According to the passage, what is the most notable feature of Kenilworth Castle?

    a.   It was built during the reign of Henry I
    b.   It has an impressive romantic history among all English ruins
    c.   It is the only castle of its time to be sufficiently preserved
    d.   It is still used as a sacred monastery
    e.   It has been exhaustively researched by British historians

Directions: *The questions in this section are based on the reasoning contained in brief statements or passages. For some questions, more than one of the choices could conceivably answer the question. However, you are to choose the one that provides the most complete and accurate answer. You should not make assumptions that are implausible, superfluous, or incompatible with the passage.*

15. The Warren County Hospital Chief of Staff claims that his chief surgeon, Dr. Hannah Right, is the best surgeon in Warren County. Inexplicably, a much lower percentage of Dr. Right's surgical patients survive their operations and enjoy a full recovery than those of other surgeons at the hospital.

Which of the following explains Dr. Right's low survival rate and the Chief of Staff 's continual confidence in her?

    a.   Since the Warren County Hospital Chief of Staff appointed Dr. Right as his chief surgeon, his judgment would be questioned if he didn't claim that Dr. Right is the best.
    b.   The Chief of Staff promoted Dr. Right to chief surgeon because of their close affiliation in medical school.
    c.   Several years ago, Dr. Right trained a number of the physicians who are currently on staff.
    d.   At the Warren County Hospital, the most difficult cases are usually assigned to Dr. Right.
    e.   Dr. Right's survival stats are much better than those of the previous chief surgeon.

16. Since 2006, the demand for new cars has risen by 20% each year. At the same time, the demand for Freon, which is used by most air conditioning units in cars, has decreased by the same amount.

If the statements above are both true, which of the following statements must also be true?

    a.   Laboratory scientists are investigating safer alternatives to Freon.
    b.   Freon has become too expensive to manufacture and buy.
    c.   Air conditioning units are less efficient in warmer climates.
    d.   The federal government has banned the use of Freon in hybrid vehicles.
    e.   Most new cars do not contain air conditioners.

17. Kristina is rolling in money. She's a fashion model.

Which one of the following uses reasoning that is most similar to the above argument?

    a.   Rachel is attractive because she is thin.
    b.   George cannot afford an oceanfront condo because he is a policeman.
    c.   The IRS is an evil entity of dubious origins.
    d.   David is a hedge fund manager. Thus, he is dishonest.
    e.   I do not trust big businesses. They are all corrupt.

18. In the den, the designer could easily replace the inefficient track lighting with fluorescent tube lighting. However, he would be better off installing a crystal chandelier, even though it would be more expensive than installing fluorescent tube lighting. The beauty it would add to the den, which is the most important room in the house, is well worth the additional cost.

Which one of the following is an assumption on which the argument depends?

    a.   Crystal chandeliers are too expensive for most single family homes.
    b.   A crystal chandelier would be more aesthetically pleasing than fluorescent lighting.
    c.   Designers choose lighting based primarily on cost and efficiency.
    d.   Lighting must be inexpensive, efficient, and beautiful.
    e.   Fluorescent tube lighting is the most popular choice in dens.

19. The only authors who receive large advances are those that the publishing company believe will sell thousands of books at full jacket price.   So, most cookbook authors will not receive large advances, because few cookbooks are sold on amazon.com.

The conclusion above follows logically if which one of the following is assumed?

    a.   Amazon.com undermines the profitability of publishing companies by selling new books at less than full jacket price.
    b.   Unless a cookbook sells well on amazon.com, publishing companies do not believe that it will sell well at venues that charge full jacket price.
    c.   Few cookbooks are bestsellers.
    d.   As book sales falter, fewer authors will receive large advances from their publishers.
    e.   Unless an author receives a large advance, he cannot afford to promote his book and achieve the aggressive sales targets that his publisher demands.

20. Patients with kidney cancer who consume citrus fruits such as oranges and pears often suffer from dire complications during chemotherapy, such as nausea and dizziness. Over time, they are unable to tolerate such high doses of these cancer fighting drugs. In contrast, patients with liver cancer who consume a comparable amount of citrus fruits such as oranges and pears do not suffer from similar complications during chemotherapy.

Which one of the following, if true, does the most to resolve the apparent discrepancy in the argument above?

    a.   Patients with liver cancer are deficient in Vitamins A and C, which citrus fruit provides.
    b.   Most chemotherapy drugs contain iron, which makes the vitamins in citrus fruit impossible to absorb.
    c.   Patients with kidney cancer have an enzymatic abnormality that causes nausea and dizziness when they consume citrus fruit .
    d.   Females are far more likely than males to contract kidney cancer.
    e.   The reaction is far less likely to occur if chemotherapy is administered in the earliest stages of tumor growth.

21. Most contractors who are experienced plumbers are flexible, but some non-flexible contractors are also experienced plumbers. In addition, every experienced plumber is a licensed electrician.

Which one of the following statements follows logically from the statements above?

    a.   Some licensed electricians are flexible.
    b.   Every licensed electrician is flexible.
    c.   Some licensed electricians are contractors.
    d.   Every licensed electrician is a contractor.
    e.   The experienced plumbers who are flexible are also licensed electricians.

22. The Atkins Diet, although expensive, is more effective than the Southside Diet for patients with heart disease and high blood pressure. The Atkins Diet is also endorsed by a majority of physicians.

What is the logical conclusion for the argument?

    a.   The Southside Diet is a lower cost version of the Atkins Diet.
    b.   The Atkins Diet is the best choice for a patient with high cholesterol.
    c.   Neither the Atkins Diet nor the Southside Diet is 100% reliable.
    d.   Different diets have different pros and cons.
    e.   The Atkins Diet is better than the Southside Diet.

23. E-Commerce Specialist: In the past five years, brick-and-mortar bookstores have lost most of their market share to online competitors such as amazon.com. Additional brick-and-mortar bookstores are unlikely to be built, because the upfront costs of construction and inventory are excessive for many entrepreneurs. But worldwide demand for books has been increasing steadily, largely to the proliferation of university textbooks. Hence, online retailers such as amazon.com are likely to enjoy record profits.

Which of the following most accurately describes the role played in the e-commerce specialist's argument by the claim that online retailers like amazon.com are likely to enjoy record profits?

    a.   It is the main conclusion of the argument.
    b.   It is an intermediate conclusion, which the e-commerce specialist presents as evidence for his main conclusion.
    c.   It is pure speculation that is not rooted in fact.
    d.   It is a valid prediction that is meant to ignite the reader's interest.
    e.   It is a piece of evidence that support's the e-commerce specialist's conclusion.

24.   Rover must be a weimaraner. He is silver gray.

The argument relies on what unstated assumption?

    a.   Rover is a dog.
    b.   Weimaraners are dogs.
    c.   Weimaraners are silver gray.
    d.   Weimaraners are not silver gray.
    e.   Some dogs are weimaraners.

25.   The Sheraton has no vacant rooms because they are hosting the Mary Kay convention. The Hilton, on the other hand, has no vacancies because they are host the tri-state job fair. So, the visitors from the technical conference will have to stay at the Radisson, which is the only five-star hotel in Baltimore besides the Sheraton and Hilton.

The argument depends on which of the following assumptions?

    a.   If the Mary Kay convention was cancelled, the Sheraton could accommodate the visitors from the technical conference.
    b.   There is a shortage of hotel rooms for business travelers in Baltimore.
    c.   The Hilton and Sheraton offer attractive discounts to corporate travelers.
    d.   The visitors from the technical conference can only stay at a five-star hotel in Baltimore.
    e.   The Radisson in Baltimore is less popular than the Sheraton and Hilton.

Directions: The following sentences test correctness and effectiveness of expression. Part of each sentence (or the entire sentence) is underlined; beneath each sentence are five ways of phrasing the underlined material. Choice A repeats the original phrasing; the other four choices are different. If you think the original phrasing produces a better sentence than the alternatives, select choice A; if not, select one of the other choices. In making your selection, follow the requirements of standard written English, such as grammar, choice of words, sentence construction, and punctuation. Your selection should result in the most effective sentence – clear and precise, without awkwardness or ambiguity.

Example: Most teenagers struggle to be free both of parental domination but also from premature responsibilities.

    a.   both of parental domination but also from premature responsibilities.
    b.   both of parental domination and also from premature responsibilities.
    c.   both of parental domination and also of premature responsibilities.
    d.   of parental domination and premature responsibilities.
    e.   both of parental domination and their premature responsibilities as well.

The correct answer is Choice D.

26.   The use of cell phones, along with other wireless devices, make other methods of communication, such as pay phones and "snail mail," seem downright obsolete.

    a.   make other methods of communication, such as pay phones and "snail mail," seem downright obsolete.
    b.   make pay phones and "snail mail" seem like obsolete methods of communication.
    c.   makes pay phones and "snail mail" seem like obsolete methods of communication.
    d.   makes other methods of communication appear to be obsolescent, like pay phones and "snail mail."
    e.   when compared to other methods of communication, such as pay phones and "snail mail," make them seem downright obsolete.

27. People convicted for fraud never have nor ever will be honest.

    a.   never have nor ever will be honest.
    b.   never have been, and never will be, honest.
    c.   never have been honest and never will be honest.
    d.   never have and never will be honest.
    e.   have and will never be honest.

28. The day care center has no objection to him joining the staff, as long as he is willing to assume the same duties as the female employees on staff.

    a. to him joining the staff, as long as he is willing to assume the same duties as the female employees
    b. to him joining the staff, so long as he is willing to assume the same duties as the women
    c. to his joining the staff, as long as he is willing to assume the same duties as the female employees
    d. to his joining the staff, so long as he will assume the same duties as the female employees
    e. to him joining the staff, providing that he is willing to do the same job as the female employees

29. Carolyn asked Elizabeth to mail her application immediately, because she was afraid it would arrive after the deadline.

    a. Carolyn asked Elizabeth to mail her application immediately, because she was afraid it would arrive after the deadline.
    b. Carolyn asked Elizabeth to mail her application immediately, to avoid missing the deadline.
    c. Carolyn asked Elizabeth to mail her application immediately, because she was afraid that Elizabeth would miss the deadline.
    d. Carolyn advised Elizabeth to mail her application immediately, because it would arrive after the deadline.
    e. Carolyn advised Elizabeth to mail her application immediately, to ensure that it arrived before the deadline.

30. Swimming two miles in heated pool is significantly easier than to swim the same distance in the choppy ocean.

    a. Swimming two miles in a heated pool is significantly easier than to swim the same distance in the choppy ocean.
    b. Swimming two miles in a heated pool is significantly easier than swimming the same distance in the choppy ocean.
    c. To swim two miles in a heated pool is significantly easier than for one to swim the same distance in the choppy ocean.
    d. To swim two miles in a heated pool is significantly easier than swimming the same distance in the choppy ocean.
    e. It is significantly easier to swim two miles in a heated pool than in the choppy ocean.

31. To avoid airport delays, our plans were that we would catch the red eye.

    a. To avoid airport delays, our plans were that we would catch the red eye.
    b. To avoid airport delays, our plans were for catching the red eye.
    c. To avoid airport delays, we planned to catch the red eye.
    d. Our plans were to catch the red eye so that we could avoid airport delays.
    e. We planned to catch the red eye, that's how we would avoid airport delays.

32. The five surviving U.S Presidents were formerly honored at a ceremony in Boston, where the current President praised them for their distinguished service to our nation.

    a. The five surviving U.S. Presidents were formerly honored at a ceremony in Boston, where the current President praised them for their distinguished service to our nation.
    b. At a formal ceremony in Boston, the President formally honored the five surviving U.S. Presidents, whom he praised for their distinguished service to our nation.
    c. The five surviving U.S. Presidents, who served our nation with distinction, were formally honored by our current President at a ceremony in Boston.
    d. The current President formally honored the five U.S. Presidents in Boston and praised them for their distinguished service to our nation.
    e. At a ceremony in Boston, the current President formally honored the five surviving U.S. Presidents and praised them for their distinguished service to our nation.

33. After a three-hour delay, the opening chorus of the musical was heard throughout the large auditorium.

    a.   the opening chorus of the musical was heard throughout the auditorium.
    b.   the opening chorus of the musical were heard throughout the auditorium.
    c.   the large auditorium heard the opening chorus of the musical.
    d.   the audience heard the opening chorus of the musical throughout the auditorium.
    e.   the auditorium heard the opening chorus of the musical.

34. Rather than choose between three equal candidates, the committee decided to award scholarships to all of them.

    a.   Rather than choose between three equal candidates,
    b.   Rather than choose among three equal candidates,
    c.   Rather than choose between three equally qualified candidates,
    d.   Rather than choose among three equally qualified candidates,
    e.   Rather than choose among the three candidates,

35. Although she was a mediocre student, Sara studied diligently to earn the kind of grades that her friends in the honor society did.

    a.   the kind of grades that her friends in the honor society did.
    b.   the type of grades that her friends in the honor society did.
    c.   honor society grades.
    d.   grades like her honor society friends.
    e.   grades that were comparable to those of her friends in the honor society.

36. The eminent director, whose childhood in Canada was the inspiration for his many films about rural challenges.

    a.   The eminent director, whose childhood in Canada was the inspiration for his many films about rural challenges.
    b.   The eminent director, whose childhood in rural Canada was the inspiration for his many films about challenges.
    c.   The eminent director's challenging childhood in Canada, which was the inspiration for his many films.
    d.   The eminent director, who was raised in Canada and inspired by the rural challenges he depicted in his films.
    e.   The eminent director's childhood in Canada was the inspiration for his many films about rural challenges.

37. After careful deliberation among all parties, including a heated discussion about the true spirit of community, a decision was made to proceed with the development.

    a.   After careful deliberation among all parties, including a heated discussion about the true spirit of community, a decision was made to proceed with the development.
    b.   After careful deliberation between all parties, including a heated discussion about the true spirit of community, a decision was made to proceed with the development.
    c.   After careful deliberation among all parties, including a heated discussion about the true meaning of community, the committee decided to proceed with the development.
    d.   After carefully deliberating, including a heated discussion about the true spirit of community, a decision was made to proceed with the development.
    e.   After careful deliberation among all parties about the development, including a heated discussion about the true spirit of community, a decision was made to proceed.

38. The contract that the union workers agreed with was an inspiration to its myriad members.

   a. that the union workers agreed with was an inspiration to its myriad members.
   b. that the union workers agreed to was an inspiration to its myriad members.
   c. which the union workers agreed with was an inspiration to its myriad members.
   d. that the union workers agreed with was an inspiration to myriad members.
   e. which the union workers agreed with was an inspiration to its many members.

39. The guests at the funeral became angry and confused when the flag failed to raise in honor of the decorated war veteran.

   a. became angry and confused when the flag failed to raise in honor of the decorated war veteran.
   b. reacted with anger and confusion when the flag failed to raise in honor of the decorated war veteran.
   c. became angry and confused when the flag did not raise in honor of the decorated war veteran.
   d. became angry and confused when the flag failed to rise in honor of the decorated war veteran.
   e. became angry and confused because the flag failed to raise in honor of the decorated war veteran.

40. The Field Museum in Chicago includes historical exhibits and artifacts, which are complimented by native drawings from each region.

   a. includes historical exhibits and artifacts, which are complimented by native drawings from each region.
   b. includes historical exhibits and artifacts, which is complimented by native drawings from each region.
   c. includes historic exhibits and artifacts, that are complimented by native drawings from each region.
   d. includes historical exhibits and artifacts, which are complimented by regional drawings.
   e. includes historical exhibits and artifacts that are complemented by native drawings from each region.

41. Because the flight was delayed by weather, we stood over at the airport hotel.

   a. Because the flight was delayed by weather, we stood over at the airport hotel.
   b. Being that the flight was delayed by weather, we stayed over at the airport hotel.
   c. In lieu of the fact that our flight experienced a weather delay, we stayed over at the airport hotel.
   d. Because our flight experienced a weather delay, we stayed overnight at the airport hotel.
   e. Because of the weather delay, we stood over the airport hotel.

Answer Key for Verbal Section 7

Critical Reading

1. Choice A is correct. All of the other choices are mentioned in the first paragraph of Passage A.

2. Choice D is correct. In this context, *deficit* means deficiency.

3. Choice D is correct. All of the other choices are mentioned in the passage.

4. Choice B is correct. In this *context*, audit means examination.

5. Choice C is correct. The author explains his position in Lines 53 – 55.

6. Choice E is correct. The author is objective in tone.

7. Choice B is correct. The other choices are either too broad or too narrow in scope.

8. Choice B is correct. The passage discusses the ownership and use of Kenilworth Castle from ancient

times until modern day

9. Choice E is correct. All of the other answer choices are mentioned in Lines 4 – 5.

10. Choice D is correct. In context, *partisans* means followers.

11. Choice A is correct. All of the other answer choices are mentioned in Lines 10 – 17. Choice A is actually a trick question, though – it contains the name of the wrong Earl (Clarendon versus Leicester). Be careful.

12. Choice C is correct. The answer is stated directly on Line 22.

13. Choice E is correct. In context, *priory* means monastery.

14. Choice B is correct. The answer is stated directly in Line 27.

Critical Reasoning

15. Here, we are asked to pick an explanation for why all things are not equal, which will allow two contradictory statements in the passage to be supported. If Dr. Right is assigned the most difficult cases, it is reasonable that her patients' will enjoy a lower survival rate than those of other surgeons. Choice D is correct.

16. The question is asking us to infer why these two seemingly contradictory events have occurred. Choice E offers a plausible answer. If the demand for cars increases at the same time that the demand for Freon decreases, then many of those cars must not contain air conditioners. The other answer choices, although interesting, do not explain the contradiction.

17. This argument presumes that a person's profession determines his/her disposable income. Choice B uses the same reasoning.

18. Choice B is correct. The argument depends on the assumption that the crystal chandelier is more beautiful than fluorescent lighting.

19. Choice B is correct. Unless a cookbook sells well on amazon.com, publishing companies do not believe that it will sell well at venues that charge full jacket price.

20. The argument makes sense – and the discrepancy is explained – if patients with kidney cancer (but not liver cancer) have an enzymatic abnormality that causes nausea and dizziness when citrus fruit is consumed. Choice C is correct.

21. Choice A is correct. The original argument is in the form: "most A (contractors) who are B (experienced plumbers) are C (flexible), but some non-C As (non-flexible contractors) are B (experienced plumbers). In addition, every B (experienced plumber) is a D (licensed electrician)." Therefore, logically, we can state that some D (licensed electricians) are C (flexible).

22. The logical conclusion is Choice E, the Atkins Diet is better than the Southside Diet.

23. Choice A is correct. It is the main conclusion of the argument.

24. The argument presumes that weimaraners are silver gray. Choice C is correct.

25. Choice D is correct. The argument presumes that the visitors from the technical conference can only stay at a five-star hotel in Baltimore.

Sentence Correction

26. Choice C is correct. He singular subject *use* requires a singular verb *makes*. The other answer choices that make this correction also introduce other errors.

27. Choice C is correct. The sentence includes two phrases with different verb tenses; hence, each must be

stated in full: *People convicted for fraud never have been honest and will never be honest.*

28. Choice C is correct. In this sentence, the pronoun is the subject of the gerund *joining*. As such, it must be in the possessive case, *his*.

29. Choice C is correct. This sentence contains two ambiguous pronouns (*her* and *she*). The correct answer choice must clarify to whom each refers without changing the meaning of the sentence. Of the possibilities, Choice C is the only option that fixes the error without altering the original sentence.

30. Choice B is correct. The original sentence contains an error in parallelism. The word *swimming* should be used in both parts of the sentence. Although Choice C uses *to swim* in both parts of the sentence, it introduces a new error.

31. In sentences with modifiers, try to determine the noun that is being modified. In this case, the implied noun is *we*, **not** *our plans*. Hence, the correct answer choice must use *we* as a noun. This narrows our answer choices to C, D, and E. Of the three, answer choice C is best.

32. The correct answer is Choice E, which eliminates the passive verb and replaces *formerly* with *formally*. The other answer choices either eliminate information or introduce new errors.

33. This sentence contains a passive verb. The correct answer, Choice D, corrects the mistake and uses the correct subject (*the audience*). The other choices either fail to correct the verb error or use an incorrect subject.

34. Choice D is correct. Because there are three candidates, the correct word is *among*, not *between*. Further, the candidates themselves are not equal; their qualifications are.

35. Choice E is correct. The expression *kind of grades* is incorrect; it should be replaced by *comparable*.

36. The original statement is not a complete sentence because it lacks a verb. The best revision is Choice E: *The eminent director's childhood in Canada was the inspiration for his many films about rural challenges.*

37. The original sentence is written in the passive voice. Choice C is the best revision because it uses an active verb and identifies who made the decision: *After careful deliberation among all parties, including a heated discussion about the true meaning of community, the committee decided to proceed with the development.*

38. In the original sentence, there is an idiomatic mistake: "agreed with," which should be "agreed to." This question is tricky because the phrase "agreed with" is not *always* wrong. In this context, however, the correct expression must capture the union's response to the contract terms. They did not *agree with* them; they *agreed to adhere to them*. The distinction is subtle, but valid. Choice B is correct.

39. The original sentence uses the wrong verb. Choice D is correct (*rise*, not *raise*).

40. The original sentence uses the verb *complimented*, rather than *complemented*. Choice E is the best revision.

41. Choice D is best, because it eliminates the passive verb (*was delayed*) and uses the correct version of the verb *stay*.

Directions: *The passage below is followed by questions based on its content. Answer the questions, based on what is* stated *or* implied *in the passage and any introductory material that may be provided.*

Passage 1

At WorldCom, there was a colossal gap between the company's Code of Ethics and the actual behaviors observed at the firm. In fact, WorldCom's story is an example of an enterprise in which the Code of Ethics was a purely theoretical document that had nothing to do with the actual conduct of its top executives. Management's behavior towards the company's employees, clients, prospects, auditors, investors, bankers, and financial community was the antithesis of the outstanding principles that they touted in their public relations materials. No doubt, this repulsive behavior revealed the organization's true priorities, and served as a warning for other business enterprises in their fields of operation.

8

In his article entitled "Lessons from WorldCom," Mark McCormack explains that WorldCom's story represents a trend that has existed in the United States over the last twenty-five years. Far too often, Western corporations rely on short-term versus long-range results in order to influence the Wall Street community. Today's investors unrealistically expect business enterprises to consistently generate large profits quarter after quarter. WorldCom simply exploited this rigid measurement system to its fullest capacity.

14

According to McCormack, it is unlikely that Wall Street investors will change their obsession with short-term numbers anytime soon. However, this does not mean that WorldCom should adhere to its questionable management tactics regarding investor expectations. By creating and spinning off quasi-owned subsidiaries, companies create opportunities for dishonest and creative accounting, which will eventually be traced back to the parent company. Even legitimate subsidiaries should be established sparingly. Far too often, enterprises that devote significant interest to their side businesses can create possible conflicts of interest.

21

Businesses also need to be able to trust their bottom-line numbers. Top executives should not encourage the company accountants to "pretty up" the numbers to deliver an artificial result. Further, executives need to be able to discuss the company's numbers with the public in an open and honest manner. Some executive officers believe that a bit of data manipulation is needed to be competitive in today's market. However, as McCormack explains, "Today, people are more than willing to assume that where there is smoke, there is fire." A firm must show that it values character, which can only be accomplished by encouraging open communication, giving the employees more responsibility, and working towards the company goals without relying too heavily on favors. Companies who value performance will reveal their true profits, unlike Enron, which suffered severe consequences for putting a deceptive spin on their actual performance.

31

In 2002, Congress and the Securities Exchange Commission created the Sarbanes-Oxley Act to "force corporate executives to be proactive and accountable regarding the communication of their firm's financial position." This regulation was created to restore investors' faith in the integrity of corporate America and public markets. Kelly Financial Resources confirms that effective business communication is critical to educate the public about the problems surrounding their company. The scandals at Enron, WorldCom, and Tyco have encouraged the executives of other corporations to provide fair information about their organizations to Wall Street, which has improved their bottom-line. Ultimately, better communication yields happier, more engaged employees, which increases productivity and profits.

40

Strong and positive ethics have also been identified as one of the most important qualities in Bill Gates and Steve Jobs, who are two of the most ethical and exemplary business leaders in corporate America. Without exception, ethics and integrity govern how these executives conduct all aspects of their day-to-day business. By bringing a sense of fairness, respect and credibility to their interactions, Gates and Jobs set the tone for their organizations' cultures. Further, their strong positive ethics and open business communications help to build their corporations' brand names, which draw new customers and create sustained, long-term profits.

47

Competition and profit maximization have an adverse impact on ethics and communication in business, but being ethical does not have to mean losing profits. Generating wealth is necessary to make a good and positive impact on the community, but communicating ethically is also in the best interest of corporations and their stakeholders. Furthermore, such integrity can not be imposed by the law; it is a mindset that business leaders choose to adopt when making and communicating their everyday business decisions.

1. In the passage, what trend has Mark McCormack observed over the past twenty-five years?

    a.   Companies rely on short-term results to deliver higher profits
    b.   Companies move operations offshore to avoid taxation
    c.   Companies use subsidiaries for unethical purposes
    d.   Companies use creative accounting practices
    e.   Corporate executives earn ridiculously high salaries

2. In Line 23, what does "*pretty*" mean?

    a.   minimize
    b.   highlight
    c.   exaggerate
    d.   falsify
    e.   sanitize

3. What is the implication of Mark McCormack's quote on Line 26: *"Today, people are more than willing to assume that where there is smoke, there is fire."*

    a.   Thanks to WorldCom, investors think all corporate executives are corrupt.
    b.   As long as a company has good numbers, investors will remain loyal.
    c.   The minute the SEC announces a company is under investigation, investors flee.
    d.   If investors see a corporation's true financial numbers, they will assume the worst and take their money elsewhere.
    e.   Investors only trust financial statements that are verified by an independent third party.

4. According to the passage, implementation of the Sarbanes-Oxley Act will accomplish all of the following EXCEPT:

    a.   Improve the quality and quantity of information provided to Wall Street
    b.   Encourage the use of outside accounting firms
    c.   Improve employee happiness
    d.   Improve productivity
    e.   Restore investors' faith in corporate America

5. According to the author, which of the following corporate directives would Kelly Financial Resources be most likely to support?

    a.   Formal training in ethics for all corporate CEOs
    b.   Lower salaries and fewer perks for CEOs
    c.   Stronger penalties for the illegal use of subsidiaries
    d.   Annual IRS audits for all Fortune 1000 companies
    e.   A communication campaign to educate the public about a company's problems

6. Which of the following does the author attribute to Bill Gates?

    a.   Strong ethics and integrity
    b.   Open communication
    c.   Commitment to cross-cultural training
    d.   A and B
    e.   A, B and C

7. According to the author, what is the impact of competition on business?

    a.   Positive impact on profits
    b.   Negative impact on ethics and communication
    c.   Positive impact on employee morale
    d.   Negative impact on investment community
    e.   Savvy leadership

8. What is the overall objective of the passage?

    a. To find viable ways to prevent similar scandals to the one at WorldCom.
    b. To discuss WorldCom's Code of Ethics.
    c. To explain why all corporations are essentially corrupt.
    d. To warn the investment community.
    e. To explain the ramifications of the WorldCom scandal on the company's executives.

Passage 2

Until the thirteenth century, the juggling profession was a lucrative one in most European cities. There was no public or private feast of any importance without the profession being represented. Jugglers were the principal attraction at the Cours Plénières, and, according to the testimony of one of their members, they frequently retired from business loaded with presents, such as riding-horses, carriage-horses, jewels, cloaks, fur robes, clothing of violet or scarlet cloth, and, above all, with large sums of money.

6

Jugglers are also the subject of many noble stories, both veracious and fanciful. Before the battle of Hastings, Norman Taillefer was said to have advanced alone on horseback between the two armies about to commence the engagement, and drew off the attention of the English by singing them the Song of Roland. He then began juggling, and taking his lance by the hilt, he threw it into the air and caught it by the point as it fell; then, drawing his sword, he spun it several times over his head, and caught it in a similar way as it fell. After these skilful exercises, during which the enemy were gaping in mute astonishment, he forced his charger through the English ranks, and caused great havoc before he fell, positively riddled with wounds.

14

Notwithstanding this noble instance, not to belie the old proverb, jugglers were never received into the order of knighthood. They were, after a time, as much abused as they had before been extolled. Their licentious lives reflected itself in their obscene language. Their pantomimes, like their songs, showed that they were the votaries of the lowest vices. The lower orders laughed at their coarseness, and were amused at their juggleries; but the nobility were disgusted with them, and they were absolutely excluded from the presence of ladies and girls in the châteaux and houses of the bourgeoisie. The clergy, and St. Bernard especially, denounced them in one of his sermons written in the middle of the twelfth century: "A man fond of jugglers will soon enough possess a wife whose name is Poverty. If it happens that the tricks of jugglers are forced upon your notice, endeavor to avoid them, and think of other things. The tricks of jugglers never please God."

24

Thus, throughout this period, jugglers wandered about the country with their trained animals nearly starved; they were half naked, and were often without anything on their heads, without coats, without shoes, and always without money. The lower orders welcomed them, and continued to admire and idolize them for their clever tricks, but the bourgeois class, following the example of the nobility, turned their backs upon them. In 1345 Guillaume de Gourmont, Provost of Paris, forbade their singing or relating obscene stories, under penalty of fine and imprisonment. Thus, by 1350, the lucrative days of juggling in France were all but forgotten.

30

9. Which of the following is the main point of the passage?

    a. Jugglers were the most highly compensated street entertainers in thirteenth century Europe
    b. Jugglers, although talented, were not expert swordsmen
    c. The clergy took a dim view of jugglers in thirteenth century Europe
    d. Jugglers were never respected by the bourgeois class
    e. In the thirteenth century, jugglers descended from an exalted social position to one of mockery and contempt

10. In Line 7, what does "*veracious*" mean?

    a. Dull
    b. Audacious
    c. Fallacious
    d. Truthful
    e. Objective

11. Norman Taillefer did all of the following EXCEPT:

    a.   Riddled the English army with wounds
    b.   Forced his charger through the English ranks
    c.   Diverted the English by singing the Song of Roland
    d.   Threw his lance in the air and caught it by the point as it fell
    e.   Rode alone on horseback between the two armies

12. In Line 15, what does "*belie*" mean?

    a.   Affirm
    b.   Contradict
    c.   Justify
    d.   Exacerbate
    e.   Extol

13. Which of the following best conveys St. Bernard's impression of the jugglers?

    a.   Audacious
    b.   Baneful
    c.   Amusing
    d.   Melodious
    e.   Debauched

14. According to the author, which of the following groups always admired the jugglers?

    a.   The French army
    b.   The bourgeois class
    c.   The lower orders
    d.   The ladies and girls in the châteaux
    e.   The nobility

Directions: The questions in this section are based on the reasoning contained in brief statements or passages. For some questions, more than one of the choices could conceivably answer the question. However, you are to choose the one that provides the most complete and accurate answer. You should not make assumptions that are implausible, superfluous, or incompatible with the passage.

15. In a recent survey by pageant officials, the fifty contestants in the Miss America pageant were asked to choose between two hypothetical situations. In the first scenario, the Miss America pageant would be the most popular pageant in the world, with a global viewing audience of 50 million people, while the Miss USA pageant would trail slightly behind, with a global viewing audience of 45 million people. In the second scenario, the Miss USA pageant would be the most popular pageant in the world, with a global viewing audience of 75 million people, while the Miss America pageant would trail slightly behind, with a global viewing audience of 60 million people. Ironically, although the second situation offered the Miss America contestants a larger viewing audience than the first situation, ninety percent of the contestants preferred the first situation.

Which answer choice, if true, would best explain these results?

    a.   Most of the Miss America contestants want their pageant to be more popular than the Miss USA pageant, regardless of the total number of viewers.
    b.   Few of the Miss America contestants had anything to gain by either scenario.
    c.   Most of the Miss America contestants had also competed in the Miss USA pageant.
    d.   The ten percent of Miss America contestants who voted for the second situation did not understand the question.
    e.   Most of the contestants will earn a significant bonus if the number of global viewers exceeds 45 million.

16. In most states, a student can enroll at a community college if (s)he pays the tuition and passes a basic entrance exam. At first, enrollment was low. Eventually, college administrators developed new courses that generated additional applications for admission and higher tuition and fees.

Which of the following conclusions is most strongly suggested by the paragraph above?

    a. In most states, community colleges spend little to recruit candidates.
    b. Community colleges are non-profit entities.
    c. Financial considerations played a key role in the expansion of the community college system.
    d. For most community colleges, the entrance exam is not an obstacle to enrollment.
    e. Community colleges are a low-cost alternative to private universities.

17. Clarissa waits tables at the classiest restaurant in town. Therefore, Clarissa must be beautiful.

Which of the following correctly states the omitted assumption in the argument?

    a. Most waitresses are beautiful.
    b. Clarissa's sister is beautiful.
    c. Clarissa won a beauty pageant.
    d. All beautiful girls are waitresses.
    e. All waitresses at the restaurant are beautiful.

18. At the American Kennel Club dog show, the coordinators of the event conducted a fundraiser for abused and abandoned dogs. As they left the show ring, all three hundred participants were asked to place their donations in a cup at the side of the ring. At the end of the show, the coordinators made an interesting observation: the owners whose dogs won a prize in the show were significantly less likely to donate than the owners of the dogs who did not win a prize.

This situation supports which one of the following propositions?

    a. There was a direct correlation between the performance of the dog and the generosity of the dog owner.
    b. There was an inverse correlation between the performance of the dog and the generosity of the dog owner
    c. There was no correlation between the performance of the dog and the generosity of the dog owner.
    d. The study is flawed, because the participants did not know that their behavior was being observed.
    e. The study is flawed, because the evidence is anecdotal.

19. Economist: Every year, the federal government spends billions of dollars on esoteric research projects, such as an investigation into the mating habits of tropical bumblebees. Although these studies may offer tangential benefits to the academic community, they have no useful benefits to the taxpayers who fund them. At the same time, more practical and worthwhile research studies, such as an investigation into a possible vaccine for HIV/AIDS, are woefully under funded. Ideally, funding for esoteric research projects should be reduced in favor of medical projects that would offer immediate health benefits to taxpayers.

Which one of the following principles, if valid, most helps to justify the economist's reasoning?

    a. Research into esoteric topics should be funded by private industry, rather than the federal government.
    b. The top priority in government research should be human health.
    c. Research that offers immediate and practical benefits to the taxpayers is more worthwhile than esoteric projects that only benefit the academic community.
    d. Research that benefits the academic community should be executed in a more practical and cost-effective manner.
    e. Academic researchers and government agencies should work in tandem to ensure that research goals achieve both practical and esoteric objectives.

20. Indonesia and Spain have dramatically different attitudes about fitness. In Spain, citizens set aside one hour every day to exercise, and many corporations provide elaborate gyms for their employees. In contrast, few Indonesian corporations have organized fitness programs. Recent studies show that the Spanish worker is more productive than the Indonesian worker. Thus, we must conclude that the productivity of Indonesian workers will lag behind their Spanish counterparts until mandatory exercise programs are introduced.

The conclusion of the argument is valid if which one of the following is assumed?

- a. Fitness programs will improve the Indonesian worker's health.
- b. The productivity of all workers can be increased by exercise.
- c. Spanish workers are happier than Indonesian workers.
- d. Exercise is an essential factor in the Spanish worker's superior productivity.
- e. Indonesian corporations don't have the funds to build elaborate gyms.

21. All cats have fleas. This creature is scratching. Therefore, this creature must have fleas.

Which of the following uses a similar type of reasoning?

- a. All kitchens have stoves. This house has a kitchen. Therefore, this kitchen must have a stove.
- b. All carpenters wear pants. This man is wearing pants. Therefore, this man must be a carpenter.
- c. All books have titles. This item has a title. Therefore, this item must be a book.
- d. All toads have webbed feet. This creature cannot jump. Therefore, this creature must be a toad.
- e. All rodents have teeth. This creature is chewing. Therefore, this creature must have teeth.

22. The Governor's opponents claim that his policies only benefit the wealthiest residents of the state, but that is an unfair assessment. During his tenure in office, many of the Governor's policies have benefited low income residents. The Governor fought mightily to lower the state's sales tax rate, which was the most onerous in the nation. He also championed the availability of low cost health care for uninsured residents. Thanks to these changes, all state residents have more discretionary income at their disposal, along with affordable medical care.

Which of the following most accurately expresses the main conclusion of the argument?

- a. The Governor is often criticized for favoring the rich.
- b. The Governor's opponents cannot evaluate his performance objectively.
- c. The Governor's support for socialized medicine is troubling to his opponents.
- d. The Governor's opponents are not aware of his position on sales tax and health care reform.
- e. The Governor's policies do not only benefit wealthy residents.

23. Twelve hundred female graduates of a prestigious MBA program completed a survey about their employment prospects after graduation. The results for the survey were puzzling, Ninety percent of the respondents reported that they had received at least one job offer by the time they graduated, when the actual number was only 60%.

Which one of the following provides the most helpful explanation for the apparent contradiction in these survey results?

- a. Several respondents misread the survey.
- b. Not all participants received the survey.
- c. The survey did not include volunteer or unpaid positions.
- d. The unemployed graduates were more likely to return the survey.
- e. The respondents with job offers were more likely to return the survey.

24. Diane: Organic produce offers tangible benefits to health conscious consumers, including less exposure to dangerous chemicals and pesticides. Although organic produce is expensive, the improved safety gives me greater peace of mind, which is well worth the additional cost.

Cindy: I agree that safety and peace of mind are well worth the cost, but I do not think that I need to buy organic produce in order to attain them. By washing regular produce in cold water before I serve it, I can attain the same benefits as organic produce at a fraction of the cost.

These statements reveal that Diane and Cindy disagree about whether

   a. Quality food needs to be expensive.
   b. The chemicals and pesticides used to treat produce are dangerous for their families.
   c. Washing regular produce eliminates the dangerous chemicals and pesticides that are used in its growth.
   d. Organic produce is properly tested and monitored for chemical and pesticide levels.
   e. Peace of mind can be bought at any price.

25. The spiritual writings of death row inmates, who express profound remorse for their crimes, suggest that most prisoners "find God" within the confines of their jail cells.

The reasoning in the argument is vulnerable to criticism on what grounds?

   a. It presumes to understand the inner workings of the criminal mind.
   b. It ignores the fact that death row inmates are inherently dishonest.
   c. It does not define the expression "find God"
   d. It generalizes from a small sample that is not unrepresentative of the whole.
   e. It uses circular reasoning.

Directions: The following sentences test correctness and effectiveness of expression. Part of each sentence (or the entire sentence) is underlined; beneath each sentence are five ways of phrasing the underlined material. Choice A repeats the original phrasing; the other four choices are different. If you think the original phrasing produces a better sentence than the alternatives, select choice A; if not, select one of the other choices. In making your selection, follow the requirements of standard written English, such as grammar, choice of words, sentence construction, and punctuation. Your selection should result in the most effective sentence – clear and precise, without awkwardness or ambiguity.

Example: Most teenagers struggle to be free both of parental domination but also from premature responsibilities.

   a. *both of parental domination but also from premature responsibilities.*
   b. *both of parental domination and also from premature responsibilities.*
   c. *both of parental domination and also of premature responsibilities.*
   d. *of parental domination and premature responsibilities.*
   e. *both of parental domination and their premature responsibilities as well.*

The correct answer is Choice D.

26. According to recent polls, the top three consumer concerns are jobs, health care, and inflation, respectfully.

   a. According to recent polls, the top three consumer concerns are jobs, health care, and inflation, respectfully.
   b. Consumers are most concerned about jobs, health care, and inflation, respectfully, according to recent polls.
   c. According to recent polls, the top three consumer concerns, respectfully, are jobs, health care, and inflation.
   d. According to recent polls, the top three consumer concerns are jobs, health care, and inflation, respectively.
   e. Recent consumer polls proved that consumers are most concerned about the availability of jobs, health care, and inflation, respectively.

27. After years of backbreaking work in the fields, for which she was paid little money, Clara's hands became inflicted with arthritis.

    a.   for which she was paid little money, Clara's hands became inflicted with arthritis.
    b.   for which Clara was paid little money, her hands became afflicted by arthritis.
    c.   when Clara was paid little money, her hands became afflicted by arthritis.
    d.   when she was paid little money, Clara became inflicted with arthritis of the hands.
    e.   for which Clara was paid little money, her hands became afflicted with arthritis.

28. Carrie, Samantha and Charlotte are all great actresses, but Samantha has the wider emotional range.

    a.   Carrie, Samantha and Charlotte are all great actresses, but Samantha has the wider emotional range.
    b.   Although Carrie, Samantha and Charlotte are all great actresses, Samantha has the wider emotional range.
    c.   Carrie, Samantha and Charlotte are all great actresses, but Samantha has the widest emotional range.
    d.   Between Carrie, Samantha and Charlotte, Samantha has the wider emotional range.
    e.   Samantha has more emotion than Carrie and Charlotte.

29. Media reps from twelve television networks will meet on Saturday to lay out their strategy for covering political news.

    a.   to lay out their strategy for covering political news.
    b.   to lie out their strategy for covering political news.
    c.   to lay out their strategy to cover political news.
    d.   to lay out their political strategy.
    e.   to lie out their strategy to cover political news.

30. To snap back at one's angry husband is a less effective course than attempting to reconcile with him.

    a.   To snap back at one's angry husband is a less effective course than attempting to reconcile with him.
    b.   To snap back at your angry husband is less effective than reconciling with him.
    c.   To snap back at one's angry husband is a less effective course than to attempt to reconcile with him.
    d.   Snapping back at one's angry husband is a less effective course than to attempt to reconcile with him.
    e.   To snap back at one's angry husband is less effective than reconciling with him.

31. If Maria would of been home when the fire started, she would have saved the old photographs that her mother dearly loved.

    a.   If Maria would of been home when the fire started, she would have saved the old photographs that her mother dearly loved.
    b.   If Maria was home when the fire started, she would have saved the old photographs that her mother dearly loved.
    c.   Had Maria been home when the fire started, she would of saved the old photographs which her mother had dearly loved.
    d.   If Maria had been home when the fire started, she would have saved the old photographs that her mother dearly loved.
    e.   If Maria would be home when the fire started, she could have saved the old photographs that her mother dearly loved.

32. President Abraham Lincoln <u>disregarding the fervent advice of his own Cabinet regarding</u> the controversy surrounding slavery in the American colonies.

    a.   disregarding the fervent advice of his own Cabinet regarding
    b.   disregarding the fervent advice of the nation's Cabinet regarding
    c.   disregarded the fervent advice of his own Cabinet, ending
    d.   disregarding the fervent advice of his own Cabinet about
    e.   disregarded the fervent advice of his own Cabinet about

33. Ross Perot is a respected American businessman and financier, <u>and is best known for running</u> for President in 1992.

    a.   and is best known for running
    b.   and he is best known because he was running
    c.   who was best known when he was running
    d.   who everyone knows ran
    e.   who is best known for running

34. Connie would have accepted Bill's invitation to the dance, <u>if he waited for her reply.</u>

    a.   if he waited for her reply.
    b.   if he had waited for her reply.
    c.   if he would have waited for her reply.
    d.   if he only would have waited for her reply.
    e.   if he took the time to wait for her reply.

35. <u>Having sunk all of their money into a losing investment, which he had promised not to do, Rick was afraid to tell his parents.</u>

    a.   Having sunk all of their money into a losing investment, which he had promised not to do, Rick was afraid to tell his parents.
    b.   Having sank all of his parents' money into a losing investment, Rick was afraid to tell them because he promised not to do.
    c.   After sinking their money into a losing investment, which his parents had made him promise, Rick was afraid to tell them.
    d.   Having sank all of their money into a losing investment, which he had promised not to do, Rick was afraid to tell his parents.
    e.   Rick was afraid to tell his parents that he sunk all of their money into a losing investment, which he had promised not to do.

36. <u>Between the doctor, my wife and me, there is full disclosure.</u>

    a.   Between the doctor, my wife and me, there is full disclosure.
    b.   Between the doctor, my wife and I, there is full disclosure.
    c.   The doctor, my wife and me agree to fully disclose all information.
    d.   The doctor agreed to disclose all information to my wife and I.
    e.   The doctor, my wife and I agree to full disclosure.

37. Dr. Davis was advised to give the assignment <u>to whoever he believed was best qualified</u> for the job.

    a.   to whoever he believed was best qualified
    b.   to whomever he believed was best qualified
    c.   to whoever was qualified best
    d.   to the person who, in his belief, was best qualified
    e.   to the person, whom, in his belief, we best qualified

38. <u>The candidate reacted with quickness and eloquently to her opponent's misleading statements.</u>

    a.   The candidate reacted with quickness and eloquently to her opponent's misleading statements.
    b.   With quickness and eloquence, the candidate responded to statements from her opponent, which she believed were misleading.
    c.   The candidate reacted quickly and eloquence to the misleading statements by her opponent.
    d.   The opponent's misleading statements were met with quickness and eloquent by the candidate.
    e.   The candidate reacted quickly and eloquently to her opponent's misleading statements.

39. <u>If I was her, I would lay my glasses on the table</u> before I greeted the dog.

    a.   If I was her, I would lay my glasses on the table
    b.   If I was she, I would lay my glasses on the table
    c.   If I were her, I would lie my glasses on the table.
    d.   If I were she, I would lay my glasses on the table
    e.   If I were she, I would lie my glasses on the table

40. <u>Janice was so excited about being named Prom Queen that she couldn't hardly get to sleep that night.</u>

    a.   Janice was so excited about being named Prom Queen that she couldn't hardly get to sleep that night.
    b.   When she was named Prom Queen, Janice was so excited that she couldn't hardly get to sleep that night.
    c.   Janice was so excited about being named Prom Queen that she could hardly get to sleep that night.
    d.   Janice was so excited to be named Prom Queen that she couldn't hardly sleep that night.
    e.   The night Janice was named Prom Queen, she was so excited that she couldn't hardly get to sleep.

41. <u>In spite of Jenny wanting to go to the mall, her mother drove her straight home from school to work on her assignment.</u>

    a.   In spite of Jenny wanting to go to the mall, her mother drove her straight home from school to work on her assignment.
    b.   In spite of Jenny's desire to go to the mall, her mother drove her straight home from school to work on her assignment.
    c.   Jenny's mother drove her straight home from school to work on her assignment in spite of her wanting to go to the mall,
    d.   Jenny's mother drove her straight home from school in spite of her wanting to go to the mall, to work on her assignment.
    e.   Although Jenny wanted to go to the mall, her mother drove her straight home from school to work on her assignment.

Answer Key for Verbal Section 8

Critical Reading

1. Choice A is correct. The answer is in Lines 10 – 12.

2. Choice D is correct. In this context, *pretty up* means to falsify (to deliver an artificial result).

3. Choice D is correct. McCormack was referring to the investor response to poor financial numbers.

4. Choice B is correct. All of the other choices are mentioned in Lines 32 – 39.

5. Choice E is correct. The answer is mentioned in Lines 35 – 36.

6. Choice D is correct. The answer is in Lines 41 – 46. Cross-cultural training is not mentioned.

7. Choice B is correct. The answer is in Line 48.

8. Choice A is correct. The goal of the passage was to suggest ways to prevent similar scandals in the future.

9. Choice E is correct. The remaining choices are not the correct scope to be the main idea of the passage.

10. Choice D is correct. In this context, veracious means truthful.

11. Choice A is correct. All of the other choices are mentioned in the third paragraph (Lines 8 – 13).

12. Choice B is correct. In this context, belie means contradict.

13. Choice E is correct. St. Bernard thought the jugglers were debauched or amoral (Lines 20 – 23).

14. Choice C is correct. The answer is presented in Line 27.

Critical Reasoning

15. Choice A is correct. The contestants would prefer to be in the most popular pageant, regardless of the total number of viewers.

16. Choice C is correct. By increasing the number of courses they offer, community colleges increased both their enrollment and revenue. A natural conclusion is that the desire for economic gain fueled the expansion. The other answer choices are not supported by the text.

17. In this argument, the assumption is that all waitresses at the restaurant are beautiful, which is Choice E.

18. Choice B is correct. Those who contributed were the ones whose dogs did not win a prize.

19. Choice C is correct. According to the argument, the most worthwhile research offers immediate and practical benefits to the taxpayers who fund it.

20. The unstated premise of the argument is that fitness is an integral part of productivity and that Spanish workers are more productive than Indonesian workers because they exercise more. Choice D is correct.

21. The original argument is in the following form: "All X have Y. This item is doing Z. Therefore, this item must have Y." Choice E is correct.

22. Choice E is correct. The conclusion of the argument is that the criticism against the Governor is unwarranted, because his policies do not simply benefit the rich.

23. Choice E best explains the discrepancy.

24. Choice C is correct. Diane and Cindy both want safe, clean produce. They disagree about whether or not washing regular (non-organic) produce can provide those benefits.

25. Choice D is correct. It generalizes from a sample that is likely to be unrepresentative.

Sentence Correction

26. Choice D is correct. The original sentence uses the word respectfully instead of respectively. Only Choices D and E correct this mistake. Choice E, unfortunately, changes the meaning of the sentence.

27. Choice E is correct. The original sentence contains two errors. First, there is a misplaced modifier (Clara was paid little money, not her hands). Second, the word *inflicted* in used instead of *afflicted*. The correct answer choice must correct both mistakes. Only Choice E corrects the modifier AND uses the correct phrase *afflicted with*.

28. Choice C is correct. When three or more people are being compared, the correct term is *widest*, not

wider.

29. The correct choice is A, which is the best option of all five choices. Choice D is tempting, but it omits the words "for covering," which are essential in this sentence.

30. The error in the sentence is the inconsistency between *to snap back* and *attempting to reconcile with him.* Answer choices B and E shorten the sentence quite nicely, but they do not correct this inconsistency. The only answer choice that makes the correction is C, which is the correct answer. Although the sentence is long-winded, it is grammatically correct.

31. Answer choice D is correct, because it contains the correct verb tense in both parts of the sentence.

32. In its original form, this statement was not a complete sentence, because it lacked a verb. Although both C and E add a verb, answer choice C adds an error in the latter part of the sentence. The best answer to the question is choice E.

33. The error in this sentence is that the second clause is not joined logically to the first. The best answer choice will subjugate one clause in favor of the other in a grammatically correct manner. Of the five answer choices, E is the best.

34. Choice B is correct. The verb in the second clause should be had waited.

35. Choice D is correct. The only error in this sentence is the verb *sunk*, which should be *sank.*

36. As written, there is a pronoun error; the sentence also uses *between,* rather than *among.* The best solution is choice E, which eliminates the mistake and uses the active voice.

37. The sentence is correct as written (Choice A). Whoever is the correct pronoun, because it is the subject of the subordinate clause.

38. Choice E is correct. The words *quickness* and *eloquently* are not parallel in the original sentence. Choices B and E correct this mistake, but Choice B is not as concise.

39. The original sentence used the wrong pronoun. Because the first clause is not fact, we must use the subjunctive form of the verb (If *I were*, not If *I was*). Further, the phrase "to be" requires that the pronoun be a subject, not an object (*she*, not *her).* Choice D is correct because it makes this change without introducing an error with the verbs lie and lay.

40. The original sentence uses a double negative (*couldn't hardly).* Choice C is the best revision.

41. Choice E is correct because it replaces the awkward introductory phrase with *Although Jenny wanted.*

Passage 1

In recent years, people have demonstrated an insatiable appetite for technology that enables them to remain in touch on the go. As a result, individual consumers, along with countless public, private, and government organizations, have purchased a plethora of mobile and hand-held devices that offer sophisticated software applications, Internet and e-mail access, instant messaging, voice calls, and networking features that are accessible in a portable package. The biggest reason, however, for such explosive growth in mobile technologies is the potential cost savings for the organizations that use them. Advanced mobile and wireless devices allow firms to communicate independently of their physical locations. In addition, by 2010, wireless technology is forecasted to outperform wired networks due to its preferable cost, reliability, and functionality. Despite these benefits, however, mobile devices pose ever-changing security challenges for a corporation's top management to ensure the integrity, privacy, and security of their corporate data.

11

Mobile devices provide remote access to a company's data, which provides tremendous flexibility to their users. This flexibility, however, leaves the company's networks and data vulnerable to security breaches and viruses. Furthermore, many companies are struggling to find ways to protect the increasing amount of sensitive information that is stored in laptops, PDAs, BlackBerries, cell phones, USB drives, and other portable devices, which can be easily stolen, lost, or carried away due to their small size. And, sadly, once a mobile device is lost, the subsequent costs extend far beyond the physical replacement of the unit. In many cases, the greatest threat is the loss of sensitive or proprietary data that has been stored on the device.

19

Due to their portability, laptops, PDA's, smart phones, and USB memory sticks are far more difficult to secure than traditional workstation computers. Every day, employees at private, public, and government organizations transfer sensitive information from secured networks to mobile devices and remove them from the company premises. Although some companies prohibit CD burners at their workstation computers, laptops, PDAs, and USB drives are as commonplace as house keys. Even more troubling, when cheap USB memory devices are missing, employees may not even report it.

26

Unfortunately, the loss of these devices is all too common. Last year, about 750,000 laptops were stolen; about 97% of stolen PC's are never recovered. Every month, thousands of mobile phones are also stolen. If they are smart phones, they could contain private information like computer files and email messages, which could spark an unwanted leak of sensitive company information. According to a survey performed by the Yankee Group in 2005, 37% of respondents attributed the disclosure of company information to USB drives.

32

In a survey last year, the Technology Security Institute of the Federal Bureau of Investigation reported that 75% of respondents experienced laptop and mobile device theft, which was more than any other type of attack or misuse, including denial of service attacks, telecommunications fraud, unauthorized access of information, viruses, system penetration, sabotage, website defacement, and misuse of a public web application.

37

According to a survey performed by the Weiss Institute, 81% of information security professionals reported that their companies had experienced the loss of one or more laptops containing sensitive information. The study also reported that hand-held devices and laptops posed the greatest risk of data loss, followed by USB memory sticks. Sensitive information could include customer data, employee records, vendor information, intellectual property (such as product or research data, corporate plans, and strategies), and even the secret personal correspondence of key employees, which might make them vulnerable to blackmail.

44

Currently, there are numerous products and services to recover missing or stolen devices. Companies like SmartProtec provide software that can trace stolen property and return it to its rightful owner. Mr. Shively, an inventory manager for a company that processes medical records, recently installed SmartProtec software on more than 900 computers that are used by employees who travel between hospitals to scan patient records. If a computer is stolen, Mr. Shively simply has to call a hotline; the next time that laptop is connected to the internet, it will automatically send a message to the servers at SmartProtec headquarters that identifies its location. Immediately afterwards, the same information is forwarded to the police, who can retrieve the stolen laptop.

52

SmartProtec provides a similar service for cell phones, which allows users to register their devices. This simple step makes it dangerous for thieves to possess or re-sell stolen items. SmartProtec works with the police and other authorities to recover stolen devices, and offers rewards to the individuals who find them. The serial numbers of all devices are stored in a SmartProtec database, so there is no need for the owner to write it on a piece of paper and worry about losing it. The moment the device is lost or stolen, the owner must immediately change its status from "In Possession" to "Lost" or "Stolen." When police recover a stolen item, or someone finds a lost device, SmartProtec allows them to contact the owner through the serial number, without disclosing any personal information. Moreover, SmartProtec collaborates with FedEx to deliver the recovered device directly to the owner's doorstep.

62

Executives must keep these security services in their proper perspective. Although SmartProtec can trace stolen property and return it safely to its rightful owner, no amount of technology can substitute completely for the actions of people. Ultimately, security is only as good as each company's individual policies.

66

1. According to the author, what is the main reason for the fast growth of mobile technologies?

    a. Computer networking
    b. Voice mail applications
    c. Potential cost savings
    d. Internet access and email
    e. Instant messaging

2. By 2010, what technological change do industry experts expect?

    a. Corporations will no longer allow employees to store sensitive data on mobile devices
    b. SmartProtec will capture more than eighty-percent of the wireless security market
    c. The theft of mobile devices will spark a corresponding rise in identity theft
    d. Due to problems associated with theft, USB memory devices will be prohibited at most major corporations
    e. Wireless technology will outperform wired networks

3. According to the passage, what percentage of stolen computers is recovered?

    a. 3%
    b. 37%
    c. 75%
    d. 81%
    e. 97%

4. The passage mentions all of the following mobile devices EXCEPT:

    a. Smart phones
    b. USB drives
    c. BlackBerries
    d. Memory sticks
    e. Portable microchips

5. In Line 41, what does "*sensitive*" mean?

    a. Easily hurt
    b. Classified
    c. Clandestine
    d. Delicate
    e. Reactionary

6. Which organization conducted a survey to determine how sensitive company information was erroneously disclosed?

    a. Yankee Group
    b. Federal Bureau of Investigation
    c. Weiss Institute
    d. SmartProtec
    e. Technology Security Institute

7. In the survey conducted by the Weiss Institute, which of the following is NOT mentioned as a type of record kept on corporate computers?

    a.   Vendor information
    b.   Corporate strategies
    c.   Secret personal correspondence
    d.   Health and medical records
    e.   Employee records

8. In which scenario would the SmartProtec system NOT be helpful?

    a.   The thief takes the laptop outside the United States
    b.   The owner forgets the hotline number
    c.   The thief does not attempt to log onto the Internet
    d.   The laptop is dropped
    e.   The laptop is sold to a pawn shop

9. In Line 59, what does "*serial*" mean?

    a.   identifying
    b.   in order
    c.   repetitive
    d.   rank
    e.   production

10. Which of the following best conveys the author's attitude about the security of mobile devices?

    a.   There is no realistic way to secure them.
    b.   The risks are minimal compared to the benefits these devices offer.
    c.   Portable storage devices should be banned at most companies to prevent security risks.
    d.   Their security depends on each company's policies.
    e.   A system like SmartProtec provides adequate protection for most users' needs.

Passage 2

In 2005, scientists at Yale University were awarded a patent for "GeneTropy," a home-based DNA analysis kit. The practical implications of the kit are enormous to law enforcement groups, as GeneTropy makes a positive DNA match in just thirty minutes, compared to the minimal three-week period required by previous testing methodologies. Since GeneTropy's introduction, federal, state and local law enforcement agencies have used the test to solve over 400 rapes, 120 assaults and 6,100 burglaries. In Illinois, the test has also been used to reverse the wrongful convictions of eleven murderers, including three on Death Row.

7

The burgeoning market for home-based paternity testing offers another revenue stream for GeneTropy that its developers are eager to explore. During their initial promotional work, they discovered that traditional lab-based tests cost over $650 and offer results in three weeks. Of the five accredited labs in the United States, backlogs are usually so severe that the turnaround time can be five weeks or longer. In contrast, GeneTropy costs just $100, provides reliable results in 24 hours, and can be used in the privacy of a buyer's home. The developers' primary goal for 2007 is to get FDA approval for the over-the-counter distribution of the test. From a societal perspective, the potential financial and psychological benefits to families in America are too important to ignore.

15

11. What is the main point of the passage?

    a.   To convince customers of traditional DNA labs to use GeneTropy as a lower cost option
    b.   To encourage families to have paternity tests run on their children
    c.   To discuss the low cost and fast speed of GeneTropy's DNA analysis kit
    d.   To explain what GeneTropy can offer law enforcement groups
    e.   To demonstrate Yale's financial interest in GeneTropy technology

12. According to the author, what is GeneTrophy's main advantage to law enforcement?

    a. small sample size
    b. low cost
    c. fast results
    d. reliability
    e. FDA approved

13. In line 8, what does "*burgeoning*" mean?

    a. unexpected
    b. lucrative
    c. sophisticated
    d. expanding
    e. consumer

14. According to the author, law enforcement agencies have used GeneTropy to solve all of the following crimes EXCEPT:

    a. forgery
    b. rape
    c. murder
    d. burglary
    e. assault

15. For paternity tests, which of the following is NOT a benefit provided by GeneTrophy?

    a. reliable
    b. low cost
    c. privacy
    d. over-the-counter access
    e. fast results

16. The author's attitude toward GeneTrophy can be best described as?

    a. neutral
    b. cynical
    c. envious
    d. enthusiastic
    e. laconic

Directions: The questions in this section are based on the reasoning contained in brief statements or passages. For some questions, more than one of the choices could conceivably answer the question. However, you are to choose the one that provides the most complete and accurate answer. You should not make assumptions that are implausible, superfluous, or incompatible with the passage.

17. Jeeps must be expensive. Doctors drive them.

The argument relies on what unstated assumption?

    a. Jeeps are prestigious cars.
    b. Doctors have a lot of money.
    c. Doctors like sports utility vehicles.
    d. Jeeps are overpriced.
    e. Nurses cannot afford jeeps.

18. For the past forty years, investigators have known little about the U.S. Air crash in 1969, which killed more than three hundred people. However, a recent study of the fuselage that was recovered from the Atlantic Ocean revealed that the only portion of the plane that was damaged was the left wing, which had mysteriously detached from the plane. The rest of the aircraft was intact at the bottom of the ocean. This debris was eerily similar to that of an American Airlines jet that was hit by lightning on the left wing, which caused it to plummet from the sky and sink to the bottom of the Pacific Ocean. Therefore, it is likely that the U.S. Air jet was also hit by lightning on the left wing.

Which of the following, if true, best justifies this argument?

    a.   Lightning is known to destroy aircraft at the weakest joint.
    b.   If two effects are similar, their causes are probably also similar.
    c.   In aviation disasters, the most logical conclusion is generally true.
    d.   Both planes encountered heavy rain on their reported flight paths.
    e.   Since 2009, when the wing of the plane was re-designed, no other crashes have occurred.

19. Taco salad gets its zesty flavor from the addition of chili powder. Therefore, enchiladas must also get their zesty flavor from the addition of chili powder.

The flawed reasoning in the argument above most closely parallels the reasoning in which of the following?

    a.   Direct TV pays extra money to offer its viewers premium channels such as HBO and Showtime. Consequently, the Movie Channel must also cost Direct TV extra money.
    b.   Alice earned more money from stocks than bonds. Therefore, her broker must receive a smaller commission on stocks than bonds.
    c.   Supermarkets charge more for cosmetics than drug stores. Consequently, the quality of cosmetics at supermarkets must be higher than those in drug stores.
    d.   Gina smells great because she wears the newest fragrance by Britney Spears. Consequently, Doris must also smell great because she wears the newest fragrance by Britney Spears.
    e.   Popcorn is low in fat unless you add butter. Therefore, products that contain butter must contribute to weight gain.

20. Barbara ate a bowl of ice cream, despite its high caloric content.

Which one of the following can be inferred from the argument?

    a.   Ice cream is fattening.
    b.   Barbara is lactose intolerant.
    c.   Barbara is on a diet.
    d.   Barbara dislikes ice cream.
    e.   Barbara is fat.

21. Research suggests that most people with normal HDL/LDL levels have no problem consuming high cholesterol diets. Whatever cholesterol they do not need for their basic metabolic functions is simply excreted in their feces and does not cause an increase in their blood cholesterol levels. Thus, the only people who need to restrict their cholesterol intake are those who have high HDL/LDL levels and cannot excrete excess cholesterol in their feces.

Which of the following, if true, would most seriously weaken this argument?

    a.   The less cholesterol people consume, the more they crave foods that contain it.
    b.   Excessive cholesterol intake has been linked to male pattern baldness in mice.
    c.   As people age, their caloric needs decrease by 5% each year.
    d.   Stress fractures in the elderly have a direct correlation with the amount of calories they consume.
    e.   Over time, people who consume excessive cholesterol lose their ability to metabolize it efficiently.

22. Olivia: eBay is the best place to buy all types of software, because the prices are nearly 80% below those of retail stores. Although the shipping costs are not always reasonable and some products are inferior knockoffs, I am more than willing to take the risk.

Justine: I agree that most software packages sell for 80% below retail on eBay, but few of the items are original copies that can be registered with the manufacturer. Rather than pay a little less and get an illegal copy of a program, I would rather buy my software in a retail store and eliminate the risk of viruses, spyware, and inferior performance.

These statements reveal that Olivia and Justine disagree about whether

    a. It is preferable to pay retail prices for software to avoid the risks of viruses, spyware, and inferior performance from illegal products on eBay.
    b. eBay violates the law by selling illegal copies of software packages.
    c. Registered software protects the owner from viruses, spyware, and inferior performance.
    d. People who purchase illegal software on eBay are at increased risk of encountering viruses, spyware, and inferior performance.
    e. You get what you pay for.

23. Girls that consume a high level of coconut oil in cosmetics such as lip balm and dental floss develop gum line infections that are resistant to antibiotics. If left untreated, premature tooth loss is inevitable. Unlike girls, boys who consume an equal amount of coconut oil from lip balm and dental floss do not get similar gum line infections.

Which one of the following, if true, does the most to resolve the apparent discrepancy in the argument above?

    a. Most boys do not use cosmetic products such as lip balm and dental floss.
    b. In nations where lip balm and dental floss are cost prohibitive, the rate of gum line infections is negligible.
    c. Female patients who contract mononucleosis are ten times more likely to spread the infection than those who do not.
    d. Salivary enzymes that react with coconut oil to form gum line infections are found in females, but not males.
    e. Most girls are resistant to antibiotics because they are over-prescribed for acne treatment.

24. Mrs. Davis ordered the breakfast special at Denny's. Therefore, Mrs. Davis must have received a free cup of coffee.

Upon what assumption does this argument rely?

    a. Mrs. Davis is a senior citizen.
    b. All breakfasts come with free coffee.
    c. Mrs. Davis likes coffee.
    d. Denny's has good coffee.
    e. Coffee is the most popular beverage at Denny's.

25. Of course Helen is smart. She went to Harvard.

Which one of the following uses reasoning that is most similar to the above argument?

    a. Grace is a lawyer. She must be articulate.
    b. Elizabeth is a dynamo. She graduated with six job offers.
    c. Joe got into law school. He must be wealthy.
    d. Of course Liza is popular. She's a blonde.
    e. Joe was rejected by the state university. He is not particularly intelligent.

Directions: The following sentences test correctness and effectiveness of expression. Part of each sentence (or the entire sentence) is underlined; beneath each sentence are five ways of phrasing the underlined material. Choice A repeats the original phrasing; the other four choices are different. If you think the original phrasing produces a better sentence than the alternatives, select choice A; if not, select one of the other choices. In making your selection, follow the requirements of standard written English, such as grammar, choice of words, sentence construction, and punctuation. Your selection should result in the most effective sentence – clear and precise, without awkwardness or ambiguity.

Example: Most teenagers struggle to be free <u>both of parental domination but also from premature responsibilities.</u>

a. both of parental domination but also from premature responsibilities.
b. both of parental domination and also from premature responsibilities.
c. both of parental domination and also of premature responsibilities.
d. of parental domination and premature responsibilities.
e. both of parental domination and their premature responsibilities as well.

The correct answer is Choice D.

26. Rick and Steve will meet <u>Bonnie and me</u> at the dance at 8 o'clock.

    a.   Bonnie and me
    b.   Bonnie and I
    c.   I and Bonnie
    d.   me and Bonnie
    e.   both I and Bonnie

27. <u>Despite Bill's reservations, the party went on as planned.</u>

    a.   Despite Bill's reservations, the party went on as planned.
    b.   Despite the fact that Bill had reservations, the party went on as planned.
    c.   Although Bill had reservations, the party went on.
    d.   Despite Bill's reservations, they did not prevent the party.
    e.   Despite Bill's reservations, he went to the party as planned.

28. <u>Using a typewriter in the computer age is in many ways like when we use a slide rule instead of a calculator.</u>

    a.   Using a typewriter in the computer age is in many ways like when we use a slide rule instead of a calculator.
    b.   Using a typewriter in the computer age is like when we use a slide rule instead of a calculator.
    c.   Using a typewriter in the computer age is similar to using a slide rule instead of a calculator.
    d.   Using a typewriter in the computer age is similar to when we use a slide rule instead of a calculator.
    e.   Using a typewriter in the computer age is the same as when we use a slide rule instead of a calculator.

29. <u>It was reported by Channel 12 that the identity of the deceased would not be revealed until the next of kin had been notified.</u>

    a.   It was reported by Channel 12 that the identity of the deceased would not be revealed until the next of kin had been notified.
    b.   It was reported by Channel 12 that the authorities would not reveal the identity of the deceased until their next of kin were notified.
    c.   Channel 12 reported that the authorities will not reveal the identity of the deceased until after their next of kin have been notified.
    d.   Channel 12 would not reveal the identity of the deceased until the authorities notified their next of kin.
    e.   Channel 12 reported the authority's decision not to reveal the identity of the deceased until after the next of kin had been notified first.

30. When they found $50 in the parking lot, Joe and Ted decided to divide the money equally among themselves.

    a.   equally among themselves
    b.   equally between themselves
    c.   equally
    d.   between the two of them equally
    e.   equally between them

31. Only two of the job candidates exceeded the required typing speed of 75 words per minute; not surprisingly, even the slowest of the two was an excellent typist.

    a.   Only two of the job candidates exceeded the required typing speed of 75 words per minute; not surprisingly, even the slowest of the two was an excellent typist.
    b.   Only two of the job candidates typed faster than the required typing speed of 75 words per minute; not surprisingly, even the slowest of the two was an excellent typist.
    c.   Only two of the job candidates typed faster than 75 words per minute; even the slower one was an excellent typist.
    d.   Only two job candidates typed faster than 75 words per minute; not surprisingly, even the slowest candidate was an excellent typist.
    e.   Only two of the job candidates typed faster than the required speed of 75 words per minute; not surprisingly, even the slower candidate was an excellent typist.

32. Kyle turned down the job offer for several reasons, beside the disappointing salary.

    a.   Kyle turned down the job offer for several reasons, beside the disappointing salary.
    b.   Kyle turned down the job offer for several reasons, besides the disappointing salary.
    c.   Kyle turned down the job offer on account of the disappointing salary, along with several other reasons.
    d.   Kyle turned down the job offer because of the disappointing salary, and several other reasons.
    e.   Kyle turned down the job offer for many reasons, not to mention the disappointing salary.

33. In his cautionary speech about the economy, the Senator eluded to problems with inflation, interest rates, and the depressed housing market.

    a.   the Senator eluded to problems with inflation, interest rates, and the depressed housing market.
    b.   the Senator eluded to problems relating to inflation, interest rates, and the depressed housing market.
    c.   the Senator eluded to problems relating to inflation and interest rates, along with the depressed housing market.
    d.   the Senator alluded to problems with inflation, interest rates, and the depressed housing market.
    e.   the Senator alluded to inflation, interest rates, and the depressed housing market, which are all problematical.

34. Buying retail is more expensive and less satisfaction than to buy at a wholesale warehouse.

    a.   Buying retail is more expensive and less satisfaction than to buy at a wholesale warehouse.
    b.   Buying retail is more expensive and less satisfactory to me than to buy at a wholesale warehouse.
    c.   Buying retail is more expensive and less satisfying than buying at a wholesale warehouse.
    d.   To buy retail is more expensive and less satisfaction than to buy at a wholesale warehouse.
    e.   Buying at a wholesale warehouse is less expensive but less satisfactory than retail.

35. By the time Alicia retires, which will probably be in 2007, her granddaughter <u>will have been living</u> with her for nine years.

    a.   will have been living
    b.   will have lived
    c.   will be living
    d.   would have lived
    e.   would have been living

36. <u>The phenomena. although intriguing, was a source of frustration for the eminent scientists.</u>

    a.   The phenomena, although intriguing, was a source of frustration for the eminent scientists.
    b.   The intriguing phenomena was a source of frustration for the imminent scientists.
    c.   The phenomenon, although intriguing, were a source of frustration for the imminent scientists.
    d.   The phenomenon, although intriguing, was a source of frustration for the imminent scientists.
    e.   The phenomena, although intriguing, were a source of frustration for the eminent scientists.

37. Bill can give the prize to <u>whomever he wants.</u>

    a.   whomever he wants
    b.   whoever he wants
    c.   whichever person he chooses
    d.   whomever works the hardest
    e.   whoever is best

38. If my great-grandfather <u>was to see</u> our family farm today, he would be stunned by the high prices of utilities and real estate.

    a.   was to see
    b.   were to see
    c.   had seen
    d.   will see
    e.   would see

39. <u>Although the principal praised the students' ability to handle change, never before has their violations of the rules been more apparent.</u>

    a.   Although the principal praised the students' ability to handle change, never before has their violations of the rules been more apparent.
    b.   Although the principal praised the students' ability to handle change, never before have their violations of the rules been more apparent.
    c.   Although the principal praised the students' ability to handle change, their violations of the rules has never been more apparent.
    d.   Despite the principal's praising the students' ability to handle change, never before has their violations of the rules been more apparent.
    e.   Although the principal has praised the students' ability to handle change, never before has their violations of the rules been more apparent.

40. <u>Long before she went to the emergency room, Emily had suspected that her leg was broken.</u>

    a.   Long before she went to the emergency room, Emily had suspected that her leg was broken.
    b.   Before she went to the emergency room, Emily had suspected that her leg was broken.
    c.   For a long time before she went to the emergency room, Emily suspected that her leg might be broken.
    d.   Long before the emergency room confirmed it, Emily had suspected that her leg was broken.
    e.   Long before her visit to the emergency room, Emily's leg was broken and she knew it.

41. The football coach, along with several key players, are scheduling a conference to lay down next season's recruitment regulations.

 a. The football coach, along with several key players, are scheduling a conference to lay down next season's recruitment regulations.
 b. The football coach and several key players is scheduling a conference to lay down next season's recruitment regulations.
 c. The football coach, along with several key players, are scheduling a conference to lie down next season's recruitment regulations.
 d. The football coach, along with several key players, is scheduling a conference to lay down next season's recruitment regulations.
 e. The football coach and several key players are scheduling a conference to lie down the recruitment regulations for next season.

Answer Key for Verbal Section 9

Critical Reading

1. Choice C is correct. The answer is in Line 6.

2. Choice E is correct. The answer is in Line 8.

3. Choice A is correct. On Line 28, the author reports that 97% of stolen computers are NOT recovered.

4. Choice E is correct. All of the other devices are mentioned in the passage.

5. Choice B is correct. In this context, *sensitive* means classified.

6. Choice A is correct. The answer is in Line 30.

7. Choice D is correct. The other choices are mentioned in Lines 41 - 43.

8. Choice C is correct.   According to Lines 49 - 50, the laptop can only be traced if the thief logs onto the Internet, at which time its location can be determined from its IP number. If the thief does not log onto the Internet, the unit cannot be traced.

9. Choice A is correct. The *serial* number corresponds with the ownership certificate, which identifies the registered user of the laptop.

10. Choice D is correct. The author states this conclusion in the final sentence of the passage.

11. Choice C is correct. The other answer choices are either too broad or too narrow in scope.

12. Choice C is correct. In Line 3, the author cites the fast speed of the test, which is the greatest advantage for law enforcement applications.

13. Choice D is correct. In this context, *burgeoning* means expanding.

14. Choice A is correct. The passage mentions all of the other crimes in the first paragraph.

15. Choice D is correct. The FDA has not yet approved the test for over-the-counter sales.

16. Choice D is correct. The final statement in the passage confirms the author's enthusiasm about GeneTropy.

Critical Reasoning

17. The argument presumes that doctors have a lot of money. Choice B is correct.

18. Choice B is correct. If the effects are similar (and somewhat unique), the causes are probably also similar.

19. Choice D is correct. The argument presumes that a requirement in one situation should be the same for a similar situation.

20. In this case, we are dealing with an inference question. The correct answer choice will be a piece of information that is essential to the argument; without it, the author's position will no longer make sense. In this case, the correct choice is C. The argument infers that Barbara is on a diet.

21. Choice E is correct. The argument fails to consider the long-term consequences of excessive cholesterol consumption or the possibility that it may weaken the body's ability to metabolize it.

22. Choice A is correct. Their disagreement is about the cost of buying software on eBay versus the underlying risks.

23. Choice D is correct. The argument makes sense – and the discrepancy is explained – only if girls (but not boys) have salivary enzymes that react with coconut oil to form gum line infections.

24. In this argument, the assumption is that all breakfasts come with free coffee, which is Choice B.

25. This argument presumes that a person's alma mater determines indicates his/her intelligence. Choice E uses the same reasoning.

Sentence Correction

26. Choice A is correct. The sentence is correct as written

27. Choice A is correct. This question is tricky because the statement is so vague. Although answer choices D and E provide more information, we do not know (as readers) if the information is accurate. We only know that Bill had reservations about the party. We don't know if he actually attended it. Hence, the best answer choice is A.

28. The original sentence makes an awkward comparison. Choice C presents the best correction. *Using a typewriter in the computer age is similar to using a slide rule instead of a calculator.*

29. The initial phrase *it was reported* is in the passive voice, which Choices C – E correct. Of the three, choice D is the only version that also corrects the second passive verb *had been notified.*

30. Choice C is correct. Although the original sentence uses the word *among* incorrectly (rather than *between*), neither word is necessary in the sentence.

31. Choice E is correct. When comparing two people, the word comparing their speeds should be *slower*, not *slowest*. Choice E makes this correction in the most concise and straightforward way, without omitting key information.

32. Choice B is correct. The word *beside* means "next to," while *besides* means "in addition to."

33. Choice D is correct. The correct word is *alluded*, not *eluded*. Choices D and E both make this correction, but Choice E is too wordy and awkward (particularly the word *problematical).*

34. Choice C is correct. The original sentence has two errors. First, the phrase *and less satisfaction* is not correct. Second, *buying* and *to buy* are not parallel. Choice C corrects both errors without changing the original meaning of the sentence.

35. The sentence is projecting into the future; it is correct as originally written. Choice A.

36. This sentence, as originally written, contains an error in subject/verb agreement. Because the word *phenomena* is plural, it requires the plural verb *were*, rather than *was*. The answer choices offer several subject and verb combinations, but they agree in number only in choices D and E. Interestingly, the writers have further confused the issue by including answer choices with the word *imminent* in place of *eminent*.

The correct answer choice is E, which offers the correct agreement between subject and verb and the correct adjective (eminent).

37. In this sentence, the word *whomever* is used correctly. Choice A is correct.

38. This sentence is presenting a hypothetical situation. The correct verb is *were to see*, which is Choice B.

39. The original sentence includes the wrong verb, which should be *have* (rather than *has*). Choice B is correct.

40. Choice A is correct. The sentence is correct as written.

41. The subject of the sentence is singular and therefore requires the singular verb *is scheduling*. Choice D is correct.

Directions: *The passage below is followed by questions based on its content. Answer the questions, based on what is stated or implied in the passage and any introductory material that may be provided.*

Passage 1

During the sixteenth century, the most celebrated sheep in France were those of Berri and Limousin; and of all butchers' meat, veal was reckoned the best. In fact, calves intended for the tables of the upper classes were fed in a special manner: they were allowed for six months, or even for a year, nothing but milk, which made their flesh most tender and delicate. Contrary to the present taste, kid was more appreciated than lamb, which caused the rôtisseurs frequently to attach the tail of a kid to a lamb, so as to deceive the customer and sell him a less expensive meat at the higher price. This was the origin of the axiom which described a cheat as "a dealer in goat by halves."

8

In other places, butchers were far from acquiring the same importance which they did in France and Belgium, where much more meat was consumed than in Spain, Italy, or even in Germany. Nevertheless, in almost all countries there were certain regulations, sometimes eccentric, but almost always rigidly enforced, to ensure a supply of meat of the best quality and in a healthy state. In England, for instance, butchers were only allowed to kill bulls after they had been baited with dogs, no doubt with the view of making the flesh more tender. At Mans, it was laid down in the trade regulations that "no butcher shall be so bold as to sell meat unless it shall have been previously seen alive by two or three persons, who will testify to it on oath; and, anyhow, they shall not sell it until the persons shall have declared it wholesome."

17

To the many regulations affecting the interests of the public must be added that forbidding butchers to sell meat on days when abstinence from animal food was ordered by the Church. These regulations applied less to the vendors than to the consumers, who, by disobeying them, were liable to fine or imprisonment, or to severe corporal punishment by the whip or in the pillory. We find that Clément Marot was imprisoned and nearly burned alive for having eaten pork during Lent. In 1534, Guillaume des Moulins, the Count of Brie, asked permission for his mother, who was then eighty years of age, to cease fasting; the Bishop of Paris only granted dispensation on the condition that the old lady should take her meals in secret and out of sight of every one, and should still fast on Fridays.

26

The severity of the punishment for these transgressions increased during times of religious dissensions. Erasmus says, "He who has eaten pork instead of fish is taken to the torture like a parricide." An edict of Henry II, 1549, forbade the sale of meat during Lent to persons who should not be furnished with a doctor's certificate. Charles IX forbade the sale of meat to the Huguenots; and it was ordered that the privilege of selling meat during the time of abstinence should belong exclusively to the hospitals. Orders were given to those who retailed meat to take the address of every purchaser, although he had presented a medical certificate, so that the necessity for his eating meat might be verified. Subsequently, the medical certificate had to be endorsed by the priest, specifying what quantity of meat was required. Even in these cases, the use of butchers' meat alone was granted, pork, poultry, and game being strictly forbidden.

36

1. What is the main point of the passage?

    a. To explain the best ways to tenderize meat
    b. To explain the reasoning for attaching a kid to a lamb
    c. To explain the religious implications of meat consumption in sixteenth century Europe
    d. To discuss the regulations regarding meat consumption in Europe during the sixteenth century
    e. To explain the extreme tyranny of Charles IX regarding the consumption of food

2. According to the author, in France, what was the best way to ensure that a calf's meat was tender?

    a. They were baited by dogs before they were killed
    b. They were declared wholesome by two people before they were killed
    c. The meat was cooked slowly with moisture
    d. They were fed nothing but milk for at least six months before slaughter
    e. The meat was consumed within 24 hours of the calf's slaughter

3. In Line 6, what does "*axiom*" mean?

   a. Maxim
   b. Law
   c. Irony
   d. Allegation
   e. Corollary

4. Customers who ate illegal meat were punished in all of the following ways EXCEPT:

   a. Fines
   b. Starvation
   c. Whipping
   d. Imprisonment
   e. Pillory

5. In Line 28, what does "*parricide*" mean?

   a. Death via food poisoning
   b. Death by starvation
   c. Murder of a relative
   d. Religious execution
   e. Animal sacrifice

6. What is the most likely source of the passage?

   a. A food journal
   b. A history book
   c. A cookbook
   d. A religious sermon
   e. A print ad for the beef industry

Passage 2

The coffee tree, scientifically known as Coffea arabica, is native to Abyssinia and Ethiopia, but grows well in Java, Sumatra, and other islands of the Dutch East Indies; in India, Arabia, equatorial Africa, the islands of the Pacific, in Mexico, Central and South America, and the West Indies. The plant belongs to the large sub-kingdom of plants known scientifically as the Angiosperms, which means that the plant reproduces by seeds which are enclosed in a box-like compartment, known as the ovary, at the base of the flower. The word Angiosperm is derived from two Greek words, sperma, a seed, and aggeion, a box or ovary.

7

This large sub-kingdom is subdivided into two classes. The basis for this division is the number of leaves in the little plant which develops from the seed. The coffee plant, as it develops from the seed, has two little leaves, and therefore belongs to the class Dicotyledoneæ. This word dicotyledoneæ is made up of the two Greek words, di(s), two, and kotyledon, cavity or socket. It is not necessary to see the young plant that develops from the seed in order to know that it had two seed leaves; because the mature plant always shows certain characteristics that accompany this condition of the seed.

14

In every plant having two seed leaves, the mature leaves are netted-veined, which is a condition easily recognized even by the layman; also the parts of the flowers are in circles containing two or five parts, but never in threes or sixes. The stems of plants of this class always increase in thickness by means of a layer of cells known as a cambium, which is a tissue that continues to divide throughout its whole existence. The fact that this cambium divides as long as it lives, gives rise to a peculiar appearance in woody stems by which we can, on looking at the stem of a tree of this type when it has been sawed across, tell the age of the tree.

21

In the spring the cambium produces large open cells through which large quantities of sap can run; in the fall it produces very thick-walled cells, as there is not so much sap to be carried. Because these thin-walled open cells of one spring are next to the thick-walled cells of the last autumn, it is very easy to distinguish one year's growth from the next; the marks so produced are called annual rings.

26

The flower of the coffee plant is separated into sub-classes according to whether the flower's corolla is all in one piece, or is divided into a number of parts. The coffee flower is arranged with its corolla all in one piece, forming a tube-shaped arrangement, and accordingly the coffee plant belongs to the sub-class Sympetalæ, or Metachlamydeæ, which means that its petals are united.

31

Within the Dicotyledoneæ classification, plants are separated into orders according to their varied characteristics. The coffee plant belongs to an order known as Rubiales. These orders are again divided into families. Coffee is placed in the family Rubiaceæ, or Madder Family, in which we find herbs, shrubs or trees, represented by a few American plants, such as bluets, or Quaker ladies, small blue spring flowers, common to open meadows in northern United States; and partridge berries (Mitchella repens).

37

The Madder Family has more foreign representatives than native genera, among which are Coffea, Cinchona, and Ipecacuanha (Uragoga), all of which are of economic importance. The members of this family are noted for their action on the nervous system. Coffea, as is well known, contains an active principle known as caffeine which acts as a stimulant to the nervous system and in small quantities is very beneficial. Cinchona supplies us with quinine, while Ipecacuanha produces ipecac, which is an emetic and purgative.

43

All botanists do not yet agree in their classification of the species and varieties of the Coffea genus. M.E. de Wildman, curator of the Royal Botanical Gardens at Brussels, in his Les Plantes Tropicales de Grande Culture, says the systematic division of this interesting genus is far from finished; in fact, it has only yet begun.

47

7. What is the main point of the passage?

    a.   To explain the economic value of the Madder Family
    b.   To explain the botanical classification of the coffee plant
    c.   To explain the origin of Dicotyledoneæ
    d.   To explain the significance of annual rings
    e.   To differentiate between Dicotyledoneæs and Rubiales

8. Coffee grows naturally in all of the following locations EXCEPT:

    a.   Africa
    b.   Slovakia
    c.   India
    d.   Mexico
    e.   West Indies

9. According to the author, where is the aggeion?

    a.   Within the seed
    b.   On a netted-veined leaf
    c.   At the base of the flower
    d.   Within the woody stem
    e.   In a one-piece tube

10. What is the purpose of the cambium?

    a.   It holds the ovary
    b.   It stimulates the nervous system
    c.   It allows us to classify plants by their number of leaves
    d.   It allows us to determine the age of a tree
    e.   It supplies the seeds for reproduction

11. In Line 27, what is a "*corolla*"?

    a. Stem
    b. Leaf
    c. Petal
    d. Root
    e. Seed

12. All of the following are Rubiaceæ EXCEPT:

    a. Cacao
    b. Bluets
    c. Partridge berries
    d. Shrubs
    e. Herbs

Directions: *The questions in this section are based on the reasoning contained in brief statements or passages. For some questions, more than one of the choices could conceivably answer the question. However, you are to choose the one that provides the most complete and accurate answer. You should not make assumptions that are implausible, superfluous, or incompatible with the passage.*

13. Cats are simple animals that do not have a savvy worldview, which means that cats will never be cynical.

Which one of the following is an assumption on which the argument depends?

    a. Savvy people are usually cynics.
    b. The more you see of the world, the less impressed you are likely to be.
    c. Cats are delightfully simple creatures.
    d. Being cynical requires the capacity to have a savvy worldview.
    e. Savvy people are less happy than those with a limited worldview.

14. Olives are not green, because green things are yucky and olives are usually not yucky.

Which of the following arguments is most similar in its pattern of reasoning to the argument above?

    a. Babies are plump, which is suggestive of jaundice, but adults are rarely plump.
    b. Daises are white, while roses are red, yet both are seldom pungent.
    c. Karen is wealthy, but not terribly happy, because money cannot buy happiness.
    d. Power is not a bad thing, for bad things are criminal, yet powerful people are rarely criminals.
    e. Music is soothing, except at funerals, where it is downright inspirational.

15. Dina must be intelligent. She's not blonde.

The argument relies on what unstated assumption?

    a. Dina is smart.
    b. Dina is blonde.
    c. Dina dyes her hair.
    d. Blondes are intelligent
    e. Blondes are not intelligent.

16. Scientist: To investigate the impact of aspartame in the diet, Researcher X wants to conduct a study with 1,000 elderly men who have dangerously high blood pressure. The six-month study will randomly assign these participants to one of three diets, which have varying levels of aspartame. During this time, the participants' vital signs, including blood pressure, will be monitored on a daily basis. Frankly, I have reservations about this study. Nutritional research should only be permitted if it is likely to reveal relevant information about the dietary implications of aspartame intake on blood pressure. It should also pose no risk to the subjects who have agreed to participate. Therefore, I believe that Researcher X's proposed study on aspartame should be prohibited.

Which of the following, if true, would most help to justify the scientist's argument?

a. Elderly men are the greatest consumers of dietary products that contain aspartame. As such, they have a vested interest in the results of this study.
b. Researcher X has conducted preliminary studies to assess the risk of aspartame intake on teenagers.
c. The participants have agreed to sign waivers that release Researcher X of any liability for the study.
d. Researches cannot determine the effects of aspartame in a reliable manner without conducting tests with human participants.
e. The long-term effects of aspartame intake by elderly patients with high blood pressure have never been evaluated. Accordingly, the risks are unknown.

17. The candidate's opponents claim that his position on health care will bankrupt the national surplus, but that is blatantly false. In nations that utilize the candidate's proposed health care program, the initial costs are offset by a modest yet consistent profit. Additionally, by providing preventive care to uninsured citizens at the earliest stages of a disease, patients will enjoy better outcomes and lower costs because the treatments will be less invasive. Eventually, under the candidate's plan, citizens will enjoy better, more affordable care without draining the national surplus.

Which of the following most accurately expresses the main conclusion of the argument?

a. The candidate's health care plan is the best choice for the nation.
b. The candidate's opponents are not aware of the financial benefits of his health care plan.
c. The candidate's position on heath care will not bankrupt the national surplus.
d. The candidate's opponents cannot evaluate his performance objectively.
e. The candidate's support for socialized medicine is troubling to his opponents.

18. All job candidates must pass a random drug screening in order to be hired by Microsoft.   Joe was not hired by Microsoft, which means that he failed to pass the drug screening.

What is the flaw in this conclusion?

a. It presumes that Joe wanted to work at Microsoft.
b. It uses circular reasoning.
c. It ignores other possible reasons that Joe was not hired by Microsoft.
d. Microsoft is not hiring this year.
e. It presents contradictory evidence.

19. At a national grocery chain, a customer can obtain a discount on her purchases if she enrolls in a frequent shopper plan that requires a minimum number of purchases per month.   At first, enrollment in the plan was high. Eventually, however, the store decreased the types and amounts of discounts that the customer could obtain with the frequent shopper card.

Which of the following conclusions is most strongly suggested by the paragraph above?

a. The original plan was costing the store too much money.
b. The store eliminated the frequent shopper plan in favor of double coupons.
c. Most customers are not loyal to a single grocery store.
d. For most customers, frequent shopper plans are not worth the trouble.

e. Frequent shopper plans are a financial necessity for most cash-strapped families.

20. All cooks eat shrimp. Joy is a cook. Therefore, Joy must eat shrimp.

Which of the following statements uses a similar type of reasoning?

a. All laws are regulations. Rules are also regulations. Therefore, rules must be laws.
b. All begonias are flowers. Some begonias are yellow. Therefore, this begonia is a flower.
c. All models have passports. Patricia is a model. Therefore, Patricia must have a passport. .
d. All coins are nickel. Nickel is a natural metal. Therefore, all coins are natural metal.
e. All buses seat twenty. Cars seat four. Therefore, one bus seats four carloads..

21. Canaries are smaller, prettier, and more intelligent than parakeets. They are also cheaper to feed.

What is the conclusion for the argument?

a. Canaries are better than parakeets.
b. Canaries are the best house pets.
c. Parakeets are not worth the investment.
d. Different birds require different types of diets.
e. Neither canaries nor parakeets can be fully domesticated.

22. Today's dairies only produce a few flavors of whole milk, such as white, chocolate, and strawberry. As a result, consumers who want more exotic flavors must add their own syrup into basic whole milk. Hence, a savvy entrepreneur could make a huge profit by developing and marketing a line of exotic flavorings for whole milk products.

Which of the following, if true, would most weaken this argument?

a. Fruity flavorings tend to taste sour in milk.
b. The FDA would require full approval of the manufacturing process for all exotic flavorings.
c. The most popular flavorings are alcoholic, which children cannot consume.
d. In recent years, customers have become enchanted by exotic flavorings in coffee, thanks to the proliferation of chains such as Starbucks.
e. In previous years, dairies stopped making milk in exotic flavors because there was limited demand for them.

23. College Administrator: Every fall, the university struggles to recruit the best professors in highly competitive areas, such as computer science, medicine, and finance, because academic salaries in these fields lag far behind those in the private sector. Instead, to ensure fairness, we have limited our compensation packages in these areas to those we offer to professors in less competitive fields, such as history, sociology, and the humanities, which offer few opportunities in the private sector. As a result, it is becoming increasingly difficult to attract the best professors in highly competitive fields, who can help us to maintain our top rankings. Ideally, academic salaries in computer science, medicine, and finance should be increased to match what is offered in the private sector.

Which one of the following principles, if valid, most helps to justify the college administrator's reasoning?

a. The most important criterion for the university is retaining its top ranking.
b. Academic salaries in all disciplines should be comparable to those in the private sector, to allow the university to attract the highest caliber of talent in all fields.
c. The university should make highly competitive fields, such as computer science, medicine, and finance, its top priority.
d. To attract the top talent in any academic discipline, universities must offer the highest starting salaries.
e. The top professors in computer science, medicine, and finance attract considerable research funding from public and private sources, which offsets their need for a high salary.

24. Evidence suggests that female mechanics groom themselves nearly one hour per day, while female secretaries devote only ten minutes to their daily grooming. It seems, therefore, that female mechanics are cleaner than female secretaries.

Which one of the following statements, if true, most seriously weakens the argument?

    a. Female mechanics get dirtier and sweatier in their jobs than female secretaries; as a result, they must spend additional time grooming themselves to maintain the optimal level of cleanliness.
    b. Female mechanics are exposed to fewer germs than female secretaries.
    c. Most grooming products are aimed at a feminine audience.
    d. Most female secretaries wear clothes that require dry cleaning; due to the prohibitive cost, they clean the items as infrequently as possible.
    e. Most female mechanics have short hair because it is easier to manage and style.

Directions: The following sentences test correctness and effectiveness of expression. Part of each sentence (or the entire sentence) is underlined; beneath each sentence are five ways of phrasing the underlined material. Choice A repeats the original phrasing; the other four choices are different. If you think the original phrasing produces a better sentence than the alternatives, select choice A; if not, select one of the other choices. In making your selection, follow the requirements of standard written English, such as grammar, choice of words, sentence construction, and punctuation. Your selection should result in the most effective sentence – clear and precise, without awkwardness or ambiguity.

Example: Most teenagers struggle to be free both of parental domination but also from premature responsibilities.

a. both of parental domination but also from premature responsibilities.
b. both of parental domination and also from premature responsibilities.
c. both of parental domination and also of premature responsibilities.
d. of parental domination and premature responsibilities.
e. both of parental domination and their premature responsibilities as well.

The correct answer is Choice D.

25. The players will eat dinner with the cheerleaders and me after the game.

    a. cheerleaders and me
    b. cheerleaders and I
    c. me and the cheerleaders
    d. I and the cheerleaders
    e. both I and the cheerleaders

26. Irregardless of the cost, Sophie continued to select the attire she wanted for her dream wedding, which was scheduled for New Year's Eve.

    a. Irregardless of the cost, Sophie continued to select the attire she wanted for her dream wedding, which was scheduled for New Year's Eve.
    b. Irregardless of the cost, Sophie selected the attire she wanted for her dream wedding, which was scheduled for New Year's Eve.
    c. Regardless of the cost, Sophie selected the attire she wanted for her dream wedding, which was scheduled for New Year's Eve.
    d. Irregardless of the cost, Sophie continued to select the attire she wanted for her dream wedding, scheduled for New Year's Eve.
    e. Irregardless of the cost, Sophie continued to select the attire she wanted for her dream wedding on New Year's Eve.

27. There is ongoing debate about how much of the decrease in teen pregnancies is due to the availability of inexpensive birth control and how much is the result of abstinence programs.

    a.   There is ongoing debate about how much of the decrease in teen pregnancies is due to the availability of inexpensive birth control and how much is the result of abstinence programs.
    b.   There is ongoing debate about how much of the decrease in teen pregnancies is due to the availability of inexpensive birth control and how much is abstinence programs.
    c.   There is ongoing debate about whether teen pregnancies are due to the availability of inexpensive birth control and abstinence programs.
    d.   There is ongoing debate about how many teen pregnancies are due to the availability of inexpensive birth control and how much is the result of abstinence programs.
    e.   There is ongoing debate about how much of the decrease in teen pregnancies is due to birth control and abstinence programs.

28. Before she bought the sweater, Christine asked her husband if he wanted it in plaid or stripes.

    a.   if he wanted it in plaid or stripes.
    b.   if he wanted plaid or stripes.
    c.   about wanting plaid or stripes.
    d.   if he could want plaid or stripes.
    e.   whether he wanted it in plaid or stripes.

29. Jane works during the day and go to school at night.

    a.   Jane works during the day and go to school at night.
    b.   During the day, Jane works, but she go to school at night.
    c.   Jane works during the day and goes to school at night.
    d.   Jane will work during the day and goes to school at night.
    e.   Jane work during the day and go to school at night.

30. Since no one understands the project as well as her, no one but her should give the oral presentation.

    a.   Since no one understands the project as well as her, no one but her should give the oral presentation.
    b.   Because no one understands the project as well as her, no one but her should give the oral presentation.
    c.   Since no one understands the project as well as she, no one but she should give the oral presentation.
    d.   Because no one understands the project as well as her, no one but she should give the oral presentation.
    e.   Since no one understands the project as well as she, no one but her should give the oral presentation.

31. At the job fair, Mr. Davis met two candidates who, he believed, could do the job.

    a.   who, he believed
    b.   both of who, he believed
    c.   which, he believed
    d.   whom, he believed
    e.   for whom, he believed

32. <u>When the election results, including those for the contentious Senate race in District 3, were announced,</u> <u>Senator Smith conceded defeat.</u>

    a. When the election results, including those for the contentious Senate race in District 3, were announced, Senator Smith conceded defeat.

    b. When the election committee announced the results, including those for the contentious Senate race in District 3, Senator Smith conceded defeat.

    c. When the election results were announced, including those for the contentious Senate race in District 3, Senator Smith conceded defeat.

    d. Senator Smith conceded defeat when the election results, including those for the contentious Senate race in District 3, were announced.

    e. Because the election results, including those for the contentious Senate race in District 3, looked grim, Senator Smith conceded defeat.

33. <u>The hiring manager did not encourage the applicant any, although her credentials were a perfect fit for</u> <u>the opening at the firm.</u>

    a. The hiring manager did not encourage the applicant any, although her credentials were a perfect fit for the opening at the firm.

    b. Despite the fact that her credentials were a perfect fit for the opening at the firm, the hiring manager did not encourage the applicant any.

    c. The hiring manager did not encourage the applicant, although her credentials were a perfect fit for the opening at the firm.

    d. The hiring manager did not encourage the applicant any, despite the fact that her credentials were a perfect fit for the opening at the firm.

    e. Although her credentials were a perfect fit for the opening at the firm, the hiring manager did not encourage the applicant any.

34. After school, Juan works as a maintenance manager at a car wash, <u>where he is expected to solve a</u> <u>large amount of mechanical problems.</u>

    a. where he is expected to solve a large amount of mechanical problems.

    b. in which he is expected to solve a large amount of mechanical problems.

    c. because he can solve a large amount of mechanical problems.

    d. where he is expected to solve a large number of mechanical problems.

    e. in which he is expected to find solutions for a large amount of mechanical problems.

35. <u>Although she tried to be brave, the little girl would undoubtedly be effected by her parents' divorce.</u>

    a. Although she tried to be brave, the little girl would undoubtedly be effected by her parents' divorce.

    b. Although she was brave, the little girl would undoubtedly be effected by her parents' divorce.

    c. Although she tried to be brave, the little girl would unquestionably be effected by her parents' divorce.

    d. Despite her bravery, the little girl was undoubtedly affected by her parents' divorce.

    e. Although she tried to be brave, the little girl would undoubtedly be affected by her parents' divorce.

36. Despite the risks, <u>Greg laid his expensive camera on top of his car, where it could easily have been</u> <u>damaged.</u>

    a. Greg laid his expensive camera on top of his car, where it could easily have been damaged.

    b. Greg lay his expensive camera on top of his car, where it could easily have been damaged.

    c. Greg had lay his expensive camera on top of his car, where it could easily have been damaged.

    d. Greg lain his expensive camera on top of his car, where it could easily be damaged.

    e. Greg had lain his expensive camera on top of his car, where it could easily be damaged.

37. After having completed his degree in History, Alex sought a job at a museum in Paris, which would value his knowledge of medieval times.

   a. After having completed his degree in History, Alex sought a job at a museum in Paris, which would value his knowledge of medieval times.
   b. After having completed his degree in History, Alex sought a job at a museum in Paris, which would have valued his knowledge of medieval times.
   c. After completing his degree in History, Alex sought a job at a museum in Paris, which would value his knowledge of medieval times.
   d. After having completed his degree in History, Alex sought a job at a museum in Paris, which will value his knowledge of medieval times.
   e. After completing his degree in History, Alex sought a job at a museum in Paris, that would value his knowledge of medieval times.

38. Clara will stop at nothing in her efforts at eradicating discrimination in the workplace.

   a. Clara will stop at nothing in her efforts at eradicating discrimination in the workplace.
   b. Clara will stop at nothing at eradicating discrimination in the workplace.
   c. In her efforts at eradicating discrimination in the workplace, Clara will stop at nothing.
   d. Clara will stop at nothing in her efforts to eradicate discrimination in the workplace.
   e. Clara will not stop her efforts at eradicating discrimination in the workplace.

39. If George Washington, who was a great proponent of firearms, was to come back to life, he would probably be appalled by the anti-gun movement.

   a. who was a great proponent of firearms, was to come back to life, he would probably be appalled by the anti-gun movement.
   b. a great proponent of firearms, was to come back to life, he would have probably been appalled by the anti-gun movement.
   c. a great proponent of firearms, was to come back to life, he would probably be appalled by the anti-gun movement.
   d. who was a great proponent of firearms, was to come back to life, he would have been appalled by the anti-gun movement.
   e. who was a great proponent of firearms, were to come back to life, he would probably be appalled by the anti-gun movement.

40. Opinions on Hilary Clinton are usually divided, with Democrats regarding her as a political dynamo, while Republicans chastising her as a disingenuous carpetbagger.

   a. Opinions on Hilary Clinton are usually divided, with Democrats regarding her as a political dynamo, while Republicans chastising her as a disingenuous carpetbagger.
   b. Opinions on Hilary Clinton are usually divided, with Democrats regarding her as a political dynamo and Republicans chastising her as a disingenuous carpetbagger.
   c. Democrats regard Hilary Clinton as a political dynamo, while Republicans chastising her as a disingenuous carpetbagger.
   d. Democrats are regarding Hilary Clinton as a political dynamo, while Republicans chastise her as a disingenuous carpetbagger.
   e. Opinions are divided on Hilary Clinton, with Democrats regarding her as a political dynamo, while Republicans chastising her as a disingenuous carpetbagger.

41. <u>Charred remains found in the debris extending from Fifth Avenue to the Brooklyn Bridge suggests that the fire started as early as 9 pm.</u>

    a. Charred remains found in the debris extending from Fifth Avenue to the Brooklyn Bridge suggests that the fire started as early as 9 pm.
    b. Charred remains in the debris that extend from Fifth Avenue to the Brooklyn Bridge suggests that the fire started as early as 9 pm.
    c. Charred remains found in the debris from Fifth Avenue to the Brooklyn Bridge suggests that the fire started as early as 9 pm.
    d. Charred remains found in the debris extending from Fifth Avenue to the Brooklyn Bridge suggest that the fire started as early as 9 pm.
    e. Charred remains that were found in the debris extending from Fifth Avenue to the Brooklyn Bridge suggests that the fire started as early as 9 pm.

Answer Key for Verbal Section 10

Critical Reading

1. Choice D is correct. The main point of the passage is to discuss the regulations regarding meat consumption in Europe during the sixteenth century.   The other answer choices are wrong in scope.

2. Choice D is correct. The answer is presented in Lines 3 – 4.

3. Choice A is correct. In this context, axiom means a maxim, saying, or proverb.

4. Choice B is correct. The other answer choices are all presented in Lines 20 - 21.

5. Choice C is correct. Parricide means the murder of a relative.

6. Choice B is correct. The passage is an excerpt from a history book.

7. The main point of the passage is to explain the botanical classification of the coffee plant. Choice B is correct.

8. Lines 1 -3 mention all of the places that are listed except Slovakia. Choice B is correct.

9. Lines 5 -6 state that the aggeion is at the base of the flower. Choice C is correct.

10. According to Lines 18 – 20, the cambium produces the cells that create the annual ring, which allow us to age the tree. Choice D is correct.

11. A corolla is a petal. Choice C is correct.

12. According to Lines 34 – 36, all are Rubiaceæ except cacao. Choice A is correct.

Critical Reasoning

13. Choice D is correct. The argument depends of the assumption that cynicism requires a savvy worldview.

14. Choice D is correct. Both arguments are in the form "A not B because B are C and A are not C."

15. The argument presumes that blondes are not intelligent. Choice E is correct.

16. The research can only be justified if it reveals new information and poses little risk.   Choice E is the best answer choice, because it reveals that these criteria have not been met.

17. Choice C is correct. The conclusion of the argument is that the criticism against the candidate's health care plan is unwarranted, because it will not bankrupt the national surplus.

18. The argument fails to consider other reasons that Joe was not hired, including a lack of experience.

Choice C is correct.

19. Choice A is correct. The store decreased the discounts even though the program was very popular. This suggests that the costs to the store were not offset by the increase in volume. The other answer choices, although interesting, are not supported by the text.

20. The argument in the question stem can be symbolized as follows: "All A do B. C is an A. Therefore, C must do B." Of the five possibilities, Choice C is the best answer.

21. The logical conclusion is Choice A; canaries are better than parakeets.

22. Choice E is correct. The argument presumes that there is an untapped market for exotic flavorings in milk, which is not necessarily the case.

23. Choice B is correct. According to the argument, academic salaries should be comparable to those in the private sector to ensure that the university can recruit top talent in highly competitive fields.

24. Choice A is correct, because it explains why female mechanics need additional grooming time to maintain the same level of cleanliness as female secretaries.

Sentence Correction

25. The correct pronoun is *me*; the sentence is correct as written, which is Choice A.

26. Choice C is correct. The word *irregardless* is not standard English; it should be replaced by *regardless*.

27. Choice A is correct. The other options change the meaning of the sentence.

28. Choice E is correct. The original sentence makes a common error by using the word *if* instead of *whether*. (*Whether* introduces a choice, while *if* introduces a condition.)

29. Choice C is correct. *Jane works during the day and **goes** to school at night.*

30. Choice E is correct. *Since no one understands the project as well **as she**, no one **but her** should give the oral presentation.*

31. Choice A is correct. The sentence is correct as written.

32. The original sentence contains the passive voice and a misplaced modifier. The best correction is Choice B.

33. In the original sentence, the word *any* is extraneous. Choice C is the best correction.

34. The original sentence uses the wrong word to describe the scope of Juan's job. It should read *a number of problems* or *many problems*, not *a large amount of* problems. Choice D is correct.

35. The original sentence should say *affected*, not *effected*. Choice E is correct.

36. Choice A is correct. This sentence contains no errors.

37. The original sentence should say *after completing*. Choice C is correct.

38. The original sentence uses an infinitive instead of a gerund. The sentence should read: *Clara will stop at nothing in her efforts to eradicate discrimination in the workplace.* Choice D is correct.

39. This question employs a rare, contrary-to-fact conditional statement beginning with an "if" clause. The correct answer is Choice E, because the verb must be in the past subjunctive form (*were*).

40. Choice B is correct. The original sentence uses the wrong verb form.

41. In this sentence, the subject (remains) is plural, which requires the verb *suggest that*, rather than *suggests that*. Choice D is correct.

Directions: *The passages below are followed by questions based on their content. Answer the questions, based on what is* <u>stated</u> *or* <u>implied</u> *in the passage and any introductory material that may be provided.*

Passage 1

Jealousy is an accidental passion, for which the faculty indeed is unborn. In its nobler form and in its nobler motives it arises from love, and in its lower form it arises from the deepest and darkest Pit of Satan. Jealousy arises either from weakness, which from a sense of its own want of lovable qualities is not convinced of being sure of its cause, or from distrust, which thinks the beloved person capable of infidelity. Sometimes all these motives may act together.

6

The noblest jealousy, if the term noble is appropriate, is a sort of ambition or pride of the loving person who feels it is an insult that another one should assume it is possible to supplant his love, or it is the highest degree of devotion which sees a declaration of its object in the foreign invasion, as it were, of his own altar. Jealousy is always a sign that a little more wisdom might adorn the individual without harm.

11

The lowest species of jealousy is a sort of avarice of envy which, without being capable of love, at least wishes to possess the object of its jealousy alone by the one party assuming a sort of property right over the other. This jealousy, which might be called the Satanic, is generally to be found with old withered "husbands," who the devil has prompted to marry young women and who forthwith dream night and day of cuckold's horns. These Argus-eyed keepers are no longer capable of any feeling that could be called love, they are rather as a rule heartless house-tyrants, and are in constant dread that someone may admire or appreciate his unfortunate slave.

18

The general conclusion will be that jealousy is more the result of wrong conditions which cause uncongenial unions, and which through moral corruption artificially create distrust than a necessary accompaniment of love. Jealousy is a passion with which those are most afflicted who are the least worthy of love. An innocent maiden who enters marriage will not dream of getting jealous; but all her innocence cannot secure her against the jealousy of her husband if he has been a libertine. Those are wont to be the most jealous who have the consciousness that they themselves are most deserving of jealousy. Most men in consequence of their present education and corruption have so poor an opinion not only of the male, but even of the female sex, that they believe every woman at every moment capable of what they themselves have looked for among all and have found among the most unfortunate, the prostitutes. No libertine can believe in the purity of woman; it is contrary to nature. A libertine therefore cannot believe in the loyalty of a faithful wife.

29

There may be occasions where jealousy is justifiable. If a woman's confidence has been shaken in her husband, or a husband's confidence has been shaken in his wife by certain signs or conduct, which have no other meaning but that of infidelity, then there is just cause for jealousy. There must, however, be certain proof as evidence of the wife's or husband's immoral conduct. Imaginations or any foolish absurdities should have no consideration whatever, and let everyone have confidence until his or her faith has been shaken by the revelation of absolute facts.

36

No couple should allow their associations to develop into an engagement and marriage if either one has any inclination to jealousy. It shows invariably a want of sufficient confidence, and that want of confidence, instead of being diminished after marriage, is liable to increase, until by the aid of the imagination and wrong interpretation the home is made a hell and divorce a necessity. Let it be remembered, there can be no true love without perfect and absolute confidence, jealousy is always the sign of weakness or madness. Avoid a jealous disposition, for it is an open acknowledgment of a lack of faith.

43

1. What is the main point of the passage?

   a. Jealousy is a sign of weakness or madness
   b. Jealousy is justifiable when infidelity has occurred
   c. Jealousy is a misguided form of personal pride
   d. Jealous people believe that others are jealous as well
   e. Jealous people are incapable of honest communication

2. In Line 8, what does "*supplant*" mean?

   a. Mollify
   b. Repudiate
   c. Diminish
   d. Prove
   e. Supersede

3. In Lines 15 - 16, to whom does the author refer as "Argus-eyed keepers?

   a. People who suffer from unrequited love
   b. Old husbands who do not trust their younger wives around other men
   c. Unfaithful spouses who flaunt their extramarital affairs
   d. Unfaithful spouses who presume their spouses are also cheating
   e. Spouses who lack confidence in their romantic appeal

4. In Line 23, what does "*libertine*" mean?

   a. Withholding affection
   b. Sociopath
   c. Self-involved
   d. Morally depraved
   e. Morally superior

5. The author states all of the following about jealousy EXCEPT:

   a. Those who are most jealous are least worthy of love
   b. Those who are most jealous believe that they are also deserving of jealousy
   c. Most men who seek the company of prostitutes believe that women will also seek the same type of immoral companionship
   d. Jealous is a necessary accompaniment of love
   e. Moral corruption artificially creates distrust

6. What is the likely source of the passage?

   a. A religious sermon
   b. A newspaper article about marriage
   c. A documentary about sexually transmitted diseases
   d. A psychology textbook
   e. An argument in a college debate

Passage 2

Arbuckle Brothers are direct importers of green coffee on a large scale, and are known also as heavy buyers "on the street." The roasting capacity of their Brooklyn plant is from 8,000 to 9,000 bags per day. The cylinder equipment of twenty-four Burns roasters is supplemented by four "Jumbo" roasters of Arbuckle build, each capable of roasting thirty-five bags at one time. The Ariosa package business grew from the smallest beginnings to more than 800,000 packages per day. Although individual brands have not held their lead of late years, the volume of the package-coffee business is greater than ever. Many jobbers now pack brands of their own, besides handling the Arbuckle brands.

8

To ship more than one hundred cars of coffee and sugar in a single day calls for shipping facilities that could be had only by organizing a railroad and waterfront terminal, known as Jay Street Terminal, equipped with freight station, locomotives, tugboats, steam lighters, car floats, and barges. City deliveries of coffee and sugar call for a fleet of thirty-five large motor trucks that are housed in the firm's own garage and repaired in their own shops.

14

Within the company's Brooklyn plant, a printing shop vibrates with the whirr of epic printing presses turning out thousands of coffee-wrappers and circulars; in fact, the first three-color printing press was expressly designed and built for Arbuckle Brothers. Then, there is a sunny first-aid hospital on top of the Pearl Street warehouse where a physician is ready to relieve sudden illness and accidental injuries. On the eleventh floor there is a huge dining room where the Brooklyn clerical forces get their noonday lunches. This feeding of the inner man (and woman) is matched by the power-house where twenty-six large steam boilers must be fed their quota of coal. In the winter months, when warmth must come for the workers as well as power for the wheels, the coal consumption runs up as high as four hundred tons per day.

23

The barrel factory, with a daily capacity of 6,800 sugar barrels, is located about a mile away, where barrel staves and heads are received from the firm's own stave mill in Virginia, made from logs cut on their own timber lands in Virginia and North Carolina. A more self-contained plant would be hard to imagine. During the busy sugar season, the firm dumps from eight to ten thousand bags of raw sugar per day, and these bags are washed and dried daily as they are emptied. A huge rotary drier of the firm's own design does the work of about three miles of clothes lines.

30

Even after the coffees have been sold and paid for, there still remains an important task, and that is to redeem the signature coupons which the consumers cut from the packages and return for premiums. Lest some regard this as an insignificant phase of the business, it may be stated that in a single year the premium department has received over one hundred and eight million coupons calling for more than four million premiums, including handkerchiefs, lace curtains, shears, and Torrey razors. Finger rings are perennial favorites, and so insistent is the demand for the rings offered as premiums, that Arbuckle Brothers are regarded as the largest distributors of finger rings in the world. One of their premium rings is a wedding ring; and if all the rings of this pattern serve their intended purpose, it is estimated that the firm has assisted at more than eight hundred thousand weddings.

40

Turning from the utilities at the plant to the trades and professions represented, other than the trained sugar and coffee workers, the facility also employs various engineers, chauffeurs, teamsters, machinists, coppersmiths, carpenters, masons, painters, plumbers, riggers, typesetters and pressmen, and last but not least, the chef and table waiters. One of the most remarkable things about the growth of this business enterprise is that it is not the result of buying out, or consolidating with, competitors; but has resulted from a steady wholesome growth along conservative business lines. Consolidations are often desirable and effective; but when a great business has been built without any such consolidations, the conclusion is inevitable that somewhere in the establishment there must have been a corresponding amount of wisdom, foresight, energy, and honorable business dealing. Those were the things for which John Arbuckle stood firm, and for which he will always be remembered.

51

7. What is the main point of the passage?

    a.   To explain the economic impact of the Arbuckle Brothers facility on the city of Brooklyn
    b.   To explain why John Arbuckle became the "king of coffee"
    c.   To explain the size and scope of the Arbuckle Brothers coffee facility in Brooklyn
    d.   To explain the complexity of producing and selling a natural commodity such as coffee
    e.   To explain why Arbuckle Brothers is the largest employer in Brooklyn

8. According to the author, all of the following functions are performed at the Brooklyn facility EXCEPT:

    a.   Feeding the workers
    b.   Washing the raw coffee beans
    c.   Providing First Aid
    d.   Printing wrappers and circulars
    e.   Redeeming premium coupons

9. In Line 15, what does "epic" mean?

    a.   Illustrious
    b.   Proprietary
    c.   Antiquated
    d.   Massive
    e.   Efficient

10. In Line 25, what does "*stave*" mean?

    a. Base
    b. Lid
    c. Spigot
    d. Liner
    e. Opening

11. According to the author, what is the most popular premium?

    a. Handkerchiefs
    b. Curtains
    c. Rings
    d. Razors
    e. Shears

12. According to the author, what is John Arbuckle's legacy?

    a. He was the largest and most reliable employer in Brooklyn
    b. He grew his business steadily and honorably, without consolidating with competitors
    c. By keeping most functions in-house, he kept the price of his products low and the quality high
    d. He developed and built his own roasters, which gave him an edge in a competitive market
    e. By offering premiums, he built a level of customer loyalty that no competitor could match

Directions: The questions in this section are based on the reasoning contained in brief statements or passages. For some questions, more than one of the choices could conceivably answer the question. However, you are to choose the one that provides the most complete and accurate answer. You should not make assumptions that are implausible, superfluous, or incompatible with the passage.

13. The number of high school graduates who eventually complete a four-year college degree has steadily increased in recent decades. In 1980, the percentage of high school graduates who completed college was 35%; in 2008, the percentage had increased to 58%. These statistics prove that a college education is essential to succeed.

Which one of the following does the author assume in reaching his conclusion?

    a. Most prestigious firms recruit their employees from top universities.
    b. Job opportunities are plentiful in most fields.
    c. Success is measured primarily by financial status.
    d. College graduates are more successful than those without degrees.
    e. The highest paid professions are medicine and the law.

14. I do not trust politicians. They take money from lobbyists.

Which one of the following uses reasoning that is most similar to the above argument?

    a. Liberals support social welfare programs. They are nicer than Conservatives.
    b. I trust the government to make decisions in my best interest.
    c. Taxes are evil. They should be rescinded.
    d. Doctors receive kickbacks from drug companies. They cannot be trusted.
    e. Attorneys cannot win if they tell the truth.

15. Student: Financial management is the best career option for analytical types who like to work with numbers. Although the field is highly competitive, it provides the best opportunity to earn astronomical bonuses right out of graduate school.

Guidance Counselor: I agree that financial management provides the best opportunity to earn astronomical bonuses right out of graduate school, but it is also an unusually risky profession. In contrast, careers in accounting require similar personal and educational skills, but offer less stress, volatility, and uncertainty.

These statements reveal that the Student and Guidance Counselor disagree about whether

    a.   Smart, driven analytical types have the stomach for financial management.
    b.   Students right out of graduate school deserve astronomical bonuses.
    c.   Stable fields are boring.
    d.   It is preferable to choose a career that offers astronomical bonuses over a more secure and stable path.
    e.   It is preferable to make astronomical money as soon as possible, in order to retire early.

16. Eating a low-fat diet will improve a student's math skills, since students who consume the fewest calories tend to score best on quantitative exams.

The flawed pattern of reasoning in the argument above is most similar to that in which of the following?

    a.   Singing in nightclubs is a great way to launch a musical career, since talent scouts are known to visit these establishments on a regular basis.
    b.   Working outside your field is ill-advised, since it is hard to explain on your resume.
    c.   Applying for jobs is a tedious activity, because it requires a lot of menial tasks.
    d.   Marrying for love is ill-advised, because emotions can change over time.
    e.   Owning a dog will improve your stamina, since people who own dogs tend to be in better physical shape than those who do not.

17. Only a fool would oppose the President's economic bailout plan. No one else has offered a ray of hope to the millions of people who have lost their homes, jobs, and retirement savings. You would have to be cruel or heartless to deny them a reprieve.

In presenting his position the author does which one of the following?

    a.   Presents an illogical contradiction.
    b.   Attacks the character of his opponents.
    c.   Uses the positions of noted social commentators to support his position
    d.   Claims that his position is correct because others cannot disprove it.
    e.   Argues in a circular manner.

18. The only language classes offered on weekends are those that school administrators believe will attract enough students to be profitable. So, most Latin classes will not be offered on weekends because few people speak Latin in the community.

The conclusion above follows logically if which one of the following is assumed?

    a.   Latin is a "dead" language that is only studied by history and philosophy majors.
    b.   All classes should be profitable.
    c.   Weekend classes are reserved primarily for working adults, whose needs are more practical and goal oriented than those of traditional college students.
    d.   School administrators are more interested in earning a profit than in serving the social, educational and linguistic needs of their student body.
    e.   Foreign language classes are only popular if many people in the community speak that particular language.

19. Toyota recalled nearly one million Corollas because of faulty wiring in the headlights. Therefore, they will undoubtedly recall a similar number of Camrys for the same reason.

The flawed reasoning in the argument above most closely parallels the reasoning in which of the following?

    a.   American Airlines raised its domestic fares by 40%. Therefore, they will surely raise their international fares by a similar amount.
    b.   Obese people are far less likely to eat whole grains and fresh fruits and vegetables. Therefore, they are far more likely to be unfit.
    c.   The cost of gas is expected to rise dramatically this summer. Therefore, the cost of airfares will also rise by a similar amount.
    d.   As property values rise, so do tax revenues.
    e.   Jim landed a great job after college. Therefore, he can afford to buy a house.

20. Brides who purchase their wedding attire at David's Bridal are significantly more likely to report their shopping experience as "overwhelmingly positive" than brides who purchase their wedding attire elsewhere. However, bridesmaids who shop at David's Bridal are far more likely to be grouchy and argumentative throughout the shopping experience.

Which one of the following, if true, best resolves the apparent discrepancy in the argument above?

    a.   The prices at David's Bridal are exorbitant in most markets.
    b.   David's Bridal offers a free spa treatment to relax the prospective brides, but does not provide the bridesmaids with a similar amenity.
    c.   The selection at David's Bridal is limited.
    d.   David's Bridal offers attractive prices for brides who purchase their gowns off the rack.
    e.   Most wedding apparel is ugly and expensive.

21. All fabrics that are lacy and sheer are used for bridal gowns, so there are bridal gowns that are boring.

The conclusion of the argument follows logically if which one of the following is assumed?

    a.   Some sheer fabrics are boring, but not lacy.
    b.   All boring fabrics are lacy.
    c.   Some lacy fabrics are boring, but not sheer.
    d.   Bridal gowns should not be boring.
    e.   Some fabrics that are lacy and sheer are boring.

22. The cat is small. It must be sickly.

Which one of the following uses reasoning that is most similar to the above argument?

    a.   The hotel is enormous. It must be popular.
    b.   The defendant is guilty. He must be poor.
    c.   The candy is sweet. It must contain sugar.
    d.   The larger the dog, the better its health.
    e.   The alumni are rich. They must be successful.

23. To win a triathlon, athletes must be excellent swimmers, runners, and bicyclists. Jane cannot swim, but she is an excellent runner and bicyclist, so she would undoubtedly win a triathlon.

In presenting her position the author does which one of the following?

    a.   Makes an illogical comparison.
    b.   Confuses causation with correlation.
    c.   Relies on false assumptions.
    d.   Contradicts herself.
    e.   Argues in a circular manner.

24. Fifteen months after a hurricane, local business owners completed a survey about their participation in FEMA's national recovery program. The results for the survey were puzzling. Forty percent of the respondents reported that they had participated in the program, when the actual number that participated was 75%.

Which one of the following provides the most helpful explanation for the apparent contradiction in these survey results?

    a.   Not all participants responded to the survey.
    b.   Several respondents misread the survey.
    c.   Almost all local businesses who participated in FEMA's program responded to the survey.
    d.   A disproportionately small number of business owners who participated in FEMA's program responded to the survey.
    e.   The FEMA program had rigid requirements that only a small percentage of business owners could meet.

Directions: The following sentences test correctness and effectiveness of expression. Part of each sentence (or the entire sentence) is underlined; beneath each sentence are five ways of phrasing the underlined material. Choice A repeats the original phrasing; the other four choices are different. If you think the original phrasing produces a better sentence than the alternatives, select choice A; if not, select one of the other choices. In making your selection, follow the requirements of standard written English, such as grammar, choice of words, sentence construction, and punctuation. Your selection should result in the most effective sentence – clear and precise, without awkwardness or ambiguity.

Example: Most teenagers struggle to be free <u>both of parental domination but also from premature responsibilities.</u>

a.   both of parental domination but also from premature responsibilities.
b.   both of parental domination and also from premature responsibilities.
c.   both of parental domination and also of premature responsibilities.
d.   of parental domination and premature responsibilities.
e.   both of parental domination and their premature responsibilities as well.

The correct answer is Choice D.

25. <u>If the author would have edited her manuscript better, she might have sold it to a national women's magazine.</u>

    a.   If the author would have edited her manuscript better, she might have sold it to a national women's magazine.
    b.   If the author would have edited her manuscript better, she would have sold it to a national women's magazine.
    c.   If the author edited her manuscript better, she could have sold it to a national women's magazine.
    d.   If the author might have edited her manuscript better, would have sold it to a national women's magazine.
    e.   If the author had edited her manuscript better, she might have sold it to a national women's magazine.

26. To select the optimal profession, <u>one must be insightful enough to assess their own talents and wise enough to identify a way to market them</u> in an increasingly competitive economy.

    a.   one must be insightful enough to assess their own talents and wise enough to identify a way to market them
    b.   one must be insightful enough to assess his own talents and wise enough to identify a way to market them
    c.   he must be insightful enough to assess their own talents and market them
    d.   one must be insightful enough to assess one's own talents and wise enough to identify a way to market them
    e.   one must be insightful enough to assess his own talents and wisely market them

27. The shark presents a compelling danger to coastal areas, where tourism and ocean sports are a vital part of the economy; in these densely populated regions, their eradication is imperative.

   a. The shark presents a compelling danger to coastal areas, where tourism and ocean sports are a vital part of the economy; in these densely populated regions, their eradication is imperative.
   b. The shark presents a compelling danger to coastal areas, where tourism and ocean sports are a vital part of the economy; in these densely populated regions, its eradication is imperative.
   c. The shark presents a compelling danger to densely populated coastal areas, where tourism and ocean sports are a vital part of the economy and should be eradicated.
   d. The shark presents a compelling danger to coastal areas and should be eradicated where tourism and ocean sports are a vital part of the economy.
   e. In densely populated coastal regions, where tourism and ocean sports are a vital part of the economy, their eradication is imperative.

28. To gain support for her candidate, Diane attended the television debate, which was watched by millions of people in a political t-shirt.

   a. Diane attended the television debate, which was watched by millions of people in a political t-shirt.
   b. Diane attended the television debate, which was watched by millions of people wearing a political t-shirt.
   c. Diane, in a political t-shirt, attended the television debate, which was watched by millions of people.
   d. Diane wore her political t-shirt to the television debate, which millions of people watched.
   e. Diane attended the television debate in a political t-shirt, which millions of people watched.

29. A primary cause of side collisions is when drivers pull into intersections without checking for the presence of ongoing traffic.

   a. is when drivers pull into intersections without checking for the presence of ongoing traffic.
   b. is when drivers pull into intersections and don't check for the presence of ongoing traffic.
   c. is that drivers pull into intersections without checking for the presence of ongoing traffic.
   d. is that drivers fail to check for the presence of ongoing traffic when they are pulling into intersections.
   e. is when drivers pull into intersections and fail to check for the presence of ongoing traffic.

30. Because of an equipment malfunction, the chorus could not be heard by the occupants of rows six through twelve in the massive auditorium.

   a. Because of an equipment malfunction, the chorus could not be heard by the occupants of rows six through twelve in the massive auditorium.
   b. Because of an equipment malfunction, the occupants of rows six through twelve could not hear the chorus in the massive auditorium.
   c. Because of an equipment malfunction, the occupants of rows six through twelve in the massive auditorium could not be heard by the chorus.
   d. Because of an equipment malfunction in the massive auditorium, the chorus could not be heard by the occupants of rows six through twelve.
   e. Because of an equipment malfunction in the massive auditorium, the occupants of rows six through twelve could not hear the chorus.

31. To save money, the trend in airline service is to offer more electronic interactions and less people.

   a. To save money, the trend in airline service is to offer more electronic interactions and less people.
   b. To save money, the trend in airline service is to offer more electronic interactions and fewer people.
   c. To save money, the trend in airline service is to offer more electronic interactions and fewer interactions with people.
   d. The trend in airline service is to offer more electronic interactions and less people to save money.
   e. The trend in airline service is to offer more electronic interactions and less interactions with people who save money.

32 . Due to a scheduling conflict, several participants missed the meeting at which John tendered his resignation.

    a. Due to a scheduling conflict, several participants missed the meeting at which John tendered his resignation.
    b. Due to a scheduling conflict, several participants missed the meeting when John tendered his resignation.
    c. Due to a scheduling conflict, several participants missed the meeting where John tendered his resignation.
    d. Because of a scheduling conflict, several participants missed the meeting at which John tendered his resignation.
    e. Because of a scheduling conflict, several participants missed the meeting where John tendered his resignation.

33. Perspective buyers of the condominiums on Fourth Street were justifiably concerned about the impact of construction noise from nearby factories, which operate twenty-four hours each day.

    a. Perspective buyers of the condominiums on Fourth Street were justifiably concerned about the impact of construction noise from nearby factories, which operate twenty-four hours each day.
    b. Perspective buyers of the condominiums on Fourth Street, which were near the impact of noise from nearby factories that operate 24 hours each day, were justifiably concerned.
    c. Perspective buyers of the condominiums on Fourth Street were justifiably concerned about the twenty-four hour per day impact of construction noise from nearby factories.
    d. Prospective buyers of the condominiums on Fourth Street were justifiably concerned about the impact of construction noise from nearby factories, which operate twenty-four hours each day.
    e. Prospective buyers of the condominiums on Fourth Street were justifiably concerned twenty-four hours each day about the impact of construction noise from nearby factories.

34. Diana did what she was expected to do when she canceled the class due to insufficient enrollment.

    a. Diana did what she was expected to do when she canceled the class due to insufficient enrollment.
    b. Diana did what she expected by canceling the class due to insufficient enrollment.
    c. Due to insufficient enrollment, which she expected, Diana canceled the class.
    d. Diana did what the class expected when she cancelled it due to insufficient enrollment.
    e. Due to insufficient enrollment, Diana canceled the class and did what they expected.

35. Stephanie embarked on a weight loss program in an attempt at attracting an eligible bachelor.

    a. Stephanie embarked on a weight loss program in an attempt at attracting an eligible bachelor.
    b. Stephanie embarked on a weight loss program in an attempt to attract an eligible bachelor.
    c. In an attempt at attracting an eligible bachelor, Stephanie embarked on a weight loss program.
    d. In an attempt at attracting an eligible bachelor, Stephanie attempted to embark on a weight loss program
    e. To attract an eligible bachelor, Stephanie attempted to embark on a weight loss program.

36. David could easily have earned an Olympic medal for gymnastics, if he had trained the same long hours as his competitors.

    a. David could easily have earned an Olympic medal for gymnastics, if he had trained the same long hours as his competitors.
    b. David could earn an Olympic medal for gymnastics, if he had trained the same long hours as his competitors.
    c. David could easily have earned an Olympic medal for gymnastics, if he trained as many hours as his competitors.
    d. David might have earned an Olympic medal for gymnastics, if he trained the same long hours as his competitors.
    e. David could earn an Olympic medal for gymnastics, had he been training the same long hours as his competitors.

37. The kittens that George and Cindy purchased from a backyard breeder were more even-tempered and healthy than the local pet shop.

    a. The kittens that George and Cindy purchased from a backyard breeder were more even-tempered and healthy than the local pet shop.
    b. The kittens which George and Cindy purchased from a backyard breeder were more even-tempered and healthy than the local pet shop.
    c. The kittens that George and Cindy purchased from a backyard breeder were more even-tempered and healthy than those from the local pet shop.
    d. The kittens which George and Cindy purchased from a backyard breeder were more even-tempered and healthier than the local pet shop.
    e. The kittens that George and Cindy purchased from a backyard breeder were even-tempered and healthy, more than the local pet shop.

38. After the science fair, Mrs. Chaney praised Alison for her appearance, choice of topic and because she was organized.

    a. for her appearance, choice of topic and because she was organized.
    b. for her appearance, choice of topic and organization.
    c. for her appearance, choosing a good topic, and being organized.
    d. for looking professional, choosing a good topic and because she was organized.
    e. for her organization, appearance, and because she chose a good topic.

39. Although I understand that not all hotels can offer smoke-free rooms, I do not understand why I was assigned a room by a desk clerk that reeked of cigarette smoke.

    a. Although I understand that not all hotels can offer smoke-free rooms, I do not understand why I was assigned a room by a desk clerk that reeked of cigarette smoke.
    b. Although all hotels cannot offer smoke-free rooms, I do not understand why I was assigned a room by a desk clerk that reeked of cigarette smoke.
    c. I understand that some hotels cannot offer smoke-free rooms; however, I do not understand why a desk clerk assigned me a room that reeked of cigarette smoke.
    d. Although I understand that not all hotels can offer smoke-free rooms, I do not understand why I was assigned a room that reeked of cigarette smoke by a desk clerk.
    e. Although some hotels do not offer smoke-free rooms, I do not understand why I was assigned a room by a desk clerk that reeked of cigarette smoke.

40. Rather than tell the truth, which would place her in a bad light, the disingenuous politician hedging her bets by remaining silent.

    a. Rather than tell the truth, which would place her in a bad light, the disingenuous politician hedging her bets by remaining silent.
    b. Rather than be truthful, which would place her in a bad light, the disingenuous politician be silent.
    c. Rather than place herself in a bad light, the disingenuous politician hedging her bets by remaining silent, not truthful.
    d. Rather than tell the truth, which would place her in a bad light, the disingenuous politician hedged her bets by remaining silent.
    e. Rather than tell the truth, the disingenuous politician hedged her bets by remaining silent, which ran the risk of placing her in a bad light.

41. <u>Contrary to what many of Mary's neighbors suspected, the dog's aggressive behavior was not provoked from the taunts of the neighborhood children.</u>

    a. Contrary to what many of Mary's neighbors suspected, the dog's aggressive behavior was not provoked from the taunts of the neighborhood children.
    b. Contrary to what many neighbors suspected, Mary's dog's aggressive behavior was not provoked from the taunts of the neighborhood children.
    c. Contrary to the suspicions of Mary's neighbors, the dog's aggressive behavior was not provoked from the taunts of the neighborhood children.
    d. Contrary to Mary's neighbors, the dog's aggressive behavior was not provoked by the taunts of the neighborhood children.
    e. Contrary to what many of Mary's neighbors suspected, the dog's aggressive behavior was not provoked by the taunts of the neighborhood children.

Answer Key for Verbal Section 11

Critical Reading

1. Choice A is correct. The answer is stated directly in Line 41.

2. Choice E is correct. In context, supplant means supersede.

3. Choice B is correct. The answer is stated in Lines 14 – 17.

4. Choice D is correct. In this context, libertine means morally depraved or dissolute.

5. Choice D is correct. All of the other answer choices are presented in Lines 19 – 28.

6. Choice D is correct. The passage is an excerpt from a psychology textbook. The tone and subject matter of the passage do not match the other four answer choices.

7. Choice C is correct. The other answers are either too broad or narrow in scope.

8. Choice B is correct. All of the other answer choices are presented in the passage.

9. Choice D is correct. In context, epic means large or massive.

10. Choice A is correct. In context, the word stave means base or bottom.

11. Choice C is correct. The answer is stated in Lines 35 – 39.

12. Choice B is correct. The answer is stated directly in Lines 44 – 49.

Critical Reasoning

13. The unstated assumption the author makes is that the students who graduate from college are more successful than those who do not. Choice D is correct, because it correctly states this assumption.

14. This argument presumes that a specific type of professional cannot be trusted because they receive money from a special interest group. Choice D uses the same reasoning.

15. Choice D is correct. The disagreement is over immediate bonuses versus stability.

16. Choice E is correct. The original argument has the form "Doing A should cause B, since people who A tend to be B."

17. The author attacks the character of his opponents.   Choice B is correct.

18. Choice E is correct. Unless many people in the community speak a foreign language, school administrators do not believe that classes in that language would be popular enough to attract a significant number of students.

19. Choice A is correct. The argument presumes that a company that makes a specific decision for one product will make a similar decision for another product.

20. Choice B is correct. The argument makes sense – and the discrepancy is explained – only if the brides receive an amenity that the bridesmaids do not.

21. Choice E is correct. The argument only makes sense if we assume that some fabrics that are lacy and sheer are boring.

22. The argument assumes that the size of an animal indicates its health status. Choice D uses the same reasoning.

23. The author contradicts herself. Choice D is correct.

24. Choice D is correct because it best explains the apparent contradiction.

Sentence Correction

25. Choice E is correct. The correct phrase is *had edited*.

26. The original sentence uses inconsistent pronouns. Choice D is the best revision.

27. The original sentence includes a pronoun error, which Choice B corrects.

28. The original sentence contains a misplaced modifier. Choice D is the best correction, which also eliminates a passive verb.

29. The original sentence uses the word *when* incorrectly. The correct proposition is *that*. Choice C is correct.

30. The original sentence contains the passive voice. The best revision is Choice E.

31. The original sentence should state *fewer interactions with people*. Choice C makes the correct revision.

32. Choice D is correct. Sentences should never begin with the phrase *due to*. Use *Because* instead.

33. The original sentence includes an error in word choice (it should be *prospective buyers*, not *perspective buyers)*. Choice D is correct.

34. Choice A is correct. The sentence is correct as written.

35. In this sentence, a gerund should be used rather than an infinitive: *Stephanie embarked on a weight loss program in an attempt to attract an eligible bachelor.* Choice B is correct.

36. Choice A is correct. This sentence contains no errors.

37. The original sentence includes an illogical comparison. The correct revision is Choice C, *than those from the local pet shop.*

38. The original sentence has an error in parallelism, Choice B is correct. *After the science fair, Mrs. Chaney praised Alison for her appearance, choice of topic and organization.*

39. The original sentence contains a misplaced modifier. As a result, it is unclear whether the room or the desk clerk reeked of cigarette smoke. The sentence should be re-written to place the modifier closer to the noun that it modifies. Choice C is the best option: *I understand that some hotels cannot offer smoke-free rooms; however, I do not understand why a desk clerk assigned me a room that reeked of cigarette smoke.*

40. The original statement is not a complete sentence. The best revision is choice D.

41. The original sentence contains an idiomatic mistake. Choice E presents the correct revision (*provoked by*, rather than *provoked from).*

Directions: *The passages below are followed by questions based on their content. Answer the questions, based on what is* <u>stated</u> *or* <u>implied</u> *in the passage and any introductory material that may be provided.*

English pioneers found an instrument for colonization in companies of merchant adventurers, which had long been employed in carrying on commerce with foreign countries. Such a corporation was composed of many persons of different ranks of society--noblemen, merchants, and gentlemen--who banded together for a particular undertaking, each contributing a sum of money and sharing in the profits of the venture. It was organized under royal authority; it received its charter, its grant of land, and its trading privileges from the king and carried on its operations under his supervision and control. The charter named all the persons originally included in the corporation and gave them certain powers in the management of its affairs. When the members of the corporation remained in England, as in the case of the Virginia Company, they operated through agents sent to the colony. When they came over the seas themselves and settled in America, as in the case of Massachusetts, they became the direct government of the country they possessed. The stockholders in that instance became the voters and the governor, the chief magistrate.

12

Four of the thirteen colonies in America owed their origins to the trading corporation. It was the London Company, created by King James I in 1606, that laid during the following year the foundations of Virginia at Jamestown. It was under the auspices of their West India Company, chartered in 1621, that the Dutch planted the settlements of the New Netherland in the valley of the Hudson. The founders of Massachusetts were Puritan leaders and men of affairs whom King Charles I incorporated in 1629 under the title: "The governor and company of the Massachusetts Bay in New England." In this case, the law incorporated a group drawn together by religious ties. Far to the south, on the banks of the Delaware River, a Swedish commercial company in 1638 made the beginnings of a settlement, christened New Sweden; it was destined to pass under the rule of the Dutch, and finally as the proprietary colony of Delaware.

22

In a certain sense, Georgia may be included among the "company colonies." It was, however, originally conceived by the moving spirit, James Oglethorpe, as an asylum for poor men, especially those imprisoned for debt. To realize this humane purpose, he secured from King George II, in 1732, a royal charter uniting several gentlemen, including himself, into "one body politic and corporate," known as the "Trustees for establishing the colony of Georgia in America." In the structure of their organization and their methods of government, the trustees did not differ materially from the regular companies created for trade and colonization. Though their purposes were benevolent, their transactions had to be under the forms of law and according to the rules of business.

31

A second agency which figured largely in the settlement of America was the religious brotherhood, or congregation, of men and women brought together in the bonds of a common religious faith. The Mayflower Compact, so famous in American history, was a written and signed agreement, incorporating the spirit of obedience to the common good, which served as a guide to self-government in Plymouth until it was annexed to Massachusetts in 1691. Three other colonies, all of which retained their identity until the eve of the American Revolution, likewise sprang directly from the congregations of the faithful: Rhode Island, Connecticut, and New Hampshire They were founded by small bodies of men and women, "united in solemn covenants with the Lord," who planted their settlements in the wilderness. These pioneers agreed that "the Scriptures do hold forth a perfect rule for the direction and government of all men."

41

The third colonial agency was the proprietor, who was granted property by the king in North America to have, hold, use, and enjoy for his own benefit and profit, with the right to hand the estate down to his heirs in perpetual succession. The proprietor was a rich and powerful person, prepared to furnish or secure the capital, collect the ships, supply the stores, and assemble the settlers necessary to found and sustain a plantation beyond the seas. Sometimes the proprietor worked alone. Sometimes two or more were associated like partners in the common undertaking.

48

Five colonies, Maryland, Pennsylvania, New Jersey, and the Carolinas, owe their formal origins, though not always their first settlements, nor in most cases their prosperity, to the proprietary system. Maryland, established in 1634 under a Catholic nobleman, Lord Baltimore, and blessed with religious toleration by the act of 1649, flourished under the mild rule of proprietors until it became a state in the American union. New Jersey, beginning its career under two proprietors, Berkeley and Carteret, in 1664, passed under the direct government of the crown in 1702. Pennsylvania was, in a very large measure, the product of the generous spirit and tireless labors of its first proprietor, the leader of the Friends, William Penn, to whom it was granted in 1681 and in whose family it remained until 1776. The two Carolinas were first organized as one colony in 1663 under the government and patronage of eight proprietors, including Lord Clarendon; but after more than half a century both became royal provinces governed by the king.

60

1. What is the main point of the passage?

   a. To document the role of the King of England in the development of the thirteen colonies
   b. To explain the role of religion in the thirteen colonies
   c. To discuss the three different ways that the original thirteen colonies were established
   d. To explain the role of trading companies in colonial times
   e. To document the superiority of the proprietary system in establishing the thirteen colonies

2. In Line 1, what does "*instrument*" mean?

   a. Justification
   b. Mechanism
   c. Exception
   d. Escape
   e. Obligation

3. According to the passage, all of the following are true about charters EXCEPT:

   a. The members included nobleman, merchants, and gentleman
   b. The charter, land, and trading privileges all came from the king
   c. The king supervised and controlled all operations of the venture
   d. All profits were retained by the king
   e. The charter defined the specific powers of each member

4. According to the passage, what is the primary difference between the corporations in Virginia and Massachusetts?

   a. The members of the Massachusetts corporation were Pilgrims, while the members of the Virginia corporation were primarily merchants and noblemen
   b. The members of the Virginia corporation remained in England, while the members of the Massachusetts corporation actually settled in the colony
   c. The members of the Virginia corporation had no religious affiliation, while the members of the Massachusetts corporation were Christian
   d. The members of the Massachusetts corporation remained in England, but hired the chief magistrate to govern the colony
   e. The corporations were similar in organization and structure, but very different in size

5. Which of the following American colonies owed their origins to the trading corporation?

   a. Massachusetts, Virginia, New Hampshire, Rhode Island
   b. Virginia, Delaware, Maryland, Pennsylvania
   c. Connecticut, Virginia, New Jersey, Rhode Island
   d. Virginia, Massachusetts, Delaware, Rhode Island
   e. Virginia, Massachusetts, Delaware, Georgia

6. Which colony was once christened New Sweden?

   a. Virginia
   b. Massachusetts
   c. Delaware
   d. Georgia
   e. New England

7. Which ruler was associated with the work of James Oglethorpe?

    a. King James I
    b. King Charles I
    c. King George I
    d. Lord Clarendon
    e. King George II

8. All of the following are true about the settlement of Georgia EXCEPT:

    a. It was conceived by a moving spirit
    b. It was conceived as an asylum for poor men
    c. Its charter was issued by King Charles II in 1732
    d. It is considered a company colony
    e. The purposes of its organization were benevolent

9. Which of the following colonies were settled by the religious brotherhood?

    a. Massachusetts
    b. Massachusetts, Rhode Island, Connecticut, and New Hampshire
    c. Rhode Island, Connecticut, and New Hampshire
    d. Massachusetts, Rhode Island, Connecticut, and New Hampshire
    e. None

10. In Line 39, what does "*covenants*" mean?

    a. Scriptures
    b. Subservience
    c. Agreement
    d. Aristocracy
    e. Obligation

11. All of the following are true about proprietors EXCEPT:

    a. They were the first settlers of five of the first thirteen colonies
    b. The king granted them the right to use property in America for their own benefit
    c. They could leave their property in America to their own heirs
    d. They were required to secure the capital, collect the ships, supply the stores, and assemble the settlers onto their plantations
    e. They included Berkeley, Carteret, Lord Clarendon and William Penn

12. Which of the following colonies were affiliated with proprietors?

    a. Maryland, Pennsylvania, Virginia, New York, and the Carolinas
    b. New Jersey, Georgia, Virginia, Delaware and the Carolinas
    c. Maryland, Pennsylvania, Virginia, North Carolina, and South Carolina
    d. Pennsylvania, New Jersey, Virginia, North Carolina, and South Carolina
    e. New Jersey, Maryland, Pennsylvania, North Carolina, and South Carolina

Directions: *The questions in this section are based on the reasoning contained in brief statements or passages. For some questions, more than one of the choices could conceivably answer the question. However, you are to choose the one that provides the most complete and accurate answer. You should not make assumptions that are implausible, superfluous, or incompatible with the passage.*

13. Samantha must be pregnant. Only a pregnant woman would eat pickles with ice cream.

The argument relies on what unstated assumption?

    a. Samantha is married.
    b. Samantha likes pickles and ice cream.
    c. Samantha ate pickles with ice cream.
    d. Few people enjoy pickles with ice cream.
    e. Samantha is overweight.

14. All trees have leaves. Shrubs do not have leaves. Therefore shrubs cannot be trees.

Which of the following choices uses a similar type of reasoning?

    a. All drugs have side effects. Pain is a side effect. Therefore, drugs cause pain.
    b. All fans have blades. Lamps do not have blades. Therefore, lamps cannot be fans.
    c. Every lion has claws. Animal X has claws. Therefore, Animal X cannot be a lion.
    d. All requirements have deadlines. Honesty is not a requirement. Therefore, truth has no deadline.
    e. All leopards have spots. Zebras have fewer spots. Therefore, leopards cannot be zebras.

15. The leanness of Russian supermodels suggests that the dietary habits of people in Soviet countries are not as healthy and robust as reported by nutritionists.

The reasoning in the argument is vulnerable to criticism on what grounds?

    a. It does not consider the dietary habits of people in other parts of Europe.
    b. It ignores the economic conditions in Russia, which influence people's dietary habits.
    c. It does not define which countries are "Soviet"
    d. It relies on the advice of self-appointed experts.
    e. It generalizes from a small sample that is not representative of the whole.

16. Hurricanes in Louisiana are often preceded by tropical depressions off the coast of Africa. Therefore, tropical storm conditions in Africa are valid predictors of the onset of subsequent storms on the Louisiana coast.

Which selection contains the same type of flaw?

    a. Students who participate in sports in high school often become attorneys. Therefore, participating in high school sports is a good predictor of whether someone will enroll in law school.
    b. Snowboarders tend to have large biceps. Therefore, snowboarders typically have large hands.
    c. Runners tend to run slower when they wear leather shoes than when they wear vinyl shoes. Therefore, runners win more races when they wear vinyl shoes.
    d. Music videos can impact the fashion choices of high school girls. Therefore, if a pop star wears revealing clothes in a music video, then high school girls will also start wearing revealing clothes.
    e. During the hottest part of the day, mice do not play. Therefore, mice must play before dawn.

17. Joining the glee club will improve your artistic skills, since students who belong to the glee club tend to be more artistic than those who do not.

The flawed pattern of reasoning in the argument above is most similar to that in which of the following?

    a.   Flying in bad weather is downright scary, since the pilots are rarely prepared to make emergency landings.

    b.   Reading Shakespeare's work will improve your understanding of history, because it captured the social mores of the time better than the work of any other author.

    c.   Visiting the doctor for an annual physical will improve your health, since the doctor can detect abnormalities faster than you could find them at home.

    d.   Wearing cowboy boots will improve your romantic prospects, since men who wear cowboy hats tend to attract more women than men who do not.

    e.   Playing a musical instrument will make you more attractive, since teenage girls tend to idolize rock stars.

18. According to meteorologists, the East Coast is struck by a Category 5 hurricane, which is enough to cause total annihilation of all physical structures, on an average of once every three hundred years. The last such incident occurred in 1992, when Hurricane Andrew decimated several South Florida communities. Hence, we can reasonably expect that the East Coast will not be struck by another Category 5 hurricane until 2292, when preventive measures will be markedly different than what we have now. This clearly negates any need for coastal communities to develop disaster plans for Category 5 hurricanes in the near future.

The reasoning in the argument is most subject to criticism on what grounds?

    a.   It fails to consider the human implications of failure.

    b.   It uses evidence about the average frequency of an event to make a specific prediction about when the next such event will occur.

    c.   It does not consider the usefulness of disaster plans for other types of emergencies.

    d.   It does not consider the frequency of Category 5 hurricanes in other parts of the United States.

    e.   It fails to consider alternative statistical explanations.

19. Designers predict that as women mature, their taste in home furnishings will become more conservative, which will inspire them to trade in their casual and contemporary decor for more traditional and ornate styles. Thus, these designers conclude, there will be increased demand for formal accessories, such as punch bowls, chandeliers, and crystal, which had previously fallen into disfavor. Although these designers would benefit financially if this prediction came true, I believe that they will be sorely disappointed. As women age, they are less resistant to change and more likely to stick with what is comfortable and familiar to them. As a result, they would be highly unlikely to embrace a total change in home décor.

The argument does which of the following?

    a.   Discredits the argument of the designers by manipulating the use of statistics.

    b.   Agrees with the conclusion of the designers, but suggests that they are overly optimistic.

    c.   Attempts to undermine the argument of the designers by drawing an alternative conclusion from their premises.

    d.   Attempts to undermine the argument of the designers by using circular reasoning.

    e.   Attempts to discredit the underlying premise of the designers' argument.

20.   Samantha must be Gemini. She is not moody.

The argument relies on what unstated assumption?

    a.   Samantha believes in astrology.

    b.   Samantha is a twin.

    c.   Twins are not moody.

    d.   Geminis are not moody.

    e.   Geminis are moody.

21. The number of murder convictions has dramatically decreased in recent years. In 1999, three thousand defendants were convicted of first degree murder in U.S. courthouses. In 2009, however, there were only two thousand murder convictions. These statistics prove that law enforcement agencies failed to convict a significant number of murderers between 1999 and 2009.

Which one of the following does the author assume in reaching his conclusion?

    a. The decrease in the number of convictions was not due to a reduction in the number of murders.
    b. Law enforcement agencies had insufficient resources to bring most murder cases to trial.
    c. The murder rate is higher in the U.S. than it other countries.
    d. In states that allow the death penalty, it is rarely imposed.
    e. Many juries convict murder defendants of lesser charges, such as manslaughter.

22. Athletes are famous, but not terribly wise, because fame cannot buy wisdom.

Which of the following uses a similar pattern of reasoning as the argument above?

    a. Models are thin but not always fit, because thinness cannot create fitness.
    b. Dogs are feisty, but hard to control, because they are not particularly intelligent.
    c. Sequins add beauty to any outfit, except for pajamas, which require less flamboyant fabrics.
    d. Television is boring and not entertaining because passivity is lame and unhealthy.
    e. To see is to know, but to hear is divine, because the ears are far more perceptive.

23. Jonathan plays the lead in a Broadway musical. Therefore, Jonathan must be a Julliard graduate.

Which one of the following, if added to the passage, will make the conclusion logical?

    a. Julliard has the best theatrical program.
    b. Jonathan's brother graduated from Julliard.
    c. All leads must be Julliard graduates.
    d. All Broadway actors are leads.
    e. Jonathan attended Julliard.

24. In a recent study, researchers divided a room full of teachers into two groups and videotaped their subsequent lectures. Before they began, the first group of teachers was told that their performance would be used strictly to evaluate the quality of the textbook they were using. In contrast, the second group of teachers was told that the researchers would actually be evaluating their skills as educators. Without exception, the first group of teachers performed significantly better in all areas of evaluation than the second group of teachers.

This situation supports which one of the following propositions?

    a. Subjects perform better when they know they are being observed.
    b. Subjects perform better if they are evaluated independently, rather than as part of a group.
    c. Teaching is a complex task that cannot be evaluated in an objective manner.
    d. Subjects perform better when they do not know that their skills are being evaluated.
    e. Subjects performed poorly when they are misled about the evaluation criteria.

Directions: The following sentences test correctness and effectiveness of expression. Part of each sentence (or the entire sentence) is underlined; beneath each sentence are five ways of phrasing the underlined material. Choice A repeats the original phrasing; the other four choices are different. If you think the original phrasing produces a better sentence than the alternatives, select choice A; if not, select one of the other choices. In making your selection, follow the requirements of standard written English, such as grammar, choice of words, sentence construction, and punctuation. Your selection should result in the most effective sentence – clear and precise, without awkwardness or ambiguity.

Example: Most teenagers struggle to be free <u>both of parental domination but also from premature responsibilities.</u>

a. both of parental domination but also from premature responsibilities.
b. both of parental domination and also from premature responsibilities.
c. both of parental domination and also of premature responsibilities.
d. of parental domination and premature responsibilities.
e. both of parental domination and their premature responsibilities as well.

The correct answer is Choice D.

25. <u>In nursing school, Diane studied the proper way to dress a wound, the way to minimize bacterial infections and relieving pain through the use of pharmaceuticals.</u>

a. In nursing school, Diane studied the proper way to dress a wound, the way to minimize bacterial infections and relieving pain through the use of pharmaceuticals.
b. In nursing school, Diane studied the proper way to dress a wound, minimize bacterial infections and relieving pain through the use of pharmaceuticals.
c. In nursing school, Diane studied the proper way to dress a wound, minimize bacterial infections and using pharmaceuticals.
d. In nursing school, Diane studied the proper way to dress a wound, the way to minimize bacterial infections and the way to relieving pain through the use of pharmaceuticals.
e. In nursing school, Diane studied the proper way to dress a wound, minimize bacterial infections and relieve pain through the use of pharmaceuticals.

26. <u>By practicing every weekend, including nights when several parties were held, her performance improved dramatically.</u>

a. By practicing every weekend, including nights when several parties were held, her performance improved dramatically.
b. By practicing every weekend, including nights when several parties were held, she improved her performance dramatically.
c. By practicing every weekend, including several party nights, her performance improved dramatically.
d. By practicing every weekend, her performance improved dramatically, including nights when several parties were held.
e. By practicing on nights and weekends when several parties were held, her performance improved dramatically.

27. <u>Clinical psychologists investigating the disturbing increase in murder rates among pregnant women have documented the sad reality that many expectant fathers are more than capable to killing their wives and unborn children.</u>

a. Clinical psychologists investigating the disturbing increase in murder rates among pregnant women have documented the sad reality that many expectant fathers are more than capable to killing their wives and unborn children.
b. Clinical psychologists investigating the disturbing increase in murder rates amongst pregnant women have documented the sad reality that many expectant fathers are more than capable to kill their wives and unborn children
c. Clinical psychologists investigating the disturbing increase in murder rates among pregnant women have documented the sad reality that many expectant fathers are more than capable of killing their wives and unborn children
d. Clinical psychologists who investigate the disturbing increase in murder rates among pregnant women have documented the sad reality that many expectant fathers are more than capable to killing their wives and unborn children
e. Clinical psychologists investigating the disturbing increase in murder rates among pregnant women have documented the sad reality that many expectant fathers frequently killing their wives and unborn children

28. Because of an unexpected budget cut, the grocery chain will hire less employees in 2009.

    a.   Because of an unexpected budget cut, the grocery chain will hire less employees in 2009.
    b.   Because of an unexpected budget cut, the grocery chain will hire fewer employees in 2009.
    c.   Thanks to an unexpected budget cut, the grocery chain will hire less employees in 2009.
    d.   In 2009, because of an unexpected budget cut, the grocery chain will hire less employees.
    e.   The grocery chain, thanks to an unexpected budget cut in 2009, will hire less employees.

29. When they least expected, a drug was found to mitigate the spread of cancer.

    a.   When they least expected, a drug was found to mitigate the spread of cancer.
    b.   A drug, which was found to mitigate the spread of cancer, was found when they least expected.
    c.   To everyone's surprise, the spread of cancer was mitigated by a drug.
    d.   When they least expected, scientists found a drug to mitigate the spread of cancer.
    e.   When no one expected, a drug was found to mitigate the spread of cancer.

30. Despite the influx of Federal money into urban schools, there are many inner city students who do not receive a good education.

    a.   Despite the influx of Federal money into urban schools, there are many inner city students who do not receive a good education.
    b.   Despite the influx of Federal money into urban schools, there are many inner city students that do not receive a good education.
    c.   Despite the influx of Federal money into urban schools, there is many inner city students who do not receive a good education.
    d.   Despite the influx of Federal money into urban schools, many inner city students do not receive a good education.
    e.   There are many inner city students who do not receive a good education despite the influx of Federal money into urban schools.

31. In rural Brazil, most designer shoes are made by unskilled workers, few of which could ever hope to purchase a pair for their own use.

    a.   few of which could ever hope to purchase a pair for their own use.
    b.   few of whom could ever hope to purchase a pair for their own use.
    c.   few of which could purchase a pair for their own use.
    d.   few of which could ever hope to purchase a pair for his own use.
    e.   few of whom could ever hope to purchase a pair for his own use.

32. Even if they are extremely clever, most escaped criminals cannot allude the law for an extended period of time.

    a.   Even if they are extremely clever, most escaped criminals cannot allude the law for an extended period of time.
    b.   Unless they are extremely clever, most escaped criminals cannot allude the law for an extended period of time.
    c.   Unless they are extremely clever, most escaped criminals cannot allude the law for long.
    d.   Unless you are extremely clever, most escaped criminals cannot elude the law for an extended period of time.
    e.   Even if they are extremely clever, most escaped criminals cannot elude the law for an extended period of time.

33. <u>After several years of circuit weight training, Jason's stamina and muscle tone are like those of a seasoned athlete</u>.

    a. After several years of circuit weight training, Jason's stamina and muscle tone are like those of a seasoned athlete.
    b. After several years of circuit weight training, Jason's stamina and muscle tone are like a seasoned athlete.
    c. After several years of circuit weight training, Jason's stamina and muscle tone is like those of a seasoned athlete.
    d. After several years of circuit weight training, Jason's stamina and muscle tone is like a seasoned athlete.
    e. After several years of circuit weight training, Jason is as muscular as a seasoned athlete.

34. In a national interview, the actress <u>stated that she had had a great admiration for the work of Katharine Hepburn, who she considered an icon</u>.

    a. stated that she had had a great admiration for the work of Katharine Hepburn, who she considered an icon.
    b. stated that she had had a great admiration for the work of Katharine Hepburn, whom she considered an icon.
    c. stated that she had a great admiration for the work of Katharine Hepburn, who she considered an icon.
    d. stated that she used to have a great admiration for the work of Katharine Hepburn, whom she considered an icon.
    e. stated that she admired Katharine Hepburn, who she considered an icon.

35. <u>The President, as well as the Senate and House, is trying to affect positive changes in education, health care and international policy.</u>

    a. The President, as well as the Senate and House, is trying to affect positive changes in education, health care and international policy.
    b. The President, as well as the Senate and House, is trying to effect positive changes in education, health care and international policy.
    c. The President, along with the Senate and House, are trying to affect positive changes in education, health care and international policy.
    d. The President, Senate and House are trying to affect positive changes in education, health care and international policy.
    e. The President, with support from the Senate and House, are trying to effect positive changes in education, health care and international policy.

36. On opening night, the cast members gave a terrific performance, <u>although there wasn't hardly anyone in the audience.</u>

    a. although there wasn't hardly anyone in the audience.
    b. although there was anyone in the audience.
    c. although there was hardly no one in the audience.
    d. although there was hardly anyone in the audience.
    e. although there wasn't hardly no one in the audience.

37. <u>If Grace would have lain her purse on the table, it might not have been stolen in the robbery.</u>

    a. If Grace would have lain her purse on the table, it might not have been stolen in the robbery.
    b. If Grace would have laid her purse on the table, it might not have been stolen in the robbery.
    c. If Grace would have lain her purse on the table, it would not have been stolen in the robbery.
    d. If Grace had lay purse on the table, it would not have been stolen in the robbery.
    e. If Grace had laid her purse on the table, it might not have been stolen in the robbery.

38. If any soldier from the Civil War was to observe our computerized weapons, he would be amazed by such cutting-edge technology.

    a.   If any soldier from the Civil War was to observe our computerized weapons, he would be amazed by such cutting-edge technology.

    b.   If any soldier from the Civil War was to observe our computerized weapons, he would have been amazed by such cutting-edge technology.

    c.   Any soldier from the Civil War who was to observe our computerized weapons would be amazed by such cutting-edge technology.

    d.   If any soldier from the Civil War were to observe our computerized weapons, he would be amazed by such cutting-edge technology.

    e.   Were any soldier from the Civil War to observe our computerized weapons, they would be amazed by such cutting-edge technology.

39. The new bridal boutique on Seventh Avenue employs the most unique premise: renting, rather than selling, different forms of designer bridal attire.

    a.   The new bridal boutique on Seventh Avenue employs the most unique premise: renting, rather than selling, different forms of designer bridal attire.

    b.   The new boutique on Seventh Avenue rents different forms of bridal attire rather than selling it, which we think is the most unique premise.

    c.   The new bridal boutique on Seventh Avenue rents designer bridal attire, rather than selling it, which is the most unique premise.

    d.   The new bridal boutique on Seventh Avenue uses the most unique premise: renting, rather than selling, different forms of designer bridal attire.

    e.   The new bridal boutique on Seventh Avenue employs a unique premise: renting, rather than selling, different forms of designer bridal attire.

40. The licensing requirements for physicians include a test of the candidate's didactic learning, clinical skills and research proficiency.

    a.   include a test of the candidate's didactic learning, clinical skills and research proficiency.

    b.   includes a test of the candidate's didactic learning, clinical skills and research proficiency.

    c.   test the candidate's learning, clinical, and research proficiency.

    d.   are didactic, clinical, and research.

    e.   measures your proficiency in the classroom, clinic, and research lab.

41. When she packed for the trip, Diane did not realize that the rainfall in Madrid would be just like Sydney that time of year.

    a.   would be just like Sydney

    b.   would be identical to Sydney

    c.   might be similar to Sydney

    d.   would be the same as Sydney

    e.   would be similar to that in Sydney

Answer Key for Verbal Section 12

Critical Reading

1. Choice C is correct. The others are too broad or narrow in scope.

2. Choice B is correct. In context, instrument means mechanism.

3. Choice D is correct. All of the other answer choices are presented in the first paragraph of the passage.

4. Choice B is correct. The answer is presented in Lines 8 – 11.

5. Choice E is correct. The answer is presented in Lines 13 - 23.

6. Choice C is correct. The answer is presented in Lines 20 – 21.

7. Choice E is correct. The answer is presented in Line 25.

8. Choice C is correct. All of the other answer choices are presented in Lines 23 – 29.

9. Choice B is correct. The answer is given in Lines 33 – 38.

10. Choice C is correct. In context, covenant means agreement.

11. Choice A is correct. All of the other answer choices are presented in Lines 42 – 59.

12. Choice E is correct. The answer is presented in Line 49.

Critical Reasoning

13. The unstated assumption is that Samantha did, indeed, eat pickles with ice cream. Choice C is correct.

14. The argument in the question stem can be symbolized as follows: "All X have Y. Z does not have Y. Therefore, Z cannot be an X."   Of the five possibilities, Choice B is the best answer. The other four answers all deviate slightly from the original argument.

15. Choice E is correct. It generalizes from a sample that is likely to be unrepresentative.

16. Choice A is correct, as it uses the same false correlation. Other weather conditions could lead to the heavy storms and hurricane in Louisiana. Likewise, attorneys are inspired to attend law school for reasons other than their athletic experiences in high school.

17. Choice D is correct. The original argument has the form "Doing A should cause B, since people who A tend to be B. "

18. Choice B is correct. "Average frequency" data cannot be used to predict the likelihood of a specific event happening in the future.

19. Choice E is correct. The argument disagrees with the underlying premise that women will change their décor as they age.

20. The argument presumes that Geminis are not moody. Choice D is correct.

21. The argument tells us that the number of murder convictions decreased between 1999 and 2009. As evidence, the author presents actual numbers to support his conclusion. The unstated assumption that the author makes is that the reduction in the number of convictions was *not* due to a reduction in the number of murders - it was strictly because law enforcement agencies failed to build a successful case against the guilty parties. Choice A is correct, because it correctly states the assumption that the author makes in this passage.

22. Choice A is correct. Both arguments are in the form "A are B but not C because B cannot create C."

23. In this argument, the the assumption is that all leads must be Julliard graduates, which is Choice C.

24. Choice D is correct. The teachers who thought their skills were being evaluated (rather than the textbook) did not perform as well as the teachers who did not believe their skills were being evaluated.

Sentence Correction

25. The original sentence includes an error in parallelism. Choice E is correct, which reads *how to relieve pain*.

26. In this sentence, the phrase *by practicing every weekend*, modifies the wrong noun (the student is practicing, not her performance). Choice B offers the best revision: *By practicing every weekend, including*

nights when several parties were held, she improved her performance dramatically.

27. The original sentence contains an idiomatic mistake. The correct phrase is *capable of killing*, which is presented in Choice C.

28. Choice B is correct. The correct word is *fewer*.

29. The original sentence contains a passive verb. The best correction is Choice D, *When they least expected, scientists found a drug to mitigate the spread of cancer.*

30. The subject of the sentence is *inner city students*, not *there*. the correct revision is Choice D, *Despite the influx of Federal money into education, many inner city students do not receive a good education.*

31. The original sentence contains an error in pronoun usage. The correct revision is Choice B, *few of whom*.

32. Choice E is correct. The correct verb is *elude*, rather than *allude*.

33. The original sentence contains no errors. Choice A is correct.

34. The original sentence contains an error in verb expression. There are several possible corrections, depending on whether or not the actress still admires Katharine Hepburn. If her admiration is current, the clause should read, *that she had.* If it is strictly in the past, then the clause should read *that she used to have.* Choice C is correct, because it makes this correction without introducing another error into the sentence.

35. The original sentence contains the wrong verb. Choice B offers the best revision (*to effect*, not *to affect*).

36. The original sentence includes a double negative. Choice D offers the best revision.

37. The original sentence uses the wrong verb (lie vs. lay) and has conjugated it incorrectly. The correct revision is Choice E: *If Grace had laid her pursue on the table, it might not have been stolen in the robbery.*

38. The original sentence employs a contrary-to-fact conditional statement that begins with the word "if." Hence, it requires the past subjunctive form of the verb, "were to observe." Choice D is correct.

39. This is about as subtle as sentence correction questions get on the GMAT. The original sentence makes an error in comparison. The word *unique* implies one of a kind. Hence, there is no need to add the word *most*. Choice E is correct.

40. Choice A is correct. The sentence is correct as written.

41. The original sentence makes a faulty comparison. Choice E is correct. - *would be similar to that in.*

Quantitative Section 1: 37 questions   75 minutes

Use the following answer choices for questions 1 – 8 below:

A.   Statement 1 alone is sufficient but Statement 2 alone is not sufficient to answer the question asked.
B.   Statement 2 alone is sufficient but Statement 1 alone is not sufficient to answer the question asked.
C.   Statements 1 and 2 together are sufficient to answer the question but neither statement is sufficient alone.
D.   Each statement alone is sufficient to answer the question.
E.   Statements 1 and 2 are not sufficient to answer the question asked and additional data is needed to answer the question.

1. A restaurant received 112 cans of Coca-Cola for their busy lunch shift. How many cans were remaining at the end of the shift?

(1) Waitress A served 18 cans of Coca-Cola and Waitress B served 11 cans.
(2) Each member of the cooking staff consumed two cans each.

2. Greg will split his winning lottery prize evenly with his brothers, after 30% is deducted in taxes.   How much will each man receive?

(1) Greg has three brothers.
(2) Greg's winning ticket was worth $1,000.

3. What is the sum of the prime numbers between x and y?

(1) y = 30
(2) x = y/3

4. Jenny's monthly budget includes $600 for rent, $300 for her car payment, $100 for insurance, $300 for utilities, and $300 for groceries. How much does she have left for discretionary spending?

(1) Jenny's monthly take-home pay is $3,000.
(2) Jenny pays 20% of her gross income in taxes.

5. What is the area of the square?

(1) The side length is 13
(2) The perimeter is 52

6. What is the value of R?

(1)   R is an integer greater than 29 but less than 33.
(2)   R/6 is an integer

7. What is the square root of (M + N)?

(1) M - N = 3
(2) M and N are different prime integers between 20 and 24.

8. Is X > 19?

(1) X > 2Y
(2) Y < 3^3

9. If x = 10, what is the value of $x^2 + 1/x^2$?

    a. 100.001
    b. 100.010
    c. 100.100
    d. 101.010
    e. 110.010

10. If F = {1, 2, 4, 5, 8}, G = {4, 5, 6, 9,}, and H = {2, 6, 7, 10}, what is (F ∪ G) ∩ H?

    a. {2}
    b. {2, 6}
    c. {2, 4, 5}
    d. {2, 5}
    e. {9, 10}

11. Leslie added Y dolls to her large collection, which gave her a total of Z dolls. Then, Leslie sold Y – 96 of her dolls to a local collector. How many dolls did Leslie have left?

    a. Y - Z + 96
    b. Z + Y - 96
    c. Z - Y + 96
    d. Z - Y - 96
    e. (Y + Z – 96)/2

12. How much greater than 10 – 8y is 5y - 3?

    a. 3y - 11
    b. 13y - 5
    c. 13y - 13
    d. -3y - 11
    e. 13y + 11

13. The Boston Philharmonic invited the top five student violinists to perform on their national tour. Only the top three would be offered a chance to play solos. How many possible ways are there to order the top three finalists?

    a. 3
    b. 9
    c. 15
    d. 27
    e. 60

14. How many positive integers less than 50 are evenly divisible by 3, 6 and 9?

    a. 1
    b. 2
    c. 3
    d. 4
    e. 5

15. A chef must blend a type of oregano that costs $25 per pound with one that costs $10 per pound to make 2000 pounds that cost $20 per pound. How many pounds of the $25 oregano can the chef use?

      a.   668
      b.   998
      c.   1002
      d.   1332
      e.   1667

16. The sides of a hexagonal shaped lot are 24.5 ft, 12.0 ft, 9.75 ft, 11.9 ft, 34.0 ft and 21.6 ft. If the cost of chain link fencing is $36.00 per linear yard, how much will it cost the owner of the lot to buy a fence to secure the entire lot?

      a. $1,222
      b. $1,365
      c. $1,643
      d. $4,086
      e. $4,104

17. $(1/36)(44 + 22)^2 =$

      a.   0.02776
      b.   0.1666
      c.   1.8333
      d.   120
      e.   121

18. If x + 7 is an even integer, the sum of the next three even integers is:

      a.   3x + 4
      b.   3(x +7)
      c.   3x + 28
      d.   3x + 33
      e. $(x + 7)^3$

19. If 4x + 9y = 55 and 2x + 7y = 11, what is the value of (x+y)/2?

      a.   4
      b.   7
      c.   9
      d.   11
      e.   22

20. Which of the following sets of numbers *cannot* represent the lengths of the sides of a right triangle?

      a.   10, 24, 26
      b.   3.7, 11.9, 12.5
      c.   9, 26, 31
      d.   4, 15, 15.5
      e.   15, 36, 39

21. If a square of side 9 and a circle of radius r have equal areas, what is the value of the radius, r (use π = 3.1416)?

    a. 5
    b. 6
    c. 9
    d. 12
    e. 18

22. The perimeter of a rectangle is 25x. If one side has a length of x/4, what is the area of the rectangle?

    a. $125x^2/16$
    b. $5x^2/2$
    c. 100x
    d. $100x^2$
    e. $49x^2/8$

23. A line segment has endpoints of (6, 14) and (8, 21), What are the coordinates of its midpoint?

    a. (7, 17)
    b. (7, 17.5)
    c. (6, 17)
    d. (6, 17.5)
    e. (17, 7)

24. What is the largest integer that will divide evenly into 63 and 117?

    a. 1
    b. 7
    c. 9
    d. 11
    e. 13

25. What is the product of (3/8)(4/5)(9/3)?

    a. 106/120
    b. 54/64
    c. 108/122
    d. 9/10
    e. 54/56

26. Two individual price reductions of 10% and 15% are equal to a single price reduction of:

    a. 12.5%
    b. 20%
    c. 24.5%
    d. 25%
    e. 27.5%

27. Sara is completely broke when she receives a $74 parking ticket. When Sara's brother gives her $125 for her birthday, she pays the ticket and buys $26 in gas. How much money does Sara have left?

     a. $25
     b. $26
     c. $51
     d. $99
     e. $101

28. How many positive integers less than 75 are evenly divisible by 3, 5 and 6?

     a. 1
     b. 2
     c. 3
     d. 4
     e. 5

29. Gina decides to save money by making her bridal outfit from scratch. She buys 5 yards of a beautiful silk fabric that costs $35 per yard. After studying her pattern, Gina concludes that she will need 6/4 yards of the fabric for her dress, 5/2 yards for her jacket, and 1/3 yard for her veil. How many yards of material will Gina have left over?

     a. 2/5
     b. 1/2
     c. 2/3
     d. 1
     e. 5/2

30. A buffet table contains 7 entrees, 3 soups and 2 specialty salads. The remaining ¼ of the items are desserts. What percent of the items on the buffet table are specialty salads?

     a. 3.125%
     b. 6.25%
     c. 12.5%
     d. 16.67%
     e. 20%

31. If it takes a robot thirty-six minutes to travel the 18 blocks between the police station and the fire house, how long will it take the same robot (in minutes), traveling at the same rate per block, to travel from the police station to the train station that is 64 blocks away?

     a. 10
     b. 32
     c. 128
     d. 648
     e. 2304

32. For three consecutive integers, three times the sum of the first and second is 27 more than twice the third. What is the smallest of these three integers?

     a. 6
     b. 7
     c. 8
     d. 9
     e. 11

33. Nathan is seven years older than his sister Claire, who is three years younger than Jayne, who is 28 years old. How old is Nathan?

     a. 22
     b. 25
     c. 28
     d. 29
     e. 32

34. The Big Red Boat and the Carnival Cruise Ship left Port Canaveral at the same time and sailed in opposite directions. If the Big Red Boat traveled 35 miles per hour slower than the Carnival Cruise Ship, and they were 490 miles apart after sailing for 10 hours, how fast was the Carnival Cruise Ship sailing (in miles per hour)?

     a.   7
     b.   15
     c.   40
     d.   42
     e.   50

Refer to the following table for questions 35 – 37.

Number of Items Sold (in thousands)

	Macys	Dillard's
Clothes	425	550
Furniture	375	300
Jewelry	421	400

Total Sales (in millions)

	Clothes	Furniture	Jewelry
Macys	19.125	56.250	25.250
Dillard's	22.750	60.000	12.000

35. Which items sell for the twice as much at Macys than at Dillard's?

     a. Clothes
     b. Furniture
     c. Jewelry
     d. None
     e. Cannot be determined from the information given

36. Which item commands the highest price per unit?

     a. Furniture at Macys
     b. Furniture at Dillard's
     c. Clothes at Macys
     d. Clothes at Dillard's
     e. Jewelry at Dillard's

37. If both stores earn 35% profit on all jewelry sales, how much profit did Macy and Dillard's both earn from jewelry in the time period this table represents?

     a. $4,200,000
     b. $8,400,000
     c. $8,837,500
     d. $10,037,500
     e. $13,037,500

Answer Key for Quantitative Section 1

1. In this case, we know that some of the cans were served by the waitresses and some were consumed by the kitchen staff. Unfortunately, we do not know how many people work in the kitchen so we do not have enough information to answer the question. Choice E is correct.

2. To answer this question, we need to know the number of brothers Greg has and the amount of his winning lottery ticket. Statement 1 gives us the first quantity, while Statement 2 provides the second. Choice C is correct.

3. To answer this question, we simply need to know the actual values of x and y. Statement 1 gives us the value of y; Statement 2 gives us a way to calculate the value of x. Hence, with both statements, we can solve the problem. Choice C is correct.

4. In this question, all we need to know is Jenny's take-home pay, which is given in Statement 1. Statement 2 allows us to calculate her gross pay, which is extraneous information. Hence, Choice A is correct.

5. To calculate the area of a square, we simply need the length of a side, which Statement 1 provides. We can also get the same answer from the perimeter, which Statement 2 provides. Hence, Choice D is correct – either statement alone would give us enough information to answer the question.

6. To solve, we need to know the value of R. From Statement 1, we know that R is 30, 31, or 32. From Statement 2, we know that R must be 30. Choice C is correct.

7. Choice B is correct. Statement 2 gives us enough information to answer the question. (M and N are 21 and 23, respectively, which makes their sum = 44 and the square root = 6.63.)

8. Choice E is correct. Statements 1 and 2 are not sufficient to answer the question.

9. If $x = 10$, then $x^2 + 1/x^2 = 100.+ 0.01 = $ **100.01**. Choice B is correct.

10. $F \cup G = \{1, 2, 4, 5, 6, 8, 9\}$. $\{1, 2, 4, 5, 6, 8, 9\} \cap \{2, 6, 7, 10\} = $ **{2, 6}**. Choice B is correct.

11. The fastest way to solve this problem is to substitute numbers for the variables. Then, we can convert the relationship back to letters. Let's say Y = 100 and Z = 200. Therefore, (Y – 96) = 4. When Leslie sold the dolls, she reduced her collection by the following amount: 200 – (Y – 96) = 200 – Y + 96. Converting this back to letters, she had **Z – Y + 96** dolls left. Choice C is correct.

12. Here, we are simply being asked to find the difference between the two quantities: 5y – 3 - (10 - 8y) = 5y - 3 – 10 + 8y = **13y – 13**. Choice C is correct.

13. For situations in which the *order matters*, the correct formula is 5!/(5- 3)! = 5! / 2! = (5 x 4 x 3 x 2 x 1) / (2 x 1) = **60**. Choice E is correct.

14. Choice B is correct. The **two** integers are 18 and 36.

15. In this case, we can write two equations – one for the amount of each type of oregano and the other for their cost. As always, we must first define our variables. We will let = x the amount of $25 oregano and y = the amount of $10 oregano.

The first equation, which defines the *amount* of oregano, is simply x + y = 2000
The second equation, which defines their *cost*, is 25x + 10y = 20
To solve the problem for x, we must combine the equations in a way that eliminates y.

We can re-write equation 1 as y = 2000 – x and substitute this value for y into equation 2. When we do, we get: 25x + 10(2000 – x) = 20. 25x + 20,000 – 10x = 20. 15x = -19980. x = **1,332** pounds of $25 oregano. Choice D is correct.

16. The perimeter of the lot is the sum of its six sides, or 24.5 + 12 + 9.75 + 11.9 + 34 + 21.6 = 113.75 feet / 3 = 37.9 yards. 37.9 x $36 = **$1,365**. Choice B is correct.

17. $(1/36) (44 + 22)^2 = 1/36 (66)^2 = $ 4356/36 = **121**. Choice E is correct.

18. $(x + 9) + (x + 11) + (x + 13) = $ **3x + 33**. Choice D is correct.

19. $4x + 9y = 55$ and $2x + 7y = 11$. After subtracting the two equations, we have $2x + 2y = 44$, or $x + y = 22$, so $(x + y) / 2 = $ **11**. Choice D is correct.

20. According to the Pythagorean theorem. *The squares of the two shorter sides MUST equal the square of the third side.* For these five answer choices, we discover that they are all correct answer choices, except for choice C. If we square 9 and 26 and add those numbers together, they do NOT equal the square of 31. Since the question asks us to identify the *one incorrect answer*, we must choose C.

21. Area of square is 81, or S^2 Area of circle $= \pi r^2$ Thus, $81 = \pi r^2$ Radius r = the square root of $(81/\pi)$= 5.08 = **5**. Choice A is correct.

22. The perimeter 25x = sum of all 4 sides. Two of the sides are $x/4 + x/4$, or $x/2$. This means that the other two sides add up to $25x – x/2$, or $50x-1x = 49x$. One side, therefore, is $49x/2$. Area $= (x/4)(49x/2) = $ **$49x^2/8$**. Choice E is correct.

23. (6,14), (8, 21). Midpoint = (6+8)/2, (14 +21)/2 = 14/2, 35/2 = **7, 17.5**   Choice B is correct.

24. The fastest way to solve this problem is to try each answer choice. Choice C is correct.

25. (3/8)(4/5)(9/3) = 108/120. Choice D is correct, **9/10**.

26. Two price reductions = 0.9 x 0.85 = 0.765, which is **24.5%.** Choice C is correct.

27. To answer this question, subtract the amount of money that Sara spent from the total amount she had available. 125 – 74 – 26 = **25.** Choice A is correct. The trap in this question is the inclusion of alternative answer choices that match the answers you WOULD have gotten if you had subtracted incorrectly.

28. The question asks us to determine how positive integers less than 75 are divisible by 3, 5 and 6. First, we will list the integers that are evenly divisible by our largest number, which is 6: 6, 12, 18, 24, 30, 36, 42, 48, 54, 60, 66, 72. (Note: Because they are all multiples of 6, they are also divisible by 3.) In this group, we must then select the numbers that are ALSO evenly divisible by 5, which are 30 and 60. Our correct answer is Choice B. There are **two** positive integers less than 75 that are divisible by 3, 5, and 6.

29. First, we must determine how much fabric Gina will need to sew her entire outfit, which is 6/4 + 5/2 + 1/3 yards. To add these fractions together, they must all have the same denominator. In this case, the least common denominator (which is evenly divisible by 2, 3, and 4) is 12, which makes our equation:

18/12 + 30/12 + 4/12 = 52/12 = 4- 4/12 yards = 4 -1/3 yards. Now, we must determine how many yards of fabric Gina will have left over. If she has purchased 5 yards of the fabric, she will have 5 – 4- 1/3 = **2/3** yards left over. Choice C is correct. (As far as the price of the fabric ($35 per yard), you didn't need to know it. It's completely extraneous information.)

30. 7 + 3 + 2 = 12 items = ¾ of the total number of items. Hence, the overall total is 16.   2/16 = 1/8 = **12.5%.** Choice C is correct.

31. We can solve this using a proportion. 36/18 = x/64.   x = **128** minutes. Choice C is correct.

32. The three consecutive integers are x, x + 1 and x + 2. From the problem, we can write the following equation: 3 {x + (x + 1)} = 2 (x + 2) + 27. Thus, 6x + 3 = 2x + 31. 4x = 28
x = **7**, x + 1 = 8 x + 2 = 9. Choice B is correct.

33. In this case, we can start with Jayne, whose actual age we are given. Then, we can work backwards to determine Nathan's age. Jane = 28. Claire = 28 – 3 = 25. Nathan = 25 + 7 = **32**. Choice E is correct.

34. The first step for this type of problem is to draw a quick chart of what we know:

Driver	Distance	Rate	Time
Big Red Boat	10(x - 35)	x - 35	10
Carnival Cruise	10x	x	10

In this case, we will let x = the rate (or speed) of the Carnival Cruise ship, which is what we are asked to find. The speed of the Big Red Boat is therefore x - 35. Since they both travel for 10 hours, we can complete the Distance entry for the Big Red Boat and the Carnival Cruise ship as 10(x - 35) and 10x, respectively.

Next, we must write our equation to solve for the speed of the Carnival Cruise ship. Although both ships started in the same place and sailed for the same amount of time, they traveled at different speeds. The 490 miles distance is the TOTAL distance that the two of them sailed. Mathematically, it can be represented by the SUM of the Big Red Boat's distance, 10(x - 35), and the Carnival Cruise ship's distance, 10x. Hence, our equation becomes: 10x + 10(x - 35) = 490. 20x − 350 = 490. 20x = 840. X =**42** miles per hour = speed of the Carnival Cruise ship. Choice D is correct.

35. Jewelry at Dillard's sells for $30 per unit ($12,000,000/400,000 = $30), while jewelry at Macys sells for $15 per unit ($25,250,000/421,000 = $60). Choice C is correct.

36. Choice B is correct. Furniture at Dillard's costs $200 per unit ($60,000,000/300,000 = $200).

37. Macys profit from jewelry = ($25,250,000)(0.35) = $8,837,500
Dillard's profit from jewelry = ($12,000,000)(0.35) = $4,200,000
Total profit = $8,837,500 + $4,200,000 = **$13,037,500**. Choice E is correct.

Quantitative Section 2:   37 questions   75 minutes

Use the following answer choices for questions 1 - 8 below:

A.   Statement 1 alone is sufficient but Statement 2 alone is not sufficient to answer the question asked.
B.   Statement 2 alone is sufficient but Statement 1 alone is not sufficient to answer the question asked.
C.   Statements 1 and 2 together are sufficient to answer the question but neither statement is sufficient alone.
D.   Each statement alone is sufficient to answer the question.
E.   Statements 1 and 2 are not sufficient to answer the question asked and additional data is needed to answer the question.

1. What is the largest integer less than p that leaves a remainder of 1 when divided by 17?

(1) p = 100
(2) p = 10^2

2. How many two-digit positive integers are multiples of a and b?

(1) a and b are different odd integers that are less than 10
(2) a and b are both greater than 6

3. How many nuggets are in an X-lb. bag of chicken nuggets?

(1) X = 5
(2) Each nugget weighs between 2 ounces and 4 ounces

4. A restaurant sold 150 chicken dinners during the evening rush. How many chicken cutlets were remaining?

(1) Each dinner used 3 cutlets per dinner.
(2) The number of cutlets sold equals 5/6 of the restaurant's original stock of chicken cutlets.

5. What is the perimeter of rectangle ABCD?

(1) The area of rectangle ABCD is 48
(2) AB = CD.

6. What is the sum of A + B?

(1)   A is an integer greater than 9 but less than 11.
(2)   B is an odd positive integer less than ten that is not a prime number.

7. How much money did Wendy and Wanda earn in tips on Saturday night?

(1) Wendy earned 30% more than Wanda.
(2) Wendy earned 17.5% of her total sales for the night, which were $547.50.

8. What is Integer B?

(1)   Integer B = Integer A + 4
(2)   The cube of Integer B is 1,000

Directions: For each problem, decide which answer is the best of the choices given.

9. How many inches are there in X yards, Y feet and Z inches?

    a. 36X + 12Y + Z
    b. 3X + 12Y +12 Z
    c. 3X + 36Y +12 Z
    d. (X + Y + Z)/12
    e. (X +Y)/12 + Z

10. Beth's Bridal Shop sells two designer gowns online: Victorian Lady and Summer Delight. Selling just these two products, the company makes $44,995 in profits each year on the sale of 450 gowns. If the profit per gown is $75 and $140 for Victorian Lady and Summer Delight, respectively, how many Victorian Lace gowns does the shop sell per year?

    a.   173
    b.   177
    c.   273
    d.   277
    e.   303

11. If y is g less than h times x, what is the value of x?

    a. (y - g)/h
    b. (y + g)/h
    c. hy + 20
    d. hy - 20
    e. h/g y

12. If the average of nine consecutive odd integers is 999, what is the smallest of the nine integers?

    a.   987
    b.   989
    c.   991
    d.   993
    e.   997

13. The sum of two numbers is 12. When four times the larger number is subtracted from 6 times the smaller number, the difference is 2. What is the larger number?

    a.   4
    b.   5
    c.   6
    d.   7
    e.   9

14. Which of the following is equal to 0.0000543?

    a. 54.3×10^5
    b. $54.3 \; 10^{-7}$
    c. 543×10^{-8}
    d. 5.43×10^{-6}
    e. 5.43×10^{-5}

15. At the company picnic, each of the firm's 20 employees placed a raffle ticket into a bowl. At the end of the night, the company president picked one ticket randomly from the bowl and awarded the first prize to Greg. He then picked another ticket randomly from the bowl and awarded the second prize to Pete. Finally, after awarding two more prizes in the same manner, the president picked a fifth random ticket from the bowl and awarded the fifth prize to Jim. Assuming that the first four tickets were not placed back into the bowl after the first four prizes were awarded, what was the probability of Jim winning the fifth prize?

    a.   1.25%
    b.   2.50%
    c.   5.00%
    d.   5.25%
    e.   6.25%

16. If the following series continues in the same pattern, what will the next term be?
          3, 5, 4, 7, 5, 9, 6, 11………

    a.   3
    b.   5
    c.   6
    d.   7
    e.   13

17. Equilateral triangle XYZ has an area of 36. If U is the midpoint of XY and V is the midpoint of XZ, what is the area of triangle XUV?

    a.   3
    b.   6
    c.   9
    d.   12
    e.   18

18. In quadrilateral ABCD, the sum of angles B, C and D = 5A. What is the value of angle A?

    a.   15
    b.   20
    c.   36
    d.   45
    e.   60

19. Line Q contains five points: A, B, C, D and E. How many different line segments do these five points form?

    a.   4
    b.   5
    c.   6
    d.   10
    e.   11

20. If $x \wedge y = xy - y + y^2$, then $2 \wedge 4 =$

    a.   4
    b.   16
    c.   20
    d.   24
    e.   68

21. On her way to the Post Office, Claire spent 10 minutes in her car, 11 minutes at the drugstore and another 11 minutes talking on her cell phone to her boyfriend. If she arrived at the Post Office at exactly 11:04 am, what time did Claire leave for the Post Office?

    a.   10:22 am
    b.   10:32 am
    c.   10:33 am
    d.   10:34 am
    e.   10:35 am

22. What is the largest integer that will divide evenly into 97 and 117?

    a.   1
    b.   7
    c.   9
    d.   11
    e.   13

23. Ken listed his car for sale on EBay for $8,000 but did not receive any bids. Later, he re-listed it for $6,400. What fraction of the original price does this represent?

    a.   2/3
    b.   3/4
    c.   4/5
    d.   5/6
    e.   7/8

24. Eight hundred people answered a newspaper ad to audition for American Idol. Forty percent of them were assigned Whitney Houston songs. Of this 40%, one-quarter of the people sang "I Will Always Love You." How many people sang "I Will Always Love You?"

    a.   40
    b.   60
    c.   80
    d.   120
    e.   160

25. What is the sum of the following fractions: 1/15, 2/10, 2/5, 1/3, 3/30

    a.   11/10
    b.   29/30
    c.   14/15
    d.   31/30
    e.   32/30

26. The sum of two numbers is 18. When three times the larger number is subtracted from 5 times the smaller number, the difference is 2. What is the larger number?

    a.   7
    b.   8
    c.   9
    d.   10
    e.   11

27. Jocelyn weighs 60% as much as Connie. If Jocelyn gains 8 pounds, she will weigh 75% as much as Connie. What is Jocelyn's weight (in pounds)?

  a.   32.0
  b.   35.5
  c.   40.0
  d.   43.3
  e.   53.3

28. A US Air commercial jet and a Sea Hawk helicopter left the Chicago airport at the same time and headed in opposite directions. If the US Air jet flew at an average rate of 500 miles per hour and the Sea Hawk helicopter flew at an average rate of 100 miles per hour, how many hours would it take the two flights to be 4,200 miles apart (assuming no stops to re-fuel)?

  a.   7
  b.   8
  c.   10
  d.   12
  e.   20

29. The Zippy Cheese Company has established a quality control program to minimize the number of underweight bars of cheese that leave their plant. During the first six weeks of the program, the number of bars that failed, by week, was 324, 119, 267, 219, 553, and 189. If management's goal is to have an overall average of 300 failing bars or less during the first seven weeks of the program, what is the highest number of bars that can fail during week seven?

  a.   297
  b.   307
  c.   359
  d.   429
  e.   548

30. How much greater than $11 - 9y$ is $7y + 4$?

  a.   16y -7
  b.   −2y -7
  c.   2y +15
  d.   6y -15
  e.   −16y +1

31. $(3/6 + 4/2)^3 =$

  a.   6.25
  b.   8
  c.   15.625
  d.   16.525
  e.   48

32. Which of the following is a multiple of 10, 15 and 35?

  a.   70
  b.   150
  c.   350
  d.   525
  e.   1050

33. Jenny has twice as many swimming medals as Cindy. If the sum of the squares of each number is 180, how many medals does Jenny have?

    a. 6
    b. 8
    c. 12
    d. 16
    e. 24

34. A pet shop had an inventory of 150 animals - 105 of the animals were cats and the rest were dogs. If 85 of the animals are female and 80% of the dogs are female, how many of the pets are male cats?

    a. 9
    b. 36
    c. 45
    d. 49
    e. 56

Refer to the following chart for questions 35 – 37.

Number of Items Sold (in thousands)

	Macys	Dillard's
Clothes	425	550
Furniture	375	300
Jewelry	421	400

Total Sales (in millions)

	Clothes	Furniture	Jewelry
Macys	19.125	56.250	25.250
Dillard's	22.750	60.000	12.000

35. If Macy's sells 50% additional furniture items next year and earns 30% profit on them, how much total profit from furniture will Macys earn (assuming the price per unit does not change)?

    a. $1,687,500
    b. $20,250,000
    c. $25,312,500
    d. $21,167,500
    e. $84,375,000

36. What is the difference between the average cost of a piece of clothing at Macys and Dillard's?

    a. The average price of an item of clothing at Macys is $10 higher than at Dillard's
    b. The average price of an item of clothing at Dillard's is $10 higher than at Macys
    c. The average price of an item of clothing at Dillard's is $5 higher than at Macys
    d. The average price of an item of clothing at Macys is $5 higher than at Dillard's
    e. It cannot be determined from the information given.

37. To sell the same dollar amount of clothing as Dillard's without increasing the number of units they sell, Macys will have to increase the average price of its clothing items to what amount?

    a. $50.00
    b. $53.50
    c. $55.00
    d. $57.50
    e. $60.50

Answer Key for Quantitative Section 2

1. Statements 1 and 2 provide the same information. Either is sufficient to answer the question. Choice D is correct.

2. When taken together, Statements 1 and 2 provide enough information for us to learn that a and b are 7 and 9, respectively. Choice C is correct.

3. To answer this question, we need to know the value of X and the weight of each nugget. Statement 1 gives us X, but Statement 2 reveals that the nuggets are not all the same eight – they range from 2 ounces to 4 ounces. Because the weights are inconsistent, we cannot determine the exact number of nuggets in the bag. Choice E is correct.

4. To answer this question, we need to know the original number of chicken cutlets and the number used in each dinner. Statements 1 and 2, if taken together, provide us with this information. Choice C is correct.

5. To calculate the perimeter of the rectangle, we need to know the four side lengths. Statement 1 gives us the area, which is the product of the side lengths, while Statement 2 simply tells us which sides are equal (which we already knew). Therefore, we do not have enough information to answer the question. Choice E is correct.

6. To solve the problem, we need to be able to identify values for A and B. Statement 1 gives us enough information to determine A. Statement 2, however, narrows us down to two values for B (1 or 9). Hence, Choice E is correct. We cannot answer the question without additional information.

7. Choice C is correct. Statements 1 and 2 together are sufficient to answer the question, but neither statement is sufficient alone

8. Choice B is correct. Statement 2 is sufficient to answer the question. Statement 1 is not necessary to determine the value of Integer B.

9. To solve, we must convert all of the terms to inches and add them together. Let's start with what we know. The term for inches is represented by Z. There are 12 inches in 1 foot. Hence, our coefficient for Y is 12. There are 3 feet in one yard and 12 inches in one foot. Hence, our coefficient for X is 3 x 12 = 36. The number of inches in a distance of X yards, Y feet and Z inches is therefore **36X + 12Y + Z.** Choice A is correct.

10. Let x = the # of Victorian Lady gowns sold and 450 – x = the # of Summer Delight gowns sold. The total profit ($44,995) is the sum of the two gowns, which makes our equation: 75x + 140 (450 –x) = 44,995. 75x + 63,000 – 140x = 44,995. - 65x = -18005. x = **277** Victorian Lady Gowns; 450 –277 = 173 Summer Delight Gowns. Choice D is correct.

11. According to the problem, y = hx – g. If we solve for x, we find x = **(y + g)/h.** Choice B is correct.

12. If 999 is the mean, then it is the fifth in the series of nine consecutive odd numbers. We can simply count back to get the first in the series, which will be **991** (999 –997- 995 – 993 - 991). Choice C is correct.

13. First, we must define our variables. For convenience, we will let the smaller number = x and the larger number = (12 – x). We also know that 6x - 4(12 – x) = 2. When we solve this equation, we find that 6x – 48 + 4x = 2, or 10x = 50, so x = 5 and 12 – 5 = **7.** Choice D is correct.

14. **5.43×10^{-5}** Choice E is correct.

15. Jim's ticket was one of 16 tickets left in the bowl during the fifth drawing. His probability of winning the prize was 1/16, or 0.0625, which is **6.25%.** Choice E is correct.

16. This problem is a combination of two sub-series. In the first one, each number increase by 1 (3,4,5,6); in the second, each number increases by 2 (5,7,9,11). The next number would be 6 + 1, or **7.** Choice D is correct.

17. The area of the triangle formed by the midpoints is ¼ of the original triangle XYZ. Therefore, the area is 36/4 = 9. Choice C is correct.

18. A + B + C + D = 360. Here, A + 5A = 360. Therefore, A = **60** degrees. Choice E is correct.

19. Choice D is correct. There are **10** possible segments: AB, AC, BC, AC, BD, CD, AE, BE, CE, DE.

20. If $x \wedge y = xy - y + y^2$, then $2 \wedge 4 = (2)(4) - 4 + 16 =$ **20.** Choice C is correct.

21. Add the minutes that Claire spent in the car; then, subtract them from the time she arrived at the Post Office. 10 + 11 + 11 = 32 minutes en route. 11:04 – 32 minutes = **10:32 am**. Choice B is correct.

22. The fastest way to solve this problem is to try each of the answer choices. When we do, we discover that the largest one that divides evenly into 97 and 117 is **1.** Choice A is correct.

23. If the original price was $8,000 and the new price is $6,400, then the relationship can be represented by $6,400/$8,000 = 8/10 = **4/5.** Choice C is correct.

24. 800 x 0.4 = 320. 320 x 0.25 = **80**. Choice C is correct.

25. Convert all fractions to the form with an LCD of 30. The sum is: 2/30 + 6/30 + 12/30 + 10/30 + 3/30 = 33/30 = **11/10**. Choice A is correct.

26. First, let's define our variables. We will let x = the smaller number and 18 – x equal the larger number. Five times the smaller number is therefore 5x. Three times the larger number is 3(18 – x). Further, we know that the difference between these two quantities is equal to 2. We must therefore solve the following equation: 5x – 3(18-x) = 2, so 5x –54 + 3x = 2, or 8x =56, or x = 7 and 18 – 7 = **11.** Choice E is correct.

27. First, we must summarize our data in a table:

Name	Current Weight	Hypothetical Weight
Connie	x	-
Jocelyn	0.6x	0.6x + 8

In this case, Connie's weight does not change. Our equation is simply the relationship between the two weights if Jocelyn gains eight pounds: 0.6x + 8 = 0.75x. Solving for x, Connie's weight = 53.3 lbs and Jocelyn's weight = **32** lb. Choice A is correct.

28. The first step for this type of problem is to draw a quick chart of what we know.

Driver	Distance	Rate	Time
US Air	500x	500	x
Sea Hawk	100x	100	x

In this case, we will let x = the time it takes for the jet and the helicopter to travel 4,200 miles. We can also enter the rates for each plane and write an expression for their respective distances. Next, we must use this information to solve for x.

The US Air jet and the Sea Hawk helicopter each traveled *a portion* of the total distance, which is 4,200 miles. Our equation, therefore, is: Jet's Distance + Helicopter's Distance = Total Distance
500 x + 100X = 4,200. 600x = 4,200. X = **7** hours. Choice A is correct

29. For this problem, we can simply use the equation for simple averages to find the missing number: 300 = (324 + 119 + 267 + 219 + 553 + 189 + x) / 7, So 300 = (1671 + x) / 7, so 2100 = 1671 + x, so x = **429.** Choice D is correct.

30. Here, we are simply being asked to find the difference between the two quantities: 7y + 4 - (11 - 9y) = 7y + 4 – 11 + 9y = **16y – 7**. Choice A is correct.

31. $(3/6 + 4/2)^3 =$ (5/2)(5/2)(5/2) = 125/8 = **15.625**. Choice C is correct.

32. Choice E, 1050.

33. First, let's define our variables.   We will let x = the number of Cindy's medals and 2x = the number of

Jenny's medals. Therefore, the squares of the two numbers are x^2 and $4x^2$. Our equation therefore becomes: $x^2 + 4x^2 = 180$. $5x^2 = 180$. $x^2 = 180/5 = 36$. $x^2 = 36$. $x = +6$ and -6
Cindy has 6 medals. Jenny has $2(6) = $ **12** medals. Choice C is correct.

34. The best way to attack this type of problem is to summarize the data you are given in a simple table. Once you do, the answer will either be obvious – or surprisingly easy to calculate. In this case, we have cats and dogs in a pet shop; some are male, while others are female. When we put the information into our chart, we get:

	Cats	Dogs	Total
Male	56	9	65
Female	49	36	85
Total	105	45	150

From the table, we can answer the question; the number of male cats is **56**. Choice E is correct.

35. Macys currently sells 375,000 units of furniture per year. If they sell 50% more, they will sell (375,000)(1.5) = 562,500 units. From the chart, we know that the price per unit is $150 ($56,250,000 / 375,000). Thus, for 562,500 units, Macys total furniture sales will be (562,500)($150) = $84,375,000. If 30% of this is profit, Macys will earn **$25,312,500** in profit from furniture. Choice C is correct.

36. At Macys, the average cost of an item of clothing = $19,125,000/425,000 = $45
At Dillard's, the average cost of an item of clothing = $22,000,000/ 550,000= $40
Thus, the average price of an item of clothing at Macys is **$5 higher** than at Dillard's. Choice D is correct.

37. Dillard's sold $22,750,000 in clothing last year, while Macys sold 425,000 clothing items. For Macys to generate $22,750,000 from 425,000 units, they will need to sell each unit for $22,750,000/425,000 = **$53.50**. Choice B is correct.

Quantitative Section 3:   37 questions   75 minutes

Use the following answer choices for questions 1 - 8 below:

A.   Statement 1 alone is sufficient but Statement 2 alone is not sufficient to answer the question asked.
B.   Statement 2 alone is sufficient but Statement 1 alone is not sufficient to answer the question asked.
C.   Statements 1 and 2 together are sufficient to answer the question but neither statement is sufficient alone.
D.   Each statement alone is sufficient to answer the question.
E.   Statements 1 and 2 are not sufficient to answer the question asked and additional data is needed to answer the question.

1. Rick grosses $6,000 per month and pays 30% in taxes. If he saves X% of his take-home pay, how much will he have at the end of the year?

(1) His mortgage payments are $1,000 per month
(2) X= 50%

2. Robert bought a condo with an unusual financing plan. He paid a down payment of X and agreed to pay the balance in 60 equal installments. What is Robert's monthly installment payment?

(1) X = $5000
(2) Robert paid no points or closing costs on the loan.

3. X college students were asked to name their favorite color. 250 said red, 225 said blue, 150 said green and Y students each said yellow, orange and white, respectively. What percentage of students chose white?

(1) X = 775
(2) No student chose black

4. Joe and Candy have a $100 gift certificate for a local restaurant, which must cover the complete cost of their meal, plus tax and tip. What is the maximum amount they can pay for their meal?

(1) They must pay 5% sales tax for alcoholic beverages
(2) There is no sales tax on food

5. What is the surface area of the cube (in square centimeters)?

(1) Its volume is 27 cubic centimeters
(2) It has a side length of 3

6. What is the length of the hypotenuse in Triangle B?

(1) Triangle B is a right triangle.
(2) Triangle B has side lengths of 4 and 8.

7. What is the value of x?

(1) The value of x quarters is equal to the value of x + 3 dimes.
(2) The value 10x pennies is equal to the value of 2x nickels.

8. What is the next term in the series?

(1)   The first five terms are 1, 1, 6, 36, 41.
(2)   The pattern continues indefinitely.

9. If a Ψ b = (1 + b) $^{1/2}$ what is aΨ 3024?

      a.   24
      b.   30
      c.   55
      d.   64
      e.   72

10.   2.05 x 8.99 x 54.22 =

      a.   99.25
      b.   487.43
      c.   974.87
      d.   999.25
      e.   1949.75

11. What is the sum of the following fractions: 1/5, 2/20, 3/5, 3/10, 3/20

      a.   23/20
      b.   12/10
      c.   27/20
      d.   27/10
      e.   29/20

12. What is the largest integer that will divide evenly into 64 and 118?

      a.   2
      b.   4
      c.   6
      d.   8
      e.   12

13. If x + 5 is an even integer, the sum of the next two even integers is:

      a.   x + 9
      b.   2(x +5)
      c.   2x + 16
      d.   2x + 27
      e.   It is impossible to determine from the information given.

14. The final exam for English Literature class is worth 1/3 of the overall grade. The average of 4 monthly exams counts for another third, while an oral presentation on sonnets is worth the final third. So far, Becky's exam scores are 68, 73, 80 and 95. She only scored a 70 on her oral presentation. What will Becky have to earn on the final exam to raise her average to 80?

      a.   87
      b.   88
      c.   89
      d.   91
      e.   92

15. Two airplanes leave the Orlando Airport at the same time and head in opposite directions. Plane A flies four times as fast as Plane B. Three hours later, they are 5,000 miles apart. How fast is Plane B flying (in miles per hour)?

    a.   300
    b.   333
    c.   500
    d.   667
    e.   900

16. The Kline Corporation had to mail a package on the day that the Post Office increased its rates. The cost is 93 cents for the first ounce and 51 cents for each additional ounce. How much did the company pay to mail a package that weighed three pounds?

    a. $22.90
    b. $22.97
    c. $23.90
    d. $23.97
    e. $24.90

17. A base angle of an isosceles triangle is 30 degrees. How many degrees are in the vertex angle?

    a.   100
    b.   110
    c.   120
    d.   140
    e.   150

18. A rectangle that measures 9 inches by 16 inches is completely inscribed in a circle. If all four corners of the rectangle touch the circumference of the circle, what is the area of the circle?

    a. 12π
    b. 36π
    c. 84π
    d. 144π
    e. 720π

19. A Brinks truck is making a special delivery of 24 gold bars to the U.S. Treasury. Each bar is 3 feet long, 6 inches wide and 12 inches deep. If the gold is certified to weigh 3 ounces per cubic inch, how many pounds does each bar weigh?

    a.   54
    b.   486
    c.   864
    d.   1,296
    e.   7,776

20. If $x = 5$, $y = 2$ and $z = 3$, what is the value of $3x^3 + 5y^4 - 2z^2$?

    a.   357
    b.   375
    c.   393
    d.   437
    e.   455

21. What are the y-intercepts of the graph for the following equation: $(x + 6)^2 + (x + 3)^2 = 1$

    a.   (6, 0) (3, 0)
    b.   (-6, 0) (-3, 0)
    c.   (0 –6) (0, -3)
    d.   (0, 6) (0, 3)
    e.   There are no y-intercepts

22. Find the area of a square with a diagonal of 8.

    a.   32
    b.   36
    c.   49
    d.   64
    e.   96

23. If x = 3, calculate $5^x - (x^3)^{x-1}$

    a.   -604
    b.   44
    c.   98
    d.   104
    e.   604

24. Simply the following expression: $(3x + y)(x + 3y) - 10xy =$

    a.   0
    b. $3x^2 - 11xy + y^2$
    c. $-21xy$
    d. $3x^2 + 3y^2$
    e. $3x^2 - 3y^2$

25. The inequality $5x - 78 > 6x + 80$ is true for what values of x?

    a. $x < 2$
    b. $x > 158$
    c. $x > -158$
    d. $x < -158$
    e. $x < 158$

26. A wholesaler shipped seven dozen roses to a flower shop for use in a window display. If Jane takes three roses for her own use, and nineteen are discarded because they are wilted, but Barb adds back an additional half-dozen roses to the group, how many roses were available for the window display?

    a.   61
    b.   64
    c.   68
    d.   71
    e.   74

27. Which of the following is the smallest integer that leaves a remainder of 1 when divided by 8?

    a.   131
    b.   137
    c.   145
    d.   153
    e.   168

28. A year ago, Julie had 62 recipes for her country cookbook. This year, she has 329 recipes. What percentage increase does this number represent?

    a.   4.306%
    b.   43.06%
    c.   430.6%
    d.   4306%
    e.   none of the above

29. The larger of two numbers is 11 more than the smaller. Double the small number equals 14 more than the larger number. What is the small number?

    a.   24
    b.   25
    c.   26
    d.   35
    e.   36

30. If the perimeter of an isosceles triangle is 64 and its base is 16, find the length of one of the equal sides.

    a.   18
    b.   20
    c.   24
    d.   26
    e.   28

31. If $f(p) = p/7 + 10 - (7^3)/p$, what is $f(14)$?

    a.   −12.5
    b.   -12
    c.   0
    d.   7
    e.   343

32. Which of the following is equal to 0.0000321?

    a. 32.1×10^7
    b. $32.1 c 10^{-7}$
    c. 321×10^{-8}
    d. 3.21×10^{-6}
    e. 3.21×10^{-5}

33. Which of the following expressions is equivalent to $(a + b - 1)(a - b - 1)$?

    a. $a^2 + 2a - 2b - b^2 + 1$
    b. $a^2 - 2a + 2b + b^2 + 1$
    c. $a^2 - 2a + 2b - b^2 + 1$
    d. $a^2 - 2a - b^2 + 1$
    e. $a^2 + 2a - b^2 + 1$

34. A research lab has a new hand pump, which can fill a bucket in 32 seconds. It also has an older pump that can fill the same bucket in 48 seconds. If both pumps are used at the same time, how many seconds will it take to fill the bucket?

    a. 18.0
    b. 19.2
    c. 28.5
    d. 36.4
    e. 40.0

35. Heidi bought U wedding favors at a bridal shop at a price of V per favor. Afterwards, Heidi had W dollars left over. Assuming that she made no other purchases, how much money (in dollars) did Heidi bring to the bridal shop for favors?

    a. UVW
    b. UV + W
    c. (U/V) + W
    d. UV – W
    e. It cannot be determined from the information given.

Refer to the chart below for questions 36 & 37.

Number of Hospitals per Million Residents

Atlanta	56
Boston	94
Chicago	87
Detroit	79
Los Angeles	99
Miami	48
Sacramento	61

36. If the population of Los Angeles decreases from 10 million to 7.5 million, how many fewer hospitals will be needed in the city?

    a. 190
    b. 240
    c. 247
    d. 743
    e. 790

37. If there are 5 million people in Miami and 20 X-ray technicians per hospital, how many X-ray technicians work in hospitals in Miami?

    a. 240
    b. 1,200
    c. 2,400
    d. 2,600
    e. 4,800

Answer Key for Quantitative Section 3

1. In this case, all we need to know to solve the problem is the value of X. Statement 2 gives us this information, while Statement 1 adds unnecessary details. Choice B is correct.

2. To answer this question, we need to know the amount of the down payment and the purchase price of the house. Statement 1 gives us the amount of the down payment, but neither statement reveals the purchase price. Hence, we do not have sufficient information to answer the question. Choice E is correct.

3. To answer the question, we need to know the values of X and Y. Statement 1 gives us X, which is enough for us to calculate Y. Statement 2 is extraneous information. Choice A is correct.

4. To answer the question, we need to know the amount they spent for the sales tax and tip. Neither statement reveals the amount of the tip. Additionally, we do not know whether or not Joe or Candy consumed alcohol, which is the only taxable item at the restaurant. Choice E is correct.

5. Each statement, on its own, provides enough information to answer the question. Choice D is correct.

6. To answer this question, we need to know whether or not Triangle B is a right triangle. We also need to know the lengths of the two other sides. Statement 1 gives us the first quantity, while Statement 2 provides the second. Choice C is correct.

7. In this case, we can answer the question using either statement. Choice D is correct.

8. To answer this question, we need to know the first several terms in the series. We also need to know whether or not the pattern continues indefinitely. Statement 1 gives us the first piece of information, while Statement 2 provides the second. Choice C is correct.

9. If $a \Psi b = (1 + b)^{1/2}$ then $a \Psi 3024 = (1 + 3024)^{1/2} = \mathbf{55}$. Choice C is correct.

10. $2.05 \times 8.99 \times 54.22 = \mathbf{999.35}$. Choice D is correct.

11. Convert all fractions to the form with an LCD of 20. The sum is:
$1/5 + 2/20 + 3/5 + 3/10 + 3/20 = 4/20 + 2/20 + 12/20 + 6/20 + 3/20 = \mathbf{27/20}$. Choice C is correct.

12. The fastest way to solve this problem is to try each answer choice. Choice A is correct.

13. $(x + 7) + (x + 9) = \mathbf{2x + 16}$. Choice C is correct.

14. Let's let x = the final exam grade. The average of Becky's four exams is $(68 + 73 + 80 + 95)/4 = 79$. Finally, her score for the oral presentation is 70. Since the final exam grade, oral presentation score and the average of her four exam grades all equal one-third of Becky's final grade, we simply need to solve the following equation for x: $1/3 (79) + 1/3 (70) + 1/3 (x) = 80$. Hence, $x = \mathbf{91}$. Choice D is correct.

15. In this case, we can write two equations – one for the speed of the planes and the other for the distance they travel. As always, we must first define our variables. We will let x = Plane B's speed and y = Plane A's speed.

The first equation, which defines the *speed* of the planes, is simply $y = 4x$
The second equation, which defines the *distance* they travel, is $3x + 3y = 5,000$
To solve the problem for x, we must combine the equations in a way that eliminates y.

The fastest way is to substitute equation 1 into equation 2. When we do, we get $3x + 3(4x) = 5,000$. $15x = 5,000$. $x = \mathbf{333.33}$ = Plane B's speed. Choice B is correct. ($4x = 1333.33$ = Plane A's speed)

16. First, we must convert the weight of the package from pounds to ounces. In this case, 3.00 pounds X (16 ounces/1 pound) = 48 ounces. The total cost is \$0.93 for the first ounce and \$0.51 for the 47 additional ounces, or $0.93 + 47 (0.51) = 0.93 + 23.97 = \mathbf{\$24.90}$ total cost to mail a 3-pound package. Choice E is correct.

17. By definition, an isosceles triangle has two equal sides. Additionally, the two opposite angles, which are called base angles, are also equal. If one of the base angles = 30 degrees, then the second base angle

also equals 30 degrees. The vertex angle is therefore 180 – 60 = **120** degrees. Choice C is correct.

18. In this situation, the diagonal of the rectangle is equal to the diameter of the circle.   Because the rectangle can also be viewed as two triangles that share the diagonal as a common side, we can use the Pythagorean theorem to calculate its length. Accordingly, the square of the diagonal is equal to (9)(9) + (16)(16) = 81 + 256 = 337. This means that the diameter of the circle is the square root of 337, or 18.36; the radius is therefore 9.18. Now, we can calculate the area of the circle, which is (9.18)(9.18)(π), = **84π**. Choice C is correct.

19. Volume = (36)(6)(12) = 2,592 cubic inches x 3 oz/ inch = 7,776 oz./16 oz. per pound = **486** lbs. Choice B is correct.

20. If x = 5, y = 2 and z = 3, then $3x^3 + 5y^4 - 2z^2$ = (3)(5)(5)(5) + (5)(2)(2)(2)(2) – (2)(3)(3) = 375 + 80 – 18= **437**. Choice D is correct.

21. None. Choice E is correct.

22. The square is the sum of two right triangles that share the diagonal as their hypotenuse. Therefore, the sum of the squares of the other two sides must equal 64. Therefore $2x^2$ = 64, where x = a side of the square. To calculate the area of the square, which is L x W, we get (5.65)(5.65) =**32**. Choice A is correct.

23. 125 – 729 = **-604**. Choice A is correct.

24. $(3x + y)(x + 3y) – 10xy = 3x^2 + 9xy + xy + 3y^2 – 10xy$ = **$3x^2 + 3y^2$**. Choice D is correct.

25. Choice D is correct. When we simplify the expression, we get **x < -158**

26. First, determine the total number of roses. Then, add and subtract according to the details in the question stem. If we do, we get: 12(7) = 84 roses - 3 – 19 + 6 = **68**. Choice C is correct. This problem requires you to add and subtract a string of numbers. As long as you convert the "dozen" terms to individual roses, and keep the signs correct when you add, you will obtain the right answer.

27. The easiest way to solve this problem is to try the answer choices in the order they are presented. When we do, we discover that 137 = **8(17) + 1**. Choice B is correct.

28. 329 - 62 = 267/62 = 4.306 x 100 = **430.6% increase**. Choice C is correct.

29. Let x = the smaller number. Therefore, the larger number = x + 11. We also know that:
2x = (x + 11) + 14.   2x = x + 25.   x = **25.** Choice B is correct.

30. Perimeter = sum of all three sides = 16 + 2x = 64. Therefore, 2x = 48. x = **24**. Choice C is correct.

31. If f(p) = p/7 + 10 – (7^3)/p , then f (14) = 14/7 + 10 – 343/14 = 2 + 10 – 24.5 = **-12.5** Choice A is correct.

32. **3.21 x 10^{-5}** Choice E is correct.

33. $(a + b – 1)(a – b – 1) = a^2 –ab –a + ab - b^2 –b –a +b + 1 = a^2 – 2a – b^2 + 1$. Choice D is correct.

34. For this problem, our unknown x is the total time required to fill the bucket if both pumps are used. Hence, our equation becomes 1/32 + 1/48 = 1/x. To solve, we must multiply both sides of the equation by 96x, which is our least common denominator: 3x + 2x = 96, so 5x = 96 and x = **19.2** seconds. Choice B is correct.

35. We can solve this problem by plugging in numbers or by doing a few simple "backwards" calculations. First, let's plug- in numbers. Let's assume that Heidi bought 10 favors at a price of 2 dollars per favor. Let's also assume that she had 5 dollars left over. Hence, U = 10, V = 2 and W = 5. Heidi therefore spent (10)(2), which is UV. If she had 5 dollars left over, then her original amount of money was **UV + W**. Choice B is correct.

36. (99)(10) = 990. (99)(7.5) = 743. 990 – 743 = **247**. Choice C is correct.

37. (48)(5)(20) = **4,800**. Choice E is correct.

Quantitative Section 4: 37 questions   75 minutes

Use the following answer choices for questions 1 - 8 below:

A.   Statement 1 alone is sufficient but Statement 2 alone is not sufficient to answer the question asked.
B.   Statement 2 alone is sufficient but Statement 1 alone is not sufficient to answer the question asked.
C.   Statements 1 and 2 together are sufficient to answer the question but neither statement is sufficient alone.
D.   Each statement alone is sufficient to answer the question.
E.   Statements 1 and 2 are not sufficient to answer the question asked and additional data is needed to answer the question.

1. Six hundred guests will either eat shrimp or roast beef at a wedding reception. How many of the guests will eat roast beef?

(1) Ten percent of the guests are allergic to seafood
(2) The ratio of shrimp eaters to roast beef eaters is 6:4.

2. A chef has a wonderful recipe for meatloaf, which uses 8 oz of garlic. How much garlic will she need to make enough meatloaf to serve 48 people?

(1) For every ounce of garlic she uses, the chef must reduce the amount of onion by one-half
(2) The original recipe requires 4 ounces of onion

3. On a snowy Sunday night, Sam, Joe, and Pete decided to compare CD collections. How many CDs does Joe have?

(1) Joe has 10 fewer CDs than Sam
(2) Pete has 12 less than four times the number of CDs that Joe has

4. Five numbers have a sum of 475. What is the middle number?

(1) The numbers are consecutive odd integers
(2) The average of the numbers is 157

5. What is the volume of a holiday shipping container (in cubic centimeters)?

(1) The container is a rectangle
(2) The container has a width of ½ foot, a length of 18 inches and a height of 2 feet

6. What is the area of square Z?

(1)The perimeter is 32.
(2)The side length is 8.

7. What is the product of A and B?

(1) A and B are both even integers between 10 and 20, inclusive.
(2) A − B = 6.

8. What is Y?

(1) X is one-third of Y
(2) $Y^3 = 125$

Directions: For each problem, decide which answer is the best of the choices given.

9. A mechanic must store his leftover antifreeze in a tank in his garage. His largest tank is a cylinder with a radius of 14 and a height of 16 inches. If the antifreeze has a density of 12 cubic inches per gallon, how many gallons of it will fit in the bucket? (Use $\pi = 3.1416$)

    a.   205
    b.   261
    c.   421
    d.   704
    e.   821

10. How many divisors of 60 are prime numbers?

    a.   2
    b.   3
    c.   4
    d.   5
    e.   6

11. For the following fractions, what is the least common denominator?
        2/3, 3/5, 4/6, 9/10, 1/3

    a.   10
    b.   15
    c.   30
    d.   36
    e.   60

12. (75% x 800) + (1/6 x 600) =

    a.   660
    b.   700
    c.   1060
    d.   1200
    e.   1400

13. What is the absolute value of twice the difference of the roots of the equation $5y^2 - 20y + 15 = 0$?

    a.   0
    b.   1
    c.   2
    d.   3
    e.   4

14. What is the next term in the following series?   85, 84, 82, 79, 75.......

    a.   71
    b.   70
    c.   69
    d.   68
    e.   64

15. What is the probability of getting a white jelly bean from a dispenser that contains 28 red jelly beans, 48 green ones, 36 purple ones, 26 pink ones, 30 blue ones and 28 white ones?

     a.   1/8
     b.   1/7
     c.   1/6
     d.   1/5
     e.   ¼

16. How many 4-inch sections of ribbon can be obtained from a roll of ribbon that is 30 yards long?

     a.   108
     b.   270
     c.   360
     d.   810
     e. 1,080

17. One hundred vacationers on a cruise ship have signed up for the ship's activities. Sixty sign up for ballroom dancing lessons. Thirty-five sign up for aerobics class. Twenty sign up for neither ballroom dancing nor aerobics class. How many have signed up for BOTH ballroom dancing and aerobics class?

     a.   5
     b.   10
     c.   12
     d.   15
     e.   18

18. Joe's monthly budget includes $1,200 for rent, $400 for his car payment, $150 for insurance, $250 for utilities, and $200 for groceries. Assuming that Joe' monthly take-home pay is $3,300, what fraction of it is left for discretionary spending?

     a. 1/5
     b. 1/4
     c. 1/3
     d. 2/5
     e. 2/3

19. What is the area of a square with a side of length 5?

     a.   5
     b.   25
     c.   50
     d.   100
     e.   125

20. The first term in a sequence is -50. Every consecutive term is 25 greater than the term that immediately preceded it. What is the value of the 75th term in the sequence?

     a. 1,750
     b. 1,775
     c. 1,800
     d. 1,825
     e. 1,850

21. Which of the following numbers is closest in value to 3/8?

    a. 3/10
    b. 4/13
    c. 5/16.
    d. 7/19
    e. 0.395

22. Jason has 1,489 nickels in a large jar in his bedroom. If he adds 324 nickels on Monday, and adds another 112 nickels on Tuesday, but removes 117 nickels on Wednesday, how much money (in dollars) does Jason have left in the jar on Thursday, assuming that there are no other additions or subtractions?

    a. $90.40
    b. $94.80
    c. $108.80
    d. $180.80
    e. $188.00

23. What is the least positive integer that is divisible by both 2 and 9 and leaves a remainder of 4 when divided by 5?

    a. 18
    b. 36
    c. 45
    d. 49
    e. 54

24. If the 6% hotel tax on a room is $4.32, what was the total price of the room (including tax)?

    a. $70.32
    b. $72.00
    c. $76.00
    d. $76.32
    e. $78.00

25. If 25 less than eight times a number is equal to 215, find the number.

    a. 20
    b. 25
    c. 30
    d. 35
    e. 40

26. Ronda borrowed $15,000 from the bank at 9% simple interest. If she pays the money back over four years, how much will she pay each month in interest?

    a. $37.50
    b. $112.50
    c. $375.00
    d. $450.00
    e. $5,400.00

27. Ben found a jar with 320 coins, all dimes and quarters, which were worth $77.90. How many of the coins were dimes?

    a.   14
    b.   15
    c.   32
    d. 210
    e. 306

28. Each of the equal sides of an isosceles triangle is four less than three times its base. If the perimeter is 90, what is the base of the triangle?

    a. 12
    b. 14
    c. 15
    d. 18
    e. 28

29. If $3x + 4y = 12$ and $x + 8y = 46$, what is the value of $2x + 6y$?

    a. 15
    b. 24
    c. 29
    d. 68
    e. 112

30. If $11 - 4x = 3$, what is the value of $6 - 4x$?

    a. -8
    b. -2
    c.   0
    d.   2
    e.   8

31. Pipe A can fill a tank in 40 hours. Pipe B can fill the same tank in 72 hours. Pipe C can empty the tank in 96 hours. If all three pipes are open at the same time, how many hours will it take to fill the tank?

    a. 20
    b. 35
    c. 40
    d. 56
    e. 60

32. If you roll a 6-sided die, which sides are numbered 1 through 6, what is the probability that you will roll a 3?

    a. 1/6
    b. 1/5
    c. 1/4
    d. 1/3
    e. ½

33. The cost to park at Yankee Stadium is J dollars for the first eight hours and P dollars for each additional hour. How much did Grace pay to park at the stadium for S hours (assuming that S is greater than eight)?

    a.   J + PS
    b.   J + 1/JPS
    c.   J + P(S − 8)
    d.   JPS - P(S − 8)
    e.   J +{(S − 8)/P}

34. What positive integer is 40% less than 15,600?

    a.   4,680
    b.   6,240
    c.   6,864
    d.   8,680
    e.   9,360

35. What is the largest integer that will divide evenly into 57 and 399?

    a.   7
    b.   13
    c.   17
    d.   19
    e.   21

Refer to the chart below for questions 36 and 37.

Percentage of Diabetics (By Age)

	China	Italy	France	Germany
Under 10	5	5	2	0
10 – 18	20	30	15	13
19 – 30	35	30	28	29
31 – 50	30	30	40	48
Over 51	10	5	15	10

36. If there are 15 million diabetics in China, how many of them are less than 31 years old?

    a. 750,000
    b. 3 million
    c. 5.25 million
    d. 9 million
    e. 10 million

37. If there are 8 million diabetics in France, and they each purchase two insulin pumps per year, how many pumps are needed by the diabetics who are 51 or older?

    a. 1.0 million
    b. 1.2 million
    c. 2.4 million
    d. 4 million
    e. 4.8 million

Answer Key for Quantitative Section 4

1. To answer this question, we need to know the ratio of shrimp eaters to roast beef eaters, which is provided in Statement 2. The information in Statement 1 is interesting, but extraneous. Choice B is correct.

2. To answer this question, we need to know the amount of people that the original recipe served. Neither statement gives us this information. Choice E is correct.

3. To answer this question, we need to know the exact number of CDs that one of the boys owns AND enough information to write an equation to solve for the number that belong to Joe. Neither of these statements gives us an exact number for any of the boys; additionally, there is insufficient information to write an equation to solve for the unknown. Choice E is correct.

4. To answer this question, we need to know the relationship of the five numbers, which Statement 1 provides. Statement 2, however, is NOT enough information for us to find the middle number, because it only gives us an average of the 5 values, not the spread. Choice A is correct.

5. The two statements, if taken together, provide enough information for us to answer the question. Choice C is correct.

6. In this case, we can answer the question using either statement. Choice D is correct.

7. Choice E is correct. We do not have enough information to determine definite values for A and B. Therefore, we cannot answer the question.

8. Choice B is correct. Statement 2 is sufficient to answer the question.

9. The problem is asking us to determine the capacity, or volume, of a cylinder. To do so, we can simply use the formula: Volume = $\pi r^2 h$ = (3.1416)(14)(14)(16) = 9,852.06 cubic inches. To convert this to gallons, we must divide by 12: 19,852.06/ cubic inches/12 cubic inches per gallon = **821** gallons. Choice E is correct.

10. Choice B is correct. The divisors of 60 that are prime numbers are **2, 3 and 5**. By definition, 1 is NOT prime.

11. Choice C is correct, **30**.

12. (3/4 x 800) + (1/6 x 600) = 600 + 100 = **700**. Choice B is correct.

13 Choice E is correct. First, factor the 5 out of the original equation which yields $5(y^2 - 4y + 3)$. The trinomial factors into (y - 3)(y - 1) = 0. Setting each term to 0 yields y = 3 and y = 1. The difference is 2. Two times two equals **4**.

14. Then first term decreases by 1, the second term decreases by 2, the third term decreases by 3, etc. The next term in the series would be 75 – 5 = **70**. Choice B is correct.

15. First, we must determine the total number of jelly beans: 28 + 48 + 36 + 26 + 30 + 28 = 196. Then, we can determine the probability of choosing one of a specific color: 28/196 = **1/7**. Choice B is correct.

16. 30 yards x 3 feet/yard x 12 inches/foot = 1,080 inches / 4 = 270 4-inch segments. Choice B is correct

17. The relationship of the groups is defined as follows: Group 1 + Group 2 + Neither – Both = 100. Once we establish this simple equation, we can plug in numbers to solve for the unknown, which in this case is the group defined as Both.

Group 1 + Group 2 + Neither – Both = 100
60 + 35 + 20 – Both = 100
Both = **15**, which is answer choice D.

18. Total expenses = 1200 + 400 + 150 + 250 + 200 = 2200. 2200/3300 = 2/3, which leaves 1/3 for discretionary spending. Choice C is correct.

19. Area = L x W = 5 x 5 = **25**. Choice B is correct.

20. For an arithmetic sequence in which the first term is A and the difference between the terms is D, the *nth* term is: An = A1 + (n − 1)D. In this case, the first term in the sequence is -50. The difference in terms is 25 and n = 75. The 75th term = -50 + (75 − 1)25 = -50 + 1,850 = 1,800. Choice C is correct.

21. 3/8 = 0.375. The closest answer choice is D, **7/19**, which is 0.368.

22. This is a simple addition and subtraction problem, with a final conversion to dollars at the end. When we add and subtract the terms, we get: 1489 + 324 + 112 − 117 = 1808 nickels x ($1.00/20 nickels) = **$90.40**. Choice A is correct.

23. To solve this problem, we must check our answer choices against both criteria in the problem. First, they must be divisible by 2 and 9. Second, they must leave a remainder of 4 when they are divided by 5. Choices C and D are not divisible by 2, so we do not need to examine them further. Of the remaining choices, only Choice E (54) meets both criteria.

24. If 0.06x = $4.32, then x = $72. Total price = **$76.32.** Choice D is correct.

25. This can be solved by a simple equation: 8x − 25 = 215. x = **30**. Choice C is correct.

26. To solve this problem, we must first calculate the total interest that Ronda will pay on the loan. To do so, we use the basic formula, Interest = Principal x Rate x Time. In this case, the Principal = $15000, the Rate = 0.09 and the Time = 4 years. Hence, Interest = ($15000)(0.09)(4) = $5,400 in total interest over 4 years. Now, we must convert this number to a monthly basis. If Ronda pays $5,400 in total interest over 4 years, then she pays $5,400/48 = **$112.50** in interest per month. Choice B is correct.

27. First, we must define our variables. In this case, x = the number of dimes. Therefore, 320 − x = the number of quarters. Since the value of these two coins is $77.90, our equation becomes:
10x + 25(320 − x) = 7790. 10x + 8000 − 25x = 7790. -15x = -210. x = **14** dimes. Choice A is correct.

28. Let x be the length of the base. Perimeter = sum of all three sides = 90 = x + 2(3x - 4) = 7x − 8. Thus, 7x = 98. x = **14**. Choice B is correct.

29. Add the equations together, then divide by 2: 2x + 6y = **29**. Choice C is correct.

30. If 11 − 4x = 3, then x = 2. 6 − (4)(2) = **-2**. Choice B is correct.

31. Our unknown is the total amount of time needed to fill the tank, which is the sum of the intake pipes, minus the drain pipe. Hence, our equation is 1/40 + 1/72 − 1/96 = 1/x. To solve, we must multiply both sides of the equation by 4320x, which is our least common denominator: 108x + 60x − 45x = 4320. 123x = 4320. x = **35.12** hours. Choice B is correct.

32. The probability is **1/6**, or Choice A.

33. This is a simple problem if we substitute numbers for letters. Let's assume that Yankee Stadium charges $20 for the first 8 hours and $5 for each additional hour. Let's also assume that Grace parked for 12 hours. If we do, then J = 20, P = 5, and S = 12. Grace's total cost will be the basic charge for 8 hours, plus the additional cost for every hour over 8. The basic cost = 20 = J. The additional cost per hour = 5(12 − 8) = P(S − 8). Therefore, Grace's total cost = 20 + 5(12 − 8) = **J + P(S − 8).** Choice C is correct.

34. (0.6) 15,600= **9,360**. Choice E is correct.

35. The easiest way to solve this problem is to try each answer choice. The largest one that divides evenly into 57 and 399 is **19,** which is Choice D.

36. (15 million)(0.05 + 0.20 + 0.35) = 9 million. Choice D is correct.

37. If France has a total of 8 million diabetics, then the number of them who are 51 or older is (8 million)(0.15) = 1.2 million. If all of these patients purchase 2 insulin pumps per year, they will require a total of 2.4 million. Choice C is correct.

Quantitative Section 5:   37 questions   75 minutes

Use the following answer choices for questions 1 - 8 below:

A.   Statement 1 alone is sufficient but Statement 2 alone is not sufficient to answer the question asked.
B.   Statement 2 alone is sufficient but Statement 1 alone is not sufficient to answer the question asked.
C.   Statements 1 and 2 together are sufficient to answer the question but neither statement is sufficient alone.
D.   Each statement alone is sufficient to answer the question.
E.   Statements 1 and 2 are not sufficient to answer the question asked and additional data is needed to answer the question.

1. What are the values of X and Y?

(1)   The difference between $(X + Y)$ and $(X - Y)$ is 10
(2)   XY is 120.

2. What is the average of five integers: A, B, C, D, and E?

(1)   The sum of A, B, C, D, and E is 850
(2)   A, B, C, D, and E are consecutive odd integers

3. Debbie put one-half of her annual take-home pay into a CD. How much will it earn in simple annual interest in one year?

(1)   The bank pays 6% annual interest on CDs
(2)   Debbie pays $15,000 of her gross annual income in taxes

4. A Laundromat emptied its vending machines at the end of the night and deposited all of the money in a local bank. How much was the deposit?

(1) The ratio of quarters to dimes was 8:3.
(2) Eighty percent of the coins were nickels and pennies

5. A cube and a rectangular solid are equal in volume. What is the length of an edge of the cube?

(1) The lengths of the edges of the rectangular solid are 8, 9, and 24
(2) The surface area of the rectangular solid is 960

6. What is the perimeter of rectangle WXYZ?

(1) The rectangle has a length of 15
(2) The rectangle is a square

7. What is the cube root of B?

(1)   B is one half of A
(2)   B is the cube of 1000

8. How much did Karen spend on her boyfriend's birthday gift?

(1) Karen bought her boyfriend a 32" plasma television.
(2) The price of the television had been reduced by 40%.

Directions: For each problem, decide which answer is the best of the choices given.

9. For the following data set, what is the mean minus the mode?
                7, 3, 15, 6, 7, 8, 9, 12, 5, 7, 6

    a.   0.127
    b.   0.727
    c.   1.127
    d.   3.000
    e.   7.000

10. A clothing shop sells six pairs of shoes and eight pairs of socks for $995. The cost for four pairs of shoes and twelve pairs of socks is $750. How much would it cost to buy one pair of shoes?

    a. $58.12
    b. $69.75
    c. $77.50
    d. $139.50
    e. $148.50

11. For the repeating decimal 0.23896238962389623896....., what is the 43rd digit to the right of the decimal point?

    a.   2
    b.   3
    c.   6
    d.   8
    e.   9

12. Which of the following expresses the ratio of 8 ounces to 10 pounds?

    a.   1/20
    b.   1/16
    c.   1/12
    d.   1/10
    e.   1/8

13. If $f(j) = j^2 + 0.002j$, what is f (0.5)?

    a.   0.2550
    b.   0.2510
    c.   0.0252
    d.   0.0250
    e.   0.0251

14. Reduce the following fraction to its simplest form: 2,000 / 2 million

    a.   1/1000
    b.   2/1000
    c.   1/100
    d.   2/100
    e.   1/10

15. $(5y^2)^3(2y^3)^2 =$

    a. $10y^6$
    b. $250y^6$
    c. $500y^6$
    d. $250y^{12}$
    e. $500y^{12}$

16. Which of the following is not a factor of 420?

    a.   10
    b.   15
    c.   40
    d.   42
    e.   60

17. In triangle ABC, AB = 3 and BC = 5. Which of the following could possibly be the length of side AC?

    a.   6
    b.   9
    c.   10
    d.   either a, b or c
    e.   none of the above

18. Which of the following polygons has all sides of equal length and all angles of identical measure?

    a.   hexagon
    b.   octagon
    c.   nonagon
    d.   pentagon
    e.   None of the above

19. The line represented by 3x −9y = 12 is parallel to which of the following lines?

    a.   y = 3x + 5
    b.   y = 12x + 1
    c.   y = 1/3x -8
    d.   y = 4/3 x -3
    e.   y = 3x + 4/3

20. What is the value of x if xy + xz = 15 and y + z = 3?

    a.   1/2
    b.   1
    c.   3
    d.   5
    e.   15

21. Which of the following are the solutions to the following equation? $x^2 -7x + 10= 0$

    a.   5, 2
    b.   2, -5
    c.   −2, -5
    d.   −2, 5
    e.   5, ½

22. Stephanie has a certain amount of money invested at 4% and three times that amount invested at 7%. If the total annual interest from her two investments is $17,500, how much does Stephanie have invested at 7%?

    a. $35,000
    b. $70,000
    c. $135,000
    d. $170,000
    e. $210,000

23. The base of a triangle is 16 more than the height. If the area of the triangle is 256 square inches, what is its base?

    a.   4
    b.   8
    c.   16
    d.   32
    e.   36

24. What is 5/4 divided by 7/6?

    a.   15/30
    b.   24/28
    c.   24/35
    d.   14/15
    e.   15/14

25. Three hundred entertainers will perform at a talent show. The group contains only singers and dancers. If the ratio of singers to dancers is 2:1, how many dancers are there?

    a.   50
    b.   100
    c.   150
    d.   175
    e.   200

26. Carla owed her university $585 in tuition. When she receives her paycheck of $116, she pays it all to the university, along with $219 that she has borrowed from a friend. Later in the day, Carla wins $947 in the lottery, and immediately pays off the rest of her tuition bill and her friend. How much money does Carla have left?

    a. $250
    b. $362
    c. $478
    d. $697
    e. $728

27. If Q is 25% of R and S is 30% of R, what is the ratio of Q to S?

    a. 3/20
    b. 1/5
    c. 11/20
    d. 3/4
    e. 5/6

28. Five consecutive even integers have a sum of 370. What is the largest of the five integers?

    a. 70
    b. 76
    c. 78
    d. 80
    e. 82

29. The length of a rectangular gift box is 4 inches shorter than its width. If the area of the box is 572 square inches, what is its length?

    a. 18
    b. 20
    c. 22
    d. 26
    e. 28

30. At a local hospice with 200 patients, 120 have HIV and the rest have cancer. If 70 of the patients are under 18 and one quarter of the cancer patients are over 18, how many of the patients are under 18 with HIV?

    a. 10
    b. 20
    c. 60
    d. 70
    e. 80

31. In a jar containing dimes and nickels, the ratio of nickels to dimes is 3:5. If there are 80 coins, what is value of the nickels (in dollars)?

    a. $0.10
    b. $0.50
    c. $1.00
    d. $1.50
    e. $2.50

32. Professor Davis can write a book manuscript in 5 days. His graduate student Miguel can write the same manuscript in 10 days. After working alone for 3 days, Professor Davis was called away on urgent business, which left Miguel alone to finish the manuscript. How many days did it take Miguel to finish it?

    a. 2
    b. 3
    c. 4
    d. 5
    e. 6

33. If the following series continues in the same pattern, what will the next term be?

        5, 9, 6, 11, 7, 13, 8, 15.....

    a. 7
    b. 9
    c. 11
    d. 12
    e. 13

34. What is the total cost (in cents) of W watermelons, which cost X dollars each, and Y apples, which cost Z cents each?

    a.   WXYZ/100
    b.   100WX + YZ
    c.   WX + 100YZ
    d.   W + YZ/100
    e.   100WX/YZ

Refer to the following charts to answer questions 35 – 37.

Number of Financial Products Sold

	Traditional Brokerage	Online Brokerage
CD	200	350
Annuity	50	105
401-K	85	409

Total Value of Financial Product Sold (in millions)

	CD	Annuity	401-k
Traditional Brokerage	54	23	10
Online Brokerage	92	27	31

35. For the time period represented by these charts, what was the average value of an Annuity sold at the traditional brokerage house (in millions of dollars)?

    a.   0.23
    b.   0.25
    c.   0.46
    d.   0.50
    e.   0.75

36. For the time period represented by these charts, what was the average value of a 401-K sold at an online brokerage house (in millions of dollars)?

    a.   0.076
    b.   0.088
    c.   0.100
    d.   0.295
    e.   0.358

37. For the time period represented by these charts, what was the total value of all financial products sold by the online brokerage (in millions of dollars)?

    a.   87
    b.   146
    c.   150
    d.   237
    e.   864

Answer Key for Quantitative Section 5

1. Statements 1 and 2, if taken together, will allow us to write an equation to solve for both X and Y. Neither is sufficient on its own. Choice C is correct.

2. To answer this question, we need to know the sum of the numbers and their relationship to each other. Statement 1 provides the sum, while Statement 2 defines their relationship. If taken together, they allow us to answer the question. Choice C is correct.

3. To answer this question, we need to know the principal, the rate, and the time. Statement 1 tells us the rate and the question stem tells us the time. However, neither statement gives us enough information to calculate the amount of Debbie's original investment. Choice E is correct.

4. To answer this question, we must know (or be able to calculate) the total number of coins in the machines. Neither statement provides this information. Therefore, Choice E is correct.

5. Each statement, on its own, provides enough information to answer the question. Choice D is correct.

6. To answer this question, we need to know the length and width of the rectangle. Statement 1 gives us the length, while Statement 2 tells us that the rectangle is a square (which means that its width is also 15). Taken together, we have enough information to answer the question. Choice C is correct.

7. Choice B is correct. Statement 2 is sufficient to answer the question. Statement 1 is extraneous information.

8. Choice E is correct. Statements 1 and 2 are not sufficient to answer the question.

9. The mean of these numbers is 85/11 = 7.727. The mode is 7. 7.727 – 7 = **0.727**. Choice B is correct.

10. In this case, we can write one equation for the first condition and a second equation for the second condition. As always, we must first define our variables. We will let = x the cost of one pair of shoes and y = the cost of one pair of socks.

The first equation, which defines the first condition, is 6x + 8y = 995
The second equation, which defines the second condition, is 4x + 12y = 750
To solve the problem for x, we must combine the equations in a way that eliminates y.

We can do this by multiplying the first equation by 3 and the second equation by 2. When we do, we get: 18x + 24y = 2,985. 8ex+ 24y = 1,500. If we subtract the second equation from the first, we get 10x = 1,485. Therefore, x = **$148.50** = the cost of one pair of shoes. Choice E is correct.

11. The repeating pattern is 23896, which includes 5 digits. The 43rd[th] digit is the third digit in the string, which is **8**, or Choice D.

12. 10 pounds = 160 oz. 8/160 = **1/20**. Choice A is correct.

13. If f(j) = j^2 + 0.002j, then f (0.5) = (0.5)(0.5) + (0.002)(0.5) = 0.25 + 0.001 = **0.251**. Choice B is correct.

14. 2,000 / 2,000, 000 = **1/1000**. Choice A is correct.

15. $(5y^2)^3(2y^3)^2$ = $(125y^6)(4y^6)$ = **500y^{12}**. Choice E is correct.

16. Choice C, **40**.

17. The length of the third side of the triangle must be less than the sum of the other two sides. Thus, the length must be less than 5 + 3 = **8.** Choice A is correct.

18. Octagon. Choice B is correct.

19. Parallel lines have the same slope. In this case, the slope of 3x –9y = 12 is 1/3, because the equation simplifies to 9y = 3x – 12, or y = 1/3x – 4/3. Choice C also has a slope of **1/3.**

20. xy + xz = 15, so x (y + z) = 15. Since (y + z) = 3, 3x = 15 and x = **5**. Choice D is correct.

21. If x^2 -7x + 10= 0, then (x – 2)(x - 5) = 0. So, x = 5, or **2**. Choice A is correct.

22. To solve, we must first determine how much interest Stephanie earns on each investment separately.

For simplicity, we will x = the amount she has invested at 4%. Therefore, 3x = the amount that she has invested at 7%. The interest on the account that pays 4% = 0.04x. The interest on the account that pays 7% = (0.07)3x = 0.21x.

According to the problem, 0.04x + 0.21x = $17,500.
Therefore, 0.25x = $17,500, so x = $70,000 = amount invested at 4%.
3x = **$210,000** = the amount invested at 7%. Choice E is correct.

23. Area = ½(Base)(Height). Here, we will let x = the height and x+16 = the base. Therefore,
256 = ½ x(x + 16)
512 = x² + 16x
0 = x² + 16x – 512
0 = (x - 16)(x + 32). The height = 16 inches. The base = X + 16 = **32** inches. Choice C is correct.

24. Choice E is correct, **15/14**.

25. For a 2:1 ratio, the whole is 3. 2/3 of 300 = 200 singers;1/3 of 300 =**100** dancers. Choice B is correct.

26. The easiest way to solve this problem is to keep a running total of what Carla has. When she pays the first part of her tuition bill, she winds up owing 250 (585 – 116 – 219 = 250). Then, after Carla wins the lottery and settles up with both the school and her friend, she has 947 – 250 – 219 = **478**. Choice C is correct.

27. Q = 0.25R. S = 0.3R. Thus, Q/S = 0.25/0.30 = 5/6. Choice E is correct.

28. From the data in the problem, we can write the following equation: x + (x + 2) + (x + 4) + (x + 6) + (x + 8) = 370, so 5x + 20 = 370, so 5x = 350, x = 70. x + 8 = **78**. Choice C is correct.

29. First, let's define our variables. We will let x = the length of the gift box. Therefore, its width = x + 4 and its area (Length x Width) = x(x + 4). Our equation becomes: x(x + 4) = 572. x² + 4x - 572 = 0. (x – 22)(x +26) = 0. Therefore, x = 22 and -26. Since a length cannot be negative, we can discard the -26 root. The length of the rectangle is **22** and the width is 22 + 4 = 26. Choice C is correct. .

30. The best way to attack this type of problem is to summarize our data in a simple table.
In this case, the hospice patients either have HIV or cancer. Some of the patients are under 18, while others are over 18. When we put the information into our chart, we get:

	HIV	Cancer	Total
Under 18	10	60	70
Over 18	110	20	130
Total	120	80	200

From the table, we can answer the question; the number of HIV patients under 18 is **10**. Choice A is correct.

31. In this case, the test writers have thrown us a curveball by presenting the number of nickels to dimes as a ratio. Don't be intimidated by it – just use the information to define the variables. In this case, since the ratio of nickels to dimes is 3:5, we will let 3x = the number of nickels and 5x = the number of dimes. Since their total is 80, our equation becomes: 3x + 5x = 80. 8x = 80. x = 10. Therefore, the number of nickels is 3(10) = 30; their value is 5(30) = **$1.50**. Choice D is correct.

32. To solve, we must first calculate the amount of work that Professor Davis did in 3 days, which is (1/5)(3) = 3/5. Miguel, therefore, only had to complete 2/5 of the book. Since Miguel's rate is 1/10, our equation becomes 1/10 = (1/x)(2/5), or 1/10 = 2/5x. 1/10 = 2/5x. x = **4** days. Choice C is correct

33. This problem is a combination of two sub-series. In the first one, each number increase by 1 (5, 6, 7, 8); in the second, each number increases by 2 (9, 11, 13, 15). The next number would be **9**. Choice B is correct.

34. Let's substitute numbers for the variables and see what we get. Let's assume that we have 10 watermelons that cost $3.00 each and 5 apples that cost 60 cents each. Hence, W = 10, X = 3.00, Y = 5 and Z = 0.60.

The total cost of W watermelons is 100(10)(3) = 100WX
The total cost of C apples is (5)(60) = YZ
Therefore, the total cost of the watermelons and apples is 100(10)(3) + (5)(6) = **100WX + YZ**. Choice B is correct.

35. The average value = 23/50 = **0.46** million dollars. Choice C is correct.

36. The average value = 31/409 = **0.076** million dollars. Choice A is correct.

37. Total value of financial products sold by online brokerage = 92 + 27 + 31 = **150** million. Choice C is correct.

Quantitative Section 6: 37 questions   75 minutes

Use the following answer choices for questions 1 - 8 below:

A.   Statement 1 alone is sufficient but Statement 2 alone is not sufficient to answer the question asked.
B.   Statement 2 alone is sufficient but Statement 1 alone is not sufficient to answer the question asked.
C.   Statements 1 and 2 together are sufficient to answer the question but neither statement is sufficient alone.
D.   Each statement alone is sufficient to answer the question.
E.   Statements 1 and 2 are not sufficient to answer the question asked and additional data is needed to answer the question.

1. Joe borrowed $25,000 from the bank. How much will his monthly payments be?

(1) The term of the loan is two years
(2) The interest rate is fixed at 4.9%

2. A general admission ticket to a concert costs $32, while a student ticket costs $10. On Saturday night, the concert hall generated $12,400 in total ticket sales. How many students attended?

(1) The concert hall holds 1,000 people
(2) There were a total of 800 tickets sold

3. Nancy is three years younger than her brother Cane, who is eight years older than Jake. How old is Nancy?

(1) Jake is 27
(2) Cane is 35

4. Gary and Bill decide to work together to mow a two-acre lawn. How many hours will it take them to complete the job?

(1) Gary can mow a one-acre lawn in 3 hours
(2) Bill works half as fast as Gary

5. What is the value of 5x?

(1) x is an integer greater than 3 but less than 6.
(2) 5x is even

6. How much time does a doctor need to complete his house calls?

(1) He needs to visit three patients.
(2) All three patients live on the same street.

7. What is the value of S?

(1) $43 < S < 46$
(2) X is an even integer

8. Is X < 16?

(1) $X < Y$
(2) $4^2 < Y < 5^2$

Directions: **For each problem, decide which answer is the best of the choices given.**

9. To get a grade of A in Spanish, Sara must achieve an average of 90 or above on six exams. Thus far, Sara's scores on the first five exams are 96, 81, 79, 87 and 100. What is the lowest possible score that Sara can get on the final exam to get an A grade in Spanish?

    a. 95
    b. 96
    c. 97
    d. 98
    e. 99

10. A business executive and his client are charging their dinner tab on the executive's expense account. The company will only allow them to spend a total of $50 for the meal. Assuming that they will pay 7% in sales tax for the meal and leave a 15% tip, what is the most that their food can cost?

    a. $39.55
    b. $40.03
    c. $40.63
    d. $41.15
    e. $43.15

11.   What is the sum of the integers between 11 and 39, inclusive?

    a. 525
    b. 625
    c. 725
    d. 1,400
    e. 1,500

12. The graph of $y = 4x^2 - 12$ is:

    a. A straight line
    b. A parabola opening upward
    c. A parabola opening downward
    d. A circle
    e. None of the above

13. A city park is frequently used as an exercise path. If the park is a square, with each side 2,400 feet long, how many minutes would it take someone walking 600 feet per minute to walk the entire perimeter of the park?

    a. 8
    b. 12
    c. 16
    d. 20
    e. 40

14. There are five possible electives for Julie to take at her local community college this summer: English, Math, Statistics, History and Social Studies. Her counselor has advised Julie to choose two of them. How many possible combinations of the two courses are there?

    a. 30
    b. 25
    c. 15
    d. 12
    e. 10

15. When a store owner compiled her weekly sales records, she had a stack of invoices numbered 014567 through 019876. Upon further examination, however, the store owner realized that invoice numbers 014876 and 018999 were missing. How many invoices did the store owner have available for her weekly calculations?

   a. 5307
   b. 5308
   c. 5309
   d. 5310
   e. 5311

16. In the xy-plane, a circle is centered at the origin and passes through the point (-7,0). What is the area of the circle?

   a. $49/\pi$
   b. $3.5\,\pi$
   c. $7\,\pi$
   d. $49\,\pi$
   e. $81\,\pi$

17. If $f(a) = a^2 - 4a + 3$, what is f(-1) ?

   a. -2
   b. 0
   c. 7
   d. 8
   e. 9

18. What is the mean of the following set of numbers? 44, 33, 58, 22, 16, 66

   a. 35.8
   b. 38.5
   c. 38.9
   d. 39.8
   e. 39.9

19. 23/42 – 35/84 =

   a. −12/84
   b. −11/84
   c.   11/84
   d.   12/84
   e.   12/42

20. For the repeating decimal 0.04321043210432104321....., what is the 49th digit to the right of the decimal point?

   a. 0
   b. 1
   c. 2
   d. 3
   e. 4

21. If p =3 and q is 2, what is $(9^p)(27^q)$ =

     a. 3^9
     b. 3^{14}
     c. $(729)^2$
     d. 6561 x 2
     e. 9^5

22. If m (8)(10)(12)(14)= (4)(5)(6)(7), what is the value of m?

     a. 1/16
     b. 1/8
     c. ½
     d. 8
     e. 16

23. Which of the following are the solutions to the following equation? $x^2 + 3x - 18 = 0$

     a. −2, 9
     b. 2, -9
     c. -3, 6
     d. 3, -6
     e. 3, -9

24. 12.67 =

     a. 37/4
     b. 38/3
     c. 72/6
     d. 72.5
     e. 100/6

25. Which of the following expresses the ratio of 12 ounces to 6 pounds?

     a. 1/16
     b. 1/12
     c. 1/8
     d. 1/6
     e. ¼

26. If 86,868,686 is divided by 6,868, what is the remainder?

     a. 2222
     b. 3434
     c. 4343
     d. 6832
     e. 12648

27. The Glenview Airport offers two parking lots: long-term and short-term. Long-term parking costs a flat rate of $7.00 per day. Short-term parking costs $1.00 for the first two hours, and 50 cents for each additional hour. If a visitor plans to park for 6 hours at the airport, what will be the additional cost of parking in long-term parking versus short-term parking?

    a. $1.00
    b. $3.00
    c. $4.00
    d. $6.00
    e. $7.00

28. What is the product of the prime numbers between 10 and 20?

    a.   60
    b.   3,536
    c.   4,199
    d. 46,189
    e. 508,079

29. Carrie added M coins to her large collection, which gave her a total of N coins. Then, Carrie sold M – 180 of her coins to a local collector. How many coins did Carrie have left?

    a. M - N + 180
    b. N + M - 180
    c. N - M + 180
    d. N - M - 180
    e. (M + N – 180)/2

30. A stock decreases in value by 20 percent. By what percent must the stock price increase to reach its former value?

    a. 20%
    b. 25%
    c. 30%
    d. 40%
    e. 50%

31. The amount of sugar in a cake batter varies directly as the weight of the batter. If there are 42 pounds of sugar in a one-ton quantity of batter, how many pounds of sugar would there be in 325 pounds of batter?

    a. 3.412
    b. 6.825
    c. 13.650
    d. 27.30
    e. 54.60

32. The sum of two numbers is 238. Their difference is 46. What is the smaller number?

    a. 96
    b. 104
    c. 136
    d. 142
    e. 150

33. What is the thirteenth even positive integer minus the twelfth odd positive integer?

    a. 1
    b. 2
    c. 3
    d. 12
    e. 13

34. The mean of two numbers is $11d + 5$. If one of the numbers is d, what is the other number?

    a. $(11g - 5)/d$
    b. $(g + 5)/d$
    c. $(g - 5)/10$
    d. $(g - 5) /(10 - d)$
    e. it cannot be determined from the information given

Refer to the chart below for questions 35– 37

	2005	2006	2007	2008
Number of snow plows sold (thousands)	50	70	75	80
Annual snowfall (inches)	110	150	140	175

35. In what year was the number of snow plows sold per foot of snow 5600?

    a. 2005
    b. 2006
    c. 2007
    d. 2008
    e. It cannot be determined from the information given

36. In which year was the number of snowplows sold per inch of snow the highest?

    a. 2005
    b. 2006
    c. 2007
    d. 2008
    e. It cannot be determined from the information given

37. In which two years were the number of snowplows sold per foot of snowfall nearly identical?

    a. 2005 and 2006
    b. 2006 and 2007
    c. 2007 and 2008
    d. 2005 and 2008
    e. 2005 and 2007

Answer Key for Quantitative Section 6

1. To answer this question, we need to know the principal, the rate, and the time. Statement 1 tells us the time, Statement 2 tells us the rate, and the question stem tells us the principal. Choice C is correct.

2. To answer this question, we simply need to know the total number of tickets sold, which is provided in Statement 2. Statement 1, although interesting, is extraneous. Choice B is correct.

3. Either statement is sufficient to answer the question. Hence, Choice D is correct.

4. To solve this problem, we need to know the individual rates for Gary and Bill. Statement 1 gives us Gary's rate, while Statement 2 gives us Bill's rate. Choice C is correct.

5. To solve, we need to know the value of x. From Statement 1, we know that x is either 4 or 5. From Statement 2, we know that x must be 4. Choice C is correct.

6. To solve, we need to know the number of house calls the doctor will make and the amount of time he needs to complete each one. Neither statement gives us the second quantity, which means that we do not have enough information to solve the problem. Choice E is correct.

7. Choice C is correct. When considered together, Statement 1 and Statement 2 give us enough information to answer the question.

8. Choice C is correct. When considered together, Statements 1 and 2 give us enough information to answer the question.

9. To solve, we can use the following equation: $90 = (x + 96 + 81 + 79 + 87 + 100) / 6$. When we solve the equation for x, we find that it is **97**, which is Choice C.

10. The total bill, which can be no more than $50, includes the cost of the meal, 7% sales tax and a 15% tip. If we let x = the cost of the food, then the tax = 0.07x. The tip is 15% of the total cost of the food and the 7% tip. Algebraically, we can represent the tip as $0.15 (x + 0.07x) = 0.1605x$. Since the total bill can be no more than $50, our final equation for the meal is: Meal + Tax + Tip = 50, or $x + 0.07x + 0.1605x = 50$. Solving for x, the cost of the meal must be less than **$40.63**. Answer Choice C is correct.

11. The find the sum of the integers between 11 and 39, inclusive, we must use the formula, Sum = Average x Number of terms. The Average = 11 + 39 / 2 = 25. Number of terms = 39 – 11 + 1 = 29. The Sum = 25 x 29 = **725**. Choice C is correct.

12. A parabola opening upward. Choice B is correct.

13. If the park is a square with a side length of 2,400 feet, the perimeter is 2,400 (4), or 9,600 feet. Someone walking 600 feet per minute would take 9,600/600, or **16** minutes to walk the perimeter of the park. Choice C is correct.

14. For 5 items, there are **10** possible combinations of any 2 of them (5 x 2 = 10). In this case, they are: English/Math, English/Statistics, English/History, English/Social Studies, Math/Statistics, Math/History, Math/Social Studies, Statistics/History, Statistics/Social Studies, and History/Social Studies. Choice E is correct.

15. To find the original number of invoices in the series, we must subtract the endpoints and add one: 019876 – 014567 + 1 = 5310. Next, we must subtract the two missing invoices: 5310 - 2 = **5308**. Choice B is correct.

16. A circle that is centered at the origin and passes through point (-7, 0) has a radius of 7. Therefore, its area is **49 π,** which is answer Choice D.

17. If f (a) = a^2 - 4a + 3, then f(-1) = (-1)(-1) - 4(-1) + 3 = 1 + 4 + 3 = **8**. Choice D is correct.

18. The mean is **39.8**, or Choice D.

19. Choice C is correct, **11/84**.

20. The repeating pattern is 04321, which includes 5 digits. The 49th digit is **2**, or Choice C.

21. If p =3 and q is 2, then $(9^p)(27^q) =$ (9)(9)(9) (27)(27) = 531,441, which is **$(729)^2$**. Choice C is correct.

22. m =**1/16**. Choice A is correct.

23. If x^2 + 3x – 18= 0, then (x + 6)(x - 3) = 0. So, **x = 3, -6**. Choice D is correct.

24. 12.67 = **38/3**. Choice B is correct.

25. 6 pounds = 96 oz. 12/96 = **1/8**. Choice C is correct.

26. We can solve this problem by dividing the two quantities: 86868686/6868 = 12648.323529. 0.323529 x 6868 = 2222. Choice A is correct. To check: 12648 x 6,868 = 86866464 + **2222**

27. Short-term parking for 6 hours costs $1.00 + 4(0.50) = $3.00. Long-term parking costs $7.00, which is **$4.00** more. Choice C is correct.

28. The prime numbers between 10 and 20 are 11, 13, 17, and 19. Their product is (11)(13)(17)(19)= **46,189**. Choice D is correct.

29. The fastest way to solve this problem is to substitute numbers for the variables. Then, we can convert the relationship back to letters. Let's say M = 200 and N = 500. Therefore, (M − 180) = 20.

When Carrie sold the coins, she reduced her collection by the following amount: 500 − (M − 180) = 500 − M + 180. Converting this back to letters, she had **N − M + 180** coins left. Choice C is correct.

30. Let's solve this by using $100 as the initial price of the stock: The 20% decrease reduced the stock price to $80. For the stock to reach $100 again, there must be a $20 increase. $20 is what % of $80? 20/80 x 100 = 25%. Choice B is correct.

31. 42 / 2000 = x / 325. x = **6.825** lb. Choice B is correct.

32. First, let's define our variables. We will let one number = x. Therefore, the second unknown is x − 46. The sum of these two numbers is 238. Hence, our equation becomes: x + (x − 46) = 238. 2x = 284. x = 142. x − 46 = 142 − 46 = **96**. Choice A is correct.

33. We can solve this using the formulas for arithmetic sequences:

13th even: 2 + (13-1)(2) = 2 + 24 = 26.
12th odd: 1 + (12 − 1)(2) = 1 + 22 = 23.
26 − 23 = **3**. Choice C is correct.

34. In this case, we know that there are two numbers being averaged, one of which is d. We do not know the value of the other number, so we must "assign" an arbitrary value. Since the answer choices all include a term with the variable g, let's use g to represent our unknown. By definition, their sum divided by two = the average. Mathematically, (d + g) / 2 = 11d + 5. 2d + 2g = 22d + 10. 2g -10 = 20d. g − 5 = 10d. **d = (g - 5)/10**. Choice C is correct.

35. In 2006, the number of snowplows sold per foot of snow = 5600. 70,000/12.5 feet = **5,600**. Choice B is correct.

36. In 2007, the number of snowplows sold per inch of snow was 75,000/140 inches = **535.71**. Choice C is correct.

37. In 2005, the number of snowplows sold per foot of snow = 50,000/9.17 feet = 5,454. In 2008, the number of snowplows sold per foot of snow = 80,000/14.58 feet = **5,486**. Choice D is correct.

Quantitative Section 7:   37 questions   75 minutes

Use the following answer choices for questions 1 - 8 below:

A.   Statement 1 alone is sufficient but Statement 2 alone is not sufficient to answer the question asked.
B.   Statement 2 alone is sufficient but Statement 1 alone is not sufficient to answer the question asked.
C.   Statements 1 and 2 together are sufficient to answer the question but neither statement is sufficient alone.
D.   Each statement alone is sufficient to answer the question.
E.   Statements 1 and 2 are not sufficient to answer the question asked and additional data is needed to answer the question.

1. Sam is five times as old as Greg. Lori is 15 years older than Sam. How old is Greg?

(1) Four years ago, Lori was six times as old as Greg
(2) The combined age of Sam, Greg, and Lori is 81.

2. Two delivery trucks are 640 miles apart. At midnight, they start to travel toward each other. In how many hours will they pass?

(1) Truck 1's speed is twice that of Truck 2
(2) Truck 1 travels at a rate of 50 miles per hour

3. How long will it take two stenographers to type a manuscript that is 1,000 pages long?

(1) Stenographer 1 can type four times as fast as Stenographer 2
(2) Stenographer 2 can type 50% faster than Stenographer 3, who can type 10 pages per hour

4. A bartender will mix Liquor A, which is X% alcohol, with Liquor B, which is Y% alcohol, to yield a 1,500 gallon batch of Liquor C, which is Z% alcohol. How many gallons of Liquor B must he use?

(1) $X = 5$
(2) $Y = 20$

5. How many people are needed to wrap one hundred holiday gifts in two hours?

(1) Six people can wrap five large boxes on one hour.
(2) The gifts include twenty small boxes and eighty large boxes.

6. How much did Cameron spend on gas?

(1) The cost of gas is $2.95 per gallon.
(2) Cameron topped off his 22-gallon tank.

7. What is the product of G and H?

(1) G and H are different prime integers between 10 and 15.
(2) $H - G = 2$

8. What is the numerical value of Y/X?

(1) X is one-third of Y
(2) $Y^5 = 125$

9. If $f(v) = 5v^2 - 1/8v - 3$, what is $f(v^3)$?

    a. $5v^5 - 1/8v^4 - 3v^3$
    b. $5v^5 - 1/8v^4 - 3$
    c. $15v^5 - 3/8v^4 - 9$
    d. $(5v^2 - 1/8v - 3)^3$
    e. $(5v^5 - 1/8v^4 - 3)^{-3}$

10. What is the slope of the line that contains points (2,3) and (8, 10)?

    a. 5/4
    b. 6/7
    c. 7/6
    d. 4/5
    e. 1

11. Square X has a side of 17 inches, while square Y has a side of 27 inches. How much greater is the area of square Y than square X (in square inches)?

    a. 100
    b. 270
    c. 289
    d. 440
    e. 729

12. What is the next term in the following series? 1, 7, 13, 19.......

    a. 13
    b. 21
    c. 25
    d. 27
    e. 29

13. In a family of eight children, half are girls and half are boys. If the average height of the girls is 56 inches and the average height of the boys is 42 inches, what is the average height of all eight children?

    a. 48
    b. 49
    c. 50
    d. 51
    e. 52

14. At the end of the day, the clerk in a Laundromat has 3,500 coins that are a combination of nickels and quarters. If the coins are worth $750, how many of them are nickels?

    a. 625
    b. 750
    c. 1,350
    d. 2,750
    e. 2,875

15. A parallelogram with an area of 36 has a base of $(x + 8)$ and a height of $(x - 8)$. What is the exact measure of its height?

    a.   2
    b.   4
    c.   8
    d.   10
    e.   18

16. A parallelogram has an interior angle of 60 degrees. What is the measure of the adjacent angle?

    a.   90
    b.   120
    c.   180
    d.   300
    e.   It cannot be determined from the information given

17. What is the diameter of a circle with an area of 144π

    a.   7
    b.   12
    c.   15
    d.   24
    e.   48

18. Find the number of sides in a polygon if the measure of an interior angle is twice as great as the measure of an exterior angle.

    a.   4
    b.   5
    c.   6
    d.   7
    e.   8

19. If $f(j) = j^2 + 0.001j$, what is $f(0.05)$?

    a.   0.00025
    b.   0.00250
    c.   0.00255
    d.   0.00300
    e.   0.00350

20. Which of the following numbers CANNOT be even?

    a.   The sum of two odd numbers
    b.   The sum of an odd number and an even number
    c.   The product of two even numbers
    d.   The product of an odd number and an even number
    e.   The sum of two even numbers

21. Reduce the following fraction to its simplest form: 50,000 / 5 million

    a.   1/1000
    b.   5/1000
    c.   1/100
    d.   5/100
    e.   1/10

22. What number, when cubed, is equal to the square of 125?

    a.   5
    b.   15
    c.   25
    d.   35
    e.   50

23. Solve for x: $(x + 5) - (4/2)(6/3) = 12$

    a. -2
    b. 4/5
    c. 8
    d. 11
    e. 13

24. Solve the following equations for y: $2x + 4y = 18$, $4x - 6y = 8$.

    a.   2
    b.   3
    c.   4
    d.   5
    e.   6

25. What is the value of $(x + 2)(x + 5) - (x + 1)(x + 3)$?

    a.   3x + 7
    b.   3x - 7
    c.   5x - 10
    d.   5x + 10
    e.   5x - 7

26. If $6x < 1{,}000$, what integer is the largest possible value of x?

    a. 1
    b. 2
    c. 3
    d. 4
    e. 5

27. A shopkeeper reduced the price of a refrigerator from $1000 to $500. A week later, he reduced the sales price by an additional 15%. What was the new price for the refrigerator?

    a. $350
    b. $375
    c. $400
    d. $425
    e. $450

28. After decreasing by 23% after a tsunami, the population of Sri Lanka is now 578,845. What was the original population?

    a. 445,710
    b. 548,224
    c. 674,315
    d. 711,979
    e. 751,746

29. An online store sells two products: a hardcover and soft cover book of sonnets. Altogether, the company earned $65,000 in profits last year on the sale of 5000 units. If their profit on the hardcover book is $5 and their profit on the soft cover version is $15, how many soft cover books did they sell?

    a. 1000
    b. 1500
    c. 2000
    d. 3500
    e. 4000

30. Adam earns twice as much per hour as Josh. Josh earns $5 more per hour than Connie. Together, they earn $75 per hour. What is Adam's hourly wage?

    a. $15
    b. $20
    c. $25
    d. $30
    e. $40

31. W, which is a positive integer, is the first term in a sequence. After W, each term in the sequence is 2 greater than one-half the preceding term. What is the ratio of the second term to W?

    a. $1/2W/(W + 2)$
    b. $(W + 4)2W$
    c. $(W + 2)/2$
    d. $W/2$
    e. $4(W + 1)/2$

32. Over the summer, Bill borrowed $6,500 from the bank at 8% simple interest. If he pays the money back over three years, what total amount of interest will Bill pay on the loan?

    a. $156
    b. $520
    c. $1040
    d. $1560
    e. $2080

33. Grace had $124.50 in her cookie jar, which consisted of nickels, dimes, and quarters. If Grace had 50 more nickels than quarters and 30 more dimes than nickels, how many quarters did Grace have?

    a. 285
    b. 315
    c. 335
    d. 345
    e. 365

34. What is the value of $c(c^{a+b})/c^a$?

    a. c^{a+b}
    b. $2c^b$
    c. c^{1+b}
    d. c^{2b}
    e. c/c^b

Refer to the following charts to answer questions 35 – 37.

Number of Financial Products Sold

	Traditional Brokerage	**Online Brokerage**
CD	200	350
Annuity	50	105
401-K	85	409

Total Value of Financial Product Sold (in millions)

	CD	**Annuity**	**401-k**
Traditional Brokerage	54	23	10
Online Brokerage	92	27	31

35. What was the total number of Annuities sold at both brokerage houses for the time period represented by these charts?

    a.   23
    b.   27
    c.   50
    d.   105
    e.   155

36. What was the total number of financial products sold at the online brokerage for the time period represented by these charts?

    a.   150
    b.   155
    c.   335
    d.   864
    e.   1199

37. CDs account for what percentage of the total dollar value of financial products sold at the traditional brokerage house (for the time period represented by these charts)?

    a.   27.0%
    b.   37.0%
    c.   59.7%
    d.   62.1%
    e.   70.2%

Answer Key for Quantitative Section 7

1. Statement 2 gives us the sum of the three ages, which is enough for us to calculate Greg's age. Statement 1 is extraneous information that is designed to confuse you. Choice B is correct.

2. To answer this question, we need to know the speed of both trucks. Statements 1 and 2, if taken together, give us enough information to solve the problem. Choice C is correct.

3. This question is about as tricky as the GMAT gets. Statement 2 gives us an actual rate for Stenographer 3, who which allows us to calculate the respective rates for Stenographers 1 and 2. But, neither statement tells us which two stenographers will be typing the 1,000 page manuscript. Therefore, Choice E is correct. We do not have sufficient information to answer the question.

4. At first blush, it seems like we can solve the problem by using Statements 1 and 2, which give us the percentages of alcohol in Liquors A and B. But, we actually need a *third* piece of information to solve the problem, which is the % of alcohol in the final blend, which is Z. Since neither statement provides us with this value, Choice E is correct.

5. To solve the problem, we need to know how many of the gift boxes are large and how many are small. We also need to know how quickly people can wrap both size gift boxes. Statement 2 tells us the how many of the boxes are large and small, while Statement 1 tells us how quickly people can wrap the large boxes. Unfortunately, neither statement tells us how quickly they can wrap the small gift boxes. Hence, we cannot answer the question without additional information. Choice E is correct.

6. Choice E is correct. This is as tricky as the GMAT gets, because it uses the expression "topped off" to indicate that Cameron completely filled his gas tank. But it does NOT tell us how much gas was originally in the tank; as a result, we cannot answer the question.

7. Choice A is correct. Statement 1 gives us enough information to answer the question. (G and H are 11 and 13, respectively, which makes GH = (11)(13)= 143.)

8. Choice C is correct. Statements 1 and 2 together are sufficient to answer the question.

9. If $f(v) = 5v^2 - 1/8v - 3$, then $f(v^3) = $ **$5v^5 - 1/8v^4 - 3$**. Choice B is correct.

10. Slope = $(10 - 3)/ (8 - 2) = $ **7/6**. Choice C is correct.

11. Area of Y = 27 x 27 = 729 square inches. Area of X = 17 x 17 = 289 square inches. 729 – 289 = **440** square inches. Choice D is correct.

12. Each term in the series increases by 6. Hence, the next term will be 19 + 6 = **25**. Choice C is correct.

13. In this case, the number of girls (4) is equal to the number of boys (also 4), which means that we can simply take the average of 56 + 42 and apply it to the entire group of siblings. The result is (56 + 42)/2 = **49** inches. Choice B is correct.

14. In this case, we can write two equations – one for the number of coins and the other for their value. As always, we must first define our variables. We will let = x the number of nickels and y = the number of quarters.

The first equation, which defines the *number* of coins, is simply x + y = 3,500
The second equation, which defines their *monetary worth*, is 0.05x + 0.25y = 750.00
To solve the problem for x, we must combine the equations in a way that eliminates y.

First, we will multiply equation 2 by 100 to eliminate the decimals. When we do, we get: x + y = 3,500.
5x + 25y = 75000

Then, we can re-write equation 1 as y = 3,500 – x and substitute this value for y into equation 2. When we do, we get 5x + 25(3500 – x) = 75000. 5x + 87,500 – 25x = 75000. -20x = -12,500. x= **625** nickels. Choice A is correct. y = 3,500 – 625 = 2,875 quarters.

15. The area of a parallelogram is equal to its base times its height. Therefore, (x + 8)(x – 8) = 36. $x^2 – 64 = 36$. $x^2 = 100$. x = 10. The base of the parallelogram = 10 + 8 = 18 and its height is 10 – 8 = **2**. Choice A is correct.

16. The adjacent angle is 180 – 60 =**120**. Choice B is correct.

17. Area of circle = πr^2 In this case, the radius is the square root of 144, or 12. The diameter is 12 x 2 = **24**. Choice D is correct.

18. For a hexagon, an exterior angle = 360/6 = 60; interior angle = 180 - 60 = **120**. Choice C is correct.

19. If f(j) = j^2 + 0.001j, then f (0.05) = (0.05)(0.05) + (0.001)(0.05) = 0.0025 + 0.00005 = **0.00255**. Choice C is correct.

20. The correct answer choice MUST be odd. By plugging in numbers to test each answer choice, we can quickly determine that choice B, the sum of an odd number and an even number, is the only one that cannot produce an even number. It is therefore the correct answer.

21. 50,000 / 5, 000, 000 = 5/500 = **1/100**. Choice C is correct.

22. 25 x 25 x 25 = **125 x 125**. Choice C is correct.

23. (x + 5) – 4 = 12, thus x = **11**. Choice D is correct.

24. To solve the equations for y, we must eliminate x and add the equations together. To do so, we must multiple the first equation by two and subtract the second equation from it: 4x + 8y = 36. 4x – 6y = 8. 14y = 28 or y = **2**. Choice A is correct.

25. (x + 2)(x +5) – (x + 1) (x + 3) = (x^2 + 7x + 10) - (x^2 + 4x +3) = 3x + 7. Choice A is correct.

26. 6 x 6 x 6 = 216, while 6 x 6 x 6 x 6 = 1296. Hence, **3** is the largest integer value of x. Choice C is correct.

27. The trick to this question is to ignore the initial reduction from $1000 to $500, which is extraneous information. What we are being asked to determine is a 15% reduction of a refrigerator that is marked at $500. Our answer is 500 - (500)(0.15) = 500 – 75 = **$425.** Choice D is correct.

28. Let x = the original population. 0.77x = 578,845. Thus, x = **751,746**. Choice E is correct.

29. Let x = # of soft cover books and 5000 – x = the # of hardcover books. The sum of their individual profits equals the total annual profit, or: 15x + 5(5000 – x) = 65000. To simplify: 15x + 25000 –5x = 65000 or 10x = 40000. x = **4000** soft cover books. Choice E is correct.

30. Let x = Connie's hourly wage. Josh's wage = x + 5. Since Adam earns twice as much as Josh, his hourly wage is 2 (x + 5). Therefore: x + (x + 5) + 2 (x + 5) = 75. To simplify: 4x + 15 = 75 or 4x = 60. x = Connie's wage = $15, Josh's wage = $20. Adam's wage = $40.
As a check, we can verify that $15 + $20 + $40 = **$75**. Choice E is correct.

31. If W is the first term, then the second term is W/2 + 2. The ratio of these two values is (second term)/(first term) = (W/2 + 2)/W, which simplifies to (W + 4)/2W. To check our work, let's assume that the first term W = 100. The second term would be 2 greater than one-half of one hundred, or 52. The ratio of 52/100 = 26/50= 13/25. **(W + 4)/2W** = 104/200 = 52/100 = 26/50 = 13/25. Choice B is correct.

32. This is a straightforward problem that we can solve using the formula, Interest = Principal x Rate x Time. In this case, the Principal = $6500, the Rate = 0.08 and the Time = 3 years. Hence, Interest = ($6500)(0.08)(3) = **$1,560** in total interest. Choice D is correct.

33. To solve, we must first define our variables. In this case, x = the number of quarters, x + 50 = the number of nickels, and x + 80 = the number of dimes. Since the sum of the coins = $124.50, our equation becomes: Quarters + Dimes + Nickels = Total. 25x + 10(x + 80) + 5(x + 50) = 12450.
25x + 10x + 800 + 5x + 250 = 12450. 40x = 11400. x = **285** quarters. Choice A is correct.

34. c (c $^{a+b}$) / c^a = (c ^{1})(c $^{a+b}$) (c $^{-a}$) = c $^{1+a+b-a}$ = **c $^{1+b}$** . Choice C is correct.

35. Total Annuities = 50 + 105 = **155**. Choice E is correct.

36. Total number of products sold = 350 + 105 + 409 = **864**. Choice D is correct.

37. 54 / (54+ 23 + 10) = 54/87= **62.1%.** Choice D is correct.

Quantitative Section 8: 37 questions   75 minutes

Use the following answer choices for questions 1 – 8 below:

A. Statement 1 alone is sufficient but Statement 2 alone is not sufficient to answer the question asked.
B. Statement 2 alone is sufficient but Statement 1 alone is not sufficient to answer the question asked.
C. Statements 1 and 2 together are sufficient to answer the question but neither statement is sufficient alone.
D. Each statement alone is sufficient to answer the question.
E. Statements 1 and 2 are not sufficient to answer the question asked and additional data is needed to answer the question.

1. A cook must mix 75% chocolate liqueur with 1,200 gallons of X% chocolate liqueur to produce a 2,000 gallon mixture containing Y% chocolate liqueur. How many gallons of 75% chocolate liqueur will he need?

(1) X = 50
(2) Y = 60

2. Employees at McDonalds either cook, clean or both. X percent of the employees cook; Y percent of the employees clean. What percentage of employees cooks and cleans?

(1) Half as many employees cook as clean
(2) There are 50 employees at McDonalds

3. A coin with one side heads and the other side tails is tossed A times. What is the probability of getting 4 consecutive tails?

(1) A = 5
(2) 1/32

4. Jill's boyfriend asked her to bring X DVDs from her collection of Y to a weekend party. How many different possible combinations could she bring?

(1) Y = 20
(2) Two of the DVDs were destroyed during the long car ride to the party

5. What is the value of W?

(1) W/7 is an integer
(2) W is an integer greater than -22 but less than -19.

6. Roxie earned $12,000 in interest last year. What simple rate of interest does this represent?

(1) The money was divided equally among three accounts.
(2) The total amount of Roxie's investment is $300,000.

7. How much money did Henry and Stella earn together at the summer fair?

(1) Henry earned half as much as Stella.
(2) Stella earned three times as much as she did last summer.

8. What is the value of M + 3?

(1) M = N + 25
(2) M is a perfect square.

9. If the following series continues in the same pattern, what will the next term be?

  3, 5, 4, 7, 5, 9, 6, 11………

    a. 3
    b. 5
    c. 6
    d. 7
    e. 13

10. A delivery truck traveled west for 30 miles, then south for 50 miles, then returned directly to his starting point on a diagonal. If the truck gets 8 miles per gallon of gas, how many gallons of gas will the truck use on the trip?

    a. 10
    b. 12
    c. 16
    d. 18
    e. 20

11. If $x^2 - y^2 = 16$ and $x - y = 2$, what is the value of $x + y$?

    a. 1
    b. 2
    c. 4
    d. 8
    e. 12

12. Which of the following is not a factor of 680?

    a. 10
    b. 30
    c. 34
    d. 40
    e. 68

13. In Triangle CAT, CA = AT. If angle A = 3x – 20 and angle C = 1.5x + 115, how many degrees are in angle T?

    a. 30
    b. 45
    c. 60
    d. 75
    e. 90

14. A wholesale dairy sells blocks of butter in cubic containers that have an edge of 20 inches. If the butter weighs 32 pounds per cubic foot, what is the weight of a single cube of butter (to the nearest tenth of a pound)?

    a.   2.75
    b.   4.60
    c.   53.33
    d. 106.65
    e. 148.15

15. A + B = 50. $A^2 - B^2 = 500$. What is the larger number?

    a. 15
    b. 20
    c. 25
    d. 30
    e. 40

16. Find the number of sides in a polygon if the measure of an interior angle is three times as great as the measure of an exterior angle.

    a. 4
    b. 5
    c. 6
    d. 7
    e. 8

17. What is the length of the hypotenuse in an equilateral right triangle with an area of 121?

    a. $7\sqrt{2}$
    b. 7
    c. $11\sqrt{2}$
    d. 11
    e. 15

18. Which of the following quantities is greater than 1/7?

    a. 0.1399
    b. 2/15
    c. 3/19
    d. 0.141
    e. 4/29

19. $(4x^2)^2(3x^3)^3 =$

    a. $12x^{10}$
    b. $144x^{13}$
    c. $288x^{10}$
    d. $432x^{13}$
    e. $1296x^{13}$

20. If (d)(3)(5) = (10)(e)(3), and neither d nor e are 0, what is the value of e/d?

    a. 1/3
    b. 1/2
    c. 2/3
    d. 2
    e. 3

21. For the following system of equations, what are the possible values of a? ab = 1, a = 4b

    a. ½ or −1/2
    b. 1 or -1
    c. 2 or -2
    d. 4 or -4
    e. There is no solution to the equations

22. Rectangle CDEF has a length of 6 and a width of 2. What is its perimeter?

     a. 8
     b. 12
     c. 16
     d. 40
     e. 64

23. Find the equation of the line that is parallel to y = 14 and containing the point (9, 7).

     a. y = 7 x + 2
     b. y = 7
     c. x = 14
     d. y = -7/9 x + 14
     e. y = 7/9 x + 14

24. 15 / (3/6) =

     a. 3
     b. 5
     c. 30
     d. 90
     e. 300

25. If the diameter of a circle increases by 100%, by what percent will the area of the circle increase?

     a. 50%
     b. 100%
     c. 150%
     d. 200%
     e. 300%

26. A jeweler has 62 garnet rings in stock. The only color choices for the bands are gold and silver. Which of the following is a possible ratio of gold to silver bands for this selection of rings?

     a. 12/31
     b. 12/54
     c. 27/35
     d. 27/62
     e. 12/13

27. Liz is 42 years old and Amelia is 24. How many years ago was Liz three times as old as Amelia?

     a. 9
     b. 10
     c. 15
     d. 18
     e. 20

28. In a hospital with 39 patients, the average (mean) temperature of the male patients was 101.7 F. If the average (mean) temperature of the 23 female patients was 98.5 F, what was the average temperature of all 39 patients (in degrees F)?

    a.   98.0
    b.   98.8
    c.   99.0
    d.   99.8
    e.   100.1

29. The Wilson family measured their rectangular backyard for a privacy fence. If the ratio of the length to width was 15:36, what was the diagonal of the enclosed area (in feet)?

    a.   24
    b.   36
    c.   39
    d.   48
    e.   It cannot be determined from the information given.

30. Argon gas is pumped into a tank at a rate of 42 cubic inches per second. If the chamber's dimensions are 12 inches by 24 inches by 42 inches, how many minutes will it take for the tank to be completely filled with gas (to the nearest tenth of a minute)?

    a.   4.8
    b.   9.6
    c.   28.8
    d.   57.6
    e.   288.0

31. To adhere to local zoning laws, an architect must reduce the size of a square building by 800 square yards. When she does, the area of the building is equal to five times its perimeter. What was the original area of the building (in square yards)?

    a.   20
    b.   40
    c.   400
    d.   1,600
    e.   3,200

Refer to the following table for questions 32 – 37.

Number of Items Sold (in thousands)

	Wal-Mart	K-Mart
Dresses	325	650
Jeans	475	425
Shoes	750	500

Total Sales (in millions)

	Dresses	Jeans	Shoes
Wal-Mart	8.125	14.250	26.250
K-Mart	13.000	8.500	8.750

32. If Wal-Mart and K-Mart both earn 30% profit on jeans that they sell, what is the total profit (in millions) from jean sales at both stores for the period of time that this table represents (assuming the sales price of jeans at both stores remain the same)?

    a. $3,275,000
    b. $4,275,000
    c. $6,825,000
    d. $31,187,000
    e. $93,750,000

33. If K-Mart sells 25% more shoes next year and earns 15% profit on those sales, what would be their total profit from shoes (assuming the price per pair remains the same)?

    a. $1,181,250
    b. $1,312,500
    c. $1,575,000
    d. $1,640,625
    e. $1,968,750

34. If Wal-Mart and K-Mart both earn 20% profit on all dress sales, what is the total profit (in millions) from dress sales at both stores for the period of time that this table represents (assuming the sales price of dresses at both stores remain the same)?

    a. $1,625,000
    b. $2,600,000
    c. $3,250,000
    d. $4,225,000
    e. $6,500,000

35. Of the three items – dresses, jeans, and shoes – which commands the highest price per unit at Wal-Mart?

    a. Dresses
    b. Jeans
    c. Shoes
    d. All three items sell for the same price per unit
    e. It cannot be determined from the information given

36. Of the three items – dresses, jeans, and shoes – which two sell for the same price per unit at K-Mart?

    a. Dresses and Jeans
    b. Jeans and Shoes
    c. Shoes and Dresses
    d. All sell for the same price per unit
    e. It cannot be determined from the information given

37. Which item sells for the same price per unit at both Wal-Mart and K-Mart?

    a. Dresses
    b. Jeans
    c. Shoes
    d. None
    e. It cannot be determined from the information given

Answer Key for Quantitative Section 8

1. To solve this problem, we need to know the % of chocolate liqueur in both solutions. Statement 1 gives us one value, while Statement 2 gives us the second. Choice C is correct.

2. To answer this question, we need to know the values of X and Y; we must also know the total number of employees. Statement 2 provides the number of employees, while Statement 1 tells us the *relationship* between X and Y. Unfortunately, it does not give us an exact number for either group. Therefore, we do not have enough information to answer the question. Choice E is correct.

3. In this situation, all we need to know is the number of tosses, which is the value of A. Since Statement 1 provides it, Choice A is correct. Ironically, Statement 2 gives us the actual answer to the question to try to mislead you. (Remember, our goal is not to solve the problem, simply to determine if we have enough information to do so.)

4. To answer this question, we need to know the values of X and Y. Statement 1 tells us Y, but not X. Statement 2 is extraneous information that does not tell us anything about X (only that the number of viewable DVDs will be X − 2). Therefore, we do not have sufficient information to answer the question. Choice E is correct.

5. To solve, we need to know the value of W. From Statement 2, we know that W is -20 or -21. From Statement 1, we know that W must be -21. Choice C is correct.

6. To solve, we simply need to know the total amount of Roxie's investment, which is given by Statement 2. Statement 1 is extraneous information. Choice B is correct.

7. Choice E is correct. Statements 1 and 2 are not sufficient to answer the question.

8. Choice E is correct. Statements 1 and 2 are not sufficient to answer the question.

9. This problem is a combination of two sub-series. In the first one, each term increases by 1 (3,4,5,6); in the second, each term increases by 2 (5,7,9,11). The next number would be **7**. Choice D is correct.

10. The area the truck traveled is a right triangle with side lengths of 30 and 50. Using the Pythagorean theorem, we can use this information to determine the length of the hypotenuse: $(30)^2 + (50)^2 = x^2$ 900 + 2,500 = 3,400 = x^2 or x = 58.31 miles. The total distance traveled is the perimeter of that triangle, or 30 + 40 + 58.31 = 128.31 miles/ 8 mpg = **16** gallons. Choice C is correct.

11. If $x^2 - y^2 = 16$, then (x +y)(x - y) = 16. If (x - y) = 2, then (x + y) = 16/2 = **8**. Choice D is correct.

12. Choice B, **30.**

13. If sides CA and AT are equal, then their angles are also equal. Hence, 3x − 20 = 1.5x + 115 or 1.5x = 135. Therefore, x = **90** degrees. Choice E is correct.

14. The side length is 20 inches = 5/3 feet. Therefore, the volume of the cube = $(5/3)^3$ = 4.63 cubic feet x 32 pounds/cubic foot = **148.15** pounds. Choice E is correct.

15. First, let's define our variables. We will let x = A. Therefore, B = 50 − x. If the difference between their squares is 500, our equation becomes: $(50 - x)^2 - x^2 = 500$. $(50 - x)(50 - x) - x^2 = 500$. $2,500 - 50x - 50x + x^2 - x^2 = 500$. 2,500 − 100x = 500. 2,000 = 100x. X = 20. 50 − X = **30**. Choice D is correct.

16. For an octagon, an exterior angle = 360/8 = 45; interior angle = 180 − 45 = **135**. Choice E is correct.

17. In an equilateral right triangle, $x^2 = 121$, so the two side lengths are 11. The hypotenuse is 15.56, or **11 √2**. Choice C is correct.

18. 3/19 is greater than **1/7.** Choice C is correct.

19. $(4x^2)^2(3x^3)^3 = (16x^4)(27x^9) = $ **432x^{13}**. Choice D is correct.

20. The equation reduces to d = 2e, so e/d. = ½. Choice B is correct.

21. If ab = 1 and a = 4b, then b = 1/a. Therefore, a = 4/a or a^2 = 4. Hence, **a = 2 or –2**. Choice C is correct.

22. Perimeter = 2(6) + 2(2) = **16**. Choice C is correct.

23. y = 14 is horizontal, which means that a line parallel to it must also be horizontal. Hence, the answer is **y = 7**. Choice B is correct.

24. 15 / (3/6) = **30**. Choice C is correct.

25. The fastest way to solve is to select values for the diameter of the circle and determine the effect on the area. If the diameter is 4, the radius is 2 and the area is 4π. Increasing the diameter by 100% to 8 makes the new radius 4 and the new area 16π. The percent increase is (16 - 4)/4 = 12/4, or **300%**.

Let's confirm our answer with another set of numbers. If the diameter is 10, the radius is 5 and the area is 25π. Increasing the diameter by 100% to 20 makes the new radius 10 and the new area 100π. The percent increase is (100 - 25)/25 = 75/25, or 300%. Choice E is correct.

26. The sum of the numerator and denominator must be a factor of 62, which is the total number of rings in stock. This limits the possibilities to 1, 2, 31 and 62. The correct answer choice, C, is the only one in which the terms add up to one of these factors (**27/35**, the sum is 62). The others are mathematically impossible.

27. Here, we are given the current ages of two women and asked to calculate a time when those numbers met a specified set of criteria. Currently, Liz = 42 and Amelia = 24. Therefore, X years ago, Liz = 42 – x and Amelia = 24 – x.

The correct equation to express the relationship between their ages x years ago is therefore:
42 – x = 3 (24 – x). 42 – x = 72 – 3x. 2x = 30. x = **15** Choice C is correct. Fifteen years ago, Liz was 27 and Amelia was 9.

28. Because the number of male and female patients is not the same, we must take a *weighted average* for each of the two groups.

Average =(Sum of Males' Temperatures + Sum of Females' Temperatures/Total # Patients
Average = {(16)(101.7) + (23)(98.5)} / 39 = {1627.2 + 2265.5}/39 = 3892.7/39 = **99.8° F** Choice D is correct.

29. This is one of those annoying "trick" questions for which the GRE is notorious. Most students scramble furiously to calculate an area by using the numbers in the ratio, but it is not necessary. If the ratio of the length to width is 15:36, then the diagonal will be **39**, because it is a multiple of a 5-12-13 special triangle. Choice C is correct.

30. Volume = (12)(24)(42) = 12,096 cubic inches/42 cubic inches per second = 288 seconds = **4.8** minutes. Choice A is correct.

31. First, let's define our variables. We will let x = the side length of the building. Therefore, the perimeter = 4x. Therefore, our equation becomes: x^2 – 800 = 5(4x). x^2 – 20x – 800 = 0. (x + 20)(x - 40)= 0. Therefore, x = - 20 and +40. Since the length of a building cannot be negative, we can discard the -20 root. Therefore, the side length of the building is 40 yards and its area is (40)(40) = **1,600** square yards. Choice D is correct.

32. The profit from jeans at Wal-Mart is ($14,250,000 sales)(0.30) = $4,275,000
The profit from jeans at K-Mart is ($8,500,000 sales)(0.30) = $2,550,000
The total profit is therefore $4,275,000 + $2,550,000 = **$6,825,000**. Choice C is correct.

33. K-Mart's current shoe sales = $8,750,000. Projected sales = ($8,750,000)(1.25) = $10,937,500. 15% of this value is **$1,640,625**. Choice D is correct.

34. The profit from dress sales at Wal-Mart is ($8,125,000 sales)(0.20) = $1,625,000
The profit from dress sales at K-Mart is ($13,000,000 sales)(0.20) = $2,600,000
The total profit is therefore $1,625,000 + $2,600,000 = **$4,225,000**. Choice D is correct.

35. The item with the highest price per unit at Wal-Mart are shoes, which are **$35** per pair ($26,250,000/750,000). Choice C is correct.

36. At K-Mart, dresses and jeans both sell for **$20**. Choice A is correct.
Dresses: ($13,000,000/650,000 sold) = $20 per unit; Jeans: ($8,500,000/425,000 sold) = $20 per unit.

37. Choice D is correct. None of the items sells for the same price at both stores.

Quantitative Section 9: 37 questions   75 minutes

Use the following answer choices for questions 1 – 8 below:

A. Statement 1 alone is sufficient but Statement 2 alone is not sufficient to answer the question asked.
B. Statement 2 alone is sufficient but Statement 1 alone is not sufficient to answer the question asked.
C. Statements 1 and 2 together are sufficient to answer the question but neither statement is sufficient alone.
D. Each statement alone is sufficient to answer the question.
E. Statements 1 and 2 are not sufficient to answer the question asked and additional data is needed to answer the question.

1. Eighty students are attending summer school courses at Beaver Falls High School. X have registered for Spanish, Y have registered for Math, and Z have registered for neither Spanish nor Math. How many have registered for BOTH Spanish and Math?

(1) Thirty students are not taking Spanish
(2) Y = 40% of X, while Z = 75% of Y

2. A dispenser contains A red M&Ms, B green M&Ms, C blue M&Ms and D white M&Ms. What is the probability of getting a blue M&M?

(1) B = D = 75
(2) A = 1/2C = 2/3B

3. What is the next term in the series?

(1) The first five terms are 11, 22, 20, 40, 38.
(2) The series continues indefinitely

4. How many baskets must David score in game 7 to have an average of 8 baskets per game for the entire 7-game season?

(1) David scored a total of 58 baskets in the first six games.
(2) At the end of the 6th game, David broke his arm and could not play for the rest of the season

5. How many people are needed to prepare dinner for eighty people at the soup kitchen?

(1) Five people are needed to prepare one hundred meals.
(2) Only two people can work in the kitchen at a single time.

6. What is the value of A – B?

(1) A and B are both even integers between 10 and 20, inclusive.
(2) The product of A and B is 280.

7. What is the square root of F?

(1) E = F^5
(2) E is an prime integer between 3 and 9

8. What is X?

(1) X is one-third of Y
(2) Y^3 = (5)^5

9. If the 8% hotel tax on a room is $16.20, what was the total price of the room (including tax)?

    a. $186.30
    b. $202.50
    c. $218.70
    d. $222.50
    e. $228.70

10. If $x = 0.1$, what is the value of $(10x)^2 + 100x^2$?

    a.   0.1
    b.   1
    c.   2
    d.   10
    e.   11

11. If $x = 2$, $y = 1$ and $z = 3$, what is the value of $3x^3 - 5y^4 + 2z^2$?

    a.   1
    b.   6
    c.   23
    d.   37
    e.   42

12. In Triangle D, the length of one side is 21 and the other side is 36. Which of the following could possibly be the length of the third side?

    a.   13
    b.   14
    c.   16
    d.   60
    e.   63

13. A Greyhound bus drove down the highway at 60 miles per hour. Three hours later, a second Greyhound bus traveled the same route at 40 miles per hour. How many hours will it take the second bus to reach the first?

    a.   4
    b.   5
    c.   6
    d.   8
    e.   9

14. Gina and Hillary have a small web design business. Gina can design a web site for Client A in 2 hours. Hillary can design the same site in 3 hours. How long will it take them (in minutes) to design the site if they both work at the same time?

    a.   60
    b.   66
    c.   72
    d.   90
    e.   100

15. To dilute 300 qts of a 25% solution of garlic to a 20% solution, how many qts of water should a chef add?

    a.   15
    b.   60
    c.   75
    d.   120
    e.   125

16. What is the sum of the measure of the interior angles of a polygon having 13 sides?

    a.   360
    b.   780
    c.   1,560
    d.   1,980
    e.   2,340

17. If a wholesale dealer can buy K HD-TVs for V dollars, how much will P HD-TVs cost (in dollars)?

    a. 1/PVK
    b. (100/K)PV
    c. PK/V
    d. PV/K
    e. PVK

18. If x#y = 2xy + y, what is 3#7?

    a.   6
    b.   11
    c.   19
    d.   27
    e.   49

19. Which of these statements is/are true?

    I. The sum of the angles of a polygon is 360 degrees.
    II. In a scalene triangle, two angles may be equal.
    III. On the x-axis, all values of y are equal to 0.

    a.   I
    b.   II
    c.   III
    d.   I and II
    e.   I, II and III

20. If the prime numbers between 80 and 90 are added together, what is their sum?

    a.   81
    b.   89
    c.   164
    d.   172
    e.   176

21. Triangles with equal angles but unequal sides are called

    a. Similar triangles
    b. Congruent triangles
    c. Scalene triangles
    d. Isosceles triangles
    e. Equilateral triangles

22. What is the circumference of a circle with a diameter of $2/(9\pi)$?

    a.   3
    b.   2/9
    c. $4/9\pi$
    d.   18
    e. $18/\pi$

23. $6 + 1/3 - (4/9)^2 - (3/2)(5/6) =$

    a.   4.73
    b.   4.89
    c.   5.73
    d.   5.89
    e.   6.20

24. Donna and David both decided to participate in a race for charity. Donna had eleven sponsors who promised to donate $5 for every mile that she ran. David had fifteen sponsors who promised to donate $3 for every mile that he ran. If Donna ran six miles and David ran five miles, how much ADDITIONAL money did Donna raise for the charity than David?

    a. $105
    b. $210
    c. $225
    d. $330
    e. $555

25. Dan brought his car to the mechanic to have his engine fixed. The mechanic quoted him the following prices for parts: $350 for a new alternator, $150 for the battery and $25 for miscellaneous parts. Assuming that the minimal charge for labor is $45 per hour (rounded to the nearest half-hour) and that the shop can complete all repairs in 3.5 hours, what is the minimum amount that Dan will have to pay to have his car fixed?

    a. $157.50
    b. $525.00
    c. $682.50
    d. $705.00
    e. $727.50

26. How many positive integers less than 100 are evenly divisible by 4, 6, 8 and 12?

    a.   1
    b.   2
    c.   3
    d.   4
    e.   5

27. A tour bus at Disney World holds 124 people. If the park requires one adult for every five children on the tour bus, how many children can fit on the bus?

     a.   20
     b.   22
     c.   24
     d.   30
     e.   32

28. In a large lecture hall containing 540 female students, 27 were on birth control pills, 110 were taking antibiotics, and 220 were taking antihistamines. The remaining 193 students were not taking any medication. In simplest terms, what is the ratio of female students taking birth control pills to the total number of students in the lecture hall?

     a.   1: 100
     b.   1 : 193
     c.   1: 27
     d.   1 : 20
     e.   1 : 5

29. The cost for a pen and notebook at the campus bookstore is $10.50.   If the notebook costs $10.00 more than the pen, what does the pen cost (assuming there is no sales tax)?

     a.   25 cents
     b.   50 cents
     c.   75 cents
     d. $1.00
     e. $1.50

30. Jill and Kim leave school at the same time and drive in opposite directions. After two hours, they are 100 miles apart. How fast is Jill driving, if Kim is driving 10 miles per hour faster?

     a.   20
     b.   30
     c.   35
     d.   40
     e.   50

31. If the population of Cedar City is 500,000 and grows by 10,000 people each year, in how many years will the population quadruple?

     a.   50
     b.   75
     c.   125
     d.   150
     e.   200

32. A bookstore is preparing a display with five different novels by a best-selling author. How many possible arrangements are there in the display (assume no title is repeated)?

     a.   25
     b.   120
     c.   125
     d.   500
     e.   600

33. The mean of seven numbers is 77. If 12 is subtracted from each of five of the numbers, what is the new mean?

    a.   65.00
    b.   66.66
    c.   68.43
    d.   70.15
    e.   72.00

Use the following table to answer questions 34 – 37.

Percentage of Contact Lens Wearers (By Age)

	U.S.	U.K.	France	India
Under 10	2	5	1	0
10 – 18	21	30	15	3
19 – 30	38	35	29	19
31 – 50	29	25	40	66
Over 51	10	5	15	12

34. If there are 18 million contact lens wearers in the U.S., how many of them are less than 18 years old?

    a.   3.24 million
    b.   3.78 million
    c.   4.14 million
    d.   21 million
    e.   23 million

35. If the number of contact lens wearers in France is 5 million, and they each own exactly three pairs of lenses, how many of the pairs belong to wearers who are 51 or older?

    a.   450,000
    b.   750,000
    c.   1,500,000
    d.   2,250,000
    e.   4,500,000

36. Which of the following best explains the small percentage of teenage contact lens wearers in India, compared to those in the U.S., the U.K, and France?

    a.   They are unsafe for use
    b.   They are unavailable
    c.   They are astronomically expensive
    d.   They are legally prohibited for minors
    e.   They are not advertised on Indian television

37. Which country has the largest number of contact lens wearers between 19 and 30?

    a.   U.S.
    b.   U.K.
    c.   France
    d.   India
    e.   Cannot be determined from the information given

Answer Key for Quantitative Section 9

1. We can only solve this problem if Statements 1 and 2 give us values for X, Y, and Z (or a way to determine them). Statement 1 allows us to determine the value of X, which is $80 - 30 = 50$. Statement 2 allows us to determine the values of Y and Z as 20 and 15, respectively. Thus, Choice C is correct.

2. To answer this question, we need to know the values of A, B, C and D. Statement 1 gives us the value of B and D (both are 75). Statement 2 gives us enough information to determine the values of A and C (50 and 100, respectively). Thus, with both statements, we can solve the problem. Choice C is correct.

3. To determine the next term in a series or sequence, we need twp pieces of information: (1) the pattern that the terms follow, and (2) whether or not the pattern will continue. Statement 1 gives us the first five terms of the series, which follows a definite pattern: the terms double, then decrease by 2. Statement 2 provides the second essential piece of information, which is that the series or sequence will continue indefinitely. Therefore, Choice C is correct. With both statements, we can determine that the next term in the series will be 76.

4. To determine the number of baskets that David needs to make in game 7 to achieve a specific overall average for the entire 7-game season, we need to know the total number of baskets that he made in the 6 previous games. Statement 1 provides this information. Statement 2 seems relevant, but is actually an extraneous piece of information that is designed to confuse you. The condition of David's arm does not alter the calculation we were asked to make – or the information we need to make it. Choice A is correct.

5. To solve the problem, we need to know the number of people required to make 80 meals. Statement 1 gives us this value, while Statement 2 is extraneous information. Choice A is correct.

6. Choice C is correct. If considered together, Statements 1 and 2 give us enough information to determine the values of A and B. (If AB is 280, then A and B are 20 and 14, respectively, and $A - B = 6$.)

7. Choice E is correct. Statements 1 and 2 are not sufficient to answer the question.

8. Choice C is correct. Statements 1 and 2 together are sufficient to answer the question.

9. If $0.08x = \$16.20$, then $x = \$202.50$. Total price = **\$218.70**. Choice C is correct.

10. For $x = 0.1$, $(1)^2 + 100(0.01) =$ **2**. Choice C is correct.

11. If $x = 2$, $y = 1$ and $z = 3$, then $3x^3 - 5y^4 + 2z^2 = (3)(2)(2)(2) - (5)(1)(1)(1)(1) + (2)(3)(3) = 24 - 5 + 18 =$ **37**. Choice D is correct.

12. According to the triangle inequality theorem, the length of one side of a triangle must be greater than the difference and less than the sum of the lengths of the other two sides. Therefore, in Triangle D, the length of the third side must be greater than $36 - 21 = 15$ and less than $36 + 21 = 57$. The only answer choice between 15 and 57 is Choice C.

13. The first step for this type of problem is to draw a quick chart of what we know.

Bus	Distance	Rate	Time
One	$60(x + 3)$	60	$x + 3$
Two	$40x$	40	x

In this case, the buses travel the same distance at different speeds. Our equation is: $60(x + 3) = 40x$. $60x + 180 = 40x$, so $-180 = 20x$. $x =$ **9 hours** = amount of time it will take the second bus to reach the first bus. Choice E is correct.

14. The problem asks us to determine the total amount of time that is needed for both girls to complete the job. First, we must figure the amount of work that each girl does as a percentage of the total amount:

Gina   Work = Rate x Time   (1/2) x T = ½ T
Hillary   Work = Rate x Time   (1/3) x T = 1/3T

Now, we must add them together to figure the total time for the job: ½ T + 1/3 T = 1. So, 3/6T + 2/6T =1

228

3T + 2T = 6, or 5T = 6, so T = 6/5 hours, or 1.2 hours. Solving for T, we find that they can complete the job in 1.2 hours if they work together, or **72** minutes. Choice C is correct.

15. First, we must draw a table with the information that we know.

Quantity of Solution (qt)	% Garlic	Amount of Garlic (qt)
300	25	300(0.25)
x	0	0
x + 300	20	0.20(x + 300)

In this case, we will let x = the amount of water to be added. Therefore, the volume of the final solution (in which the water has been added) will equal x + 300. Once we have these variables, we can complete the rest of the chart, and derive our expressions for the AMOUNT of garlic in each solution. We can then use the information to write an equation to solve for our unknown. Since our only change is to add water – and to dilute the amount of garlic – our equation is: 300(0.25) + 0 = 0.20(x + 300), or 75 = 0.20x + 60. This simplifies to 0.20x = 15. x = **75** quarts of water. Choice C is correct.

16. To solve, we use the equation 180 (13-2) = **1,980**. Choice D is correct.

17. To solve, let's plug in random numbers for each variable. In this case, let's assume that the dealer bought 20 HD-TVs (K) for 100 dollars (V). The cost for a single HD-TV is therefore 100/20 or V/K or 5 dollars. The cost for any value of P will simply be that number times 5, which, in symbols, is **PV/K**. Choice D is correct.

18. If x#y = 2xy + y, then 3#7: (2)(3)(7) + 7 = **49**. Choice E is correct.

19. Only III is true. Choice C is correct.

20. Choice D is correct. 83 + 89 = **172.**

21. Triangles with equal angles but unequal sides are **similar**. Choice A is correct.

22. Circumference is π x Diameter, or $2\pi/9\pi$= **2/9**. Choice B is correct.

23. 6 + 1/3 - $(4/9)^2$ - (3/2)(5/6) = 6 + 1/3 – 0.1975 – 1.25 = **4. 89**. Choice B is correct.

24. The problem asks us to calculate the difference between the amount of money raised by Donna and David. Eleven sponsors paid $5 for each mile that Donna ran. Since she ran six miles, Donna raised (11)(5)(6) = $330. In David's case 15 sponsors paid $3 for each mile. Since he ran five miles, David raised (15)(3)(5) = $225. Therefore, Donna raised **$105 more** than David. Choice A is correct.

25. The cost of repairs = Total cost of parts + Total cost of labor. The total for the parts is $350 + $150 + $25 = $525. The total cost for labor = ($45) (3.5) = $157.50. The total cost to fix the car is $525 + $157.50 = **$682.50**, or Choice C.

26. The question asks us to determine how positive integers less than 100 are evenly divisible by 4, 6, 8, and 12. First, we will list the integers that are evenly divisible by our largest number, which is 12: 12, 24, 36, 48, 60, 72, 84, and 96. (Note: Because they are all multiples of 12, these numbers are also evenly divisible by 6.)

Next, we eliminate numbers from this group that are NOT evenly divisible by 8, which leaves us with 24, 48, 72, and 96. (Note: Because they are all multiples of 8, they are also evenly divisible by 4.) Thus, there are **4** positive integers that meet the criterion: they are 24, 48, 72, and 96. Choice D is correct.

27. If there is one adult for every five children, we must divide the capacity of the bus by 6, 124/6 = 20.6. Therefore, there can be no more than **20** children on the tour bus (4 groups, each of which contains one adult and 20 children).   Choice A is correct.

28. 27 / 550 = **1 / 20**. Choice D is correct.

29. Most students read this problem too quickly and simply choose Choice B, 50 cents. Not so fast. This problem contains a psychological trick that can easily convince you to select the wrong answer. First, let's

define our variables. We will let the cost of the pen = x. Therefore, the cost of the notebook = x + $10.00. If the cost of both items is $10.50, our equation becomes: Cost of Pen + Cost of Notebook = Total Cost. x + (x + $10.00) = $10.50. 2x + $10.00 = $10.50. 2x = $0.50. X = **$0.25** = Choice A

30. The first step is to draw a quick chart of what we know:

Girl	Distance	Rate	Time
Jill	2x	x	2
Kim	2 (x + 10)	x + 10	2

Next, we must define our variables. In this case, we will let Jill's speed = x. Therefore, Kim's speed = x + 10. We also know that both girls drive for the same amount of time, which is 2 hours. We can now write an equation to solve for Jill's time based on the distance they travelled: Jill's Distance + Kim's Distance = Total Distance: 2x + 2(x + 10) = 100, so 2x + 2x + 20 = 100, which simplifies to 4x = 80 or X = **20** = Jill's speed. Choice A is correct.

31. This problem can easily be solved using an algebraic formula. First, let's define our variables. We will let x = the # of years until the population quadruples. Mathematically, this can be expressed as: 4(500,000) = 500,000 + 10,000x. 20,000,000 = 500,000 + 10,000x. 15,000,000 = 10,000x. x = **150** years. Choice D is correct.

32. For permutations, the correct formula is 5!/(5- 5)! = (5 x 4 x 3 x 2 x 1) / 1 = **120**. Choice B is correct.

33. For the original numbers, (7)(77) = 539 = sum. New sum= 539 – (12)(5) = 479. 479/7=**68.43.** Choice C is correct.

34. (18 million)(0.02 + 0.21) = **4.14 million**. Choice C is correct.

35. If France has a total of 5 million contact lens wearers, then the number of them who are 51 or older is (5 million)(0.15) = 750,000. If all of these patients own 3 pairs each, then the number of pairs is **2,250,000**. Choice D is correct.

36. Choice D is correct. Contact lenses are obviously available and affordable in India, because older patients wear them. The more logical explanation for the large discrepancy in use is that the law restricts their use to those who are 18 and over.

37. Choice E is correct. The chart only gives the % of contact lens wearers in each nation; it does not reveal the actual numbers. Without them, we cannot answer this question.

Quantitative Section 10: 37 questions   75 minutes

Use the following answer choices for questions 1 – 8 below:

A. Statement 1 alone is sufficient but Statement 2 alone is not sufficient to answer the question asked.
B. Statement 2 alone is sufficient but Statement 1 alone is not sufficient to answer the question asked.
C. Statements 1 and 2 together are sufficient to answer the question but neither statement is sufficient alone.
D. Each statement alone is sufficient to answer the question.
E. Statements 1 and 2 are not sufficient to answer the question asked and additional data is needed to answer the question.

1. At a church raffle, the pastor will award a single cash prize to one lucky winner. What is the probability (in percent) that any one ticket will be selected for the prize?

(1) There are 40 tickets in the bowl
(2) One person bought 10 of the 40 tickets

2. What is the next term in the series?

(1) The first twelve terms are 11, 7, 23, 55, 6, 34, 85, 41, 90, 58, 13, 78
(2) The terms are randomly generated by a software program

3. What is the median number of on-time flights into and out of the Miami airport during the week of January 1 – 7?

(1) Delta Airlines had 1,250 flights into and out of Miami during the first week of January
(2) No other airline flew into or out of the Miami airport during this timeframe

4. What is the length of the third side of triangle X?

(1) The other side lengths are 4 and 8
(2) The triangle has a perimeter of 14

5. A circle is inscribed in a rectangle. What is the area of the circle?

(1) The side of the square is 48.
(2) The rectangle is a square.

6. How many green jelly beans are in the jar?

(1) There are a total of 450 jelly beans in the jar.
(2) There are three times as many green jelly beans as red ones.

7. How many prime numbers are between A and B?

(1) A is the square root of 100
(2) B is the cube root of 10,000

8. Is X < 9?

(1) X > 3Y
(2) Y < 3^2

Directions: For each problem, decide which answer is the best of the choices given.

9. What positive integer is 30% less than 1,540?

    a.   308
    b.   462
    c.   972
    d.   1,078
    e.   1,386

10. Simplify the following expression: $(x^4y^7/x^5y^6)^4$

    a. y^3x^2
    b. y^4/x^4
    c. $(y/x)^{12}$
    d. y^{28}/x^{20}
    e.   none of the above

11. A circle is inscribed in a square whose side is 48. What is the area of the circle?

    a. 24π
    b. 48π
    c. 576π
    d. $2,304\pi$
    e.   It cannot be determined from the information given.

12. In Triangle DOG, angle D is six times as large as angle O. The exterior angle at G is 140 degrees. How many degrees are in angle D?

    a.   20
    b.   40
    c.   100
    d.   120
    e.   140

13. If the radius of a circle increases by 8, how much will its circumference increase?

    a. 4π
    b. 8π
    c. 16π
    d. 32π
    e. 64π

14. Find the edge (in inches) of a cube whose volume is equal to the volume of a rectangular solid that is 2 in by 36 in by 81 in.

    a.   9
    b.   18
    c.   27
    d.   36
    e.   54

15. Integer X is equal to Integer Y + 8. If the product of Integer X and Integer Y is 20, what is Integer X?

    a. -10
    b. -5
    c. -2
    d. 2
    e. 5

16. Which of the following equations will have a horizontal line as its graph?

    a. x = 2 - y
    b. x = 2 + y
    c. x/y = 2
    d. x = 2
    e. y = 2

17. Which of the following relations is a function?

    a. {(s, d), (v, z), (v, e)}
    b. {(k, m), (v, x), (k, 9)}
    c. {(4, 7), (5j 6), (4, 3)}
    d. {(4, 3), (7, 6), (7, 8)}
    e. {(4, 5), (5, 6), (7, 8)}

18. For what value of m does 12 – m = m – 12?

    a. -12
    b. 0
    c. 12
    d. 36
    e. 144

19. Which of the following answer choices correctly lists the prime numbers between 60 and 80?

    a. 61, 63, 67, 71, 73
    b. 61, 67, 71, 73, 77, 79
    c. 61, 67, 69, 71, 73, 77
    d. 61, 67, 71, 73, 79
    e. 67, 71, 73, 77, 79

20. If X is between 0 and –1, which of the following quantities is the largest?

    a. X^3
    b. X^5
    c. X^6
    d. X^7
    e. It cannot be determined from the information given

21. If (7b – 4)/2 = 16 - b, then b =

    a. 1/2
    b. 2
    c. 3
    d. 4
    e. 9

22. If H = {6, 7, 8}, J = {9, 5, 7} and K = {7, 3, 4}, what is (H∩J)∩K?

     a.   {7}
     b.   {7, 5, 9}
     c.   {5, 6, 7, 8, 9}
     d.   {3, 4, 7}
     e.   {5, 6, 7, 8}

23. If $4y \leq 56$ and $3y \geq 36$, which of the following could be a value of y?

     a.   8
     b.   9
     c.   10
     d.   11
     e.   12

24. Diane has 18 errands to run, which take 14 minutes each, before she can go home. If Diane needs to be home by 5:00 pm, what is the latest time that she can start the errands?

     a.   11:40 am
     b.   11:48 am
     c.   12:40 pm
     d.   12:48 pm
     e.   1:40 pm

25. When x is divided by 17, the remainder is 9. What is the remainder when 5x is divided by 17?

     a.   3
     b.   7
     c.   9
     d.   11
     e.   13

26. A computer science curriculum includes 8 courses on hardware and 4 courses on software. The remaining ¼ of the courses are on web design. What fraction of the courses is devoted to software?

     a.   1/4
     b.   1/3
     c.   2/5
     d.   1/2
     e.   5/8

27. In the past year, Brad's coin collection increased from 214 to 328. What percentage increase does this number represent?

     a.   27%
     b.   33%
     c.   53%
     d.   72%
     e.   114%

28. A hallway that is 90 feet long is divided into two sections that are in the ratio of 3:2. What is the length of the shorter section?

    a. 9
    b. 18
    c. 21
    d. 27
    e. 36

29. Sue is twice as old as Grace. Lee is 5 years older than Grace. If their combined age is 65, how old is Grace?

    a. 12
    b. 15
    c. 16
    d. 18
    e. 24

30. Two motorcyclists are 540 miles apart. At 10:00 am they start traveling toward each other at rates of 65 and 70 miles per hour. At what time will they pass each other?

    a. 1:00 pm
    b. 1:30 pm
    c. 2:00 pm
    d. 3:30 pm
    e. 4:00 pm

31. Students at St. Agnes Academy either study French, Spanish or both. Sixty percent of the students study French, while fifteen percent study both Spanish and French. What percentage of the students only study Spanish?

    a. 10%
    b. 15%
    c. 20%
    d. 25%
    e. 30%

32. What is the probability that a card chosen at random from a standard deck of 52 cards is a King?

    a. 1/52
    b. 1/26
    c. 1/13
    d. 1/12
    e. 4/12

33. What is the sum of the first 150 positive integers?

    a. 10,500
    b. 11,250
    c. 11,325
    d. 11,400
    e. 15,000

34. The church must replace 6 stained glass windows that were destroyed by a hurricane. The windows are squares that measure 13 feet on each side. If the stained glass costs $5.86 per square foot, how many of the windows can the church afford to replace if they have budgeted $4000 for the project?

    a. 2
    b. 3
    c. 4
    d. 5
    e. 6

35. Investments A, B, and C yield $22,000 in total annual interest. Investment B. which earns 7% interest, is $25,000 larger than investment A, which earns 5% interest. In contrast, Investment C, which earns 9% interest, is $7,500 less than three times Investment A. How much is Investment A?

    a. $50,192.31
    b. $53,653.85
    c. $93,214.29
    d. $99,642.86
    e. $100,384.62

Refer to the following table for questions 36 and 37.

Joe's Budget for August 2009 (in dollars)

Rent	700
Car Payment	350
Utilities	185
Cell Phone	80
Insurance	55
Food	100
Credit Card	240
Clothes	75
Miscellaneous	321
Savings	35

36. Financial experts recommend that people Joe's age allocate at least 10% of their budget for savings. How much additional money would Joe have to save each month to reach this percentage?

    a. $35
    b. $79
    c. $150
    d. $179
    e. $214

37. To buy a house, Joe will have to assume a mortgage payment that is $300 per month higher than his current rent. Which expenses, if eliminated, will allow him to achieve this goal?

    a. Cell phone, Food and Clothes
    b. Credit card and Insurance
    c. Credit card and Savings
    d. Clothes and Credit card
    e. Savings, Clothes, Cell phone and Food

Answer Key for Quantitative Section 10

1. The question asks us to determine the probability of any one ticket being selected. The only information we need is the number of tickets in the bowl, which is given in Statement 1. The information in Statement 2

is misleading – and extraneous. If one person holds 10 of the 40 tickets, then his/her overall odds of winning are 1 out of 4. However, this does NOT influence the odds of any *single ticket* being drawn, which remains 1 out of 40. Choice A is correct.

2. This is as tricky as questions get on the GMAT. Statement 2 tells us that the terms in the series are randomly generated by a software program, which means that there is *no way to predict* the value of the next term. Therefore, Choice E is correct. Neither statement will allow us to answer the question.

3. This problem includes a single phrase that totally changes its meaning: it asks for the number of *on-time flights*. Between Statement 1 and Statement 2, we know the total number of flights into and out of the Miami airport during the first week in January. However, neither statement tells us how many of those flights were on-time (or how many flights there were each day). Therefore, Choice E is correct.

4. If taken together, Statements 1 and 2 give us enough information to calculate the length of the third side. Choice C is correct.

5. To solve, we need to know the type of rectangle and the side length. Statement 2 gives us the first piece of information, while Statement 1 gives us the second. When considered together, we have enough information to solve the problem. Choice C is correct.

6. Choice E is correct. Neither statement gives us enough information to answer the question.

7. Choice C is correct. Statements 1 and 2 together are sufficient to answer the question but neither statement is sufficient alone.

8. Choice E is correct. Statements 1 and 2 are not sufficient to answer the question.

9. $(1{,}540)(0.7)$ = **1,078**. Choice D is correct.

10. $(x^4 y^7 / x^5 y^6)^4 = (y/x)^4$ = $\mathbf{y^4/x^4}$. Choice B is correct.

11. If the square has a side of 48, then the diameter of the circle is also 48. The radius is therefore 24, which makes the area of the circle $\pi(24)(24)$ = **576π**. Choice C is correct.

12. By definition, the exterior angle is equal to the sum of the two remote interior angles. If angle D is six times as large as angle O, then their sum is 6x + 1x = 7x. Hence, 7x =140. x = 20 = angle O. 6x = **120** = angle D. Choice A is correct.

13. The circumference of the circle =$2\pi r$. Hence, the question is asking us to determine the difference between the first circumference and the second.
First circumference = $2\pi r$
Second circumference = $2\pi(r + 8) = 2\pi r + 2\pi(8) = 2\pi r + 16\pi$
The difference between the two circumferences – which is the amount that it increases – is equal to **16π**. Choice C is correct.

14. The volume of the rectangular solid is Length x Width x Height = 2 x 36 x 81 = 5,832 cubic inches. The volume of the cube = 5,832 = (Side length)^3
Side length = **18** inches. Choice B is correct.

15. First, let's define our variables.   We will let x = Integer X and x – 8 = Integer Y. Since their product is 152, our equation becomes: x(x – 8) = 20. $x^2 - 8x - 20 = 0$. (x – 10)(x + 2) = 0. Therefore, x = 10 and -2. Since the problem does not specify that the integers must be positive, we must test both roots in our original equation to confirm that they both hold.

If Integer X = 10, then Integer Y = 10 – 8 = 2. (10)(2) = 20
If Integer X = -2, then Integer Y = -2 – 8 = -10. (-10)(-2) = 20
Hence, both roots are correct. The only answer choice that includes one of them is Choice C, **-2**.

16. Choice E is correct. y = **2**

17.   To be a function, a relation must not repeat any of the first elements of its ordered pairs. Only Choice E meets this criterion.

18. The easiest way to solve is to test each answer choice. When we do, we find that Choice C is correct. m = **12**.

19. Choice D is correct.

20. x^6 must be the largest, because it is the only answer choice that is positive. Choice C is correct.

21. (7b – 4)/2 = 16 - b, so 7b – 4 = 32 – 2b, or 9b – 36, or b =**4**. Choice D is correct.

22. (H∩J)∩K is the set of elements that are in all three sets. In this case, only **7** is in H,J, and K, which means that (H∩J)∩K = **{7}**. Choice A is correct.

23. Of the answers listed, only **12** fits both equations. Choice E is correct.

24. First, we must calculate the total number of minutes that Diane needs to complete her errands, which is 18 x 14 = 252 minutes, or 4.2 hours, which is 4 hours and 12 minutes. Therefore, Diane must leave home by **12:48** pm to complete the errands by 5:00 pm. Choice D is correct.

25. To solve this problem, simply choose a number that meets the original condition: it leaves a remainder of 9 when it is divided by 17. In this case, the number **26** meets the condition. Next, let's submit the number 26 to the second condition and see what happens. (26)(5)/17 = 130 = (17)(7) + 11. **130** leaves a remainder of 11 when it is divided by 17. Choice D is correct.

26. 12 courses (8 + 4) comprise ¾ of the curriculum, which means that there are 16 total courses. Of these, 4, or **1/4,** are on software. Choice A is correct.

27. 328 – 214 = 114/214 = **53.27%** increase. Choice C is correct.

28. For a ratio of 3:2, the whole is 5. The shorter section is therefore 2/5 of the whole. 2/5 of 90 = **36**, which is Choice E.

29. In this problem, we know the relationship among the ages of Sue, Grace, and Lee – and their combined age. We can use this information to build an equation to solve for Grace's age. For simplicity, we will let Grace's age = x. Thus, Sue's age is 2x, while Lee's age is x + 5. Since the sum of their ages is 65, our equation becomes: x + 2x + (x + 5) = 65 or 4x + 5 = 65. Thus, 4x = 60 and X = **15** = Grace's age. Choice B is correct.

30. The first step for this type of problem is to draw a quick chart of what we know:

Motorcycle	Distance	Rate	Time
A	65x	65	x
B	70x	70	x

Here, we can use the rate equation to determine the time at which the two motorcyclists will pass each other. By definition, they are traveling the same distance, which is 540 miles. Also by definition, that distance equals the SUM of the quantities (Rate x Time) for each motorcycle. Hence, our equation becomes: 65x + 70x = 540, or 135x = 540. x = **4**. They will pass after 4 hours, which will be 2:00 pm. Choice C is correct.

31. In this case, we have three distinct groups, which must add up to 100%. Since the original two groups are 60% and 15%, the remaining group must be 100 – 60 – 15 = **25%** of the total. Choice D is correct.

32. There are four kings in a deck of 52 cards. Thus, the probability of choosing a king is 4/52, or **1/13**. Choice C is correct.

33. The fastest way to solve this problem is by using the formula for the sum of the numbers in an arithmetic series: Sum = Number of Items (First Item + Last or Desired Item) / 2
Sum = 150(1 + 150)/2 = (150)(151)/2 = **11,325**. Choice C is correct.

34. Area of each window = (13)(13) = 169 square feet x $5.86 = $990.34 per window. The church can replace **4** windows for $3,961.36. Choice C is correct.

35. To solve this problem, we must first define our variables:

Investment A = x; Investment B = x + $25,000; Investment C = 3x - $7,500

Next, we must write expressions to define the amount of interest that each investment earns:
Investment A = (0.05)x; Investment B = (0.07)(x + $25,000); Investment C = (0.09)(3x − $7,500)

Finally, we must add these amounts, which − by definition − are equal to $22,000.
(0.05)x + (0.07)(x + $25,000) + (0.09)(3x − $7,500) = $22,000
(0.05)x + (0.07)x + $1,750 + (0.27)x - $675 = $22,000
(0.39)x = $20,925
x = **$53,653.85**. Choice B is correct.

36. 10% of $2141 = $214 − 35 = $179. Choice D is correct.

37. Credit Card + Clothes = $ 240 + $75 = $315. Choice D is correct.

Quantitative Section 11:   37 questions   75 minutes

1. What is the sum of the 500th term through the 505th term in the series?

(1) The first 18 terms are 4, 5, 6, 7, 8, 9, 4, 5, 6, 7, 8, 9, 4, 5. 6, 7, 8, 9
(2) The pattern continues indefinitely

2. What is the area of triangle V?

(1)   The longest side length is 15
(2)   The perimeter is 20

3. How many tiles will the decorator need to cover the entire living room floor?

(1) The perimeter of the living room is 240 feet
(2) Each individual tile measures 6 inches by 9 inches

4. How old is Shawn?

(1) Shawn is 30 years younger than Dawn
(2) The product of Dawn's age and Shawn's age is 175

5. Of the 90 students currently enrolled at Rhode Island School of Design, how many have registered for *neither* drawing nor watercolors?

(1) 55 have registered for drawing
(2) 15 have registered for both drawing and watercolors

6. How much did Grace spend on milk?

(1)   The cost of milk is $3.45 per gallon.
(2)   Grace bought 4.5 gallons of milk.

7. What is the value of X?

(1) $12 < X < 15$
(2)   X is an integer

8. What is Integer G?

(1)   The cube root of Integer G is 3
(2)   Integer G = Integer H + 9

9. What is the area (in cubic centimeters) of a trapezoid with a height of 12 cm and parallel side lengths of 16 cm and 18 cm?

    a. 84
    b. 96
    c. 192
    d. 204
    e. 216

10. What is the product of $(8/3)(5/4)(9/3)$?

    a. 4.4
    b. 40/9
    c. 10
    d. 180/9
    e. 100

11. Two individual price reductions of 20% and 30% are equal to a single price reduction of:

    a. 25%
    b. 27%
    c. 37%
    d. 44%
    e. 47%

12. $1/18 \, (22 + 33)^2 =$

    a. 9
    b. 168
    c. 336
    d. 5,450
    e. 54,450

13. If $a \, \Psi \, b = (1 + b)^{1/2}$ what is $a \Psi \, 15$?

    a. 1/2
    b. 2
    c. 4
    d. 8
    e. 16

14. Find the number of sides of a polygon if the sum of the interior angles is 2,700 degrees?

    a. 14
    b. 16
    c. 17
    d. 18
    e. 19

15. What number, when squared, is equal to the cubic root of 15625?

    a. 1
    b. 5
    c. 15
    d. 25
    e. 125

16. Which of the following is the correct factorization of $k^2 - 6k + 9$?

    a. $(k - 3)(k + 3)$
    b. $(k - 3)^2$
    c. $(k + 3)^2$
    d. $3(1/k^2 + 1)$
    e. $1/9(k - 1)(k + 1)$

17. Which of the following are the solutions to the following equation? $2x^3 - 3x^2 - 5x = 0$

    a. −1, -5/2, 2
    b. 0, 1, 2
    c. 1, 5/2, 6
    d. 0, 1, -5/2
    e. 0, -1, 5/2

18. Sara had to mail a package on the day that the Post Office increased its rates. The cost is 55 cents for the first ounce and 34 cents for each additional ounce. How much did Sara pay to mail a package that weighed three quarters of a pound?

    a. $3.74
    b. $3.95
    c. $4.08
    d. $4.29
    e. $4.63

19. An oven timer rings whenever the internal temperature reaches 425 °F. On a typical shift, the alarm rings five times every ten minutes. In a ten-hour shift, how many times will the alarm ring?

    a. 150
    b. 300
    c. 600
    d. 1500
    e. 3000

20. A number (x) is divisible by 2, 3, and 5. What is the smallest three-digit number that is divisible by 2, 3, 5, and 3x?

    a. 120
    b. 150
    c. 180
    d. 210
    e. 300

21. Three sisters took their mother for a nice dinner on Mother's Day. The total for four meals was $185.30. If the girls plan to leave a 20% tip and split the bill three ways, what dollar amount will each sister owe?

a. $46.32
b. $55.59
c. $61.76
d. $68.32
e. $74.12

22. After careful negotiations, the Zippy Insurance Company agreed to pay 75% of Chad's accident expenses, after deducting $100 in non-covered items and a $325 administrative fee. If Chad's expenses totaled $14,625, how much did he receive from Zippy Insurance?

a. $10,650
b. $10,950
c. $11,650
d. $11,960
e. $12,650

23. If Candy's age ten years from now minus her age eight years ago plus six times her age four years ago is equal to 120 years, how old will Candy be in eleven years?

a. 20
b. 21
c. 30
d. 32
e. 41

24. Jack and Jill left home at the same time and traveled to the airport using the same route. Jack drove at an average speed of 75 miles per hour, while Jill drove an average speed of 45 miles per hour. In how many hours will Jack's car be 45 miles ahead of Jill's?

a. ½
b. 1
c. 3/2
d. 2
e. 5/2

25. Olivia can transcribe three times as fast as Karen. If they both spend an equal amount of time transcribing 1200 pages of notes, how many pages will Olivia have transcribed?

a. 300
b. 450
c. 800
d. 900
e. 1000

26. Connie has two investments, A and B. Her income from A, which pays 6%, is $10,000 more than her income from B, which pays 4%. If Connie has $750 more invested in A than B, what is the TOTAL amount of Connie's two investments?

a. $497,750
b. $498,500
c. $996,250
d. $1,006,250
e. $1,026,160

27. If the population of Walnut Grove is 300,000 and grows by 5,000 people each year, in how many years will the population triple?

    a. 60
    b. 90
    c. 120
    d. 240
    e. 300

28. When a store owner compiled her weekly sales records, she had a stack of invoices numbered 014567 through 019876. Upon further examination, however, the store owner realized that invoice numbers 014876 and 018999 were missing. How many invoices did the store owner have available for her weekly calculations?

    a. 5307
    b. 5308
    c. 5309
    d. 5310
    e. 5311

29. For the following data set, what is the median minus the mode?
                7, 3, 15, 6, 7, 8, 9, 12, 5, 7, 6

    a. 0
    b. 0.7
    c. 1.0
    d. 1.7
    e. 2.0

30. X roommates agree to split the cost of utilities for their apartment, which usually cost Y per month. At the end of the year, the monthly cost of utilities increased by $250. How much did each roommate have to contribute each month for his/her total share?

    a. 250/X
    b. 250Y/X
    c. XY/250
    d. (Y + 250)/X
    e. X/Y + 250/X

31. Kelly wants to have her favorite picture enlarged to the size of a wall poster. The original picture measures 2 inches by 3 inches. If the shorter side of the poster will be 4 feet long, how long (in inches) will the longer side be?

    a. 6
    b. 36
    c. 64
    d. 72
    e. 78

32. Jake found a great deal on discontinued paint at Home Depot. When he brought the paint home, he discovered that the four cans he purchased were enough to paint three quarters of his bedroom. How many additional cans of paint will Jake need to buy to complete his bedroom and to paint three additional rooms that are the same size as his bedroom?

    a. 13.3
    b. 16.7
    c. 17.3
    d. 19.7
    e. 19.3

Refer to the following table for questions 33 – 35.

	2006	2007	2008	2009
Number of Books Sold (thousands)	54	106	189	312
Profit from Books Sold (millions)	3	11	24	21

33. In what year was the profit per book the lowest?

    a. 2006
    b. 2007
    c. 2008
    d. 2009
    e. It cannot be determined from the information given

34. In 2010, the company sold 20% fewer books than in 2009, but the profit increased by 20%. What was the average profit per book?

    a. 67.30
    b. 87.96
    c. 100.96
    d. 107.30
    e. 167.30

35. The company accountants discovered an error in the data that was presented for 2007 and 2008. The number of books sold in 2007 was understated by 50,000, while the number of books sold in 2008 was overstated by 19,000. When the data is corrected, what impact will it have on the change in the profit per book between 2007 and 2008?

    a. It will double
    b. It will increase by 50%
    c. It will decrease by 50%
    d. It will remain unchanged
    e. It is impossible to determine from the information given

Refer to the following chart for questions 36 and 37.

	1960's	1970's	1980's	1990's
Percentage of mothers in the workforce	10	30	50	120
Number of women in the workforce (millions)	15	20	30	45

36. In which decade did the number of mothers in the workforce increase the most?

    a.   1960s to 1970s
    b.   1970s to 1980s
    c.   1980s to 1990s
    d.   The increase was the same for each decade
    e.   It cannot be determined from the information given

37. In which decade was the percentage of women in the workplace the highest?

    a.   1960s
    b.   1970s
    c.   1980s
    d.   1990's
    e.   It cannot be determined from the information given

Answer Key for Quantitative Section 11

1. To determine the next term in a series or sequence, we need twp pieces of information: (1) the pattern that the numbers follow, and (2) whether or not the pattern will continue. Statement 1 gives us the first 18 terms of the series, which follows a definite pattern – the same string of six digits repeat in the same order (456789). Statement 2 provides the second essential piece of information, which is that the series or sequence will continue indefinitely. Therefore, Choice C is correct. With both statements, we can determine the sum of the 500th term through the 505th term, which will simply be the sum of 4+5+6+7+8+9 =**39**.

2. Neither statement gives us enough information to calculate the area of the triangle. Hence, Choice E is correct.

3. The two statements, when taken together, provide enough information for us to determine the number of tiles the decorator will need. Choice C is correct.

4. The two statements, if taken together, provide enough information for us to calculate Shawn's age. Choice C is correct.

5. This is a derivation of the standard grouping problem with four groups: the number of students taking Drawing, Watercolors, Both or Neither. To determine the number of students who fall into the Neither category, we must know *all* of the other totals (the total number of students, and the number who are taking Drawing, Watercolors, and Both classes). The question stem tells us the total number of students, while Statement 1 tells us how many are taking drawing. Finally, Statement 2 tells us how many students are taking both classes. Unfortunately, we do NOT know how many students were only taking the watercolors class. Without this value, we cannot answer the question. Choice E is correct.

6. To solve the problem, we need to know the cost per gallon and the number of gallons that Grace bought. Statement 1 gives us the first price of information, while Statement 2 provides the second. Choice C is correct.

7. Choice E is correct. Without knowing if X is even or odd, we do not have enough information to answer the question.

8. Choice A is correct. Statement 1 is sufficient to answer the question. Statement 2 is not necessary to determine the value of Integer G.

9. Area of Trapezoid = (Average of parallel sides) x Height. In this case, the area = {(16 + 18)/2} x (12) = (17)(12) = 204 cubic centimeters. Choice D is correct.

Alternatively, we calculate the areas of the respective parts of the trapezoid (a triangle and a rectangle) and add them together. The area of the rectangle = (12)(16) = 192. The area of the triangle is ½ (2)(12) = 12. The total area is 192 + 12 = **204** cubic inches.

10. Choice C is correct, 360/36 = **10**.

11. Two price reductions = 0.80 x 0.70 = 0.56, which is a **44%** reduction. Choice D is correct.

12. $1/18 (22 + 33)^2$ = (55)(55)/18 = 168.05 = **168**. Choice B is correct.

13. If $a \Psi b = (1 + b)^{1/2}$ then $a\Psi 15 = (1 + 15)^{1/2}$ = **4**. Choice C is correct.

14. To solve, we use the formula: 180 (X – 2) = 2,700. X = 17. Choice C is correct.

15. 5 x 5 = 25, which is the cubic root of 15,625. Choice B is correct.

16. $k^2 – 6k + 9 = (k – 3)^2$ Choice B is correct.

17. If $2x^3 – 3x^2 –5x = 0$, then $x (2x^2 – 3x –5) = 0$, so x (2x - 5) (x+1) = 0. So, x = 0, -1, 5/2. Choice E is correct.

18. First, we must convert the weight of the package from pounds to ounces. In this case, 0.75 pounds X (16 ounces/1 pound) = 12 ounces. The total cost is $0.55 for the first ounce and $0.34 for the 11 additional ounces, or 55 + 11 (34) = $4.29 total cost to mail a 12-ounce package. Choice D is correct.

19. If the alarm rings five times every ten minutes, then it rings 5(6) times, or 30, times per hour. On a ten-hour shift, it will ring 5(6)(10) times, or 300 times. Choice B is correct.

20. The first step is to find the smallest number that is evenly divisible by 2, 3, and 5, which is 30. Thus 30 = x. Our second step is to find the smallest three-digit number that is divisible by 2, 3, 5, and 90, which is 3x. The fastest way is to check the answer choices in order. When we do, we discover that Choice C, 180, is correct.

21. First, we must add the amount of the tip to the bill: $185.30 x 0.2 = $37.06. Total cost = $222.36. Each share is 222.36 / 3 = **$74.12**. Choice E is correct.

22. First, we must subtract the deductions from the total: 14625 – 100 – 325 = 14,200. Chad received 75% of this amount, or **$10,650**. Choice A is correct.

23. For age problems with a single person, our chart is:

Candy Now	Candy plus 10	Candy minus 8	Candy minus 4

Now, let's fill in our values. As always, we will let Candy's current age = x.
Her age 10 years from now will be x + 10
Her age 8 years ago was x – 8
Her age 4 years ago was x - 4

Candy Now	Candy plus 10	Candy minus 8	Candy minus 4
X	x + 10	x – 8	x – 4

By definition, our equation is: (x +10) - (x – 8) + 6(x – 4) = 120. x + 10 - x + 8 + 6x – 24 = 120.
6x = 126. x = 21 = Candy's current age. In 11 years, Candy will be **32**. Choice D correct

24. The first step is to draw a quick chart of what we know:

Driver	Distance	Rate	Time
Jack	75x	75	x
Jill	45x	45	x

In this case, Jack and Jill will drive the same amount of time at different speeds. We want to know the amount of time it will take for Jack to be 45 miles ahead of Jill, which can be represented by: 75x – 45x = 45. 30x = 45. X = 3/2 hours. Choice C is correct.

Because this is a relatively simple scenario, it is easier for some students to think it through without the chart. If Jack drives 75 miles per hour while Jill drives 45 miles per hour, then he travels 75 – 45 = 30 additional miles each hour. The time required for Jack to be 45 miles ahead of Jill is therefore 1.5 times 30 = **1.5** hours.

25. Let x = # of pages that Karen transcribes. 3x = # pages that Olivia transcribes. x + 3x = 1200, so 4x = 1200, or x = 300. Olivia transcribed 3x, or **900** pages. Choice D is correct.

26. First, we must draw a table with the information that we know.

Investment	Amount	Interest Rate	Total Return
A	x + $750	6	6(x + 750)
B	x	4	4x

Here, we are asked to determine the total amount of money invested in A + B. First, we will solve for B. We will therefore let x = the amount of money invested in B, which means that the amount of money invested in A = x + 750. From the problem, we know that Connie's income from A is $10,000 more than her income from B. Therefore, our equation is:

Income from A – Income from B = 10,000.   0.06(x + 750) – 0.04x = 10,000. 0.06x + 45 – 0.04x = 10,000. 0.02x = 9955. x = $497,750 = amount of investment B. x + 750 = $498,500 = amount of investment A. A + B = $497,750 +$ 498,500 **= $996,250.** Choice C is correct.

To check our answer, we can simply plug in the amount of interest that each investment earns to see if it matches the stipulations in the question stem.
The total return for A is 0.06($498,500) = $29,910.
The total return for B is 0.04($497,750) = $19,910.
Connie's income from A is indeed $10,000 more than her income from B.

27. This problem can easily be solved using an algebraic formula. First, let's define our variables. We will let x = the # of years until the population triples. Mathematically, this can be expressed as: 3(300,000) = 300,000 + 5,000x. 900,000 = 300,000 + 5,000x. 600,000 = 5,000x. x = **120** years. Choice C is correct.

28. To find the original number of invoices in the series, we must subtract the endpoints and add one: 019876 – 014567 + 1 = 5310. Next, we must subtract the two missing invoices: 5310 - 2 = **5308**. Choice B is correct.

29. First, we must arrange the numbers in ascending order: 3, 5, 6, 6, 7, 7, 7, 8, 9, 12, 15. Median = 7, Mode = 7.   7 – 7 = 0. Choice A is correct.

30. Let's assume that 2 roommates split the cost of utilities, which are usually $500 per month. Therefore, X = 2 and Y = 500. Every month, each roommate pays 500/2, or Y/X for his/her share of the utilities.   If the cost of utilities increases by 250, then Y increases by 250. Each roommate's cost is (Y + 250)/X. Choice D is correct.

31. We can solve this by using a ratio: 2/48 = 3/x, so x = **72** inches. Choice D is correct.

32. We can solve this using a proportion. If 4 cans covered ¾ of one room, how many cans are needed to cover 3-1/4 rooms? 4 / 0.75 = x / 3.25. Solving for x = **17.3** additional cans. Choice C is correct.

35. To find the average profit per book, we must divide the profit by the number of books sold each year. When we do, we find that the lowest average profit was in 2006. ($3 million in profits / 54,000 books = **55.5** profit per book). Choice A is correct.

34. In 2010, the number of books sold = 312,000 (0.80) = 249,600, while the profit was (21 million)(1.2) = 25.2 million). Thus, the average profit per book = 25.2million/249,600 = **100.96**. Choice C is correct.

35. In 2007, the revised profit per book = 11 million/156,000 = 70.5, while the revised profit per book for 2008 = 24 million/170,000 = 141.2. The profit per book **doubled**. Choice A is correct.

36. Choice E is correct. The table only gives us the *% increase* in working mothers – it does not given us the *number* of working mothers. Without this information, it is impossible to answer the question.

37. Choice E is correct.   The table only gives us the *number* of women in the workforce, not the percentage. Consequently, it is impossible to answer the question.

Quantitative Section 12:   37 questions   75 minutes

Use the following answer choices for questions 1 - 8 below:

A.   Statement 1 alone is sufficient but Statement 2 alone is not sufficient to answer the question asked.
B.   Statement 2 alone is sufficient but Statement 1 alone is not sufficient to answer the question asked.
C.   Statements 1 and 2 together are sufficient to answer the question but neither statement is sufficient alone.
D.   Each statement alone is sufficient to answer the question.
E.   Statements 1 and 2 are not sufficient to answer the question asked and additional data is needed to answer the question.

1. For triangle FHG, what is the value of x?

(1) One angle equals 60 degrees and the second angle equals x
(2) The third angle is equal to 3x

2. How many sides are in polygon J?

(1) The sum of the interior angles is 1,980 degrees
(2) The area of polygon is 1,980

3.   If Tina splits her lottery prize evenly with her two parents and three siblings, how much money will each person receive?

(1)The prize was $2,880 after taxes
(2)The prize was $3,600 before 20% taxes were deducted

4.   What is the largest of the five integers?

(1) Their sum is 410
(2) Their average is 64

5. Is C greater than D?

(1) C is 75% of D
(2) The ratio of D/C is 4:3

6.   What percentage of students in Dr. Lloyd's psychology class is female?

(1) There are a total of 500 students in the class.
(2) Seventy five percent of the students wear pants.

7. What is the square of X?

(1) Y is one-third of X
(2) Y = 1/2(13)(45)

8. How much money did Stephanie earn during the holiday season?

(1) Stephanie earned three times as much as Erin.
(2) Erin worked 20 hours per week for three weeks during the holiday season.

9. Which of the following are the solutions to the following equation? $x^2 + 9x + 20 = 0$

    a.   4, 5
    b.   4, -5
    c.   −4, -5
    d.   −4, 5
    e.   2, 10

10. What is the probability of getting a red jelly bean from a dispenser that contains 80 red jelly beans, 48 green ones, 36 purple ones, 26 pink ones and 210 white ones?

    a.   1/8
    b.   1/6
    c.   1/5
    d.   1/4
    e.   1/3

11. What is the next term in the following series: 11, 12, 13, 24, 15, 48……

    a.   14
    b.   17
    c.   36
    d.   96
    e.   None of the above.

12. Tim took 96 minutes to repair the engine of a customer's car. What fraction of an 8-hour work day does this represent?

    a.   1/12
    b.   1/8
    c.   1/6
    d.   1/5
    e.   3/16

13. The length of Rectangle B is six times its width. If the perimeter of Rectangle B is 280 feet, what is its length?

    a.   20
    b.   40
    c.   60
    d.   80
    e.   120

14. How much larger is the surface area (in cubic feet) of a cube with an edge of 5 feet than a cube with an edge of 3 feet?

    a.   25
    b.   27
    c.   98
    d.   125
    e.   152

15. If a rectangular Rubbermaid storage unit has an area of 63 square feet, and its length is 2 feet longer than its width, what is the width of the storage unit?

  a. 1
  b. 2
  c. 6
  d. 7
  e. 9

16. $(15 - 11)^3 =$

  a. 4
  b. 16
  c. 64
  d. 121
  e. 225

17. Which of the following is the correct factorization of $12b^2 - 12$?

  a. $12b^2 - 144$
  b. $12 (b - 1)$
  c. $12(b - 1) (b + 1)$
  d. $12(b - 1)^2$
  e. $(4b - 3)(3b + 4)$

18. At which of the following points do the following lines intersect? $y = 5x + 4$ $y = 5x - 4$

  a. (0, -4)
  b. (0, -4) (4, 0)
  c. (0, -5) (5, 0)
  d. (-4, 0)
  e. The two lines do not intersect

19. What is the diameter of a circle with area 81π?

  a. 3
  b. 9
  c. 18
  d. 36
  e. 54

20. If f (a) = 1 + 1/3 a, what is f(30)?

  a. 11/3
  b. 10
  c. 11
  d. 31/3
  e. 31

21. A cattery has 85 Persian cats, 411 Siamese cats and 103 Calico cats. For a treat, the owner of the cattery purchases 88 lbs of catnip, to be distributed evenly among all of the cats. Assuming there are no other types of cats in the cattery, how much catnip (in ounces) would each cat receive?

    a.   2.35
    b.   5.80
    c.   6.80
    d.   11.60
    e.   23.50

22. Pizza Hut offers six possible toppings for their personal pan pizzas: pepperoni, sausage, onion, cheese, mushrooms and peppers. If you choose four of these toppings, how many possible combinations are there?

    a.   4
    b.   15
    c.   26
    d.   24
    e.   30

23. Barbie's salary is $720 per week after a 20% raise. Before Barbie's raise, her supervisor Connie's salary was 50% greater than Barbie's. If Barbie and Connie receive the same dollar amount raise, what is Connie's salary after the raise?

    a. $860
    b. $900
    c. $960
    d. $1020
    e. $1200

24. Maria put $4390 into a Platinum CD at her local bank, which she left untouched for six years and nine months, when she withdrew the entire amount, plus all of the simple annual interest she had earned. If the total balance in Maria's account was $6175, what simple rate of annual interest did she earn?

    a.   3.82%
    b.   4.62%
    c.   5.52%
    d.   6.02%
    e.   7.12%

25. If three less than eleven times a whole number is equal to 140, what is the number?

    a.   11
    b.   13
    c.   14
    d.   17
    e.   19

26. Rafe is four times as old as Monica. In ten years, Rafe will be 10 times as old as Monica was 5 years ago. How old will Rafe be in five years?

    a. 19
    b. 24
    c. 25
    d. 29
    e. 45

27. The distance between Annapolis and Charlotte is 150 miles. A car travels from Annapolis to Charlotte at 75 miles per hour and returns from Charlotte to Annapolis along the same route at 50 miles per hour. What is the average speed for the round trip?

    a. 60.0
    b. 62.5
    c. 65.0
    d. 67.5
    e. 70.0

28. A tank of sugar syrup can be filled in 3 hours and drained in 6 hours. How long will it take to fill the tank if an employee forgets to close the drain valve?

    a. 1.5
    b. 3.0
    c. 4.5
    d. 6.0
    e. 9.0

29. Fifty students in a local conservatory either studied voice, piano or both. 40% of the students studied voice, while 25% studied both voice and piano. What percentage of the students studied only piano?

    a. 20%
    b. 25%
    c. 30%
    d. 35%
    e. 40%

30. A candy dish contains only Snickers bars, Mars bars, and Hershey bars. The probability of choosing a Snickers bar at random is 1/5 and the probability of choosing a Mars bar at random is 3/10. If there are 200 candy bars in the dish, how many are Hershey bars?

    a. 50
    b. 75
    c. 100
    d. 125
    e. 150

31. For the repeating decimal 0.015689015689015689...... , what is the 37th digit to the right of the decimal point?

    a. 0
    b. 1
    c. 5
    d. 6
    e. 8

32. What is the sum of the first 80 integers?

    a. 1,600
    b. 1,620
    c. 3,200
    d. 3,240
    e. 6,480

33. Jenny wants to blend a gourmet hot fudge sauce that costs 75 cents per pound with a caramel sauce that costs 95 cents per pound to make 500 pounds of a mixture that costs 80 cents per pound. How many pounds of the caramel sauce must Jenny use?

      a.   20
      b.   25
      c.   125
      d.   375
      e.   480

34. The ratio of professors to students at a private college is 1:12. If 36 new students are admitted, there will be 16 times as many students as professors. What is the new number of students at the college?

      a.   124
      b.   132
      c.   136
      d.   144
      e.   148

Use the following table to answer questions 35 – 37.

Percentage of Contact Lens Wearers (By Age)

	U.S.	U.K.	France	India
Under 10	2	5	1	0
10 – 18	21	30	15	3
19 – 30	38	35	29	19
31 – 50	29	25	40	66
Over 51	10	5	15	12

35. A leading economic journal recently estimated the number of contact lens wearers in France and India at 10 million and 20 million, respectively. If these numbers are accurate, what is the total number of people in both nations between 19 and 30 who wear contact lenses?

      a.   2.9 million
      b.   3.8 million
      c.   6.7 million
      d.   7.5 million
      e.   Cannot be determined from the information given

36. If there are currently 5 million people who wear contact lenses in France, and the French government bans their use in people under 10 and over 51, how many *fewer* people will be allowed to wear them?

      a.   50,000
      b.   80,000
      c.   160,000
      d.   500,000
      e.   800,000

37. Optometrists in the U.K. recently estimated that 40% of contact lens wearers who are under 10 years old choose blue lenses, which are not available to older patients. If the total number of contact lens wearers in the U.K. is 1.8 million, how many of them wear blue lenses?

    a.   36,000
    b.   40,000
    c.   72,000
    d.   90,000
    e.   120,000

Answer Key for Quantitative Section 12

1. If taken together, Statements 1 and 2 give us enough information to calculate the value of x. Choice C is correct.

2. To determine the number of sides in the polygon, we need to know the sum of the interior angles. Statement 1 provides this information. Statement 2 is extraneous information that is designed to confuse you. Choice A is correct.

3. We can find the answer using either Statement 1 or 2, which convey the same information. Choice D is correct.

4. In this case, Statement 1 gives us the sum of the integers and Statement 2 gives us the average. Unfortunately, this is not enough for us to determine the largest of the five integers, which may (or may not) be consecutive. Hence, Choice E is correct.

5. Either statement is sufficient to answer the question. Choice D is correct.

6. Choice E is correct. Neither statement gives us enough information to answer the question.

7. Choice C is correct. Statements 1 and 2 together are sufficient to answer the question but neither statement is sufficient alone.

8. Choice E is correct. Neither statement gives us enough information to answer the question.

9. If $x^2 + 9x + 20 = 0$, then $(x + 4)(x + 5) = 0$. So, **x = -4 or -5.** Choice C is correct.

10. First, we must determine the total number of jelly beans in the dispenser, which is 80 + 48 + 36 + 26 + 210 = 400. Then, we must calculate the probability of getting a red jelly bean, which is 80/400 = **1/5**. Choice C is correct.

11. If you look carefully, you will see that this example is actually a combination of TWO sub-series. The odd numbers (11, 13, 15 ....) form an arithmetic series, in which each number increases by two. The even numbers (12, 24, 48, ...) form an arithmetic sequence, in which each number is twice the previous one. The next number in the series will be part of the arithmetic sequence. According to the design, it is 15 + 2, or **17**. Choice B is correct.

12. An 8-hour work day contains 8(60) = 480 minutes. If Tim took 96 minutes to repair the engine, then we can represent the fraction of the day he used as 96/480 = **1/5**. Choice D is correct.

13. The perimeter of Rectangle A is 2(Length) + 2(Width). In this case, we will let the width = X and the length = 6x. Our formula for the perimeter is therefore: 2x + 2(6x) = 280. 2x + 12x = 280. 14x = 280. x = 20 = width. 6x = **120** = length. Choice E is correct.

14. Area 1 = 5 x 5 x 5 = 125 cubic feet. Area 2 = 3 x 3 x 3 = 27 cubic feet. 125 – 27 = **98** cubic feet. Choice C is correct.

15. First, let's define our variables. We will let x = the length of the storage unit. Therefore, the width = x - 2 and the area of the storage unit (Length x Width) is x(x - 2). Our equation becomes: x(x – 2) = 63. $x^2 - 2x - 63 = 0$. (x – 9)(x +7) = 0. Therefore, x = 9 and -7. Since the length of the side cannot be negative, we can discard the -7 root. The length of the storage unit is 9 and the width is 9 – 2 = **7**. Choice D is correct.

16. 4 x 4 x 4 = **64**. Choice C is correct.

17. $12b^2 - 12 = 12(b^2 - 1) = $ **12(b − 1) (b + 1).** Choice C is correct.

18. They do not intersect. Choice E is correct.

19. Area = πr^2 =π (9)(9). Diameter = 9 + 9 = **18.** Choice C is correct.

20. If (a) = 1 + 1/3 a, then f(30) = 1 + 1/ 3 (30) = 1 + 10 = **11**. Choice C is correct.

21. To solve, we must calculate the total number of cats in the cattery, which is 85 + 411 + 103 = 599 cats. Then, we must convert the amount of catnip to ounces, which is 88 lb x 16 oz/lb = 1408 oz. Finally, we must divide the total amount of catnip evenly among the total number of cats, which is 1408 / 599 = **2.35** ounces. Choice A is correct.

22. Use the factorial formula to solve: 6! / {4!(6! - 4!)} = 6!/{(4!)(2!)} = (6 x 5 x 4 x 3 x 2 x 1) / {(4 x 3 x 2 x 1)(2 x 1) = 6 x 5 / 2= 30/2 = **15**. Choice B is correct.

23. First, we must find Barbie's original salary. 720 = 1.20x, x = 600. Thus, Barbie's raise was 720 − 600 = $120. Now, we must find Connie's original salary. $600 + 0.5(600) = 900. Now, we must add Connie's raise: 900 + 120 = **$1020**. Choice D is correct.

24. In this case, we know the beginning and ending amounts and are being asked to calculate the rate of simple annual interest that was earned over 6.75 years. To solve, we will use the basic equation:

Interest = Principal x Rate x Time. The trick is to work backwards from our final total to determine the rate of interest that was paid. In this case, our total of $6157 represents the initial deposit of $4390 PLUS the interest earned.

Mathematically, $6175 = $4390 + PRT = $4390 + ($4390)(X)(6.75), so 6175 = 4390 + 29632.50X, or X =1785/29632.5 = 0.0602 = **6.02**% Choice D is correct.

25. In this case, we will let x = the whole number we are trying to find. Once we define our variable, the problem easily converts to a simple equation: 11x − 3 = 140, so 11x = 143 and x= **13**. Choice B is correct.

26. Our first step will be to draw a quick chart for the information we are given. To avoid working with fractions, we will Let Monica's current age = x. Thus, we know that Rafe's current age = 4x. Ten years from now, Monica's age will be x + 10, while Rafe's age will be 4x + 10. Five years ago, Monica's age was x − 5, while Rafe's age was 4x − 5.

Name	Current Age	Age 10 years from now	Age 5 years ago
Rafe	4x	4x + 10	4x - 5
Monica	x	x + 10	x − 5

From the table, we know that Rafe's age ten years from now = 4x + 10. From the problem itself, we ALSO know that Rafe's age ten years from now is "ten times as old as Monica was 5 years ago," which can be written mathematically as 10 (x − 5). Our equation, therefore, is: 4x + 10 = 10(x − 5). 4x + 10 = 10x − 50. 6x = 60 x =10 − Monica's current age. Rafe's current age is 4(10) = 40. Five years from now, Rafe will be 40 + 5 = **45**. Choice E is correct.

27. The first step for this type of problem is to draw a quick chart of what we know:

Route	Distance	Rate	Time
To Charlotte	150	75	2
From Charlotte	150	50	3

A car traveling at 75 mph will cover 150 miles in 2 hours. A car traveling at 50 mph covers the same 150 miles in 3 hours. The total travel time is therefore 5 hours. Average speed = Total distance / Total time. For the entire round trip, the average speed = (150 + 150) / 5 = **60** mph. Choice A is correct.

28. In this case, the rate to fill the tank is x/3, while the rate to drain it is x/6. Since the drain is emptying

the tank, our equation becomes $x/3 - x/6 = 1$. To solve, we must multiple both sides by the least common denominator, which is 6: $2x - 1x = 6$, or $x = \mathbf{6}$ hours to fill the tank. Choice D is correct.

29. In this case, we have three distinct groups, which must add up to 100%. Since the original two groups are 40% and 25%, the remaining group must be 100% - 40% - 25% = **35%** of the total. Choice D is correct. In case you are wondering, it doesn't matter how many students are enrolled in the conservatory, because we are dealing with percentages. The number 50 is extraneous information that is included strictly to confuse you.

30. If the probability of choosing a Snickers bar is 1/5 (or 2/10) and the probability of choosing a Mars bar is 3/10, then the probability of choosing EITHER a Snickers bar or a Mars bar is 2/10 + 3/10 = 5/10.

Therefore, the probability of choosing a Hershey bar is $1 - 5/10 = 5/10 = 1/2$.
If there are 200 candy bars in the dish, then there are 1/2 x 200 = **100** Hershey bars. Choice C is correct.

31. For repeating decimals, you must first determine the actual string of numbers that repeat. Then, you can simply count the number of decimal places to determine the identity of a specific digit in the string. In this case, the repeating pattern is 015689, which is a string of 6 digits. Hence, 37th digit to the right of the decimal point will be the *first* number in the series, which is 0. Choice A is correct.

32.   The fastest way to solve this problem is to use the formula for the sum of the numbers in an arithmetic series: Sum = {(Number of Items) (First Item + Last or Desired Item)} / 2. In this case,

Sum = $80(1 + 80)/2 = (80)(81)/2 = \mathbf{3,240}$. Choice D is correct.

33. First, we must draw a table with the information that we know.

Ingredient	Quantity	Price/pound	Total Cost
Hot fudge	$500 - x$	75	$75(500 - x)$
Caramel	x	95	95x
Mixture	500	80	40,000

Since the problem asks us to calculate the amount of caramel that Jenny needs, we will let that value = x. Therefore, the amount of hot fudge = $500 - x$. Once we label our variables, we can write the expression for the total cost of each ingredient. We can also calculate the cost of the final mixture. Since the cost of the hot fudge plus the cost of the caramel equals the total cost of the blend, our equation becomes:

Cost of Caramel + Cost of Hot Fudge = Total Cost. $95x + 75(500 - x) = 40,000$.
$95x + 37,500 - 75x = 40,000$. $20x = 2500$. $X = \mathbf{125}$ pounds of caramel needed. Choice C is correct.

34. The hardest part about this question is setting up the equation we need to solve it. First, it's important to acknowledge one key point: the # of professors (x) remains the same. We also know that the original number of students is 12 times this number, or 12x. Therefore, the number of new students is $12x + 36$. Finally, we also know that $12x + 36 = 16x$. Solving for x, we find that the number of professors (x) = 9. Therefore, the original number of students = $(9)(12) = 108$ and the new number of students = 108 + 36 = **144.** Choice D is correct.

35. France: 10 million wearers x (0.29) = 2,900,000 between 19 and 30. India: 20 million wearers x (0.19) = 3,800,000 between 19 and 30. Total number of people in both nations between 19 and 30 who wear contact lenses = **6.7** million. Choice C is correct.

36. 5 million (0.01) = 50,000 under age 10.   5 million (0.15) = 750,000 over age 51.   750,000 + 50,000 = **800,000** people can no longer wear them. Choice E is correct.

37. 1.8 million (0.05) = 90,000 users under age 10 x (0.4) = **36,000** wear blue lenses. Choice A is correct.

Quantitative Section 13: 37 questions   75 minutes

Use the following answer choices for questions 1 – 8 below:

A.   Statement 1 alone is sufficient but Statement 2 alone is not sufficient to answer the question asked.
B.   Statement 2 alone is sufficient but Statement 1 alone is not sufficient to answer the question asked.
C.   Statements 1 and 2 together are sufficient to answer the question but neither statement is sufficient alone.
D.   Each statement alone is sufficient to answer the question.
E.   Statements 1 and 2 are not sufficient to answer the question asked and additional data is needed to answer the question.

1. What is the new area of the circle?

(1)   The radius is decreased by 18%
(2)   The original diameter was 18

2. In quadrilateral ABCD, what is the value of angle D?

(1) The length of side AB is 12
(2) The sum of angles A, B and C = 2D.

3. A cashier had 58 pennies in her drawer at the beginning of her shift. How many pennies were remaining in the drawer at the end of her shift?

(1)   The cashier received 12 pennies from customers during the shift.
(2)   The cashier ran out of nickels twice during her shift.

4. What is the % decrease between last year and this year?

(1)   Last year, Jane won 12 Girl Scout badges
(2)   This year, Jane won 5 fewer badges than the year before

5 .How many hours will it take for a cement truck to pour 30,000 quarts of concrete mix?

(1) The truck travels at a maximum speed of 60 miles per hour.
(2) The truck can pour 600 gallons of concrete mix in 20 minutes.

6. What percentage of jelly beans in the jar is red?

(1) There are a total of 500 jelly beans in the jar.
(2) There are five different colors of jelly beans in the jar.

7. What is the value of W?

(1) $101 < W < 105$
(2)   X is an even integer

8. Is C > 16?

(1) $C > F$
(2) $4^2 < F < 5^2$

9. What is the next term in the following series: 11, 12, 13, 24, 15, 48.......

    a.   14
    b.   17
    c.   36
    d.   96
    e.   None of the above.

10. If Jake walks south for 50 yards, then west for 120 yards, then walked directly back to his starting point on a diagonal, how many yards did he walk altogether?

    a.   170
    b.   255
    c.   270
    d.   290
    e.   300

11. $46/98 - 23/196 =$

    a.   23/196
    b.   69/196
    c.   23/98
    d.   23/66
    e.   69/98

12. $8.75 =$

    a.   35/5
    b.   70/7
    c.   45/5
    d.   85/8
    e.   35/4

13. Six hundred and fifty employees at a software company have registered for classes at the corporate health center. Two hundred and seventy five have signed up for karate. Five hundred and eighty have signed up for low calorie cooking. Three hundred employees have signed up for both karate and low calorie cooking. How many employees have signed up for NEITHER karate and low calorie cooking?

    a.   95
    b.   105
    c.   125
    d.   150
    e.   200

14. Doris left her $600,000 in equal installments to her three sons. A week after Doris's death, one of her sons died before he could receive his inheritance. Instead, his portion of Doris's estate was divided equally among the man's four daughters. What fraction of Doris's original estate did each of the four granddaughters receive?

    a.   1/12
    b.   1/8
    c.   1/6
    d.   1/5
    e.   1/4

15. Roxie inherited $3 million from her maternal grandfather and placed the entire amount in account that earns 7 1/2% simple annual interest. Assuming that Roxie leaves the money in the account and does not withdraw any of the interest, how much will she have (principal + interest) exactly one year from today?

       a. $3,000,225
       b. $3,002,250
       c. $3,072,500
       d. $3,225,000
       e. $3,725,000

16. After a devastating fire, a city's population decreased by 38%. If the current population is 1.37 million, what was the original population?

       a.   931,600
       b.   1,890,600
       c.   2,209,677
       d.   2,876,900
       e.   3,605,263

17. If $f(d) = (d + 6)(d - 4)$, what is $f(9)$?

       a.   36
       b.   45
       c.   54
       d.   60
       e.   75

18. Robin's wedding anniversary is 100 days after her birthday. If her birthday is on a Wednesday this year, on what day of the week will Robin's anniversary fall?

       a.   Monday
       b.   Tuesday
       c.   Wednesday
       d.   Thursday
       e.   Friday

19. Simply $\sqrt{7}$ $\sqrt{8}$ $\sqrt{9}$

       a.   6.90
       b.   18.75
       c.   20.75
       d.   22.05
       e.   22.45

20. The mean of two numbers is $8x - 24$. If one of the numbers is x, what is the other number?

       a. $8x + 24$
       b. $3x + 8$
       c. $(2x - 4)^2$
       d. $15x - 48$
       e.   it cannot be determined from the information given

21. What is 0.005% expressed as a fraction?

    a. 5/100
    b. 5/250
    c. 5/200
    d. 1/250
    e. 1/200

22. Arrange the following fractions in descending order: 11/13, 12/15, 21/27, 32/41, 48/63

    a. 11/13, 32/41, 21/27, 12/15, 48/63
    b. 48/63, 12/15, 11/13, 32/41, 21/17
    c. 11/13, 12/15, 21/27, 32/41, 48/63
    d. 11/13, 12/15, 32/41, 21/27, 48/63
    e. 11/13, 21/27, 12/15, 32/41, 48/63

2. For the following system of equations, what is the value of y? $2x + 6y = 10$, $2x + 10y = 6$

    a. -3
    b. -2
    c. -1
    d. −1/2
    e. −1/3

24. Which of the following quantities is *greater than* 8.9×10^{-11}?

    a. 89×10^{-12}
    b. 0.89×10^{-12}
    c. 0.000000000089
    d. $0.0000000000445 \times 10^{-11} \times 2$
    e. 890000×10^{-6}

25. Grace and Edna own a small business that earned $48,000 in profits last year. If they agreed to split the profits in a 9:4 ratio, with Grace getting the larger share, how much did Edna earn from the business?

    a. $10,453.67
    b. $11,896.23
    c. $14,769.23
    d. $21,453.23
    e. $33,230.70

26. Theresa is 10 years older than Cindy. However, 5 years ago Theresa was twice as old as Cindy. How old is Cindy?

    a. 5
    b. 10
    c. 12
    d. 15
    e. 20

27. Julie drives to her grandmother's house every week at an average speed of 50 miles per hour. On the way home, she takes the same route, but averages 75 miles per hour. If Julie's total round trip is 10 hours, how far away is her grandmother's house?

    a. 30
    b. 60
    c. 150
    d. 300
    e. 600

28. Two dozen musicians auditioned for an orchestra. Fifteen played the piano, while nine played the harp. If one pianist and one harpist are chosen from the group of twenty-four, how many different pairs of musicians are possible?

    a. 24
    b. 48
    c. 96
    d. 112
    e. 135

29. Scientists recorded the daily temperature in a research aquarium. During a six-day period, the temperatures recorded (in °F) were 67, 73, 72, 56, 68, and 78. What was the median temperature (in °F)?

    a. 68.5
    b. 69
    c. 70
    d. 72.5
    e. 73

30. Jake is a wholesale dealer of foreign and vintage cars. If he can buy J cars for G dollars, how much will M cars cost (in dollars)?

    a. 1/MGJ
    b. (100/J)MG
    c. MG/J
    d. MJ/G
    e. MGJ

31. The sum of two numbers is 175 and their difference is 35. What is the smaller number?

    a. 65
    b. 70
    c. 75
    d. 100
    e. 105

32. The Boston Philharmonic charges $20 for adult tickets to their concerts and $5 for children's tickets. If they sold 1,000 tickets in a given weekend and received $11,000 in total ticket sales, how many adult tickets were sold?

    a. 300
    b. 400
    c. 600
    d. 750
    e. 800

33. The angles of a triangle are in the ratio of 3:4:5. What is the measurement (in degrees) of the smallest angle?

    a. 15
    b. 45
    c. 60
    d. 70
    e. 75

34. Jenny is making holiday decorations from a large piece of velvet fabric. How many circles, each with a 6-inch radius, can Jenny cut from a rectangular piece of the fabric, which measures 84 inches x 204 inches?

    a. 64
    b. 124
    c. 119
    d. 238
    e. 476

35. Joe will cover his bathroom floor with ceramic tiles that measure 6 inches by 12 inches. If the room is a rectangle that measures 12 feet by 14 feet, how many tiles will Joe need to cover the floor?

    a. 84
    b. 168
    c. 184
    d. 336
    e. 384

Refer to the following table for questions 36 – 37.

	2005	2006	2007	2008
Number of umbrellas sold (thousands)	A	B	C	D
Annual rainfall (inches)	E	F	G	H

36. In 2008, how many thousands of umbrellas were sold per foot of rainfall?

    a. D/H
    b. D/12H
    c. 12H/D
    d. DH/12
    e. 12D/H

37. If the number of umbrellas sold in 2006 was overstated by 25% and the annual rainfall was understated by 50%, what is the correct number of umbrellas sold per inch of rainfall that year?

    a. B/2F
    b. F/2B
    c. BF/2
    d. 0.75BF
    e. 0.75B/F

Answer Key for Quantitative Section 13

1. If we take the two statements together, we have enough information to calculate the new area of the circle. Choice C is correct.

2. In quadrilateral ABCD, the sum of the interior angles is 360 degrees. Hence, the information in Statement 2 is all we need to determine the value of angle D. Statement 1 provides extraneous information, which we do not need to answer the question. Choice B is correct.

3. To answer this question, we need to know: (1) how many pennies the cashier took in during her shift, and (2) how many pennies she paid out. Statement 1 gives us the first piece of information, but we do not know the second. Therefore, Choice E is correct. We do not have enough information to answer the question.

4. To answer this question, we need to know the number of badges Jane earned both years. Statement 1 gives us the first value, while Statement 2 gives us the second. Taken together, we have enough information to answer the question. Choice C is correct.

5. Statement 2 gives us enough information to answer the question. Statement 1 is extraneous information. Choice B is correct.

6. Choice E is correct. To answer the question, we need to know the total number of jelly beans in the jar and the number of red ones. Statement 1 gives us the first number, but neither statement gives us the second. Therefore, we do not have enough information to answer the question.

7. Choice E is correct. We do not have enough information to determine if W is 102 or 104.

8. Choice C is correct. Together, Statements 1 and 2 provide enough information for us to determine that C > 16.

9. If you look carefully, you will see that this example is actually a combination of TWO sub-series. The odd numbers (11, 13, 15 ....) increase by two, while the even numbers double (12, 24, 48, ...). The next number in the series will be 15 + 2, or **17**. Choice B is correct.

10. The area that Jake walked is a "special" right triangle with sides equal to 50, 120 and 130. Therefore, the total distance Jake walked is the perimeter of that triangle, which is 50 + 120 + 130 = **300** yards. Choice E is correct.

11. 46/98 – 23/196 = 92/196 – 23/196 = **69/196**. Choice B is correct.

12. 8.75 = **35/4**. Choice E is correct.

13. In this case, we have four groups of employees (650 total): Taking Karate: 275; Taking a cooking class: 580; Taking karate AND a cooking class: 300; Taking neither activity: ? Hence, our equation is Karate + Cooking + Neither – Both = 650. 275 + 580 + Neither - 300 = 650. Neither = **95**. Choice A is correct.

14. Doris's sons each inherited 1/3 of her $600,000 estate, or $200,000. One of the $200,000 shares was subsequently divided among one of the son's four daughters, who each received $200,000/4 or $50,000. The question asks us to determine what fraction of the *original estate* each girl received, which is $50,000/$600,000 = **1/12**. Choice A is correct.

15. $3,000,000 x 0.075 = $225,000 interest. Total = **$3,225,000**. Choice D is correct.

16. Let x = the original population. 0.62x = 1370000. Thus, x = **2,209,677**. Choice C is correct.

17. If f (d) = (d + 6)(d – 4), then f (9) = (9 + 6) (9 – 4) = (15)(5) = **75**. Choice E is correct.

18. 100/7 = 14 + 2 remainder. Her birthday will fall on a **Friday**. (Wednesday + 2). Choice E is correct.

19. (2.646)(2.828)(3) = **22.45**. Choice E is correct.

20. Let's assume the to numbers being averaged are x and y. From the problem, we know that (x + y)/2 = 8x – 24. If we "solve" this equation, we find that x + y = 16x – 48, or y = **15x – 48**, which is Choice D.

21. 0.005% = 0.5/100 = 5/1000 = **1/200**. Choice E is correct.

22. First, convert all of the fractions to decimal form. Then, arrange in descending order. The correct order

is Choice D, **11/13, 12/15, 32/41, 21/27, 48/63**.

23. If $2x + 6y = 10$ and $2x + 10y = 6$, then we can subtract the equations to get $-4y = 4$, or **y =-1**. Choice C is correct.

24. Choice E is correct.

25. $9x + 4x = \$48,000$, or $13x = 48000$, so $x = 3692.3$. Edna's share $= 4x = $ **\$14,769.23**. Choice C is correct.

26. First, we must summarize our data in a table:

Name	Current Age	Age 5 years ago
Theresa	x + 10	(x + 10) – 5
Cindy	x	x - 5

Next, we must write our equation. Five years ago, Theresa was twice as old as Cindy, which gives us the following equation: $x + 5 = 2 (x - 5)$, so $x + 5 = 2x – 10$ and $x = $ **15**. Choice D is correct.

27. The first step for this type of problem is to draw a quick chart of what we know.

Route	Distance	Rate	Time
To Grandma's	50x	50	x
From Grandma's	75(10 – x)	75	10 - x

In this case, we will let the amount of time Julie travels to her grandmother's house $= x$. Her return time is therefore $10 – x$. Once we have the expressions for the distance traveled to – and from – grandma's house, we can use them to write an equation to solve for the distance.

Distance to Grandma's = Distance from Grandma's
$50x = 75(10 – x)$ or $50x = 750 – 75x$. $125x = 750$. $x = 6$. $50x = $ **300** miles. Choice D is correct.

28. The orchestra will fill two positions – one pianist and one harpist. The possible combinations are $15 \times 9 = $ **135**. Choice E is correct.

29. To determine the median, we must first, arrange the numbers in ascending order: 56, 67, 68, 72, 73, 78. Since there is an even number of values, we must take the average of the middle two numbers as our median. Here, it is $68 + 72$, which have an average of **70**. Choice C is correct.

30. To solve, let's plug in random numbers for each variable. In this case, let's assume that Jake bought 20 cars (J) for 100 dollars (G). The cost for a single car is therefore 100/20 or G/J or 5 dollars. The cost for any value of M will simply be that number times 5, which, in symbols, is **MG/J**. Choice C is correct.

31. In this case, we can write one equation for the first condition and a second equation for the second condition.   As always, we must first define our variables. We will let $= x$ the smaller number and $y = $ the larger number.

The first equation, which defines the first condition, is $x + y = 175$
The second equation, which defines the second condition, is $y – x = 35$
To solve the problem for x, we must combine the equations in a way that eliminates y.

The fastest way is to re-write equation 1 as $y = 175 – x$ and substitute this value for y into equation 2. When we do, we get $(175 – x) – x = 35$, or $175 – 2x = 35$. Therefore, $2x = 140$. $x = $ **70.** Choice B is correct. $y = 175 – 70 = 105$.

32. In this case, we can write two equations – one for the number of tickets and the other for their cost. As always, we must first define our variables. We will let $= x$ the number of adult tickets and $y = $ the number of children's tickets.

The first equation, which defines the *number* of tickets sold, is $x + y = 1000$
The second equation, which defines the *cost* of the tickets, is $20x + 5y = 11,000$
To solve the problem for x, we must combine the equations in a way that eliminates y.

The fastest way is to re-write equation 1 as y = 1,000 – x and substitute this value for y into equation 2. When we do, we get: 20x + 5(1,000 – x) = 11,000. 20x + 5,000 – 5x = 11,000. 15x = 6000. x = **400** adult tickets sold. Choice B is correct. y = 1,000 – 400 = 600 children's sold

33.   3x + 4x + 5x = 180, so 12x = 180, x = 15, 3x = **45**, 4x = 60, 5x = 75. Choice B is correct,

34. In this case, we are cutting a rectangular piece of fabric into smaller, circular pieces. If the circles have a 6-inch radius, then their diameter is 12 inches. For a piece of fabric measuring 84 inches by 204 inches, we can lay 204/12 - or 17 - circles across the *length* of the fabric. Since the width of the fabric is 84 inches, we can make 84/12, or 7 total rows of circles. Therefore, Jenny can make 17 x 7 = **119** total circles. Choice C is correct.

35. The area of the room is 12 x 14 = 168 square feet. The area of one tile is (0.50 foot) x (1.0 foot) = 0.50 square feet. Therefore, to cover the entire floor, Joe will need: 168 square feet (1 tile/0.50 square feet) = **336** tiles. Choice D is correct.

36. In 2008, D umbrellas were sold per H inches of rainfall. The number sold per foot of rainfall = D/(H/12) =**12D/H**. Choice E is correct.

37. The number of umbrellas sold per inch of rainfall in 2006 was B/F. If B was overstated by 25% and F was understated by 50%, then the corrected number of umbrellas sold per inch of rainfall would be 0.75B/1.5F = B/2F. Choice A is correct.

Alternatively, we can plug substitute numbers for the letters and see what we get. Let's let B = 100 and F = 10. Therefore, a 25% reduction in B = 75 and a 50% increase in F = 15. The corrected ratio is 75/15 = 5. Converting back to letters, 5 = 100/(2)(10), which is **B/2F**.

Quantitative Section 14: 37 questions   75 minutes

Use the following answer choices for questions 1 - 8 below:

A.   Statement 1 alone is sufficient but Statement 2 alone is not sufficient to answer the question asked.
B.   Statement 2 alone is sufficient but Statement 1 alone is not sufficient to answer the question asked.
C.   Statements 1 and 2 together are sufficient to answer the question but neither statement is sufficient alone.
D.   Each statement alone is sufficient to answer the question.
E.   Statements 1 and 2 are not sufficient to answer the question asked and additional data is needed to answer the question.

1. How many degrees are in the smallest angle in Triangle XYZ?

(1) The triangle is scalene
(2) The angles are in a ratio of 2:3:7.

2. What is the measure of the final internal angle of enclosed figure X?

(1) The other internal angles in X total 825
(2) X is an octagon

3. At a church raffle, the pastor will award a single cash prize to one lucky winner. What is the probability (in percent) that Joe will win the prize?

(1) There are 500 tickets in the bowl
(2) Joe bought 20 of the 500 tickets

4. How much money does David have?

(1) He has 46 coins.
(2) 28 of the coins are dimes.

5. How much is the store's total bank deposit?

(1) The manager will deposit the entire amount of cash sales, which are $565.25
(2) Seventy five percent of the cash deposited is coins, rather than bills.

6. How much did Mr. Winters spend on paint?

(1) The cost of paint is $18.95 per gallon.
(2) The house he was painting had a surface area of 11,250 square feet.

7. What is the difference between H and G?

(1) H + G = 30
(2) G and H are different prime integers between 12 and 18.

8. What is the value of W?

(1)   W = V + 25
(2)   V is a perfect cube.

9. What is the set of all values of x for which $x^2 - x = 12$?

    a.   (2, 6)
    b.   (-3, 4)
    c.   (3, -4)
    d.   (-2, 6)
    e.   (2, -6)

10. F = {1, 2, 4, 5, 8}   G = {4, 5, 6, 9,}   H = {2, 6, 7, 10}. What is $(F \cup G) \cup H$?

    a.   {2}
    b.   {2, 6}
    c.   {1, 2, 4, 5, 6, 7, 10, 11, 12}
    d.   {2, 3, 4, 5, 6, 7, 8, 9, 10, 12}
    e.   {1, 2, 4, 5, 6, 7, 8, 9, 10}

11. What is the circumference of a circle that has a radius of 4444 (use π = 3.1416)?

    a. 2.22×10^3
    b. 2.79×10^4
    c. 2.22×10^7
    d. 4.44×10^7
    e. 8.88×10^7

12. How many 6 ounce rib eye steaks are in a carton of steaks that weighs 48 pounds? (Assume that all of the steaks are rib eye and that they account for the total weight of the box)

    a.   96
    b.   108
    c.   128
    d.   146
    e.   196

13. In a class of 55 students, the average waistline of the 30 girls was 24, while the average waistline of the 25 boys was 36. What was the average waistline for the entire class?

    a.   27.45
    b.   28.00
    c.   29.45
    d.   30.00
    e.   31.45

14. A teenage actress set up a trust fund for her younger brother and sister. If she gave her sister $10,000 less than three times what she gave her brother, and the total amount in the trust fund was $500,000, how much did the actress give her brother?

    a. $125,000
    b. $127,500
    c. $170,000
    d. $375,000
    e. $372,500

15. The perimeter of right triangle DEF is 144 inches. If we connect the midpoints of the three sides of DEF, we can form a smaller triangle. What will its perimeter be?

    a. 12
    b. 36
    c. 48
    d. 64
    e. 72

16. What is the equation of the line that contains the points (4, 5) and (7, 11)?

    a. $y = 2x - 1$
    b. $y = 3x - 2$
    c. $y = 2x + 3$
    d. $y = -2x - 3$
    e. $y = 2x - 3$

17.   I. The diagonal of a parallelogram always bisects the other diagonal of the parallelogram.
    II. The diagonal of a parallelogram is perpendicular to the other diagonal of the parallelogram.
    III. The diagonal of a parallelogram bisects an angle of the parallelogram.

    Which of these statements is/are true?

    a. I
    b. II
    c. III
    d. I and II
    e. I and III

18. What is the average of the following numbers: 11/5, 33/42, 4/9, 8/7, 1/11?

    a. 0.567
    b. 0.786
    c. 0.932
    d. 1.091
    e. 1.140

19. $9^5 \times 9^3 =$

    a. 3^{11}
    b. 3^{12}
    c. 27^5
    d. 81^3
    e. 81^4

20. If $(x - 5)^2 / 8 = (5 - 3)^2 / 8$, what does x equal?

    a. 2
    b. 3
    c. 6
    d. 7
    e. 9

21. Which of the following expressions is equivalent to (a + b –1) (a – b)?

    a. $a^2 - a - b^2 + b$
    b. $a^2 + a - b^2 + b$
    c. $a^2 + a + b^2 - b$
    d. $a^2 - 2a - b^2 + 2b$
    e. $a^2 - a - b^2 + b - 1$

22. What is the next term in the series? 5, 8, 7, 10, 9, 12.......

    a. 6
    b. 10
    c. 11
    d. 13
    e. 15

23. On spring break in Florida, Jennifer bought six shirts as souvenirs for her friends, which cost $14.50 each. If Jennifer works at a donut shop for $5.85 per hour, how many hours will she have to work to pay for the shirts (assuming no taxes or other deductions are withheld from her paycheck)?

    a. 5.85
    b. 6.00
    c. 8.70
    d. 14.50
    e. 14.87

24. After making preserves with her grandmother, Gayle had enough to fill 28.5 jars. If each full jar contained 23.1 oz, how many total pounds of preserves did Gayle have (to the nearest pound)?

    a. 32
    b. 41
    c. 46
    d. 56
    e. 65

25. A store sells both videos and DVDs. The average price of a video is $12.00, while the average price of a DVD is $15.00. If, last month, the store sold 40 more DVDs than videos, and the total receipts were $6000, how many DVDs did the store sell?

    a. 200
    b. 205
    c. 220
    d. 240
    e. 245

26. Three sisters, Hannah, Juliet and Patricia, have weights that are consecutive even numbers. Eighteen less than Juliet's weight equals 50 less than the sum of Hannah and Patricia's weights. What is Juliet's weight?

    a. 26
    b. 28
    c. 30
    d. 32
    e. 34

27. Wendy drove the 700 mile round trip between New York and Chicago in 12 hours. Before the 5 pm dinner rush, she averaged 70 miles per hour. Afterward 5 pm, Wendy averaged only 50 miles per hour. At what time did Wendy begin her trip?

    a.   9 am
    b.   11 am
    c.   12 noon
    d.   1 pm
    e.   It cannot be determined from the information given

28. You are arranging four brightly colored decorative tiles on the bathroom wall: they are red, green, pink and purple. How many possible ways are there to arrange them on the wall (assuming that no tile is repeated)?

    a.   4
    b.   8
    c.   16
    d.   24
    e.   64

29. For marketing purposes, Ace Hamburgers is recording the number of customers who order hot dogs during the lunch rush. For the first half of January, these are their daily values: 43, 56, 42, 56, 47, 28, 36, 65, 67, 89, 81, 45, 54, 44, 34. What is the mode?

    a.   47
    b.   52.5
    c.   54
    d.   56
    e.   65

30. There are P tenants in an apartment building, who agree to split the cost of utilities, N, in an equal manner. If the cost of utilities increases by $212 per month, how much must each tenant pay?

    a.   (P + 212)/N
    b.   (N + 212)/P
    c.   P(N − 212)/P
    d.   212/P
    e.   212P/N

31. The sum of two numbers is 24. Three times the larger number less two times the smaller number equals 17. What is the larger number?

    a.   9
    b.   11
    c.   13
    d.   15
    e.   17

32. If a triangle of base 16 has the same area as a circle of diameter 16, what is the altitude of the triangle (use $\pi = 3.1416$)?

    a.   4
    b.   8
    c.   12
    d.   16
    e.   25

33. A pizza is divided into slices of equal size, each with a side length of 7. Assuming that each slice meets at the center of the pizza, what is the pizza's circumference?

    a. 7
    b. 49
    c. 7π
    d. 14π
    e. 49π

34. If the base of a parallelogram increases by 12% and the height decreases by 18%, by what percent does the area change?

    a. 9% decrease
    b. 6% decrease
    c. 6% increase
    d. 10% increase
    e. 32% increase

35. A researcher pumps 100% nitrogen gas into an experimental chamber at a rate of 30 cubic inches per second. If the chamber's dimensions are 15 inches by 24 inches by 48 inches, how many minutes will it take the researcher to fill the chamber with nitrogen?

    a. 9.6
    b. 57.6
    c. 96
    d. 576
    e. 5,760

Refer to the following chart for questions 36 – 37.

Company Budget for September 2010 (in dollars)

Rent	1,500
Vehicle Lease	450
Utilities	200
Phone	50
Insurance	100
Advertising	300
Internet	50
Shipping	30
Computer	100
Taxes	200
Accounting	100
Attorney	150
Software	70
Miscellaneous	200

36. According to experts, the company can spend 5% of its monthly budget on technology expenses, such as internet, computer and software. By how many dollars did the company exceed this percentage in September of 2010?

    a. $30
    b. $35
    c. $40
    d. $45
    e. $50

37. In October of 2010, the company must eliminate 20% of its monthly expenses to purchase new machinery. Which of the following expenses, if eliminated, would allow the company to meet this goal?

    a.   Advertising, Attorney, Internet, Computer
    b.   Computer, Advertising, Accounting, Miscellaneous
    c.   Vehicle Lease, Shipping, Miscellaneous
    d.   Phone, Vehicle Lease, Software, and Shipping
    e.   Taxes, Advertising, Insurance, and Internet

Answer Key for Quantitative Section 14

1. Statement 2 provides enough information for us to calculate the value of the smallest angle. Statement1, while interesting, is extraneous information. Choice B is correct.

2. To answer this question, we need to know the number of sides in the figure and the sum of the remaining angles. Statements 1 and 2, when taken together, provide this information. Choice C is correct.

3. The question asks us to determine the probability of Joe winning the prize. To do so, we need two pieces of information: the number of tickets in the bowl and the number of tickets that Joe bought. Statement 1 gives us the first quantity, while Statement 2 provides the second. Choice C is correct.

4. To answer this question, we need to know the total number of coins and their respective denominations. We do not know the second piece of information, which means that we cannot solve the problem. Choice E is correct.

5. Statement 1 provides enough information for us to answer the question. Statement 2 is extraneous information. Choice A is correct.

6. To solve the problem, we need to know the cost per gallon and the number of gallons that Mr. Winters bought. Unfortunately, neither statement tells us how many gallons he bought – or the amount that was required to paint his house. Hence, Choice E is correct.

7. Choice B is correct. Statement 2 gives us enough information to answer the question. (G and H are 13 and 17, respectively, which makes their difference = 4.)

8. Choice E is correct. Statements 1 and 2 are not sufficient to answer the question.

9. $x^2 - x = 12$, or $x^2 - x -12 = 0$, or $(x+3)(x-4) = 0$. x = **(-3, 4)**. Choice B is correct.

10. $(F \cup G) \cup H$ = {1, 2, 4, 5, 6, 7, 8, 9, 10}. Choice E is correct.

11. Circumference of a circle = $2\pi r$. In this case, C = 2(3.1416)(4444) = **2.79×10^4** Choice B is correct.

12. We can solve this using a proportion. 1 steak / 6 oz = x steaks / 768 oz, so x = **128**. Choice C is correct.

13. Because the number of boys and girls is not the same, we must take a *weighted average* for each of the two groups. Average for entire class =(Sum of Girls' Waistlines + Sum of Boys' Waistlines) / Total # Students. Average = {(30)(24) + (25)(36)} / 55 = (720 + 900)/55 = 1620/55 = **29.45**. Choice C is correct.

14. In this case, we can write two equations – one for the total amount of funds and the other for the respective shares that were given to each sibling. As always, we must first define our variables. We will let = x the brother's share and y = the sister's share.

The first equation, which defines the amount of money invested, is simply x + y = 500,000
The second equation, which defines how the shares are divided, is y = 3x – 10,000
To solve the problem for x, we must combine the equations in a way that eliminates y. When we do, we get:
x + (3x – 10,000) = 500,000. 4x – 10,000 = 500,000. 4x = 510,000. x = **$127,500** = the brother's share. Choice B is correct. y = 3($127,500) - $10,000 = $372,500 = the sister's share

15. The new triangle will have sides that are one-half the length of those in triangle DEF. Hence, its perimeter will be one-half of DEF, which is **72**. Choice E is correct.

16. Slope = (11-5)/(7-4) = 6/3 = 2. y-intercept = -3. Therefore, the equation for the line is y = 2x – 3. Choice E is correct.

17. Choice A is correct.

18. The average is **0.932**, which is Choice C.

19. 9^5 x 9^3 = 9^8 = 4,304,672, which is **81^4**. Choice E is correct.

20. Just substitute each answer. **X = 7**. Choice D is correct.

21. (a + b –1) (a – b) = a^2 –ab + ab –b^2 –a +b = **a^2 – a – b^2 + b**. Choice A is correct.

22. The pattern in this series is to increase by 3, then decrease by 1. Hence, the next term will be **11**. Choice C is correct.

23. First, we must calculate the total amount that Jennifer spent on the shirts, which is $14.50 x 6 = $87.00 spent. Then, we divide this amount by her hourly pay to determine the number of hours she must work to pay for the shirts: 87/5.85 = **14.87** hours. Choice E is correct.

24. 28.5 x 23.1 = 658.35/16 = **41.14** pounds. Choice B is correct.

25. Let x be the number of videos sold and (x + 40) = the number of DVDs sold. Therefore, the value of the videos sold is 12x, while the value of the DVDs sold is 15(x + 40). Since the total sales figure is the sum of these two amounts, out equation becomes: 12x + 15(x+ 40) = 6000, or 27x + 600 = 6000. 27x = 5400. x = 200 = # of videos sold. x + 40 = **240** = number of DVDs sold. Choice D is correct.

26. We will use the information we have to build an equation to solve for Juliet's weight. Since the weights are consecutive even numbers, we can let Hannah's weight =x, Juliet's weight = (x + 2) and Patricia's weight = (x + 4). By definition, Juliet's weight less 18 equals the sum of Hannah and Patricia's weights minus 50. Mathematically, our equation becomes: (x+2) – 18 = {x + (x+4)} – 50, or x – 16 = 2x – 46 x = 30, x + 2 = 32, x + 4 = 34.   Since Juliet's weight (x+2) = **32**, Choice D is correct.

27. The first step is to draw a quick chart of what we know:

Timeframe	Distance	Rate	Time
Before the dinner rush	70x	70	x
After the dinner rush	50(12 – x)	50	12 – x

Wendy's 12 hour trip is divided into two parts: before and after the dinner rush. If we let her time traveling before the dinner rush = x, then the time she traveled after dinner = 12 – x. We can now write an equation to solve for Wendy's time based on the total distance she traveled:

Distance Before Dinner + Distance After Dinner = Total Distance
70x + 50(12 – x) = 700. 70x + 600 – 50x = 700. 20x = 100.
x = 5 hours = time Wendy travelled before 5 pm. Hence, Wendy left at **12 noon**. Choice C is correct.

28. For permutations, the correct formula is 4!/(4- 4)! = (4 x 3 x 2 x 1) / 1 = **24**. Choice D is correct.

29. The mode is the value that occurs most frequently in the set of data. To find it, we must first arrange the values in ascending order: 28, 34, 36, 42, 43, 44, 45, 47, 54, 56, 56, 65, 67, 81, 89. Here, the mode is **56**. Choice D is correct.

30. Since we are not given exact numbers for P and N, we can use the plug-in technique to determine the relationship. Let's randomly let P = 10 and N = 100. If the N increases by $212, then each tenant owes 1/10 (100 + 212), or 1/P (N+212) = **(N + 212)/P**. Choice B is correct.

31. In this case, we can write one equation for the first condition and a second equation for the second condition.   As always, we must first define our variables. We will let = x the larger number and y = the smaller number.

The first equation, which defines the first condition, is x + y = 24
The second equation, which defines the second condition, is 3x − 2y = 17

To solve the problem for x, we must combine the equations in a way that eliminates y. The fastest way is to re-write equation 1 as y = 24 − x and substitute this value for y into equation 2. When we do, we get: 3x − (2)(24 − x) = 17, so 3x − 48 + 2x = 17. 5x = 65. x = **13** = larger number. Choice C is correct. y = 24 − 14 = 11 = smaller number

32. The area of the circle is πr^2 = π(8)(8) = 64(3.1416) =201. In the triangle, the area = 1/2 (Base)(Height). We will let x = the height. Thus, for this triangle, 201 = 1/2 (16)x = 8x. Thus, x = **25**. Choice E is correct.

33. Circumference = π x Diameter If the radius is 7, the circumference= **14π.** Choice D is correct.

34. The area of the original parallelogram = Base X Height. Let B = the length of the base and H = the height of the original parallelogram. If the base increases by 12%, it becomes 1.12B. If the height decreases by 18%, it becomes 0.82H. The new area is therefore: (1.12)B (0.82)H = 0.9184BH, which is **9.18%** smaller than the original area. Choice A is correct.

35. Volume = (15)(24)(48) = 17,280 cubic inches /30 cubic inches per second = 576 seconds = **9.6** minutes. Choice A is correct.

36. 5% of 3,500 = $175. The company spent 50 + 100 + 70 = $220. The difference is **$45**. Choice D is correct.

37. 20% of $3,500 = $700. By eliminating miscellaneous ($200) + computer ($100) + advertising ($300) + accounting ($100), the company can reduce its expenses by $700. Choice B is correct.

www.ingramcontent.com/pod-product-compliance
Lightning Source LLC
Chambersburg PA
CBHW080527090426
42733CB00015B/2508